"The fourth edition of *An Introduction to the Policy Process* remains the best primer for the scientific study of public policy. It provides an accessible and accurate overview of the essential concepts and theories of the policy process with concrete illustrations. The book is ideal for undergraduate and graduate students looking for a readable and comprehensive foundation in the field."

—*Christopher Weible, University of Colorado Denver, USA*

"The fourth edition of *An Introduction to the Policy Process* provides readers with a broad perspective on American public policy, including insightful discussions of policy theory and the political processes that shape public policies. The author systematically explains his points in a clear, interesting, and accessible writing style. Birkland has made enduring contributions to the study of public policy, and in this textbook he has provided an excellent resource for teachers and students in the field of policy studies."

—*George Busenberg, Soka University of America, USA*

"*An Introduction to the Policy Process* is among the most accessible textbooks there are on policy process research and theory. This new edition clearly explains basic concepts, theories, and models, and incorporates illustrative data and empirical case study examples. Tom Birkland has the unique ability to connect conceptual and theoretical puzzles and debates with contemporary policy problems, which helps bridge the gap between theory and application. Raising questions for discussion and research, the book encourages the reader to think independently and critically about the policy process. I cannot think of a better way to inspire the next generation of public policy students and practitioners."

—*Daniel Nohrstedt, Uppsala University, Sweden*

"As it ever was—and then some! Professor Birkland's fourth edition of this introductory text to public policy continues to deliver esoteric policy theories and practical public policy content pitched at a level both casual enough for undergraduates and sophisticated enough for beginning graduate students. New to this edition are arrays of teaching and learning tools that make it almost off-the-shelf ready for instructors; new organization of the material and a focus on recent trends make the content relevant for the here and now."

—*Michael Jones, Oregon State University, USA*

"No one to my knowledge has assembled a book that covers such an expanse of the policy landscape. This volume introduces readers to the actors, outputs, models, and theories involved in deciding what government does in the name of the public."

—*Patrick Roberts, Virginia Tech, USA*

An Introduction to the Policy Process

The fourth edition of this widely-used text relates theory to practice in the public policy process. In a clear, conversational style, author Tom Birkland conveys the best current thinking on the policy process with an emphasis on accessibility and synthesis. This new edition has been reorganized to better explain the role of policy analysis in the policy process.

New to this edition:

- A new section on the role of policy analysis and policy analysts in the policy process.

- A revised and updated chapter surveying the social, economic, and demographic trends that are transforming the policy environment.

- Fully updated references to help the advanced reader locate the most important theoretical literature in policy process studies.

- New illustrations and an improved layout to clarify key ideas and stimulate classroom discussion.

The book makes generous use of visual aids and examples that link policy theory to the concrete experience of practitioners. It includes chapter-at-a-glance outlines, definitions of key terms, provocative review questions, recommended reading, and online materials for professors and students.

Thomas Birkland is the William T. Kretzer Distinguished Professor of Public Policy and Public Affairs in the School of Public and International Affairs, as well as Associate Dean for Research and Engagement in the College of Humanities and Social Science at North Carolina State University.

An Introduction to the Policy Process

Theories, Concepts, and Models of Public Policy Making

Fourth Edition

Thomas A. Birkland

Routledge
Taylor & Francis Group

NEW YORK AND LONDON

First published 2011 by M.E. Sharpe

Third edition published 2015
by Routledge

Fourth edition published 2016
by Routledge
711 Third Avenue, New York, NY 10017

and by Routledge
2 Park Square, Milton Park, Abingdon, Oxon OX14 4RN

*Routledge is an imprint of the Taylor & Francis Group,
an informa business*

Library of Congress Cataloging in Publication Data
  Birkland, Thomas A.
  An introduction to the policy process: theories, concepts, and models
  of public policy making/by Thomas A. Birkland.—Fourth Edition.
  pages cm
  Includes bibliographical references and index.
  1. Policy sciences. 2. Political planning—United States. I. Title.
  H97.B57 2015
  320.60973—dc23
  2015013571

ISBN: 978-1-138-93435-1 (hbk)
ISBN: 978-0-7656-4662-0 (pbk)
ISBN: 978-1-315-71737-1 (ebk)

Typeset in Stone Serif
by Florence Production Ltd, Stoodleigh, Devon, UK

Contents

Illustrations

FIGURES

TABLES

PHOTOS

Preface to the Fourth Edition

In a prior edition of this book, I wrote that it has long been said that one never really gets to know a subject until one has to teach it. If this is true, it's doubly true that one really learns a subject when one writes a book about it. And, indeed, one gets to know one's subject even better when one rewrites, reorganizes, and reconsiders this book. Once again, I learned a great deal about my field in the course of revising this book, particularly in reorganizing some chapters to make the book more accessible for instructors, students, and general readers. Like the prior editions, I have written this book to be a starting point in what I hope you will find to be an interesting and fruitful lifetime of thinking about and engaging in public policy making.

There are many fine books on the public policy process, many of which introduce policy theory but focus more on the actual content of public policy. One of my goals in writing this book was to fill in the gap between the end of the theoretical section and the case studies that are staples in these textbooks. Striking the right balance in the classroom between the theoretical and the substantive or "practical" is a challenge throughout the social sciences, and I hope this book helps teachers balance these two important aspects of the public policy curriculum. Indeed, one of the things I hope to stress is that there's no real separation between "theory" and "practice" or the so-called "real world." Our theories are fundamentally about explaining what happens in the real world, not simply conjectures with no basis in actual policy making. I have included many examples in the book, based on my research or on interesting things I've learned about from my colleagues, in the newspapers, or en route to learning about something else. Such serendipitous discoveries make the study of public policy fresh and fascinating, and I hope I've conveyed some of that excitement in this book.

Another motivation for this book was my interest in providing a primer in public policy for advanced undergraduates or graduate students in courses and programs that are not primarily about public policy, but in which an understanding of public policy is particularly useful. Such courses include, among others, courses on engineering and public policy, science and technology policy, social welfare policy, or, indeed, any field in which government acts, and where students would benefit from a readable but theoretically informed treatment of the policy process.

For example, for 12 years I taught in and co-directed the University at Albany's (SUNY) master's program in Biodiversity and Conservation Policy. The program included a required course in politics and policy, with an emphasis on policies relating to environmental conservation. For many students, this course was initially quite daunting, as most students have a background in biology or other sciences but little exposure to public policy ideas. In particular, the complexity (or what my students called its "messiness") and seemingly random complexity of the policy process is often confusing to students who have been trained to seek universal laws about all manner of natural phenomena, and hope for such laws in human and social behavior. My goal in writing this book is to provide an overview of the policy process that acknowledges this messiness while showing how policy scholars have developed ways that we can think more systematically about this seemingly chaotic process. This systematic thinking doesn't approach the precision of, say, a fundamental law of physics. But it helps us to focus on the important variables in policy making.

I also hope people who are returning to policy studies or are seeking to teach themselves about the process will find this book useful. Returning students, and those who are pursuing graduate studies after some years of professional experience, will find that policy studies grow and change quite quickly. This book is intended to help students, whether they are studying in a formal educational institution or on their own, to become current with some important ideas in the study of policy. I urge all readers to think of this book as a beginning or a supplement, and certainly not the final word on public policy.

I've attempted to write this book in a somewhat more conversational style than most textbooks. My goal is to provide a readable text and a useful reference that can be used to supplement or clarify concepts learned in classes, textbooks, and in daily contact with the policy process, including personal experience, the news media, and direct participation in policy making.

WHAT'S AHEAD

There are some substantial changes in the organization of this book from the third edition, while I have left in place many of the case studies and examples that students have found effective in illustrating the concepts contained in this book. This book starts with an overview of the idea of policy studies as both an academic discipline and an "applied" science. I review my thinking on what makes policy studies an appropriate endeavor for systematic or scientific study, even when the subject of study seems to be so irrational and even when we are the subject of the discipline itself!

Chapter 2 is an update of key social, economic, and demographic trends that influence and will influence policy making for some time to come. Most students of political science and of public policy have a broad sense of the ideas and trends reflected in the graphs contained in Chapter 2, but I think there will be some surprises and interesting insights as well. This chapter has been updated to the most current data available at the time of its writing in late 2014.

Chapter 3 focuses on the historical and structural features of American politics that influence public policy; this chapter contrasts with Chapter 2 in that it describes a more stable set of external variables that shape public policy. This division between dynamic and changing environmental variables reflects Paul Sabatier's thinking in his Advocacy Coalition Framework in the policy process. This discussion is particularly important, as most political scientists and policy scholars acknowledge the importance of the structure and rules under which policy making is conducted. Students are often taught—or at least are allowed to conclude—that the rules and structure are neutral, and that anyone who wants to play the game can get involved in politics and "make a difference" in their community.

By contrast, I argue that the founders of our constitutional order purposefully designed our system to favor commercial interests and property holders and to make it hard for mass publics to mobilize and seek a share of the wealth. For those interested in policy change, the structure is troubling, for it suggests that mass movements and participatory democracy are not likely to carry the day in policy debates. But, as highlighted throughout this book, there are circumstances under which policy can change, and sometimes policy changes quite rapidly. Indeed, one of the most fascinating aspects of politics comes in understanding when, against the odds, policy change based on mass mobilization is possible. And, of course, not all change is welcome, and liberals and conservatives alike have engaged in attempts—often aided by the structure of our system—to slow down policy change. I draw no normative conclusion here—we can simply observe that the system is resistant to change, as current debates over healthcare reform demonstrate, to the frustration of some and the relief of others.

The various institutions and people that make public policy are described in Chapters 4 and 5. Chapter 4 describes the official or institutional actors in the process—the legislative, executive, and judiciary. Chapter 5 continues this discussion with the unofficial actors, such as interest groups and media, and then outlines the ways in which we think about how all the actors come together—in "iron triangles," sub-governments, and issue networks—to debate and negotiate policy alternatives. Much of this sort of material, particularly in Chapter 4, will be familiar, at least in form, to students of American politics. My goal here is not simply to enumerate the various political institutions, but, instead, to explain why these institutions matter in making the public policies that govern our lives.

Groups, power, and agenda setting are reviewed in Chapter 6. This is discussed at some length, as agenda setting is among the most important stages of the policy process (and, not coincidentally, it is the "stage" of the policy process in which much of my own research has been focused). It is at this stage that groups exercise political power to achieve their goals, either by promoting change or blocking it. The use of power in politics is subtle and complex, particularly in our political system. Understanding of what power is, how it is acquired, and how it is used to prevent issues from gaining attention is key to understanding why any political system does some things while not doing others, even in the face of obvious needs or logic that would seem to compel a "superior" course of action. Again, this question of power is challenging, and raises important questions about fairness, equity, and democratic governance, which are important considerations in any policy context.

Chapter 7 then describes several different ways one can categorize the substance of policies to better understand the political process behind making these policies. Like so much in public policy studies, these descriptions of policy types are not final, but they are useful as a way of stimulating thinking about what governments do, and what we ask governments to do.

Chapters 8, 9, and 10 are newly organized to flow better, and to make the chapters more tractable—some of them were quite long! Chapter 8 combines much of the discussion of decision-making from the third edition with a new section on the role of policy analysis and policy analysts in the policy process.

Many students have wondered about the relationship between the study of the policy *process* and the profession of the policy analyst. This is unsurprising, considering that many students in the courses for which this book is assigned aspire to be policy analysts. I hope this discussion is helpful in locating their role as analysts within the broader public policy process.

Chapter 9 is now devoted to a discussion of policy design and policy tools. While this subject is inextricably related to the success or failure of policy implementation, I have made the discussion of policy implementation, failure, and learning its own chapter (Chapter 10). Policy implementation is a well-studied aspect of the policy process, which considers the oft-forgotten work that must come after the excitement of policy enactment has passed. Implementation—putting a program into effect—is often as difficult and contentious as policy design and enactment, and in some cases is more difficult to manage. Because of the difficulties inherent in policy design and implementation, many people will claim that policies have failed to meet their goals. In Chapter 10, I examine policy failure by outlining the various ways in which any policy can be said to be a failure. The complexity of policy making, with interconnectedness of policy impacts but disjointed policy design, makes real or claimed failure almost inevitable based on how one defines failure.

Chapter 11 puts all these elements of policy making together by considering modern theories of the policy process. In this edition, I have focused more on the *idea* of policy science as social science in this chapter, moving some of the material that formerly appeared in Chapter 1 to here. I think this helps ground the discussion of theory. By exploring theories and thinking of the policy process as a "system," the inputs to and outputs from the political system are summarized and discussed in terms of their relationship to the political system, or what is often called "the black box" in systems models. The second half of the chapter discusses different and complementary ways of looking inside the black box; most of these models of policy making are at the forefront of current policy theory.

PUBLIC POLICY IN THE EARLY TWENTY-FIRST CENTURY

When the first edition of this book was written, the Clinton administration was coming to an end. Eight years of relatively robust economic growth was continuing, the Internet boom seemed, to some, an unlimited engine of growth and innovation, and Americans felt reasonably secure at home and abroad. The end of the Cold War gave Americans the luxury to once again turn inward, for the first time since the dark days just before World War II. This is not to say that the nation had no policy problems, including the state of the economy. But, by and large, the nation was at peace, and was prosperous broadly (even as wealth became more unevenly distributed), and contentment was reasonably high.

This sense of contentment was replaced by an initial sense of fear, then by long-term unease, after the September 11 terrorist attacks. For weeks and months after September 11, it seemed to all of us that everything had changed. Americans were less concerned about domestic politics. We were confronted with the possibility of catastrophic terrorism of the sort that could kill millions of people. As we have learned since September 11, this threat had always existed, but the September 11 attacks were surely the most dramatic and shocking example of this sort of terrorism. Concerns were raised about the possibility of nuclear, biological, and chemical terrorism. While some of that unease was alleviated by the nation's military disengagement from Iraq and Afghanistan, the emergence of groups such as Boko Haram, in Nigeria, and the "Islamic State," in the Middle East, have rekindled concerns about foreign policy, international terrorism, and the policies that the United States and its allies can adopt to mitigate, if not eliminate, the threat of terrorism.

But for the vast majority of Americans, the primary subject of conversation between 2007 and now has been the state of the economy, both in terms of its very sharp decline in 2007 and 2008, and its apparent recovery for many— but not all—people by 2012. The costs of the "bailout" of financial institutions, and of automakers GM and Chrysler, helped cause the federal budget deficit to balloon to near-record levels. Huge deficits, and consequent government actions to raise revenues and cut expenses, had a significant effect both on the economy and on the very substance of public policy; those effects persist.

Yet people continue to demand public services from government, particularly since the federal government expanded heavily into everyday life in the 1930s in response to the Great Depression. All these matters highlight how terrorism, the economy, and many other matters influence other realms of public policy. The September 11 attacks changed, for a while at least, the *agenda* in American politics. But the attacks did not change the policy *process* that this book describes; nor has the financial crisis. Indeed, the policy process—and the actors and institutions that drive it—remain as robust as ever, even if some features of it, such as partisanship in Congress and arcane rules such as the filibuster, seem to greatly impede change. What may have changed is the nature and sophistication of our theories of the policy process.

It is a testament to the capacity and resilience of the American political and policy system that some issues remain important even in the face of challenges such as the financial crisis, terrorism, and environmental disasters. The Obama administration felt able to tackle healthcare issues, and before then, the George W. Bush administration had expanded Medicare coverage for elderly Americans. Education remains an important issue as well, as the Obama administration's "Race to the Top" program attempts to build and improve upon the Bush program known as "No Child Left Behind", even as controversy persists over the "common core" curriculum, as it often does during periods of attempted educational reform.

Other issues, such as environmental policy and climate change, remain difficult yet high-profile matters in the public and government agendas. Disease outbreaks such as Ebola, in Africa, and the return, in some places, of diseases preventable by vaccines in the United States, have once again called into question the government's role in health and safety.

Because we are a large, generally wealthy, and powerful nation founded on a set of principles that people hold dear—democracy, constitutional government, the rule of law, and liberty, to name a few—these political controversies will persist in American politics, not because we enjoy arguing (although some of us do enter politics for this reason!), but because many people passionately care about these issues, and believe just as passionately that their ideas are the ones that will work best. This passion was evident during the 2012 presidential election and the 2014 midterm elections. When you strip away the candidates' debate styles and demeanors, what was left was a remarkable discussion of *ideas* and how to translate those ideas into policies that benefit the broadest range of Americans.

In the nearly 10 years since I first began writing this book, I have been privileged to hear from many colleagues, students, and friends about how they used this book. I greatly value their comments and suggestions. The first edition would not have been possible without the extraordinary help and support of Scott Barclay, Brian Davis, Mark Donovan, Ben Fordham, Jennifer Krausnick, Regina Lawrence, Peter May, Henrik Minassians, Bob Nakamura, and Beryl Radin.

In the second edition, I acknowledged the debt I still owe to my students in my undergraduate course, Introduction to Public Policy, and in my graduate courses in Politics and Policy and Biodiversity and Conservation Policy at the University at Albany. And my friend and colleague Sarah Anderson at Albany was a helpful and patient reader and critic. At Albany, two teaching assistants, Paul Alexander and Michael Deegan, created the core of the definitions of the key terms and the discussion questions.

Since joining the faculty at North Carolina State, I have twice revised this book, with the assistance of advanced graduate students and undergraduates. For this edition, I owe a particular debt of gratitude toward another remarkable group of Ph.D. students at NC State—Susan Camilleri, Annie Izod, Emily McCartha, and Meg Warnement—who, at various times, took on the tedious work of updating citations, graphs and charts, and the other things that have improved this edition. Any errors or omissions are, of course, mine, and there would be many more were it not for the fantastic students I've worked with over the years. To those friends and colleagues whose help I have failed to acknowledge, I thank you all for your support, ideas, and friendship.

One thing hasn't changed: I still dedicate this book to my wife Molly, and my kids Oskar and Ike, for their love, patience, and tolerance of dad taking over the one really good computer in the house during writing time. I hope they, in time, find it was worth it.

CHAPTER 1

Introducing the Policy Process

OVERVIEW

This book is about how public policy is made in the United
States. As a book on a particular field of the social sciences,
it goes beyond simple description to introduce you to
theories and ways of thinking about the policy process. This
is not to deny the value of understanding the substance
of the many policies themselves. I am sure that you,
your family, and friends have often puzzled over why
the government does some of the things it does, particularly when those things are contradictory. Why does, for
example, the government provide support for tobacco
farming and discourage people from smoking? Why does
the government give people tax breaks for buying houses?
Why don't renters get similar tax breaks? Or landlords,
who could pass the savings on to renters? Why doesn't the
United States have a single-payer, comprehensive health
insurance system like many other countries? Why was the
idea of creating such a system so passionately resisted?

Why is the federal government so deeply involved in crime and education
policy when our constitutional system places the primary responsibility for
these programs in the state and local governments? Is regulation of consumer
product safety better for public safety, or would greater reliance on the market
and better information for consumers work better to promote public safety?
These are questions that motivate many people of all ideological and political
persuasions to understand public problems and find solutions to them.

One of the most interesting reasons to study public policy is that public policy making is about problem-solving. People participate in policy making because they perceive that there are problems for which government, at some level, can provide solutions. Others participate, in turn, because they believe that those problems are best handled by markets, or by families, or by nonprofit organizations, or churches, or any number of other means.

But studies of the contents of public policy—the laws and regulations themselves—is important, but it's not enough to understand the social scientific aspects of the policy process. Many scholars have developed theories of how the public policy process works: that is, theories about how public problems are discovered and how policies are created to address those problems.

This book introduces theories, frameworks, and models of the policy process. This focus on theory sets this book apart from many other textbooks on public policy. Many such textbooks contain a thin treatment of theories of public policy—and the relation of these theories to broader social scientific questions—and then provide a series of case studies on "environmental policy" or "energy policy" or "national security policy." There are many good books about all manner of policy issues, and I hope you find them in the subjects that are the most interesting to you. This book focuses on the process by which policies are made. Other public policy textbooks approach policy making from an economic perspective—as a form of policy analysis, which can be different from analysis based in politics (I take this topic up in Chapter 8). Many of these books develop new theories of the policy process, but often those theories are unique to these textbooks, and are unfamiliar to those of us who study policy making as a political activity.

An Introduction to the Policy Process describes how policy is shaped by social, institutional, political, economic, and other contexts by drawing on existing theories of the policy process. Much of this description is orthodox in political science; the discussion of the branches of government, of the Constitution, of the various groups and institutions, and the like, is similar to that found in introductory American politics textbooks. The difference between this book and an introductory American politics textbook is that I am interested in how groups, institutions, and structures work to solve problems through making public policies. And, in keeping with the interdisciplinary nature of policy studies, this book owes a debt to sociology, history, economics, public administration, and other disciplines, but with a firm grounding in studies of American politics. Readers from other countries will likely find the theories described in this book useful in their countries, but will also notice important differences between the American and other contexts.

POLITICS AND THE POLICY PROCESS

This book is about a particular way in which social scientists study public policy: by studying the public policy *process*. But the study of public policy is an important aspect of political science, so it's useful to start by asking, "What is politics?" One way to conceive of politics is as a process by which societies help figure out how to organize and regulate themselves; that is, how to govern themselves. What makes this "political" is its location in the public sphere, where decisions are made by the public to address issues that affect people in communities; all manner of other decisions are made in corporations, in families, and in other organizations that we do not consider to be part of the public sphere; sociologists tend to study these private organizations and the interactions among their members, although the line between "public" and "private" is quite blurry, which is why sociologists and political scientists often address similar questions (Kumar 2014).

The public sphere can be as small as an apartment complex, or a small village, or as large as a whole nation, or even the world. Whatever the scale, public policies address problems that are public, or, more importantly, that some number of people think *should* be public instead of private. Indeed, a key feature of politics and political decision-making is the very definition of what problems are public and which are private (Rochefort and Cobb 1994).

While these questions may, at the outset, seem simple, they are in fact very complex. People have been trying to figure out how to work together in political communities for thousands of years. Philosophers such as Socrates, Plato, and Aristotle sought to understand how one can behave in a political context to help people make decisions within human societies, while reducing the possibility of political conflict turning destructive or violent (McCool 1995). "Modern" political theory begins in the fifteenth century when Niccolò Machiavelli wrote *The Prince* for his patron, an Italian nobleman, to provide him with practical political advice. Machiavelli argued that if we understand and plan the political actions we take in pursuit of our goals, we are better prepared to seize the political opportunities that arise in the normal course of political life. *The Prince* depended on postulates—statements about how we think the political world works—and then argues that we should compare these

Enlightenment
Term used to
describe a
philosophic
movement of the
early eighteenth
century, in which
numerous theorists
and philosophers
developed new
political and social
philosophies based
on reason and on
insights from the
natural sciences.
The Enlightenment
developed the
thinking that
spurred the
American and
French
Revolutions,
among other
changes.

postulates to the conduct of "real-world" politics. Developing and testing postulates about how the political world works is consistent with the way people thought of the human and natural world during the **Enlightenment**, when thinkers turned toward modern methods of scientific inquiry in hopes of better understanding all manner of phenomena—including physics, medicine, law, and politics (Gay 1996). During this era of great scientific, political, and social foment, a host of brilliant thinkers turned their focus to understanding the use of power—a basic element of politics—in social settings.

In continuing one's exploration of political philosophy, one might read Thomas Hobbes, John Locke, and Jean-Jacques Rousseau on the nature of social and political interactions under what we call "the social contract." In the American context, the French nobleman Charles-Louis de Secondat, more commonly known as Montesqieu, greatly influenced the most influential thinkers in America at the time of the American Revolution and the ratification of the Constitution; his work is best known for the idea of the separation of powers into the legislative, executive, and judicial branches (Montesquieu 1989).

These ideas are reflected in *The Federalist*, a collection of essays written by Alexander Hamilton, James Madison, and John Jay to persuade New Yorkers to ratify the U.S. Constitution. Federalist #47 is the essay most closely associated with the separation of powers, but the entire collection of *The Federalist* is still studied to gain insights into the meaning of the Constitution and the thoughts of its framers.[1] To this foundation in American political thought we can also count the writings of, among others, George Washington, Samuel Adams, Thomas Jefferson, Abraham Lincoln, and Woodrow Wilson. All of these statesmen sought to explain, to themselves and their countrymen, how our nation came to be, and how, in their minds, it was the best equipped to preserve individual rights and harness the creative power that ultimately made the United States one of the richest and most powerful countries in the world.

European thinkers such as Karl Marx and Max Weber sought to understand how people organize their societies, and how the socially and politically strong can, by accident or design, ignore the desires of the politically weak. From there, we can move to modern theorists and philosophers such as John Dewey, who studied the question of knowledge and learning in social life, and John Rawls, whose major work, *A Theory of Justice* (1999), sought to understand fundamental questions of fairness. Postmodern philosophers such as Michel Foucault offer powerful challenges to social contract theory and explain how people come to be dominated by power structures beyond their control. These theorists have all contributed to our understanding of politics and social interactions. Their ideas help us to understand the historic and modern ways of thinking about the relationships between our governments and ourselves.

All this thinking still doesn't provide a concise definition of "politics," because such a definition is difficult to produce. Harold Lasswell (1958) defines politics as "who gets what, when, and how." This definition is simple, but we can discern on its own terms three essential aspects of politics: competition to gain certain resources, sometimes at others' expense; the need to cooperate to make decisions; and the nature of political power.

Let's look at the ways the word **politics** is defined in Merriam-Webster's online dictionary. Here are two that I find particularly interesting: "the art or science of government" and "political activities characterized by artful and often dishonest practices."

politics In this book, I define politics the same way that Harold Lasswell does: the process by which society determines who gets what, when they get it, and how they get it.

Because this dictionary defines *artful* as "skillful or wily," this definition reflects how many people focus on the devious behavior of politicians or political actors, and on the seemingly dishonest aspects of politics. They accuse people of "playing politics," as if they engage in the process simply to gain personal or group advantages and not for any particular policy goals that would broadly benefit society. The negative sense of the term is reflected in a Google News search I did while writing this section to make my point. Using the search term "playing politics with," I found the following headlines:

- Playing Politics with the Supreme Court Over ObamaCare

- Playing Politics with Chicago's Murder Epidemic

- How Democrats Are Playing Politics with Ebola

- Stop Playing Politics with Women's Rights

- Republicans Playing Politics with Secret Service Mistakes

In this definition of "politics," we can see that the term "playing politics with" is very negative, and suggests that politics, in this sense, is about scoring points and making partisan claims, not about solving problems. Indeed, the process does seem to be tawdry to many people. Clearly, there are great concerns about the motivations and honesty of politicians and lobbyists. The influence of interest group money, including very active "superPACs" that raise large sums of money, is a point of considerable concern. The legislative process often seems arcane and designed to be opaque so that ordinary people cannot understand or participate in politics.

But the problem with claims of "playing politics" reduces the word to something with a negative connotation, which is not the most fruitful way to think about politics. After all, most people and organizations that make policy arguments claim that their ideas, if implemented, would serve the public interest. One of the most fundamental questions we must confront, then, as students of politics and public policy in a "democracy," broadly defined, is whether policy making does indeed serve the public interest, and whether the public is really engaged in making it. As students of the policy process, we need to carefully and systematically understand *why* it is that money is so important in politics, why legislative processes can seem so confusing and slow, and whether and to what extent politics as currently practiced—with competing claims, expensive elections, and political partisanship—really works as a way of organizing our society. But while we can question our system and recognize that our representative democracy, as practiced in the United States and in other world democracies, may not be perfect, it also has significant advantages over autocracy and dictatorship, which is why Winston Churchill once defined democracy as "the worst form of government except for all the others."

With this in mind it remains useful to consider politics as, in the dictionary's terms, "the art or science of government." Politics is therefore a profession unto itself and an object of study. As such, it is "the total complex of relations between people living in a society," as defined by Merriam-Webster.com. What does this have to do with public policy? The study of public policy is the study of how we translate what the proponents of particular actions believe to be the popular will into practice. Of course, this is a simplification—the nature of the popular will is itself highly debatable—but it's a good general way of considering what we study, while keeping in mind that, while a single definition of "the public will" or "the public interest" may never be available, we know that proponents of policy change will make appeals to it in an effort to promote change.

WHAT IS PUBLIC POLICY?

While the study of politics has a long history, the systematic study of public policy as we understand it is a fairly recent discipline. Daniel McCool argues that modern policy studies began in 1922, when political scientist Charles Merriam sought to connect the theory and practice of politics to understanding the actual activities of government. But McCool also notes "the study of public policy did not suddenly spring into existence in the 1950s and 1960s" (1995: 1). The classic literature that founded policy studies—including much that is discussed in this book—is only about 60 years old, beginning with Harold Lasswell's call for the development of a distinctive policy science (Lasswell 1958; McCool 1995). Because the field of policy studies is so new, many of the fundamentals of the policy sciences have only begun to be well understood in the last 30 years or so. Considerable debate remains over whether there is one coherent set of principles that can govern the study and understanding of what we call the public policy process (see, for example, Howlett, Ramesh and Perl 2009, Chapter 1).

As in every field of endeavor, the definition of key terms and ideas is often very important, but it also can lead to considerable contention. There are many possible ways to define public policy. In academic studies of public policy, we offer definitions of public policy to understand the shape of the field we seek to study. For many people, defining public policy helps them define their own role in policy making, as well as that of the organization they work for. As I was writing this chapter for the first edition of this book, a member of the policy analysis office of a New York State agency called me. The agency was engaging in a strategic planning initiative; to do so, it needed to establish its mission—its very reason for existence. Because this agency influences taxation, spending, and government performance assessment—that is, public policy in the broad sense—the caller was particularly interested in defining the term *public policy*, so that her agency could know better how public policy relates to its work. The analyst ran through a list of the classic public policy texts, and asked if these were good sources of a definition of public policy.

There are many good sources for such a definition, and I urged her to look at these sources because of scholars' lack of a consensus definition of public policy. And, after all, her question was very practical. She was asking for a definition of "public policy" so that her agency could more readily distinguish what is and what is not public policy, so as to focus its efforts on its *public* policy functions. I shared with her my agreement with Thomas Dye, who argues that this search for a definition of public policy can degenerate into a word game that, eventually, adds little more understanding. It may be fruitless to look for one particular definition of public policy, and it is certainly not useful to continue to develop more definitions. I suggested to the caller that she review the texts and adopt a definition that the agency felt made the most sense in its particular context. Table 1.1 provides some examples of the definitions of public policy that the caller could draw from, and some strengths and weaknesses of these definitions.

No single definition may ever be developed, but we can discern key attributes of public policy:

- Policy is made in response to some sort of problem that requires attention.

- Policy is made on the "public's" behalf.

- Policy is oriented toward a goal or desired state, such as the solution of a problem.

- Policy is ultimately made by governments, even if the ideas come from outside government or through the interaction of government and nongovernmental actors.

- Policy is interpreted and implemented by public and private actors who have different interpretations of problems, solutions, and their own motivations.

- Policy is what the government chooses to do or *not* to do.

TABLE 1.1 Defining "Public Policy"

Definition	Author
"The term public policy always refers to the actions of government and the intentions that determine those actions."	Clarke E. Cochran et al.[a]
"Public policy is the outcome of the struggle in government over who gets what."	Clarke E. Cochran et al.
"Whatever governments choose to do or not to do."	Thomas Dye[b]
"Public policy consists of political decisions for implementing programs to achieve societal goals."	Charles L. Cochran and Eloise F. Malone[c]
"Stated most simply, public policy is the sum of government activities, whether acting directly or through agents, as it has an influence on the life of citizens."	B. Guy Peters[d]

a. Clarke E. Cochran et al., *American Public Policy: An Introduction*. 10th ed. Boston, MA: Cengage Wadsworth, 2010.
b. Thomas R. Dye, *Understanding Public Policy*. 14th ed. Boston, MA: Pearson, 2013.
c. Charles L. Cochran and Eloise F. Malone, *Public Policy: Perspectives and Choices*. 4th ed. Boulder, CO: Lynne Rienner Publishers, 2010.
d. B. Guy Peters, *American Public Policy: Promise and Performance*. 8th ed. Washington, DC: CQ Press, 2010.

PHOTO 1.1
Depending on the current state of politics, government sometimes changes what it does or does not do.

Source: © Mark Wilson/Getty Images. Used with permission.

While reaching a consensus on one *definition* of public policy has proved impossible, all the variants of the definition suggest that public policy making is *public*—it affects a greater variety of people and interests than do private decisions. This is why government and the policies made by government are sometimes so controversial, frustrating, and at the same time very important. But because the public is the source of political authority—that is, the authority to act on the public's behalf—it is clear that government is at the center of efforts to make public policy.

I define a **policy** as a statement by government—at whatever level, in whatever form—of what it intends to do about a public problem. Such statements can be found in the Constitution, statutes, regulation, case law (that is, court decisions), agency or leadership decisions, or even in changes in the behavior of government officials at all levels. For example, a law that says that those caught driving while intoxicated will go to jail for up to one year is a statement of governmental policy to punish drunk drivers. The National Environmental Policy Act (NEPA) is a statement of government policy toward the environment. The First Amendment specifies that Congress cannot abridge religious, speech, or press freedoms, by stating "Congress shall make no law . . . ." Judicial decisions are also statements of policy: the Supreme Court's decision in *Brown v. Board of Education*, 347 U.S. 483 (1954), is a statement of policy that governments cannot racially segregate schools; the Court's decision in *Citizens United v. Federal Election Commission*, 558 U.S. 310

policy A statement by government of what it intends to do, such as a law, regulation, ruling, decision, order, or a combination of these. The lack of such statements may also be an implicit statement of policy.

(2010), is a statement of policy that, as a matter of policy—specifically, policy that implements the free speech provisions of the First Amendment to the Constitution—the federal government cannot regulate the independent political speech of nonprofit organizations.

Because we also define public policy as what government chooses not to do, the lack of a definitive statement of policy may be evidence of an *implicit* policy, which is quite different from a clear and explicit statement of policy—or even a vague and broad statement of policy. The government has never declared—and our system has never enshrined in the Constitution—a right to education, or healthcare, or a living wage; therefore, we can assume that the implicit policy is that there is *no* right to these things, while some other nations do express these as rights. By not making them rights, our government puts these sorts of government or private services in a different category than, for example, the right to workshop or to have a jury trial. While we might pass policies to address the problems that arise when dealing with these policy matters, we generally do not treat them as matters of right. In the United States, one cannot claim that the failure of the federal government to provide education, healthcare, or many other things violates a right stated or implied by the Constitution.

Explicit statements of policies take many different forms. A policy might be a law, or a regulation, or the set of all the laws and regulations that govern a particular issue area or problem. This would be a sound but incomplete explanation. Anne Schneider and Helen Ingram provide a more extensive definition of policy: "Policies are revealed through texts, practices, symbols, and discourses that define and deliver values including goods and services as well as regulations, income, status, and other positively or negatively valued attributes" (1997: 2). This definition means that policies are not just contained in laws and regulations; once a law or rule is made, policies continue to be made as the people who implement policy—that is, those who put policies into effect—make decisions about who will benefit from policies and who will shoulder burdens as a result. In studying policy, then, we look at the broader sweep of politics, not simply the written laws and rules themselves.

Policy change can be detected at levels ranging from constitutional change, which is clearly very visible to most members of a political system, all the way to subtle changes in the behavior of "street-level bureaucrats" (Lipsky 2010), whose vigilance or other behaviors may be hiding by the most recent event. A good example of this is the behavior of airport screeners in the days immediately after the September 11 terrorist attacks. These screeners became much more thorough and careful in their searches for dangers or prohibited items in passenger luggage, even before the laws changed to make airport screening stricter.

IDEAS AND PROBLEMS IN THE POLICY PROCESS

Now that we know how we can think of public policy, and how we might find out what policies are, it is useful to think about *why* policies are made and why they change. One way to explain the dynamism of public policy is by understanding the relationship between ideas and problems. According to Merriam-Webster, a **problem** is "a source of perplexity, distress, or vexation." Given this definition, I am sure you can think of a lot of problems in the world that are vexing. Big problems that people are worried about as I write this are the continued health of the economy, particularly after the deep recession that began in 2008 and its uneven recovery, continuing terrorism in the Middle East (and, in particular, the group known as "Islamic State"), the uncertain outcome of the so-called "ObamaCare" health reforms, the costs of doing something about—or ignoring—global climate change, and the threats posed by infectious diseases such as Ebola or variants of influenza. Each of these things is—or is not—vexing to some number of people. Public policy is largely driven by arguments about whether something is a solvable problem, what the potential solutions are, what the costs of those solutions are, and whether the solutions will be wholly or—more likely—partially effective. There are a lot of people who work to promote an understanding of a problem, and, in framing the problem a particular way, they promote the likely set of solutions, as we will see in greater detail in Chapters 6 and 8.

problem A usually undesirable situation that, according to people or interest groups, can be alleviated by government action.

WHAT MAKES PUBLIC POLICY PUBLIC?

The dominant ideological foundation of our constitutional system (and that of other countries that were once part of the British Empire, such as Canada, Australia, and Great Britain itself) is known as **classical liberalism**. This ideology is very clearly expressed in John Locke's *Second Treatise of Civil Government* (1690). Among the many beliefs of liberalism is that power derives from the consent of the governed—that is, the people themselves. The people, and not royalty or the state, are therefore sovereign. Thus, when policy

classical liberalism In political theory, the ideological system that emphasizes individual liberty and the ownership and acquisition of private property as a means to improve overall wealth and happiness and discourage social strife. Liberalism is the political ideology on which the American political system is based.

advocates seek to induce the government to make policy (by taking an action or refusing to do so), or when government actively engages in actions these advocates support, one can make a claim that the government does so in the public interest. Indeed, many states have groups called Public Interest Research Groups, or PIRGs, which promote their interpretation of the public interest.

For example, agencies that regulate public utilities, such as electric companies, claim to regulate in the public interest by limiting rates or assuring service. Some policy advocates claim that laws that relieve tax burdens on the rich are in the public interest because they create overall public wealth, which leads to job creation, the creation of wealth, and, therefore, a more prosperous society overall (Viard 2007). Those who argue that the rich should be taxed at a higher rate than the poor claim that taxation based on ability to pay is more in the spirit of the public interest. Of course, many people will argue that making certain policies would harm the public interest. For example, Google is under considerable scrutiny in Europe for its alleged anti-competitive behavior, and the European Parliament, in a largely symbolic vote, called for Google's services, such as search and online advertising, to be broken into separate companies to promote competition, thereby serving the public interest. But Google and its defenders argue that the service, as it exists without this regulation, is in the public interest because it gives people what they want. Here's where precisely *what* the public interest is comes into the debate.

public interest
The assumed broader desires and needs of the public, in whose name policy is made. The public interest is hard to define, but is something to which all policy advocates appeal.

Public policy is related to the **public interest** because the sum total of all policies affect all of us in some way. But we are not all affected by the same policies in exactly the same way, nor is one's intensity of feeling about an issue necessarily equal to that of others. And many of us don't have any particular issue that would cause us to mobilize with others to demand policy change. Most of us do not care too much about the day-to-day workings of government because we are busy with the day-to-day workings of our lives and because the activities of government seem removed from our daily interests and needs, or even because some political actors would rather we not participate in such decisions. Still, the government, particularly the U.S. federal government, plays an important role in every aspect of our lives, from the nutrition labeling on our breakfast cereal to the standards for fire-retardant kids' clothing. And state and local governments tax us, can restrict how we use our land through land use planning and zoning, define what the schools can and cannot teach, and make rules about everything from the operation of the state fairgrounds to where and when we can own and carry firearms. Big states, such as California, are so influential that their standards are adopted by other states or in federal law. Not everyone likes rules like these, of course. But as oppressive as government is claimed to be by some interests, there are many government activities that most people ignore or support because they seem either benign or beneficial to most people, so we tend not to dwell on those policies until something goes wrong. And, as is often true in democracies, policies ultimately gain broad support so their repeal is unlikely, as with the social security program or income tax deductions for children or for mortgage interest.

You may be interested in public policy because you care intensely about particular public problems and the policies intended to address them, such as those dealing with the environment, civil rights, economic freedom, or the promotion of personal morality. But even the most intensely interested participants in the policy process are not concerned with *every* issue. There is a considerable division of labor in democratic politics; in the formal institutions of government, different people have different constitutional responsibilities, and the vast array of issues that government handles on our behalf require that even members of legislatures need to be specialists in fairly narrow fields.

In the United States, as in many democracies, people tacitly delegate policy-making responsibilities to government and to specialists because everyone cannot concern themselves with the day-to-day panoply of issues that government must address. But in delegating these responsibilities, we do not abandon our interest in what the government does or how it does it (and sometimes the procedures the government uses are at least as important as the goals to be achieved), or our right to promote our own ideas of what constitutes the public interest when we are sufficiently motivated. But we do need to ask whether, by delegating much of the policy making power to other experts or other policy proponents, we are losing our voice in policy debates. This is both a normative question—about what a good democracy should look like—and a positive question, in which we can ask, as social scientists, "Who participates in making public policy?"

WHY DO WE STUDY PUBLIC POLICY?

While the concept of the public interest varies from person to person, and one person's individual interests are likely to differ in some ways from his or her neighbors' interests, most people are concerned about the impact of policies on their lives, such as how many services they receive or how much they have to pay in taxes. That said, why do you want to study the process that leads to the decisions to make these policies? Since you are reading this book, you probably already have an idea of why you are studying or working in public policy. Perhaps you have been interested in policy and politics since you were young; many people develop their interest in politics and policy at home. You may have been exposed to policy making when an interest in which you or your family believed was threatened, or if you perceived it was threatened. For example, you or your parents may have mobilized around plans to build a shopping mall, a power plant, a jail, or a polluting industrial facility near your home. Or perhaps you mobilized around a more abstract idea, such as civil rights for women, or gay and lesbian people, or for gun rights, or for environmental protection in the entire nation.

These are all practical reasons to study public policy, and many people study books, articles, and reports on public policy to learn how to be a more effective participant in public policy making, so that their and their friends' and neighbors' voices are heard in public policy debates.

But for many people, politics and policy making are inherently fascinating regardless of the specific policy content of the debate, and regardless of actual outcome. Some people study the policy process simply because it's interesting in its own right, as a way of conceiving of politics and problem-solving in a democratic society. One might compare the pursuit of knowledge to "pure" science and the practitioner orientation to "applied" science. The practical and applied study of public policy takes its cues from theory, but seeks more actively to apply those theoretical insights to actual cases of public policy formation, thereby helping theorists improve their theories. In a course on public policy, theory may be applied to particular cases or policy areas, as often seen in the later chapters of introductory public policy texts. As knowledge filters from the more abstract to the more applied, insights from the theoretical world are employed, knowingly or not, by practitioners. Conversely, students of public policy derive theory by observing the collective activity of the practitioners of public policy. This book considers theory more extensively in Chapter 11; for now, we should consider that people do also learn about theories of the world, including politics, for *both* theoretical and applied reasons—scientific knowledge is often greatly enhanced when both motivations are present (Stokes 1997).

Some of you will become very active participants in the policy process. Some will become elected officials, appointed officials, or agency managers and staff. Others will lead interest groups, work in the news media, or provide scientific and technical information for others. Many of you, never thinking you're involved in the process, will go on to successful careers in business, the arts, or other endeavors. But some day, when you least expect it, you may get involved in policy making. Perhaps you will become active when you and your neighbors oppose the construction of a new shopping mall in your neighborhood. For some people, this is the sort of problem that public policy is intended to address. But for others, a mall is an opportunity for economic growth or an added convenience, and the problem isn't the mall, it's the opposition to the mall. Perhaps your employer will ask you to participate in a public relations campaign to support or oppose a new policy. In short, chances are very good that you will become interested in the policy process at some point in your life, and I venture to guess that you will become involved in some way, given that you are reading this book! I hope that *An Introduction to the Policy Process* will help you become a more thoughtful and effective participant.

THE PLACE OF POLICY STUDIES IN THE SOCIAL SCIENCES

Because of the focus on politics in this chapter, one might conclude that policy studies are or should be the sole province of political scientists and closely related scholars, such as those who study policy analysis or public administration. But this interpretation only holds true if we focus narrowly on the policy process. There are many ways to study policy making, as Peter May shows in his "public policy morphology" (Table 1.2).

Many programs in political science, sociology, economics, public admin-istration, law, and other disciplines allow students to specialize in the study of policy and the policy process as they work toward their bachelor's, master's, and doctoral degrees. Dozens of universities now offer master's degrees in public policy (MPP degrees), and others offer bachelor's or doctoral degrees in public policy that draw from multiple disciplines to provide training in policy studies (see, for example, the National Association of Schools of Public Affairs and Administration website: www.naspaa.org). Most of these programs are interdisciplinary and draw their faculties from across the social, behavioral, and natural science disciplines. This interdisciplinary nature is both a strength and a weakness that has perennially faced policy studies. It is a strength

TABLE 1.2 A Public Policy Morphology

Public policy education and research has four fairly distinct variants. This book focuses on the first approach, and can serve as a foundation for further study in other areas of policy study.

- Public Policy Processes—This consists of research on the formulation and implementation of public policy usually limited to the American context emphasizing national, domestic policy. Using perspectives of American politics, individuals studying public policy processes address such topics as issue emergence and policy agendas, the cultural definition of policy problems, policy formulation, political feasibility, and policy implementation.

The policy process literature can be distinguished from other flavors of public policy as follows: Unlike policy analysis, it does not emphasize the craft aspects of constructing and analyzing policies. Unlike policy research, it does not emphasize problem-solving (rather, it is the study of how *others* define and seek to solve problems). And unlike comparative public policy, it tends to be limited to American settings although good comparative work is appropriate.

The other variants of public policy are:

- Comparative Public Policy—In principle, comparative public policy applies the logic of comparative analysis to the substance of different policy problems. Current writing and analysis tends to emphasize cross-national comparisons. There is also a newly emerging literature of comparative policy work among the American states. Much of this work is descriptive, rather than theoretical.

- Public Policy Analysis—A logic of analysis and mix of techniques in support of public policy decision-making. This tradition borrows heavily from economics. The logic of "rational" analysis contains a central focus on problem specification, generation of alternative policies, and assessment of policies in support of public policy decision-making. The techniques include quantitative methods, economic analysis, welfare economics, and qualitative assessments. Most of this type of training takes place within public policy programs offering professional two-year masters degrees. Weimer and Vining's policy analysis text and Eugene Bardach's short volume on policy analysis are leading works in this field.

- Public Policy Research—This consists of applied social science research aimed at documenting policy problems and evaluating interventions. The distinctive element of policy research is that it is problem driven. As such, the appropriate approaches and range of disciplinary relevance are in principle quite broad.

Typically, policy research training includes development of expertise in the substance of one or more policy areas (e.g., health, energy, and environment). This type of training takes place across a range of programs as reflected in the diversity of substantive public policy offerings in the social, natural, and behavioral sciences.

Source: Based on work by Peter J. May at the University of Washington.

discipline A field of academic research or study. Sociology, political science, and economics are social science disciplines; electrical, civil, and mechanical engineering are engineering disciplines. Disciplines approach similar problems in different ways.

social science The branch of the sciences that studies the actions and behavior of people, groups, and institutions. Political science, sociology, anthropology, and economics are social sciences. History is sometimes considered a social science.

because the **discipline** draws upon the best insights from the natural sciences, **social sciences**, and humanities. To some people, however, it is a weakness because policy scientists do not share a language that transcends disciplinary boundaries. Our challenge as students of public policy is to understand and profitably use the insights offered by the many disciplines that study, in various ways, public policy (Table 1.3).

TABLE 1.3 Selected Disciplines That Study Public Policy

Discipline	Description	Relationship to public policy	Some important journals
Political science	The study of political relationships; that is, the study of the processes by which societies seek to allocate political power and the benefits of such power.	The political process is the process through which policies are made and enforced.	*American Political Science Review, American Journal of Political Science, Journal of Politics, Polity, Political Research Quarterly, Public Opinion Quarterly*
Sociology	"Sociology is the study of social life, social change, and the social causes and consequences of human behavior. Sociologists investigate the structure of groups, organizations, and societies, and how people interact within these contexts."*	Community and group activities are an important part of policy making, because groups of people often form to make demands.	*American Sociological Review, Contemporary Sociology, American Journal of Sociology*
Economics	The study of the allocation of resources in a community, however defined. Economists study markets and exchanges. Welfare economists seek to understand the extent to which an overall community's welfare can be maximized.	There are many economic factors that influence public policy, such as economic growth, productivity, employment, and the like. The tools of economics are often used to promote policies or to explain why policies succeed or fail.	*American Economic Review, Econometrica, Journal of Applied Economics, Journal of Political Economy*
Public administration (PA)	The study of the management of government and nonprofit organizations, including the management of information, money, and personnel in order to achieve goals developed through the democratic process.	The management of public programs is an integral part of the policy process. PA scholars study the motivation of program implementers and targets, and help research innovations to improve service delivery.	*Public Administration Review, Journal of Public Administration Research and Teaching*
Public policy	The study of what governments choose to do or not to do, including studies of the policy process, policy implementation and impact, and evaluation.	We give this label to the highly interdisciplinary study of the public policy process. Policy scholars develop theories about how the policy process works, and develop tools and methods to analyze how policy is made and implemented.	*Journal of Policy Analysis and Management, Journal of Policy History, Journal of Public Policy, Policy Studies Journal, Policy Studies Review*

* American Sociological Association, www.asanet.org/employment/careers21st_whatissociology.cfm.

This book follows in the policy process tradition, which is more grounded in traditional political science. Students of the policy process view rational, scientific, and often quantitative policy analysis as part of the raw material of policy making that participants use to advocate for their preferred policies. The interplay of this evidence, the values and belief systems of the participants in the process, the structure of the process itself, and the distribution of power within the structure all have an important influence on public policy.

EVIDENCE AND ARGUMENT IN THE POLICY PROCESS

For years, political scientists have known that government is neither monolithic—that is, one single-minded body that speaks with one voice and works toward one set of goals—nor a neutral referee that dispassionately judges between policy alternatives by weighing their costs and benefits. The participants in the policy process—whether they are considered policy entrepreneurs, brokers, analysts, interest groups, or association leaders—are not all or even primarily neutral participants in the policy process. Thus, as Giandomenico Majone (1989) and Deborah Stone (1989, 2012) note, analysis is often undertaken in the name of advocacy, and is but one part of the rhetorical tools used in political debate. In the policy process, the results of "scientific" policy analysis are often abandoned when other rhetorical tools seem to work better. Indeed, as discussed later in this book, the act of identifying a problem is as much a normative judgment as it is an objective statement of fact; thus, if analysis proceeds from the identification of a problem, and the problem is defined normatively, then one cannot say that any subsequent analysis is strictly neutral.

As I wrote this chapter for the first edition, my introductory public policy course was giving its group presentations on issues related to the apparent outbreak of school violence incidents in places such as Springfield, Oregon, and Littleton, Colorado, in the late 1990s. Sadly, such concerns have continued after incidents in colleges and schools, including Virginal Tech and the Sandy Hook elementary school in Connecticut. One of the groups chose to focus on pending federal legislation, alternative policy choices, and the group's analysis of the desirability of alternative solutions to the school violence problem. The group argued that armed guards, cameras in classrooms, metal detectors, and other measures seemed too severe. These security techniques would make schools seem like prisons and thereby damage the educational environment, in turn reducing academic performance.

During a question-and-answer period, I asked the students whether they had any information that showed a link between these stern security measures and a poorer educational environment. They answered that they did not. I then asked, "Does it matter that you have no evidence?" After some discussion, we concluded that evidence is useful in policy debate, but it is not always necessary. Sometimes, the *stories* we tell about problems and policies—including the imagery and symbolism one associates with a policy—can matter more than the "facts" behind the policy. For example, arguing that a set of policies will create a school that looks and feels like a jail may be sufficient to win an argument against the most intensive security measures. While one can gather considerable information on the relationship between school security and the educational environment, one need not necessarily have all the evidence at hand if one's argument strikes a chord with the public and decision-makers. This means, more bluntly, that relatively little evidence is needed to make an argument if it is possible to appeal to popular prejudices and common misconceptions, or to common values or interests that are not too far outside the mainstream of current thought. This sounds cynical, but there are abundant examples in American history and world history of emotion overcoming rationality in policy making, such as the imposition of Jim Crow laws on black Americans based on a scientifically unfounded belief that blacks are genetically inferior to whites in some way. But emotion and appeals to justice and fairness also played a major role in overturning those very laws. Because neither facts nor emotions are solely decisive, evidence *and* emotion play important roles in policy making, and sometimes emotion gains the upper hand.

CASE STUDY: DOES THE DARE PROGRAM WORK?

Let's consider the adoption of public policy where there is little social science evidence to suggest the policy meets its goals, but it continues to be an important policy. You may be familiar with the DARE (Drug Abuse Resistance Education) program, either by reputation or personal experience.[2] The reason for the creation of DARE, or any anti-drug program, is simple: drug abuse—including the abuse of legal drugs, alcohol, and tobacco as well as illegal drugs—is associated with poor academic achievement, crime, and significant health problems for drug abusers. The federal, state, and local governments have created drug use regulations and educated the public about drugs for decades. DARE was an innovative program that linked schools with law enforcement in a way that would, its designers believed, be more effective than existing programs in preventing school-aged children from using (or "experimenting with") illegal drugs, tobacco, and alcohol.

The program was founded in 1983 by the police and schools in Los Angeles to address local problems with drugs and gangs. It has since been implemented internationally. At its peak, DARE served 43 countries and 75 percent of school districts in the United States. Originally designed for older elementary school students, DARE programs evolved to address drug abuse, gangs, and violence with students in kindergarten through twelfth grade. The national DARE organization claims that the program helps students make good decisions and "'humanizes' the police: that is, young people can begin to relate to officers as people"; through the DARE program, students may think of police officers as friends and helpers in the community. DARE designers felt that the inclusion of police officers as instructors would increase the credibility of the instructors and the program, a result that at least one study corroborated (Hammond et al. 2008).

While the DARE organization referred to itself as the "preeminent substance abuse education program"—a reasonable claim given the number of schools that use it—scientific evidence of its effectiveness is scant. The basic question is whether using the fundamental anti-drug DARE programs reduces drug use in that population of students compared with students who did not go through DARE. In a 2001 review of drug abuse prevention programs, the U.S. Surgeon General placed DARE in the "Does Not Work" category of these programs (Office of the Surgeon General et al. 2001). A 2003 Government Accountability Office study reviewed the existing body of literature on DARE effectiveness and reported that the existing research found no significant difference in drug use between students who had completed DARE and students who had not. Research by the National Institutes of Health, Department of Education, and Department of Justice corroborated these findings. Perhaps most damaging to DARE was a study published in the *American Journal of Public Health*, which conducted an overview (a meta-analysis) of the most scientifically rigorous studies the researchers could find. They discovered that, overall, studies proved no effect from the DARE curriculum; in simple terms, the studies concluded that DARE did not have a measurable influence on drug use among school-aged children, especially when measured over time. As a result of the many studies that showed DARE's ineffectiveness, federal money supporting DARE programs was cut, and some school districts have dropped the DARE program (Weiss, Murphy-Graham, and Birkeland 2005). Many organizations continued the DARE program through local fundraising and taxation.

Several responses to the negative research findings followed. First, DARE advocates argued that the outcomes of drug prevention education are difficult to quantify, that the studies cited by researchers were flawed, and that DARE's satisfaction surveys revealed positive outcomes, including high levels of parent, student, and community satisfaction. Advocates also maintain that positive experiences with law enforcement officers are significant, though difficult to measure. However, none of these claims or objections provides an answer to the fundamental research question about DARE's effectiveness.

The second response was more subtle, but more revealing. DARE, facing the loss of federal funding and its own credibility, revised its curriculum in response to several studies. In an undated document on its website, DARE suggests that the "new DARE" reflects changes in curriculum design and delivery, and incorporates more effective instructional methods based on better science. The creation of the "new DARE" was likely motivated by the urging of DARE's proponents to avoid losing federal funding and a desire to embrace science. The new program—which emphasizes teaching middle school children—was to be evaluated by a $13.7 million study funded by the Robert Wood Johnson Foundation—a highly respected institution devoted to health issues—to track the effectiveness of the program. However, the evaluators have not yet published results of their research on the fundamental question of DARE's effectiveness. Furthermore, DARE's mission shifted, as do many organizations' missions when their fundamental rationale is questioned. A review of the DARE website reveals that the organization has broadened its programs to anti-gang and anti-bullying efforts as well.

Why, then, was DARE so popular as an anti-drug program? There are several potential reasons, and the remainder of this book will help you to understand the logic behind the continued adoption of a program that "doesn't work." The first reason DARE remained popular is because people believe it works, because they draw on anecdotal evidence—that is, personal experience—to draw conclusions about its effectiveness. DARE supporters often raise the issue of DARE's creation of good relationships between police officers and students. In one case, a county sheriff in Ohio noted that "There are studies out there that said that it didn't work, that kids still used drugs. What it doesn't measure is the relationships that are built between the kids and those officers" (Wilson 2009). A parent in Texas, reacting to the impending cut of DARE from her children's school, said, "I asked my kids, 'Do you think that program is worth it?' and they said, 'Yes.' They would never smoke—they never realized how many chemicals are in (a cigarette)—and it turned them off to drugs, too" (Meyers 2009). In another instance, a school superintendent in Suffolk County, New York, expressed his disappointment with the decision to drop DARE:

> It has had a tremendous impact on the students and has become part of our school culture. I'm concerned that when the responsibility for teaching the curriculum falls on the shoulders of the teachers, who already have a full curriculum, that it won't have the same effectiveness that it did when the police officers came to visit.
>
> (Saslow 2007)

From the schools' perspective, the DARE program fills important needs. As one police department notes:

> Having a DARE program in the local school lifts the burden off teachers and administrators to provide drug education, and gives them additional time to do

something else. It is popular with parents and the media because it conveys the idea that something is being done to combat the menace of drug abuse by children.

(Lafayette (Indiana) Police Department 2008)

This idea of "doing something" is important in politics and public policy. In the DARE case, an expert on adolescent substance abuse noted the powerful reasons why DARE persists in so many schools:

> This evidence, of course, is not popular with parents, police officers and others since many of them believe DARE works. And kids do say the "right" things after participating. But, research shows there are no long-term effects. A perfect formula for a belief-versus-science polarization. So, why the interest and support for "needing" more DARE programs . . . despite overwhelming evidence they don't work? Well, it's mostly about the comfort parents, school staff, police officers, and other adults receive when a program is delivered that is visible and, in their beliefs, helpful. It feels good to know that at least something is being done.

(Rockholz 2010)

Often, policy makers feel a great deal of pressure to "do something" about public problems, even when all the information is not available; indeed, as we will learn, information is often hard to come by. Furthermore, once a program is in place, many stakeholders—in this case, parents, teachers, the police, school boards, and local community leaders—have so much money, time, and personal belief invested in a program that it is difficult, even in the face of scientific evidence, to change the program.

Another way to understand the persistence of DARE is by reframing the essential research question: Does DARE work? One can ask, "What does 'work' mean?" As originally defined by DARE's developers, the program was supposed to keep kids from trying or using drugs. The scientific evidence suggests that this does not happen. But are there other benefits to DARE? What about the oft-cited relationships between police and children? Is this a positive benefit? How would one measure this? Do police officers benefit from meeting and interacting with the students in their communities? What about the use of police as instructors? Does this benefit teachers who may not feel comfortable teaching students about drug use and abuse? What benefits, if any, might accrue to a community as a whole for identifying, as so many signs do, particularly in small-town America, that "We are a DARE community?" Did the range of those benefits increase when DARE broadened its mission beyond drug prevention? Could a more scientifically sound program provide these benefits? Or is the drug problem so intractable—that is, hard to solve—that no program is likely to work?

The DARE case illustrates how powerful rhetoric, symbolism, and storytelling that relies on anecdotes can promote a policy even when the evidence of its effectiveness is scant.

Despite mounting evidence that the old DARE was ineffective, and the lack of evidence that the new program is effective, the curriculum continues to be used in many schools around the nation. It is very difficult to remove DARE from some schools because of the popularity of the idea of working with the police combined with the valued goal of preventing or reducing youth drug use and violence. Are there other policies that continue to be used even if they fail to achieve their goals? Are policies enacted that are unlikely to achieve the goals that their proponents claim? Why would people propose policies that they may know won't work well? How do we measure whether a policy is "good" or not? Consider these questions—and the logic behind these questions—as you read this book.

SUMMARY

This chapter has provided an overview of the endeavor on which you are about to embark: the study of public policy. We learned that the study of public policy is rooted in the study of politics, which is an ancient field of study. But we also learned that the study of public policy, as we generally define it, is a recent innovation. I hope that this introductory chapter has motivated you to study the public policy process both to satisfy your own personal curiosity about how things work, and to motivate you to understand and perhaps play a more active role in the decisions that affect you, your family, and your community.

This book is organized in three broad sections. This chapter and Chapters 2 and 3 are overviews of the policy process and of the environment in which policy is made. Chapter 3 introduces the stages model of the policy process, which serves to organize the various parts of the process so that we can analyze them. Chapters 4 and 5 are about the actors in the policy process. Chapters 6 through 10 cover the outputs and processes of public policy. Chapter 11 brings all this together by considering modern, better theories of the policy process that improve upon the stages model and develop better grounded theories.

As you read this book, I hope you will think of current ideas and events in the political world, and your own ideas about how public policy can alleviate the problems you find most concerning. As you do so, think about what you are learning from this book and how it can be applied to these problems, whether such problems are new or are perennial.

KEY TERMS

classical liberalism	politics
discipline	problem
Enlightenment	public interest
policy	social science

QUESTIONS FOR DISCUSSION, REFLECTION, AND RESEARCH

- How is public policy grounded in the study of politics? What do you think the term "politics" means in this context? Do you think it would be possible to make public policy without politics?

- Is there a real difference between "playing politics" and just the general political process of argument, negotiation, and compromise? Why do people think so negatively of politics given that this is the process by which we address public problems?

- Discuss the study of public policy. Are there other disciplines that aren't mentioned here that contribute to the study of public policy? In what way might those disciplines contribute to policy making? (Think broadly. How do scientists and engineers help make public policy? Doctors? Social workers? Other professions?)

- Ask your friends, neighbors, or family members what comes to mind when they hear the word "politics." Then, ask what they think when they hear the term "public policy." How are their responses similar to and different from the ideas discussed in this chapter?

- Find an article on a public policy issue in a newspaper. Consider carefully whether the people making arguments for or against a particular policy are making *normative* or *positive* arguments. Are they using anecdotes or evidence? How can you tell the difference? Whose arguments do you consider most persuasive? Why?

ADDITIONAL READING

In this chapter, I argue in favor of evidence-based policy advocacy. The making of public policy based on scientifically gathered evidence (by which I mean evidence from the natural sciences, social sciences, and engineering) is not a new idea; indeed, this sort of evidence is at the heart of Lasswell's call for a distinctive policy science. On this conception of policy science, see Harold D. Lasswell, *A Pre-View of Policy Sciences* (New York: American Elsevier, 1971); and Daniel Lerner and Harold D. Lasswell, *The Policy Sciences: Recent Developments in Scope and Method* (Stanford, CA: Stanford University Press, 1951). The journal *Policy Sciences* publishes research that follows Lasswell's ideas about the policy sciences. This subject is taken up in greater detail in Chapter 8.

But the role of rhetoric and argument, combined with evidence and scientific inquiry, is as important as technical argument about the substance of policy, and is a theme taken up by Giandomenico Majoine in *Evidence, Argument and Persuasion in the Policy Process* (1989). A similar work is Deborah Stone's *Policy Paradox: The Art of Political Decision Making*, 3rd edition (2012), a work that has been very influential in my thinking about policy.

There are many popular treatments of how Americans engage with the political system, and why people are often so frustrated by it. A classic in this genre is E.J. Dionne, *Why Americans Hate Politics* (New York: Simon & Schuster, 1991). The book is over 20 years old, but its central premise remains relevant: that describing public problems and solutions as "conservative" or "liberal" ignores problem definitions and solutions that could be said to be centrist, not leaning to either ideological pole. Because I tend to believe that, in many cases, governmental institutions and the political process can identify and solve problems, I particularly like Paul Light's book, *Government's Greatest Achievements: From Civil Rights to Homeland Security* (Washington, DC: Brookings Institution, 2002), which reminds us that not all government activity is futile or wasteful.

NOTES

1 Yale University's law school provides the entire Federalist Papers at http://avalon.law.yale. edu/subject_menus/fed.asp, and many fine annotated editions are available as books.
2 Unless otherwise noted, all claims about DARE's history, structure, and effectiveness come from the organization's website, www.dare.com.

REFERENCES

Gay, Peter. 1996. *The Enlightenment: An Interpretation*. New York: W.W. Norton & Company.

Hammond, Augustine, Zili Sloboda, Peggy Tonkin, Richard Stephens, Brent Teasdale, Scott F. Grey, and Joseph Williams. 2008. "Do Adolescents Perceive Police Officers as Credible Instructors of Substance Abuse Prevention Programs?" *Health Education Research* 23(4): 682–696. doi: 10.1093/her/cym036.

Howlett, Michael, M. Ramesh, and Anthony Perl. 2009. *Studying Public Policy: Policy Cycles & Policy Subsystems*. 3rd ed. New York: Oxford University Press.

Kumar, Bharat. 2014. "What Is the Relationship between Sociology and Political Science?" Preserve Articles. Accessed April 1, 2015. www.preservearticles.com/201102214068/what-is-the-relationship-between-sociology-and-political-science.html.

Lafayette (Indiana) Police Department. 2008. "D.A.R.E./SRO." Accessed February 3, 2015. www.lafayette.in.gov/egov/docs/1208202879833.htm.

Lasswell, Harold D. 1958. *Politics: Who Gets What, When, How*. New York: Meridian Books.

Lipsky, Michael. 2010. *Street-Level Bureaucracy: Dilemmas of the Individual in Public Services*. 30th anniversary expanded ed. New York: Russell Sage Foundation.

McCool, Daniel C. 1995. *Public Policy Theories, Models, and Concepts: An Anthology*. Englewood Cliffs, NJ: Prentice Hall.

Majone, Giandomenico. 1989. *Evidence, Argument, and Persuasion in the Policy Process*. New Haven, CT: Yale University Press.

Meyers, Rhiannon. 2009. "Schools want to drop DARE." *Galveston County Daily News*, April 5. Accessed February 3, 2015. www.galvestondailynews.com/news/article_cee7fac4-b427-599f-921e-202cfd128be5.html.

Montesquieu, Charles de Secondat. 1989. *The Spirit of the Laws*. Cambridge Texts in the History of Political Thought. New York: Cambridge University Press.

Office of the Surgeon General, Prevention National Center for Injury, Control, Health National Institute of Mental, and Services Center for Mental Health. 2001. *Youth Violence: A Report of the Surgeon General, Publications and Reports of the Surgeon General*. Rockville, MD: Office of the Surgeon General (US).

Rawls, John. 1999. *A Theory of Justice*. Rev. ed. Cambridge, MA: Belknap Press of Harvard University Press.

Rochefort, David A. and Roger W. Cobb, Eds. 1994. *The Politics of Problem Definition*. Lawrence, KS: University of Kansas Press.

Rockholz, Peter B. 2010. "Is DARE effective? 'Overwhelming evidence' shows DARE has no lasting impact." *The News-Times*, February 19, 2010. Accessed February 3, 2015. www.newstimes.com/opinion/article/Sunday-debate-Is-DARE-effective-Overwhelming-372445.php.

Saslow, Linda. 2007. "Suffolk Schools to Say Goodbye to DARE." *The New York Times*, November 25, 2007. Accessed February 3, 2015. www.nytimes.com/2007/11/25/nyregion/nyregionspecial2/25dareli.html?_r=0.

Schneider, Anne Larason and Helen Ingram. 1997. *Policy Design for Democracy*. Lawrence, KS: University Press of Kansas.

Stokes, Donald E. 1997. *Pasteur's Quadrant: Basic Science and Technological Innovation*. Washington, DC: Brookings Institution Press.

Stone, Deborah A. 1989. "Causal Stories and the Formation of Policy Agendas," *Political Science Quarterly* 104(2): 281–300.

Stone, Deborah A. 2012. *Policy Paradox: The Art of Political Decision Making*. 3rd ed. New York: Norton.

Viard, Alan D. 2007. "The Trouble with Taxing Those at the Top," *Tax Policy Outlook*, American Enterprise Institute for Public Policy Research, no. 2, July 2007. Accessed April 23, 2014. www.aei.org/article/economics/fiscal-policy/the-trouble-with-taxing-those-at-the-top/.

Weiss, Carol Hirschon, Erin Murphy-Graham, and Sarah Birkeland. 2005. "An Alternate Route to Policy Influence: How Evaluations Affect D.A.R.E." *American Journal of Evaluation* 26(1): 12–30. doi: 10.1177/1098214004273337.

Wilson, Dara. 2009. "D.A.R.E. cut back statewide." *The Columbus Dispatch*. Accessed June 30, 2015. www.dispatch.com/content/stories/local/2009/08/30/nodare.ART_ART_08-30-09_B1_OFETO5N.html.

CHAPTER 2

Elements of the
Policy Making System

OVERVIEW

The term "policy process" suggests that there is some sort of system that translates policy ideas into actual policies that are implemented and have positive effects. Traditionally, public policy textbooks have presented what is known as the "textbook model" or "stages model" of the policy process. The process is shown in Figure 2.1.

   This figure serves both as an overview of the process, and, to some extent, the organization for this book. In this model, public problems emerge in a society through various means, including sudden events such as disasters or through the advocacy activities of concerned citizens and interest groups. If the issue gains sufficient attention, it is said to have reached the agenda, a process described in Chapter 6. Given the size and complexity of governance in the United States and the number of governments— over 80,000, from the federal government to the smallest local water district—there are lots of problems and lots of ideas on many agendas. Once an issue moves up on an agenda, it moves to the development of alternative policy responses—some might call them solutions—to public problems. From there, we move to alternative policy selection; that is, the choice of policy tools we will use to address the problem, whereupon policies are enacted. Enactment means that a law is passed, a regulation is issued, or some other formal decision is reached to take a particular action to solve a

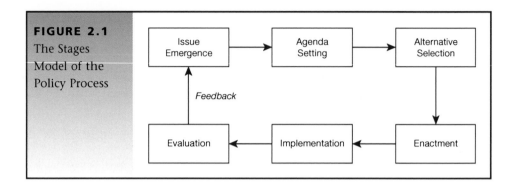

FIGURE 2.1
The Stages
Model of the
Policy Process

problem. After that decision is reached, the policy is implemented, a process described in Chapter 10. The policy is then evaluated and the results of evaluation provide feedback to the process, where it begins anew.

This model has been subject to considerable critique. A main critique of the stages, or textbook model of policy making, is that it implies that policy making proceeds step by step, starting at the beginning and ending at the end (Nakamura 1987). Critics point out that a policy idea may not reach every stage. For example, policy ideas often reach the agenda, but move no further than that. Others argue that one cannot separate the implementation of a policy from its evaluation, because evaluation happens continuously as a policy is implemented. These critics suggest that the stages model does not constitute a workable theory of how the policy process works. (These critiques are taken up when we delve into advanced theories of the policy process, including a discussion of what a theory means, in Chapter 10.) But I used the stages model to organize this book because it remains a remarkably helpful way to structure our thinking about the policy process. As political scientist Peter deLeon notes, many scholars have written extensive studies that describe each stage of the process (deLeon 1999). Thinking of policy making in stages is a way of organizing our thinking and of isolating and understanding the most important elements of the process.

systems thinking
A way of thinking
about natural or
social phenomena
as a system, in
which various
inputs into a
system are
handled, processed,
and interact with
each other to
create a set of
discernible outputs.

THE POLICY PROCESS AS A SYSTEM

The stages model of the policy process owes a great deal to **systems thinking**, a way of thinking about all manner of things—from social to biological to mechanical systems—that became much more prominent after World War

II. The simplest model of the policy process is an **input-output model**. The inputs are the various issues, pressures, information, and the like to which the actors in the system react. The outputs are, in simplest terms, public policy decisions to do or not do something. David Easton's book *A Systems Analysis of Political Life* was among the first works to describe politics in this way (Easton 1965; Greenberg et al. 1977; Gunnell 2013). A simplified depiction of this system is shown in Figure 2.2.

The challenge in thinking about policy as the product of a system lies in understanding how policy makers translate sets of inputs into outputs. The major criticism of Easton's systems model is that most depictions of this model treat the political system as a **black box** (that is, a system in which the internal workings are unexplained), rather than opening the box to understand the processes that occur within it. A black box in a systems model is something that performs a translating or processing function, but where the actual workings of that system are unclear. The stages model of the policy process is one way of opening up that black box to more thorough analysis.

Easton and the systems modelers argue that we can think of the public policy process as the product of a system that is influenced by and influences the environment in which it operates. This chapter focuses on this policy-making environment and describes the social, political, and economic system in which public policy making takes place. The political process relates to its environment much as a plant or animal does: it is both influenced by and influences its environment. One must be careful with this analogy, however; the boundary between the political system and its environment is blurry, as the system and the environment overlap. The strength of the systems

input-output model A model of the policy process that assumes a set of policy demands or inputs, which are then processed by the political system into laws, programs, and the goods and services government provides.

black box The part of any system model or theory that just assumes its operation without explaining how that part of the system translates inputs into outputs.

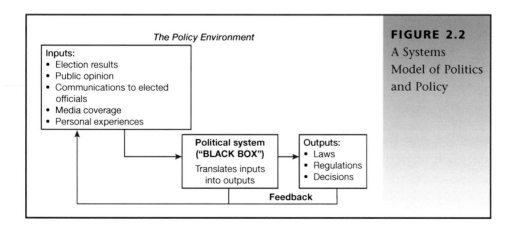

FIGURE 2.2
A Systems Model of Politics and Policy

policy environment The structural, social, economic, political, and other factors that influence and are influenced by policy making.

separation of powers The constitutional division of power between the legislative, executive, and judicial branches of the government.

federalism A system of government in which power is shared between a central or federal government and other governments, such as states or provinces.

open public meetings Laws that mandate that most public meetings and hearings should be open to the public, in decision-making.

Administrative Procedure Act A federal law (5 U.S.C. 551 et seq.) that requires regulatory agencies to follow particular procedures in rule making, such as public notice of new rules, public comment periods, publication of rule making activity in the *Federal Register*, and the like.

approach is its value in helping us isolate important things worthy of study. For example, within this general notion of the **policy environment**, we can isolate four "environments" that influence policy making: the structural environment, the social environment, the economic environment, and the political environment.

The Structural Environment

The basic structural features of American government are those taught in high school civics or introductory American politics courses. These features include the **separation of powers** into three branches of government and the system of state and federal government known as **federalism**. Beyond the basic constitutional framework, there are traditional and legal structures that establish rules of policy making, many of which are described in Chapter 3.

But government structures are not simply formal; a structural environment involves rules that dictate how government goes about its business. In the past three decades, laws such as **open public meetings** laws, the **Administrative Procedure Act**, and the **Freedom of Information Act** have opened up government to considerable scrutiny. These laws allow people greater access to government. They have helped to root out some unseemly practices in government, since the participants in a policy arena know that their actions are on the public record. These benefits come with the cost of slowing down policy change as agencies and policy proponents must seek and address public comment, scrutiny, and sometimes opposition. In other words, an agency cannot simply regulate without any public scrutiny, and that scrutiny can sometimes lead to conflict and delay. In our system, as in many democracies, citizens and policy makers must seek a broadly accepted balance between legislative speed and efficiency, on the one hand, and a respect for democracy and the rights of all citizens to participate, on the other.

The Social Environment

The social aspect of the policy environment involves the nature and composition of the population and its social structure. **Demographers** study the composition of the population by looking at the distribution of age, race, gender, and other attributes. Our nation's founders enacted a constitutional mandate for a census to be taken every 10 years, which allowed for the collection of a vast amount of demographic data. The U.S. Census Bureau and other agencies collect a huge amount of data between the censuses, so we have very good indicators of social trends. These trends have an important influence on public policy making.

A Growing, but Aging, Population

The population of the United States is graying, as reflected in Figure 2.3, but the rate of growth is relatively slow compared with that of other countries. The slope of the population growth line is nearly constant until about 1990, when growth increased as the kids of baby boomers began to have kids and there was an increase in immigration. Still, since 1960, the annual growth rate has never exceeded its 1961 high of 1.67 percent annually (Figure 2.4). Of course, this growth rate is not uniform nationally, and some states, such as California and Florida, are growing faster than others, such as New York and Ohio.

This slow growth means that the nation is trending toward an older population; in 1980, over half the nation's population was under 35 years old; by 2000, more than half the population was older than 35; and by 2015, those age 50 or above will account for one-third of the nation's population, up from just over 26 percent in 1980 (Figure 2.5).

Freedom of Information Act
Federal law that allows citizens to gain information about government programs. This act is often invoked by journalists and researchers when the government is at first unwilling to provide information; it is sometimes successful in compelling the government to provide information.

demographers
Individuals who study the composition of the population by looking at the distribution of age, race, gender, and other attributes.

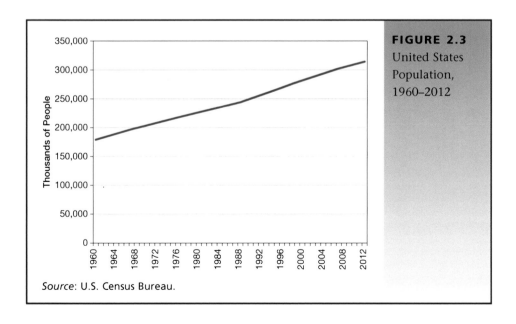

FIGURE 2.3
United States Population, 1960–2012

Source: U.S. Census Bureau.

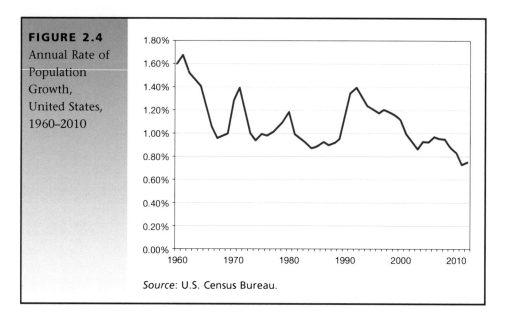

FIGURE 2.4
Annual Rate of Population Growth, United States, 1960–2010

Source: U.S. Census Bureau.

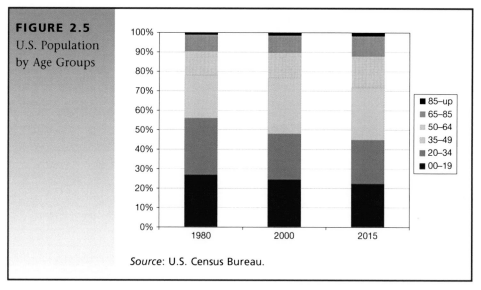

FIGURE 2.5
U.S. Population by Age Groups

Source: U.S. Census Bureau.

Race and Ethnicity

The United States has generally been a "white" country, consisting primarily of the descendants of European settlers, with a substantial African-American minority population. By the late twentieth century, these proportions were changing, as reflected in Figure 2.6. In particular, the self-identified Hispanic population was projected to grow from 12.5 percent of the population—about the same proportion as African Americans—to 17.7 percent of the population in 2009. (The "Hispanic" classification is of an ethnic group and is not a racial category on the census. Most Hispanics identify themselves as white on the census.)

Gender and Labor Force Participation

The gender distribution of the nation's population has remained relatively stable for the last 50 years, with slightly more women than men in the population, primarily because of the long life expectancy for women. But public policies do reflect changing attitudes about gender roles, which in turn have implications for families and the workforce. Indeed, we can see these trends in male and female labor force participation (Figure 2.7). While the proportion of men with jobs has slightly declined in recent years, the rate at which women are participating in the workforce has been climbing since 1975, and is leveling off or just growing slightly. These data are driven by two related but different trends: the extent to which women have gained

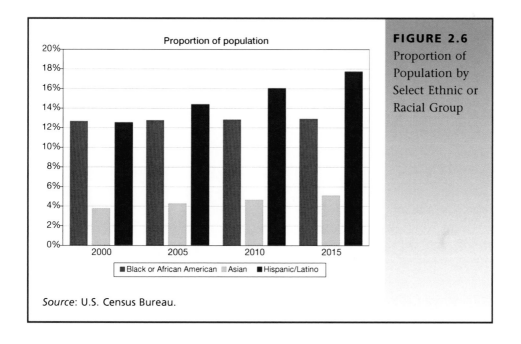

FIGURE 2.6
Proportion of Population by Select Ethnic or Racial Group

Source: U.S. Census Bureau.

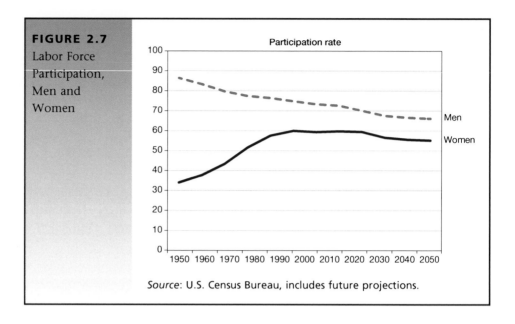

FIGURE 2.7
Labor Force
Participation,
Men and
Women

Source: U.S. Census Bureau, includes future projections.

equal access to the job market and the extent to which families depend on a second earner.

Women's labor force participation was very high during World War II, but when the war ended and millions of soldiers returned from Europe and Asia, women retreated from (or were pushed out of) the paid workforce. This trend reversed in the 1970s, when more women pressed for the right to work on an equal footing with men. About 60 percent of American women now work, up from just over 40 percent in 1975. The rate of male labor force participation declined slightly during that period. The entry of women into the workforce has led to some important trends in median family incomes, as seen in Figure 2.8.

At the same time as women were increasing their participation in the workforce, median family income among "traditional" families (in which the wife stays at home) remained fairly stagnant from the early 1970s. Only in families where women entered the workforce has there been a substantial increase in family income. While in 1970 two-earner families earned about 130 percent of the income that single-earner families earned, in 2007 two-earner families earned about 180 percent of single-earner families. Whether the increase in female labor force participation is a function of gender equity, economic necessity, or some of both is a matter that continues to be debated.

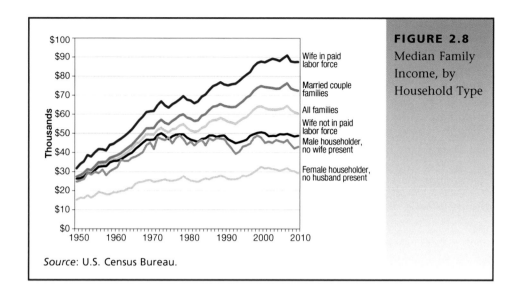

FIGURE 2.8

Median Family Income, by Household Type

Wife in paid labor force

Married couple families

All families

Wife not in paid labor force

Male householder, no wife present

Female householder, no husband present

Source: U.S. Census Bureau.

But we can say from the data that family incomes have not substantially grown where women have not entered the workforce. This stagnation in median family income has been a recurrent theme in the debates over the state of the U.S. economy.

Another major shift in the social environment that will influence policy is the increase in the number of women in professions and roles that were once held by men only. Women today attend college at a greater rate than men and attend law school at a rate nearly equal to men. The establishment of the WNBA basketball league, the very closely followed American women's World Cup soccer victory in 1999, and the considerable growth in the popularity of women's college basketball are highly visible indicators of our society's changing attitudes toward women's roles and capabilities. And more women than before are holding positions of influence at the national level; three recent U.S. secretaries of state have been women. Condoleezza Rice, the secretary of state under President George W. Bush, was the first African-American woman to hold that position; she succeeded Colin Powell, the first African American to serve as secretary. (Earlier, General Powell had been the first African-American general to chair the Joint Chiefs of Staff, the top decision-making body in the military.) Madeleine Albright was secretary of state during the Clinton administration, and Hillary Clinton was the third woman to hold the position.

The Policy Implications of Demographic Changes

Why does demographic change matter? A 2011 report for the Congressional Research Service (CRS) reviewed many of the trends outlined here, and found three broad areas where they will matter: the workforce, immigration, and intermarriage. The first is in work, retirement, and pensions. As the population becomes older, the number of people drawing social security and other old age benefits, as well as private pensions, will increase as a proportion of the overall working population. Note also that in Figure 2.7 we saw overall male participation in the workforce declining, a result in part of older men leaving the workforce with more younger women entering than before. Some of this retirement is driven by trends in "private wealth and income security," which relates both to private retirement and pension plans and to the nature of social security benefits. In particular, with many more retirees in the system:

> a major domestic political challenge of the twenty-first century will be how to adapt our old-age income security and health insurance systems to ensure financial solvency while ensuring that there is an adequate safety net to protect the most vulnerable in the population.
>
> (Shrestha and Heisler 2011: 25)

According to the report, this will result from the use of private savings. Of course, the major recession and the drop in the value of investments in 2008 through 2010 suggest at least a short-term problem with retirement income for millions of Americans. This appears to have induced many Americans to plan to work past the retirement age of 65. This, in turn, will have important implications for employment and job creation.

The aging population will also pose significant health challenges. Improvements in human health and in healthcare have shown remarkable progress. But this aging population will demand more and potentially more expensive healthcare services, at the very time when cost containment and broader availability of affordable health insurance is very high on the government's list of priorities. And as a larger proportion of Americans will be over the age of 65, there will be a particular need to provide care to people more prone to "cognitive impairment and dementia," even though the full implications are not yet clear.

The next set of policy implications relates to immigration policy. The United States will continue to grow at a faster rate than nearly all European Union nations because of a somewhat higher birth rate—particularly among recent immigrants—and because of the flow of immigrants. Americans by and large cherish the nation's self-image as a beacon of hope for people throughout the world who come to seek a better life. At the same time—just as was true 100 years ago—immigration creates social strains and resentments, as well as very strong pressures for immigrants to assimilate into American culture. Just as with the major wave of immigration in the late 1800s and early 1900s, many first-generation immigrants will retain their own language and, to some extent, their customs, but their children will rapidly become assimilated. At the same time, immigration policy must balance between encouraging immigration to ensure that population growth and its economic benefits continue, and ensuring national security, particularly after the events of September 11, 2001, after which a number of reforms were made to immigration policy and management. These policies are intended to keep criminals and terrorists out of the United States while admitting the people we want to come and live here, but these policies may have the effect of discouraging immigration.

A third trend is "America's changing color lines." As the CRS report notes, "the United States is now a society composed of multiple racial and ethnic groups." The greater diversity of the nation is combined with the growing rates of intermarriage among racial and ethnic groups, so that it is becoming less and less fruitful to speak only of specific racial and ethnic groups. What are the major policy issues?

First, the CRS report finds that the extent of assimilation of, in particular, recent Asian immigrants is low; these people maintain their own languages and cultures either because they cannot, or do not wish to, assimilate into mainstream society. For any immigrant group—and for sheer numbers, Spanish-speaking immigrants—language barriers can make gaining work or an education more challenging. The enduring question is whether and to what extent, then, we want to offer services in Spanish. Does doing so hasten or delay assimilation?

A second policy issue is income disparities between whites, blacks, and Hispanics. Blacks and Hispanics tend to earn less than whites, which makes homeownership more difficult to achieve for members of racial and ethnic minorities. Homeownership is a major policy goal in the United States. Income disparities among groups are reflected in homeownership rates. People with low incomes are less likely to own their own homes, and less able to keep their homes during economic downturns. This income disparity is also reflected in poverty rates. While the poverty rate declined among all racial and ethnic categories—with the steepest declines among African Americans—racial minorities still have higher rates of poverty than do whites.

These trends suggest that it is important for people to consider demographic change as part of the broader policy environment. But questions of race or ethnicity also raise important and sometimes controversial questions. What difference does—or should—race or ethnicity make in public policy? In a supposedly color-blind society, in which everyone, regardless of race, ethnicity, national origin, and the like, should be treated equally, why continue to consider these issues? As the trends shown here demonstrate, race and ethnicity do matter in fundamental ways. We know that policies can have different effects on different racial and ethnic minorities. As social scientists, we also know that the effect of these differences—and the effects of policies that created or alleviated these differences—will lead to group mobilization. The increasing number of Hispanic Americans is primarily accounted for by people coming to the United States for whom Spanish, not English, is their native language. However, it is important to remember that what we see here is aggregate data—recent Hispanic immigrants from Central America are culturally and economically different from Cubans who identify as Hispanic but who arrived in the country in the early 1960s.

Furthermore, the recent policy discussion about race and ethnicity tends to overlook the continuing disparities between whites and African Americans in income, housing, employment, and education. The United States has made remarkable progress in addressing problems of racial discrimination since World War II. And, of course, many people rightly point to the election of President Barack Obama, whose father was Kenyan, as a sign that Americans' attitudes toward race have changed a great deal in just the last 30 years. Yet, at the same time, we know that African Americans suffer from poverty and unemployment at a higher rate than the national average. In a nation dedicated to equality, many people find such disparities troubling and define these disparities as problems that require attention.

As noted earlier, there is rapid growth in the Asian population of the United States, with large Asian communities found in California and New York, among other places. But let's consider immigration and national origin more broadly, and consider the challenges and complexities faced by my hometown, Anchorage, Alaska. One may not consider this small, remote city (compared with the rest of the United States) to be a major magnet for immigration. Yet in this city of about 300,000 people, the Anchorage school district provides English language learning services to students who speak *94* different languages, from Danish to Tlingit. Clearly, understanding people's ethnic heritage can provide some clues about what sort of public goods and services these people may need, in big cities and small towns all over the United States.

Furthermore, as self-identified racial and ethnic groups emerge and become large enough to organize, they will, as in any democracy, seek representation in our political and social institutions. This is not to say that all racial or ethnic minorities believe that their interests are only represented by a member of their racial group. Instead, these trends, coupled with remarkable changes in Americans' attitudes toward race—arguably culminating in President Obama's election—mean that our political institutions will continue to see increased participation by nonwhite Americans. In a special election in 2009, the first Vietnamese-American member of Congress was elected from a district in Louisiana, a state to which many Vietnamese emigrated after the Vietnam War. Clearly, demographic change is ongoing, and has important policy implications.

The Political Environment

One way that policy makers and other participants in politics assess their political and policy options is by looking at public opinion polling data. Public opinion polling has come a long way from its early efforts in the 1930s and 1940s. Today, the methods for sound polling are well established, and it is possible, with a well-crafted sampling plan, to survey only about 1,700 Americans to get results within about a 4 percent margin of error. With this in mind, we can consider the following polling data as broadly reflective of public opinion. The first set of data describes the general policy issues that have dominated Americans' attention since the 1960s. Then, we consider a set of political data that reflects what John Kingdon calls "the national mood."

Pollsters have for years asked people to list what they consider to be the "most important problem" on the national agenda. Such problems tend to track very closely with media coverage of important problems, but these results are fascinating snapshots of changes in public thinking and attitudes. The data shown in Figure 2.9 are from the "Agenda Project" database, a project of the Universities of Washington and Texas. The researchers found the "most important problem" (MIP) question in a series of Gallup polls, and have normalized the data to make them comparable over time. This figure reflects the historic problems people were thinking about in these years. In

1965, civil rights matters dominated the agenda; by 1974, in the height of the energy crisis, energy concerns dominated political discussion. Over half the respondents in 1984 isolated economic issues as the key issues. Defense was also a major concern during this important era in the Cold War. Defense was an even bigger concern during the height of the Vietnam War in the mid 1960s. In 1994, health issues dominated in ways that they never had before, due in large part to President Clinton's attempts at healthcare reform. Crime and economics were equally high on the MIP list in part of the 1990s. By 2004, macroeconomic concerns were very important, but defense and health also gained a lot of attention. And in 2004, international affairs was listed as an MIP more often than any time since 1964, a result of greater international attention paid to issues such as terrorism and the wars being fought in Iraq and Afghanistan.

One can argue that the answers to the MIP are a reflection of what policy makers and, indeed, the news media are focused on, not simply what a thoughtful mass public believes. One can reply that the media cover the things that people find most important, so the influence runs from readers and viewers to the media, not the other way. This claim is addressed in Chapter 5, but for now we can say that the MIP question reflects the important issues on the government's agenda, and, therefore, reflects the areas of public policy

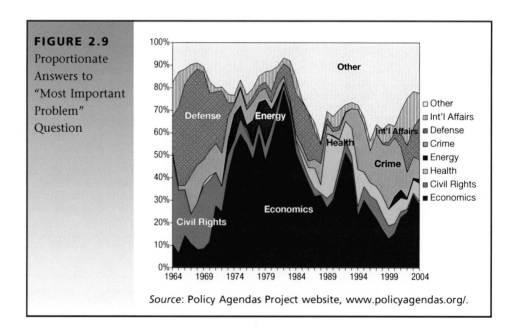

FIGURE 2.9 Proportionate Answers to "Most Important Problem" Question

Source: Policy Agendas Project website, www.policyagendas.org/.

in which one is likely to see the most activity. If we had to isolate one concern that spans the last 45 years of public policy making, that concern would be the economy.

John Kingdon describes the national mood as how we feel about government's handling of public problems (Kingdon 2011). While a national mood may be hard to measure, there are some ways to at least probe this idea. Sometimes, the national mood is generally good, such as when the economy is strong and trust in political institutions and our leaders is relatively high. From 1946 to about 1963, the national mood was broadly optimistic. The United States had emerged from World War II largely unscathed, and, after a mild postwar dip, the economy boomed after the war. Still, while the period was characterized by optimism, people were also concerned with communist expansion, fears of nuclear war (particularly in the 1950s and 1960s), and with social and political changes that seemed likely to follow World War II. An example of this anxiety was depicted by the William Wyler film *The Best Years of Our Lives*, which dealt with the postwar letdown experienced by three servicemen, their families, and their communities. Indeed, this film is one of the few post-World War II films to address these issues, and many postwar histories overlook the short-term downturn in the economy—and the accompanying postwar anxiety—that accompanied this period. Overall, and especially when the postwar economic boom took hold, people became optimistic about America's future, believed its social and political system to be superior to those of other nations, and trusted their leaders.

In the mid 1960s, the national mood began to decay. The Vietnam War began to bog down, and claims that it was being won were proven to be false. Growing antiwar sentiment and a so-called credibility gap between what government and military leaders claimed was happening in Vietnam and what journalists reported ultimately led to President Lyndon Johnson's decision not to run for re-election in 1968. Between 1968 and 1974, the war continued, Robert F. Kennedy and Martin Luther King, Jr. were murdered, and President Richard Nixon resigned in disgrace over the Watergate scandal. At the same time, inflation, unemployment, and the energy crisis combined to erode public faith in the United States' economy and its power. By the late 1970s, major American industries were facing severe competitive pressures from Europe and Japan.

The early 1980s saw little improvement in the national mood, with a major **recession** in the 1980s triggered, in part, by the Federal Reserve's stringent anti-inflation policies. By the mid 1980s, however, inflation was almost

recession
A period of economic contraction in which the value of the gross domestic product shrinks for two consecutive quarters.

entirely eliminated as a major factor in the economy, and the economy recovered. Except for a relatively mild recession in the late 1980s and early 1990s, the economy grew strong through the 1990s and early 2000s (though certainly not in all sectors), giving Americans substantial faith in the future of the nation. Indeed, most Americans believed, until 2008, that an economic **depression** was extremely unlikely. While the 2008 stock market crash and related crises in the financial markets led to a particularly severe recession, from which the economy has not, as of this writing, recovered, most economists still would hesitate to call this downturn a depression on the same scale as that which swept the world in the 1930s.

When I wrote the first edition of this book in 2000, I mentioned that "today's national mood is in many ways upbeat—with crime on the decline, the economy booming, and international tensions seemingly much less frightening than they were during the depths of the Cold War." This claim is reflected in the data shown in Figure 2.10, which show responses to a commonly asked question in an NBC/*Wall Street Journal* poll: "All in all, do you think things in the nation are generally headed in the right direction, or do you feel that things are off on the wrong track?" As you can see, most

depression
A particularly severe recession; in particular, the Great Depression in the United States and other nations from 1929 to the outbreak of World War II in 1939. It is accompanied by extremely high unemployment and significant reductions in the gross domestic product (GDP).

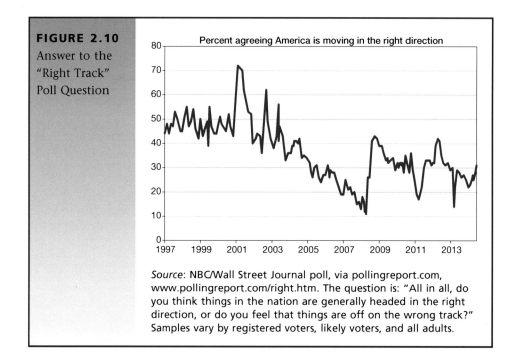

FIGURE 2.10
Answer to the "Right Track" Poll Question

Source: NBC/Wall Street Journal poll, via pollingreport.com, www.pollingreport.com/right.htm. The question is: "All in all, do you think things in the nation are generally headed in the right direction, or do you feel that things are off on the wrong track?" Samples vary by registered voters, likely voters, and all adults.

people felt good about the direction of the country until around 2000. The indicator jumped to a historic high after the September 11 terrorist attacks, in large part because of the outpouring of patriotism following the attacks. This is reflected in people thinking the country was on the right track, even as we rebounded from the worst terrorist attack in history. And we see the rally effect in 2003, when the Iraq War began. The rally effect is the tendency for people to rally around an individual president, the institutional presidency, and sometimes other national institutions in time of crisis. But as the wars in Iraq and Afghanistan dragged on and the economy grew slowly and then slid into recession, dissatisfaction began to set in.

Even with the swelling of patriotism and the renewed sense of civic purpose many people felt after September 11, many Americans still feel disconnected from government, feel they lack any voice, and, while often angry and upset, are unclear about how to participate in the policy process. This alienation is reflected in low rates of electoral participation and registration (particularly in non-presidential elections), as shown in Figure 2.11, a trend that continued in the 2002 congressional elections. To those who value voting as a form of civic participation and engagement, the relatively low participation in the 2002 congressional elections was particularly troubling, considering that at

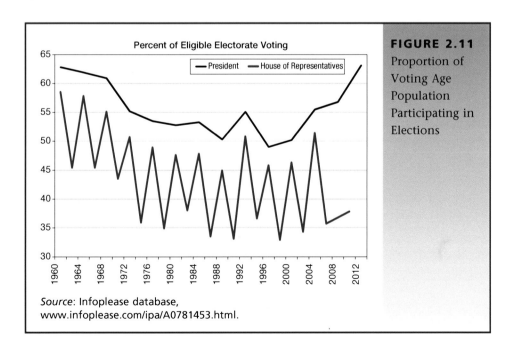

FIGURE 2.11 Proportion of Voting Age Population Participating in Elections

Percent of Eligible Electorate Voting

— President   — House of Representatives

Source: Infoplease database, www.infoplease.com/ipa/A0781453.html.

the time, the nation was debating whether or not to extend the so-called "war on terror" to an attack on Iraq in order to depose its dictator, Saddam Hussein. Such momentous decisions did not, apparently, motivate higher voter turnout in the midterm elections.

Finally, it is important to consider Americans' approval of government institutions. Since 1945, pollsters have been asking people, "Do you approve or disapprove of the job that the president is doing?" Since the mid 1970s, the same question has been asked about the U.S. Congress. Figure 2.12 shows data for public approval of the president. The data show the nearly inevitable drop in approval ratings that presidents see between their inauguration and their final approval rating when leaving office. This occurs because other candidates often come forward, and dissatisfaction is experienced about current policy and the administration's way of doing business. However, this doesn't happen to all presidents—President George W. Bush had a higher approval rating at the beginning of his second term than at the beginning of his first. What is particularly interesting is the relatively high degree of support for the president between 1953 and 1966, with only a few instances during this period of presidential approval falling below 50 percent. Presidential approval since 1966 has been subject to wide swings of opinion, even during the same presidency. In early 1991, during the Gulf War,

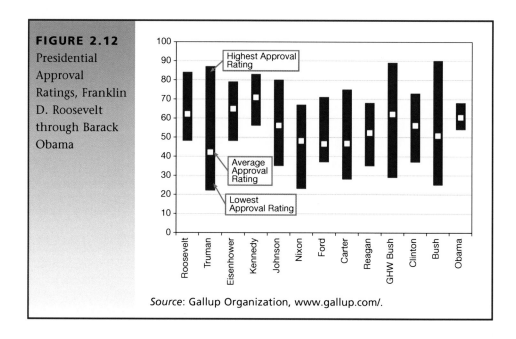

FIGURE 2.12
Presidential Approval Ratings, Franklin D. Roosevelt through Barack Obama

Source: Gallup Organization, www.gallup.com/.

President George H.W. Bush was rated as doing a good job by a whopping 89 percent of the electorate, a number matched by President George W. Bush in 2001 in the immediate aftermath of the September 11 attacks. But both Presidents G.H.W. and G.W. Bush saw very low ratings of about 25 percent, as, in the senior Bush's case, Americans were reacting to an economic recession, and, in the junior Bush's case, Americans were reflecting fears of the late 2008 economic crisis and concern about the war in Iraq.

Of course, the president is not the only person—and the presidency is not the only institution—people turn to for leadership. It is useful to consider the public's attitudes toward Congress as well. The annual average job approval ratings for Congress and the president are shown in Figure 2.13. These data date from 1990 and paint an important and interesting picture: when Congress's performance is believed to be good, the president's performance is rated lower, and vice versa. This may reflect institutional tensions between Congress and the executive branch, and, during the period in which these data are gathered, reflect partisan attitudes, particularly during periods of divided government. Recent research suggests that when Congress legislates, it appears to trigger negative reactions among the public, particularly those who are opposed to change.

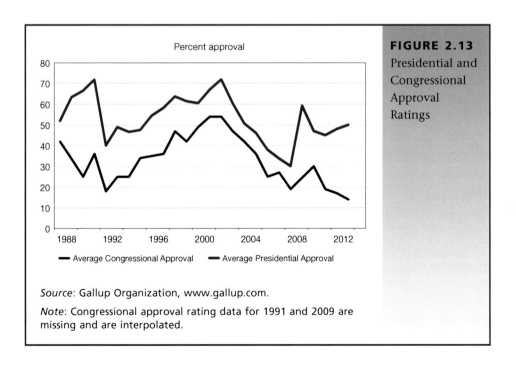

Percent approval

— Average Congressional Approval   — Average Presidential Approval

FIGURE 2.13
Presidential and Congressional Approval Ratings

Source: Gallup Organization, www.gallup.com.

Note: Congressional approval rating data for 1991 and 2009 are missing and are interpolated.

Why is the national mood and trust in government important for public policy? Because, as Ralph Erber and Richard Lau, referring to David Easton's work, state, "the legitimacy of democratic political systems depends in large part on the extent to which the electorate trusts the government to do what is right at least most of the time" (Erber and Lau 1990). The trends reflected here suggest that, as of the end of 2009, Americans' attitudes toward government are mixed, but remain guarded at best and negative at worst. Furthermore, the data I show here do not reflect partisan differences. While some social scientists and political commentators have argued that mass publics—that is, large groups of people who identify with a common interest—have become politically polarized, meaning that partisans' attitudes move to the extreme ideological positions of each party, recent research suggests that polarization is less a feature of the political system than of "party sorting," in which political parties become more closely identified with ideologically grounded policy positions (Fiorina and Abrams 2008). This partisan polarization contrasts with the 1950s and 1960s, when there were both liberal and conservative Democrats, and liberal and conservative Republicans.

gross domestic product The total value of all goods and services produced in a country.

Keynesian economics Theories and applications created or inspired by the economist John Maynard Keynes, who argued that countries should accept budget deficits and government spending during recessions so as to stimulate the economy; then, when the economy is growing, tax revenues can pay the debt so incurred.

The Economic Environment

The economic environment includes the growth of the economy, the distribution of wealth in a society, the size and composition of industry sectors, the rate of growth of the economy, inflation, and the cost of labor and raw materials. Because much of this data is specialized, we will not consider all these aspects of the economy; rather, we will consider the aspects that gain the greatest attention from policy makers and citizens.

The most common measure of economic activity is the **gross domestic product** (GDP), which is a measure of the value of all the goods and services created in the nation in a given year. Annual GDP figures are shown in Figure 2.14.

Economic factors are important because various features of the economy influence the types of policies a society makes; at the same time, we can see that during the financial crisis of 2008–2009, government policies also affected the economy, though often in unclear or unexpected ways. In **Keynesian economics** (that is, the theories of economics pioneered by the British economist John Maynard Keynes), governments spend more and run budget deficits to stimulate the economy when it is in a recession. Keynesians believe

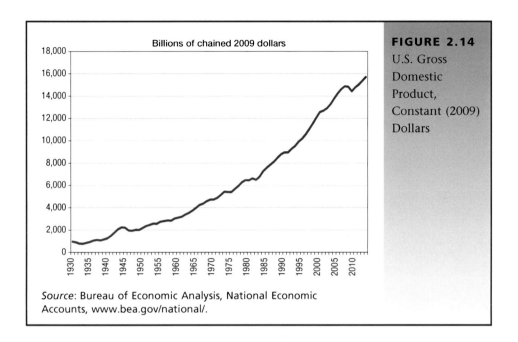

FIGURE 2.14
U.S. Gross Domestic Product, Constant (2009) Dollars

Billions of chained 2009 dollars

Source: Bureau of Economic Analysis, National Economic Accounts, www.bea.gov/national/.

that when the economy is strong, governments should run budget surpluses to make up for the deficits incurred during recessions (Keynes 1936; Heilbroner 1999). While Keynesian theories have been challenged since their publication in 1936 and came under increasing criticism when so-called supply-side theories of economic stimulus gained prominence in the 1980s, they still have an important influence on policy making, as reflected in President Obama's economic stimulus policies during his first term. Still, many economists and policy makers argued that growing federal **budget deficits** made the **national debt** grow too fast. The ultimate fear was that such spending would bankrupt the nation, an unlikely but daunting prospect. When the federal budget deficit for fiscal year (FY) 2009 neared $1.8 *trillion* dollars (Calms 2009), the deficit and the debt led to major concern about the stability of the U.S. economy, the strength of the U.S. dollar against other currencies, and the ability to pay back the debt in a slowly growing, sluggish economy. Since 2009, the economy has rebounded, and the size of annual budget deficits has declined at the same time as the GDP has grown. But the relative size of the national debt compared with the GDP continues to concern many economists and policy makers.

In the 1990s, the federal budget was in surplus for the first time since 1969, in part as a result of the booming economy. Tax collections should rise and

budget deficit
The difference between what a government spends and what it receives in revenue. When a national government runs a deficit, it must often borrow to make up the difference, thereby increasing the national debt.

national debt
The total amount of money owed to a nation's creditors, such as those who hold Treasury bills and savings bonds.

government coffers should fill during good economic times, so as to prepare for the next downturn. Starting in the early 2000s, the government ran larger deficits again due to tax cuts, slower economic growth, and the costs of two wars. Starting with FY 2009, those deficits became historically large, rivaling the budget defects incurred during World War II in terms of the dollar amount of the budget deficit, the rate at which the national debt was growing, and the fraction of the GDP accounted for by the national debt and the yearly budget deficits. These trends are illustrated in Figure 2.15, which shows the constant dollar value of the federal budget deficit or surplus since 1940, and Figure 2.16, which shows the size of the budget deficit and debt in proportion to the GDP. Figure 2.16 lends itself better to assessing the size of budgets and deficits, because it more effectively reflects the relative size of budgets and deficits and the overall economy. Federal debt and spending and economic growth are both dynamic and influence each other. Thus, in times of rapid economic growth, running a level budget deficit would yield a lower deficit-to-GDP ratio. But in 2009 and 2010, the reverse happened: the budget deficit grew as the economy contracted, yielding proportionately huge budget deficits.

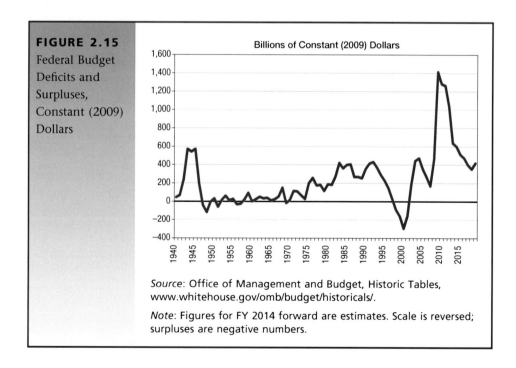

FIGURE 2.15
Federal Budget Deficits and Surpluses, Constant (2009) Dollars

Source: Office of Management and Budget, Historic Tables, www.whitehouse.gov/omb/budget/historicals/.

Note: Figures for FY 2014 forward are estimates. Scale is reversed; surpluses are negative numbers.

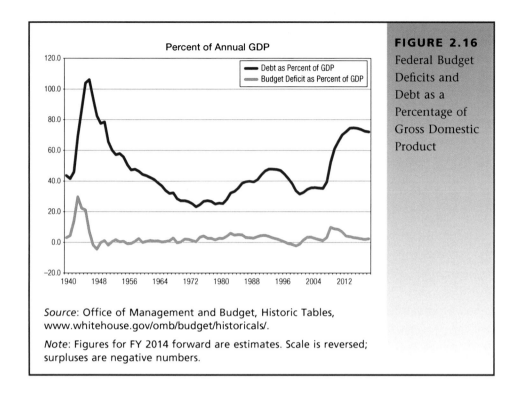

Percent of Annual GDP

Debt as Percent of GDP
Budget Deficit as Percent of GDP

FIGURE 2.16
Federal Budget
Deficits and
Debt as a
Percentage of
Gross Domestic
Product

Source: Office of Management and Budget, Historic Tables,
www.whitehouse.gov/omb/budget/historicals/.

Note: Figures for FY 2014 forward are estimates. Scale is reversed;
surpluses are negative numbers.

These trends are all very important because the policies a government makes are often a function of the overall wealth of the economy, because the resources available to government (through taxes and through its ability to compel behaviors without gravely negative economic consequences) are influenced by current and continued growth and prosperity. Wealthier societies can undertake tasks that less wealthy societies cannot. Of course, wealth is not the only determinant of policy choices. For example, the United States has no national health system or plan as of this writing, and no coherent policies to provide for public employment during economic recessions, even though the country is wealthier than many nations that do provide these services.

Public policy choices are influenced by the economy, but the policy decisions and the daily operations of government also influence the economic environment; they are very much intertwined. As Peters (2013) notes, "approximately 51 percent of all money collected in taxes by the federal government is returned to the economy as **transfer payments** to citizens." Transfer payments involve transfers of money from the government to

transfer payments
Transfers of money from the government to individual recipients, such as farm subsidies, disaster relief, and various social welfare programs.

tax expenditures
Government payments or subsidies in the form of tax deductions or credits; they are called "expenditures" because not collecting a tax is similar to collecting it and spending it.

unemployment rate The statistic generated by the federal Bureau of Labor Statistics that shows what proportion of a nation's, a state's, or a region's workers are out of work. It only counts those that are looking for work but are unable to find it, and not the underemployed or "discouraged workers" who drop out of the labor force.

recipients, such as farm subsidies, disaster relief, and various social welfare programs. The government also buys goods and services from the private sector, ranging from desks and chairs to supercomputers. And tax policies influence economic behavior: the mortgage tax deduction encourages people to buy houses and student loan interest deductions may influence people to start or continue college. These are called **tax expenditures** because allowing people to keep money that would ordinarily go to taxes is the fiscal equivalent of taxing people and then giving the money back as subsidies.

People's perceptions of their economic well-being have a significant influence on politics. While the GDP and the budget deficit are sometimes arcane statistics—particularly considering how huge the numbers are—they are often difficult to grasp and don't relate to individual experience as directly as the **unemployment rate** does. The unemployment rate is the percentage of the eligible workforce (in Figure 2.17, those aged 16 years and older) who are looking for work but cannot find it. As you can see in Figure 2.17, the unemployment rate tracks closely with recessions in the United States, as one would expect in periods of low or negative growth.

These figures do not reveal the differences in unemployment among different demographic groups. The unemployment rate for college-educated white men in their forties is much lower than the unemployment rate for

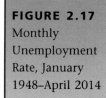

FIGURE 2.17 Monthly Unemployment Rate, January 1948–April 2014

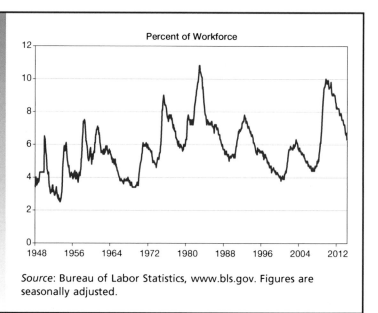

Source: Bureau of Labor Statistics, www.bls.gov. Figures are seasonally adjusted.

African-American men in their twenties with a high school diploma, or for African-American women without a diploma.

Finally, as part of the economic environment, let's consider the distribution of income between the most affluent and least affluent Americans. Wealth distribution data are shown in Figure 2.18. This figure shows the percentage of income accounted for by various groups of households. For example, since 1967, the bottom 20 percent of American households have accounted for about 4 percent of all income earned by all households. The next 20 percent of households accounted for just over 10 percent of national income. The most striking trend in Figure 2.18 is the proportion of income that is accounted for by families in the top fifth, whose share of national income grew from a low of 16.3 percent of aggregate income to 22.3 percent in 2007. This fraction has likely declined somewhat, as much of the income in the top category is from investments, the performance of which has been damaged in the 2008–2010 recession. But it remains at recent highs, a result of tax policies that benefited upper-income households but not those at lower income levels. Indeed, if we assume that the second, third, and fourth fifths of the households are the "middle class," their overall share of aggregate national income has dropped from 53.2 percent in 1968 to 46 percent in

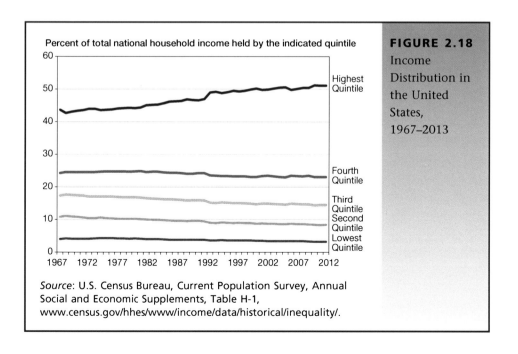

FIGURE 2.18
Income Distribution in the United States, 1967–2013

Source: U.S. Census Bureau, Current Population Survey, Annual Social and Economic Supplements, Table H-1, www.census.gov/hhes/www/income/data/historical/inequality/.

2007; this reflects many commentators' claims that the middle class is being squeezed compared with other economic classes.

How does the United States compare with the rest of the industrialized world in terms of income inequality? Figure 2.19 shows measures of income inequality among all members of the Organization for Economic Cooperation and Development (OECD), and includes the overall European Union figure. The data show the Gini Index for each country, a measure of income inequality where a score of zero means perfect income equality, and 100 means perfect income inequality (very few people earning all the income). As you can see, among the OECD member states, only Mexico shows greater income inequality than the United States. A good comparison is Canada, which looks more like European nations than the United States in terms of income equality. The Gini score for the United States reflects national tax and economic policies that favor higher-income households to a greater extent than in other countries.

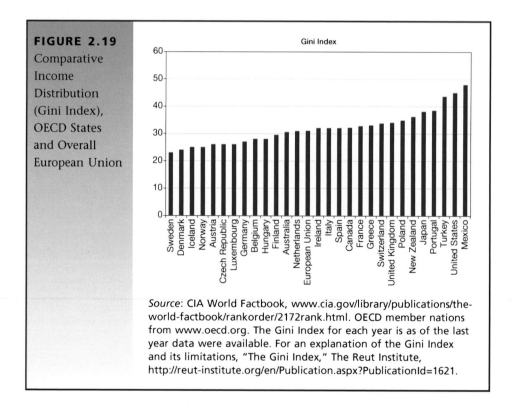

FIGURE 2.19 Comparative Income Distribution (Gini Index), OECD States and Overall European Union

Source: CIA World Factbook, www.cia.gov/library/publications/the-world-factbook/rankorder/2172rank.html. OECD member nations from www.oecd.org. The Gini Index for each year is as of the last year data were available. For an explanation of the Gini Index and its limitations, "The Gini Index," The Reut Institute, http://reut-institute.org/en/Publication.aspx?PublicationId=1621.

What does this mean in terms of public policy? On their web page dedicated to the definition of the Gini Index, the Reut Institute, an Israeli think tank, argues that there is an optimal range in which this index should fall for economic growth:

> In their study for the World Institute for Development Economics Research, Giovanni Andrea Cornia and Julius Court (2001) conclude that a Gini Index falling between 25 and 40 is optimal for growth. Extreme egalitarianism inhibits growth by reducing incentives for work and creating room for corruption in the redistribution of resources. Conversely, extreme inequality decreases growth prospects because it reduces social cohesion and stimulates social conflict.
>
> (Reut Institute 2007)

The United States falls slightly above this claimed optimal range, but political tension over income and wealth disparities has rarely had a long-term influence on public policy. Attempts to raise this issue in policy discourse are often dismissed by elected and appointed officials who, like many Americans, are wary of making distinctions based on socioeconomic classes. Most Americans define themselves as being middle class, and making political appeals to this very broad middle-class group is quite popular among interest groups and politicians. At the same time, efforts to distinguish between the benefits enjoyed by the wealthiest and the burdens suffered by the least wealthy—lack of health insurance and regressive taxation, for example—have often been dismissed as appeals to "class warfare," a specter that carries with it shades of "socialism," an ideology long in disfavor in the United States.

But the fact is that income inequality exists and has substantial political and economic implications, ranging from public dissatisfaction with current economic policy to slower economic growth as consumer spending among the middle class declines relative to the overall economy. And the growing realization that income and wealth inequality in the United States is increasing is beginning to have an influence on political discourse in the United States. As of this writing, in 2015, both Democrats and Republicans are acknowledging this inequality. President Obama made it an important theme of his State of the Union speech, and the *New York Times* reported, "Just acknowledging a wealth gap represents a significant shift in language for Republicans, who have long held that market forces driving overall economic growth will ultimately yield higher incomes without any help from government" (Weisman and Parker 2015). It is unclear whether the significant and growing gap in wealth inequality will have long-term political consequences for either party, but it is remarkable that it has reached the level it has on the political agenda.

In the case of unemployment, even though the burden of unemployment is unevenly distributed among the population, the broader public tends to view this as a universal problem, not a class-based problem. Government officials who fail to address—or to at least attempt to address—unemployment are likely to suffer at the ballot box. And, of course, the composition of government institutions has important effects on policy making. These connections, while complex, are real and worthy of attention.

Clearly, the trends shown in this section are not the only economic trends worth analyzing. As this is written, interest rates are very low and will likely remain so for the foreseeable future, although by mid to late 2015, it is likely that the Federal Reserve will move to slightly higher rates. When interest rates are very high, as in the early 1980s, the implications for consumer debt (such as credit cards and car loans), mortgages, and business credit are profound. Inflation is also quite low in large part because of Federal Reserve efforts over the past 30 years to keep inflation low through interest rate policies. Indeed, in 2014, inflation was *below* the Federal Reserve's targets for inflation (2 percent annually), and concerns were raised about deflationary trends that could create their own economic problems (Norris 2014). Were 1980s levels of inflation to become a problem again, interest rates would climb, which would have serious implications for the housing and automobile markets. It would also raise the cost of government borrowing, a very real worry in an era of persistent budget deficits. Other economic indicators that are often used include the major stock market indexes, such as the Dow Jones Industrial Average or the Standard and Poor's 500 (the S&P 500), and the NASDAQ index. These are measures of stock market performance and are related to, but are not the best indicators of, the economic health of the nation.

INPUTS

Now that we have considered key features of the policy-making environment, it's important to consider the inputs and outputs of the process. The activities of unofficial actors—generally, actors outside the government itself—are policy inputs. We can think of the official institutions, such as Congress and the executive branch, as the processors of these inputs and the creators of outputs, but the individuals who make up these institutions also provide important inputs to policy making. Public opinion—as described in the previous section—is an extremely important input. The types of policy outputs and the tools we use to achieve policy goals are described in Chapters 8 and 9. But for now let's consider broadly some inputs into the policy process.

Election Results

Considering that public policy is made in the public's name, the most obvious place to look for public input might be election results. Voting is the most common form of political participation, and elected officials and the news media often proclaim the results of elections as providing policy guidance or "mandates" to pursue particular policies. In some cases, the people are more directly involved with making laws. This is particularly true for states in which there are provisions for citizen **initiatives** or **referendums** that allow people to vote directly on policy proposals.

But interpreting voters' policy preferences in elections for public office is notoriously difficult. People have many different reasons for voting for a candidate, ranging from simple name familiarity, to appreciation for their local representatives' efforts to aid constituents with problems with federal programs (known as casework, and described in Chapter 4), to local political considerations that have little to do with national ideology or policy issues. During election campaigns, candidates can package their policy decisions in a way that they believe is most attractive to local voters, realizing that casework and redistributive spending (also known as pork-barrel spending) may have more of an influence on electoral success than legislative decisions. Furthermore, elections happen at fixed times and politicians have fixed terms: two, four, and six years for the House of Representatives, president, and Senate, respectively. Once the election is held, some elected officials need not worry about voters with respect to daily policy decisions, particularly if they represent "safe" districts. Still, while the connection between voting and policy is sometimes tenuous, elections are important because they do have an influence on the broad policy agenda and because they determine the partisan composition of Congress and other legislative bodies. Parties do have different positions on issues, and the partisan balance in the legislature can influence what policies are most likely to succeed or fail.

initiative
A process allowed in some states, by which people can propose and vote on laws via a petition and an election. Contrast with referendum.

referendum
The referral of a proposed change in law to voters for approval. Referendums (or referenda) often involve state constitutional change or local decisions on taxation or the issuance of bonds to pay for large capital projects such as roads or new public buildings.

Public Opinion

A common way to collect information about public preferences is through public opinion polls, like those cited earlier. Among the better polls are those conducted by or in conjunction with academic institutions. The National Opinion Research Center collects a great deal of public opinion information, particularly at election time. Most people are familiar with big national polls run by newspapers and television networks. Smaller newspapers and other media outlets will subscribe to poll results from reputable national polling firms such as the Gallup and Louis Harris organizations. While many people distrust public opinion polls, we know from years of experience that they are generally good snapshots of broad public opinion.

These polls look at electoral preferences, but pollsters also ask citizens about important public issues (abortion, school prayer, environmental protection) or general political questions (approval ratings of the president, Congress, and the like). Polls are important because they provide policy makers with a broad measure of public sentiments about key topics. Of course, we do not expect our public officials to be entirely driven by the results of public opinion polls, and, in fact, they weigh other information in reaching decisions. However, many elected officials are often accused of being poll-driven, and whether this is a safe political strategy is unclear. But given that elections to federal offices happen, at their most frequent, every two years, polls can provide a way of understanding public attitudes between elections. Decision-makers and interest groups can also use polling data to understand what messages will work best in advancing an opinion.

Communications to Elected Officials and Public Managers

Public opinion is not a direct form of communication from citizens to elected officials. There are numerous ways that people can communicate more or less directly with decision-makers. Among the most common are letters and email messages to elected officials. Members of Congress receive thousands of phone calls, letters, faxes, and emails every year. Much of this correspondence requests help in dealing with a problem with the government (casework), but a good proportion of these letters seeks to urge an official to vote a particular way on legislation. Indeed, many legislators, in their communications with constituents, argue that a prime source of ideas for legislation is citizen input.

This is true, but only slightly. I certainly do not wish to discourage you and other people from writing to elected officials—indeed, at the local level, your letters may lead to action on an issue, including a personal meeting to discuss your concerns, legislative hearings, and even new legislation. But the sheer volume of communication with members of Congress and most state legislators suggests that individual letters are noted, but the overall trend of the letters is more important than any single letter. In any case, representatives will often vote based on ideological or electoral concerns, because they may have other information or reason to believe that the position they take will not have bad electoral consequences. Still, elected officials know that acknowledging a letter, even with a noncommittal form letter, is important. In cases where a Member of Congress has taken a very public position on an issue, the form letter you may receive may well be very conciliatory but will explain why the member took his or her position. To overcome this tendency of individual letters getting lost in the shuffle, interest groups often mobilize members to send letters or cards to elected officials to serve as a rough gauge of public sentiment on an issue. Officials can get a very basic idea of interest group activity in their district by, in essence, weighing the pro- and anti-issue mail and using this balance as one of a number of inputs to voting and other decisions.

Interest Group Activity

Interest groups have a bad name in American politics. Allan Cigler puts this mildly, saying that "like the public at large, political scientists have often viewed interest groups with ambivalence, recognizing their inevitability but uncomfortable with their impact" (1991: 99). More bluntly, politicians and journalists often rail against the power of "special interests" and contrast their activities with a notion of a "public interest."

Regardless of one's attitudes toward interest groups, they are key actors in the policy process, as we will explore in Chapter 5. People with similar interests gather to amplify their voices in policy making; if you belong to an interest group such as the National Rifle Association, the International Brotherhood of Teamsters, or Greenpeace, you know firsthand that your group wields more power than you do individually or than even a million unconnected, unorganized people can wield independently.

The News Media

As discussed in Chapter 5, the news media are important participants in policy making, since they highlight some issues, de-emphasize others, and can therefore shape the public discourse surrounding a policy issue. Indeed, interest groups seek to get their preferred constructions of problems into the media to more broadly affect the debate over the issue; elected and appointed officials also use the media to shape the debate.

Public opinion expressed in the media—either as individual stories and anecdotes or through public opinion polling data—is an important but imprecise gauge of how the public and community leaders are thinking about issues. Politicians and policy makers are particularly sensitive to how issues are covered in the media, and, if coverage of their work is going badly, they often lash out at the news media or, more shrewdly, make changes in the course of policy making. A media outcry about a proposed plan of action can stop a policy proposal almost immediately. The agenda-setting function of the media is therefore important in shaping the government agenda.

Policy makers often use the news media as a way of floating trial balloons to assess the reaction of the public. Strategic leaks of information are common, particularly when policy makers are preparing large and complex policy initiatives. From public reaction to these trial balloons, policy makers can make adjustments to their proposals or learn whether they are likely to succeed or fail.

It is important to reiterate, however, that although the news media are very important inputs to policy making, they are not the only inputs: decision-makers have more sources of information than most citizens, and they can draw upon other information they gather in their jobs to make their decisions. But if we consider citizen demands as important inputs to the policy process, then we must be mindful of the role the news media have in shaping the terms of debate, particularly on the most visible, most controversial issues.

OUTPUTS

What does all this activity and the interaction between the environment and policy inputs produce? This produces what we can consider the political system's outputs or the basic statements of public policy that reflect the government's intent to do something. This can range from spending money, to criminalizing behavior, to mounting a public information campaign. These various policy tools are described in greater depth in Chapter 8. In this section, we consider the broad types of policy outputs.

Laws

When studying public policy, we are often interested in **statute law**: the laws that are drafted and passed in the legislature and codified in the statute books, such as United States Code or your state's statute books. **Case law** is also a policy output of the government, in this case the judicial branch. Many people decry "lawmaking by unelected judges," but under our system case law often determines the constitutional bounds under which the legislature and the executive branch operate, or explains how the Constitution requires them to make or not make particular types of policies. The landmark Supreme Court case *Brown v. Board of Education*, for example, prohibited states from segregating schools based on race and required that states desegregate their schools "with all deliberate speed." Both case laws and statute laws specify that agencies of government implement them; that is, they require that they be put into actual practice. Implementation is considered in more detail in Chapter 10.

Regulations are the rules that government agencies make to administer the various activities of government. The federal government is a vast enterprise, and laws exist that regulate everything from commercial aviation to shrimp fishing, from toy safety to nuclear power plants. With such a broad range of responsibilities, one might guess that the number of regulations is vast. The current *Code of Federal Regulations* (CFR) takes up at least 15 feet of shelf space (fortunately, much of it is now available online). A large part of what it contains is highly technical. It is unlikely that you would understand 14 CFR 121 (i.e., Title 14, part 121 of the *Code of Federal Regulations*), the regulations governing various operational aspects of commercial aviation, unless you are a pilot or other aviation professional. But if you are a professional or a well-informed citizen in a particular policy area, you can and should track the *Federal Register*—the daily newspaper of federal regulatory activity—to keep abreast of the key regulatory issues in your field.

statute law Laws made by the legislature and signed by the governor. Most such laws are codified into state codes or statutes.

case law Laws that are made as a result of judicial decisions and that influence future decisions. Contrast with statute law.

regulations The rules made by government agencies and regulatory bodies to implement the meaning of the laws under which the agencies operate. At the federal level, they are codified in the *Code of Federal Regulations* and usually have the force of law.

Oversight and Evaluation

An increasingly important part of Congress's work is the *oversight* function. Oversight involves "overseeing" programs that Congress has already enacted

legislative intent
What the legislature meant in drafting legislation, including what the language of the law should mean. Legislative intent is often difficult to discern by courts or other actors.

evaluation
The process of investigating whether and to what extent a program has its desired effect.

to ensure that they are being run efficiently and effectively, following **legislative intent**. Oversight has become a more common activity in Congress (see Chapter 4). Oversight is undertaken when Congress launches studies—performed by the Congressional Research Service, the Congressional Budget Office, or the Government Accountability Office, all bodies of the Congress—to find out how a program is working and whether and to what extent it can be improved. Congress often holds oversight hearings when there is evidence of some sort of policy failure, such as the hearings held after Hurricane Katrina (2005) and the government's apparently poor performance in that disaster.

Related to the oversight activity is policy **evaluation**, the process of determining whether and to what extent a program is achieving some benefit or its explicit or implicit goals. Policy evaluation is an important aspect of policy analysis and the policy sciences, and entire textbooks and professional courses are designed to teach the skills necessary to perform effective policy analysis and evaluation (Wholey et al. 1994; Weimer and Vining 2011). People and groups evaluate—on political and scientific bases—the performance of public policies to suggest ways to make them work better or, in some cases, to provide evidence for why a policy should no longer be pursued. While evaluation can be influential, it is not always effective in altering the course of public policy. For example, many research studies have found that the DARE (Drug Abuse Resistance Education) program did not work well in preventing schoolchildren from using marijuana and other drugs, but the program remained popular for other reasons, such as its visibility and its positive associations with law enforcement. Like any other aspect of the policy process, evaluation is a political activity that is subject to argument and interpretation.

SUMMARY

This chapter summarizes a wide range of environmental variables that influence public policy making. As Paul Sabatier notes in his work on the Advocacy Coalition Framework of the policy process, there are long-standing features of the environment, such as many features of the structural environment, and there are dynamic aspects of the policy environment that can change over time—sometimes very rapidly, as we have seen with the near-collapse of the financial system in 2008. In twenty-first-century America, these features from the eighteenth and nineteenth centuries still structure how politics and policy making are conducted in the United States. But modern trends in news gathering and distribution, telecommunications, the globalized, interconnected "flat world" economy (Friedman 2007), and its accompanying social changes mean that the policy environment—and the problems it poses— are among the most challenging faced by policy makers. However, one should not make too much of these challenges—while all people involved in the policy process must consider them it is important to understand that there have been other, perhaps more challenging, eras of American history—the Civil War, the Industrial Revolution, mass immigration, World War II, the darkest days of the Cold War—where the challenges seemed equally daunting, if not greater. While no political system is "perfect," the challenges posed by the policy environment are often met by policy makers. In the next chapter, we will see how policy makers confronted the challenges through the various eras of American policy making.

KEY TERMS

Administrative Procedure Act	legislative intent
black box	national debt
budget deficit	open public meetings laws
case law	policy environment
demographers	recession
depression	referendum
evaluation	regulations
federalism	separation of powers
Freedom of Information Act	statute law
gross domestic product	systems thinking
initiative	tax expenditures
input-output model	transfer payments
Keynesian economics	unemployment rate

QUESTIONS FOR DISCUSSION, REFLECTION, AND RESEARCH

- What are the strengths of the stages model of the policy process? What are its weaknesses?

- What are the strengths and weaknesses of any systems model of any political or social process? How might you overcome the weaknesses you have identified?

- The trends shown in this chapter are national trends. How does where you live compare with the national trends outlined here? For example, is your state, or county, or metropolitan area experiencing a higher or lower rate of unemployment? What is economic growth (defined as growth in the state domestic product) compared with the national trend? Various state economic development and budget offices should have these data.

- What are the policy implications of the trends you found in the previous question for your community?

- As tough as times are for the economy, and as contentious as politics seem to be, are there times when American politics have been more contentious? When have the policy-making challenges posed by the economic, social, political, and structural environments seemed even more daunting than they do today? How were these other eras handled by policy makers? Would you say that policy makers successfully addressed those challenges? Why or why not?

ADDITIONAL READING

Students with an interest in the systems approach to politics might consider reading David Easton's works: *A Framework for Political Analysis* (Chicago, IL: University of Chicago Press, 1968) and *A Systems Analysis of Political Life* (New York: John Wiley & Sons, 1965). However, systems analysis and system dynamics studies have evolved a great deal since the late 1960s. Recent works on systems of interest to social scientists include Donella H. Meadows and

Diana Wright, *Thinking in Systems: A Primer* (White River Junction, VT: Chelsea Green Publishing, 2008) and Virginia Anderson and Lauren Johnson, *Systems Thinking Basics: From Concepts to Causal Loops* (Cambridge, MA: Pegasus Communications, 1997).

The "textbook" model or "stages" model of the policy process is no longer a major foundation of policy theory, but its value continues as a way of formulating how we organize the policy process for ongoing analysis and study, as Peter deLeon argues in "The Stages Approach to the Policy Process: What Has It Done? Where Is It Going?" in *Theories of the Policy Process*, edited by Paul A. Sabatier (Boulder, CO: Westview, 1999). A more complete critique of the stages model is provided in Chapter 11.

Readers interested in finding the original data used to construct the charts in this chapter—or interested in finding additional information—should look to the following sources as a good starting point:

- The Bureau of Labor Statistics—www.bls.gov—data on income, labor, employment, and the like.

- Office of Management and Budget—www.whitehouse.gov/omb—key source on federal budget information, including historical data.

- *Statistical Abstract of the United States*—this book used to be published by the Census Bureau, but Congress removed funding for this valuable work in 2012. Fortunately, a private firm, ProQuest, has developed a commercial version of this book, and it may be available through your library or a nearby university's library.

REFERENCES

Calms, Jackie. 2009. "U.S. Budget Gap Is Revised to Surpass $1.8 Trillion." *The New York Times*, May 11. Accessed December 31, 2014. www.nytimes.com/2009/05/12/business/economy/12budget.html.

Cigler, Allan J. 1991. "Interest Groups: A Subfield in Search of an Identity." In *Political Science, Looking to the Future: Volume IV: American Institutions*, edited by William Crotty, 99–135. Evanston, IL: Northwestern University Press.

deLeon, Peter. 1999. "The Stages Approach to the Policy Process: What Has It Done? Where Is It Going?" In *Theories of the Policy Process*, edited by Paul A. Sabatier, 19–32. Boulder, CO: Westview.

Easton, David. 1965. *A Systems Analysis of Political Life*. New York: John Wiley & Sons.

Erber, Ralph and Richard R. Lau. 1990. "Political Cynicism Revisited: An Information-Processing Reconciliation of Policy-Based and Incumbency-Based Interpretations of Changes in Trust in Government." *American Journal of Political Science* 34(1/February): 236–253.

Fiorina, Morris P. and Samuel J. Abrams. 2008. "Political Polarization in the American Public." *Annual Review of Political Science* 11(1): 563–588.

Friedman, Thomas L. 2007. *The World Is Flat: A Brief History of the Twenty-First Century*. Rev. pbk. ed. New York: Picador.

Greenberg, George D., Jeffrey A. Miller, Lawrence B. Mohr, and Bruce C. Vladeck. 1977. "Developing Public Policy Theory: Perspectives from Emperical Research." *American Political Science Review* 71(4): 1532–1543.

Gunnell, John G. 2013. "The Reconstitution of Political Theory: David Easton, Behavioralism, and the Long Road to System." *Journal of the History of the Behavioral Sciences* 49(2): 190–201. doi: 10.1002/jhbs.

Heilbroner, Robert L. 1999. *The Worldly Philosophers: The Lives, Times, and Ideas of the Great Economic Thinkers*. New York: Simon & Schuster Trade Paperbacks.

Keynes, John Maynard. 1936. *The General Theory of Employment, Interest and Money*. London: Macmillan.

Kingdon, John W. 2011. *Agendas, Alternatives, and Public Policies*. Updated 2nd ed. Longman Classics in Political Science. Boston, MA: Longman.

Nakamura, Robert T. 1987. "The Textbook Policy Process and Implementation Research." *Policy Studies Journal* 7(1): 142–154.

Norris, Floyd. 2014. "Inflation? Deflation Is New Risk." *New York Times*, October 30. Accessed November 21, 2014. www.nytimes.com/2014/10/31/business/inflation-deflation-is-new-risk.html.

Peters, B. Guy. 2013. *American Public Policy: Promise and Performance*. 9th ed. Thousand Oaks, CA: CQ Press.

Reut Institute. 2007. "Gini Index." Accessed December 31, 2014. http://reut-institute.org/en/Publication.aspx?PublicationId=1621.

Shrestha, Laura B. and Elayne J. Heisler. 2011. *The Changing Demographic Profile of the United States*. Washington, DC: Congressional Research Service.

Weimer, David Leo and Aidan R. Vining. 2011. *Policy Analysis: Concepts and Practice*. 5th ed. Boston, MA: Longman.

Weisman, Jonathan and Ashley Parker. 2015. "Talk of Wealth Gap Prods the G.O.P. to Refocus." *New York Times*, January 21. Accessed January 30, 2015. www.nytimes.com/2015/01/22/business/economy/talk-of-inequality-prods-republicans-to-refocus.html.

Wholey, Joseph S., Harry P. Hatry, and Kathryn E. Newcomer, Eds. 1994. *Handbook of Practical Program Evaluation*. San Francisco, CA: Jossey-Bass.

CHAPTER 3

The Historical and Structural Contexts of Public Policy Making

OVERVIEW: PUBLIC POLICY AND THE AMERICAN CONSTITUTIONAL ORDER

The history of American policy making reflects considerable long-term change. If George Washington, James Madison, and Thomas Jefferson were to reappear in the United States at the beginning of the twenty-first century, they would find much that has changed in the size, nature, and scope of government, particularly the federal government, since their day. While they may not be surprised by the territorial extent of the United States (Jefferson, after all, authorized the Louisiana Purchase), they might be amazed by the ease with which we communicate in our country and around the world. At the time of the founding, it took less time for a letter or freight to move from New York to London than it took to reach Pittsburgh—and a London-bound letter or package was cheaper to ship. Today, we can use email, instant messaging, video calls, and other technologies to speak to almost anyone in the world instantly. And if we want to move freight, we have extensive roads (there were few good roads in 1789), fast trains, and faster airplanes that can move a laptop computer from a factory in China to a warehouse in Tennessee in less than 24 hours.

The history of our society and of public policy making in the United States has been characterized both by remarkable stability and remarkable change.

While a strong respect for the rule of law, the separation of powers between branches of government, and our continued commitment to concepts of federalism endure, how these ideas are put into effect has changed a great deal since 1789. These fundamental concepts have endured so that the United States—one of the youngest countries in the world—has one of the oldest written democratic constitutions in the world.

Our Constitution is not itself a guarantee of our civil rights and liberties or of political stability. Rather, the maintenance of the basic features of the American constitutional order—federalism, the separation of powers, and the rule of law, among others—relies on important cultural commitments to personal liberty, the sanctity of private property, and various civil rights, including voting and expressing one's opinion in public, organizing civic or interest groups, or holding peaceful protest marches. What all of these features have in common is the idea that the Constitution places limits on the federal government: as a matter of democratic theory, the *people*, not the government, are sovereign, and the states are important political entities, not simply administrative creations of the federal government. The political power wielded by public officers—from the president to the members school board—"derives from the consent of the governed," as John Locke argued and as is clearly stated in the Declaration of Independence.

While most Americans believe in these ideals, there is always room for improvement. Some groups, such as African Americans and women, to name two major examples, were historically denied their full rights of political participation. This sort of discrimination continues today, although much progress has been made toward open participation. And government, or, to be precise, the people who run the government, have sometimes abused their powers. One example of this abuse occurred during World War II, when the federal government moved Japanese Americans from their homes on the West Coast to detention camps based on the unfounded belief that they would be disloyal to the United States. Of course, whether the government uses its power legitimately or abuses it is a political question, often with important constitutional foundations. This nation fought a war over a central constitutional principle: that the Union is perpetually indivisible. In less dramatic but equally important ways, we expanded the right to vote to those without vast property through constitutional amendment and the creation and enforcement of statutes. At various points in our history, we have amended the Constitution to establish that black males (in 1870), all women (1920), and citizens 18 years and older (1971) are able to vote. And the meaning of the Constitution has, through the Supreme Court's major rulings, as well as through the implementation of its rulings by the legislative and executive branch, been altered, clarified, and reinterpreted as public demands or democratic principles.

Contrast the constitutional order of the United States (that is, the whole of our cultural, legal, and political commitments to the ideas contained within the Constitution) with the language contained in the constitutions of various other countries that are, as Americans understand the term, undemocratic. The constitution of the People's Republic of China provides for freedom of speech, press, association, and assembly in Article 35. Article 29 of the Russian Federation's current constitution guarantees press freedoms as well. And Article 24 of the constitution of Iran states, "Publications and the press have freedom of expression except when it is detrimental to the fundamental principles of Islam or the rights of the public. The details of this exception will be specified by law." While these are often fine sounding statements, these countries' protections of speech and press rights, while eloquently stated, are largely unheeded by their governments and courts. In these states, and many others, the extent to which speech and press liberties are guaranteed by the government and independent judiciary is much less great than what their constitutions would suggest. Restrictions on press freedoms were significant after the major protests following the June 2009 Iranian presidential elections. Journalists in Russia and China, and in many other nations, who report on sensitive issues are often suppressed and some have lost their lives while reporting on delicate matters.

Of course, even in highly democratic countries, policy makers must balance the rights and values of individuals with "public interest." Consider a country very much like our own. Canada's Charter of Rights and Freedoms states that: "The Canadian Charter of Rights and Freedoms guarantees the rights and freedoms set out in it subject only to such reasonable limits prescribed by law as can be demonstrably justified in a free and democratic society."

In the United States, we do not explicitly state that our rights are subject to reasonable limits, although in practice they are. Indeed, our clear and absolute statement of First Amendment rights of the press, speech, assembly, and religious observance (*Congress shall make no law . . .*) means that we must more overtly confront the balance between individual and community rights. For example, should self-declared Nazis be allowed to spread Holocaust denial literature? In the United States, they generally can, but in Canada and Germany it is illegal. Paradoxically, these countries' free speech rights allow for limits on personal liberty when justified to maintain the democratic order: as the Canadian Supreme Court said in *R. v. Keegstra* (3 S.C.R. 679, 1990), in which a school teacher was charged with violating what is now section 319(2) of the Criminal Code of Canada (which prohibits overt hate speech) by making virulently anti-Semitic claims. The Canadian court did indeed find that this provision of the criminal law infringed on speech rights, but that the restriction was justifiable because "there is obviously a rational connection between the criminal prohibition of hate propaganda and the objective of protecting target group members and of fostering harmonious social relations in a community dedicated to equality and multiculturalism." In the United States, on the other hand, we often consider the existence of these rights, largely unfettered, to be the essence of democratic liberty, and we rely on the political process, not legal punishment, to suppress hateful speech.

The public policy implications of this discussion are simple: the United States places a very high value on individual liberties, particularly on liberties related to political activity. And, more broadly, our constitutional order has remained remarkably stable for over 200 years. But the changes that have occurred during this time have been transformative, and, in many ways, while the United States has the same structure and philosophical foundation it had in 1789, in many other ways the nation has changed. It is as if the original builders created a very sturdy foundation and a good solid house and many additions have been made, making the structure only partially recognizable to its original architects.

THE HISTORICAL DEVELOPMENT OF THE CONSTITUTIONAL ORDER

One of the major features of our constitutional order is policy restraint—the idea that policy making should be deliberative. Indeed, while Americans commonly complain about the slow pace of action in the U.S. Congress and in other institutions, it is important to note that the slow (or, to some people, careful and deliberate) pace of policy making is intentionally built into the Constitution and the rules and practices of the House and Senate. Federalism also makes sweeping national change more difficult than it would be in a non-federal system.

In a significant study of why American politics and policy making is more constrained than expansive, Robertson and Judd lay out a history of public policy characterized by what they call "policy restraint." This history is divided into four eras: a period of divided power, an era of state activism, an era of national activism, and, finally, an era of national standards. In all these eras, some degree of policy restraint prevented government from taking action on issues when, in many cases, such action may have been warranted either by public demands, demonstrated needs and unfairness, or a combination of these factors. Policy restraint in housing and healthcare as well as other areas has distinguished the United States from other industrialized states that have more actively pursued policies that provide more services for citizens and involve greater government action. Thus one can argue that the features of our constitutional system that promote restraint—the two houses of Congress, the **separation of powers**, and **federalism**—prevent government from acting without carefully considering the costs and benefits of new policies.

Americans generally consider policy restraint to be a good thing, reflecting the framers' concerns about sudden shifts in policy being driven by the immediate "passions" of the times, rather than by more sober deliberation that addresses long-term problems. At the same time, it is also true that the features that promote stability and deliberation also promote stasis. It took the United States 75 years and one civil war to determine whether slavery should be allowed in the republic (and originally, the question was just whether or not to *contain* slavery in the South, rather than its outright abolition in the whole country). In another example, the United States started with a central bank, abolished it, and established various other central banking entities before creating a central banking system under the Federal Reserve Act of 1913, over 100 years after the demise of the First Bank of the United States. And until recently, many people argued that the failure of the United States to create a system of national health insurance put the nation "behind" other industrialized states and even some less-developed nations such as Cuba and South Africa. Even with the passage of the Patient Protection and Affordable Care Act, commonly known as the Affordable Care Act (ACA) or "ObamaCare," some argue the effort fails to effectively deliver more or better healthcare despite the time and effort involved, that its mandates violated personal liberty or were economically inefficient, or were simply too expensive (Root 2012; Heritage Foundation 2014).

The truth of these arguments and their implicit solutions are all open to debate. For now, the question to bear in mind as you read this—and as you think about policy making in general—is whether the benefits of policy restraint are greater than the costs of such restraint, particularly when rapid

separation of powers The constitutional division of powers between the legislative, executive, and judicial branches of the government.

federalism A system of government in which power is shared between a central or federal government and other governments, such as states or provinces. Key federal systems in the world include the governments of the United States, Canada, and Germany.

and decisive action seems to be necessary. Of course, even the need for rapid response to an emerging problem is a political question that is often debated. And we must bear in mind that there are two kinds of costs and benefits that must be considered: the near-term costs and benefits of creating policies to solve the immediate problem, often measured in monetary terms, and the long-term effects of such decisions on our broader understandings of civic life and the democratic order.

With this in mind, it is clear that the expansion of rights and broadening of our understanding of the Constitution has continued since the 1790s, such that the Constitution we use today is not, in fact, the same Constitution that was written and established at the founding. The Constitution has been amended several times, changing the meaning of key passages. And our understanding of what the Constitution means and what it demands of our government has also changed a great deal.

These changes in the interpretation of the Constitution can be said to have occurred in well-defined eras of the policy history of the United States. A particularly useful summary of this history is provided by David Robertson and Dennis Judd (1989) and is reviewed in this chapter. We then turn to a discussion of the features that make American politics quite stable compared with the rest of the world while allowing for long-term policy change.

Divided Power

In the first era of our nation's policy history, the era of "divided policy making power" (1787–1870), the major task facing the nation was to divide policy-making power between the states and the national government and to figure out how the federal government and states would work both together and independently of each other.

After the United States won its independence from Great Britain, many Americans thought that the newly free states would experience a period of peacetime prosperity; instead, an economic depression ensued. The economic crisis was worsened by the weakness of the national government under the **Articles of Confederation**. The national government could barely raise taxes or armies, and often too few states sent representatives to the seat of government to discuss policies. In the states, the farming interests sought loose money policies to alleviate the damage done by deflation; this meant the printing of paper money. The event that most clearly illustrated the shortcomings of the national government was **Shays' Rebellion**. Daniel Shays

Articles of Confederation
The first "constitution," of a sort, of the United States, under which the states formed a very weak federal union, with little power to tax or to exert power to regulate the economy, or to react to rebellions.

Shays' Rebellion
The name given to the uprising of poor farmers in Massachusetts who challenged civil authority in the face of growing debt, taxes, and the threat of going to debtor's prison. The uprising was one of the reasons for calling the Constitutional Convention in 1787.

was a farmer in western Massachusetts who led a group of about 1,000 men to intimidate the courts to delay foreclosures and debt collections; his band also sought to attack a federal arsenal (Richards 2002). While Massachusetts responded by providing relief for debtors, the event awakened other states to their need for strong national action to provide protection against insurrection.

The Constitution, finalized in 1787 and ratified in 1789, placed limits on the scope of the federal government, but the resulting federal government was still considerably more powerful than the skeleton government established under the Articles of Confederation. In light of economic instability and some incidents of civil disorder, which seemed to stem from federal weakness and the inability to persuade or compel states to act in their joint interests, the framers drafted provisions to protect property and the political standing of the moneyed classes against popular uprisings. Robertson and Judd call these features "structural impediments to radical policy." The historian Charles Beard went a bit further, arguing that the Constitution was a counterrevolutionary document that served to protect their economic interests in the face of populist sentiments (Beard 1956).

Whether or not you agree with Beard's thesis, there are many "structural impediments to radical policy" in the Constitution. The federal structure itself and the division of power among the three branches of government impede rapid and radical policy change. But the most important feature of the early Constitution was its relatively limited grant of power to the federal government and the reservation, under the Tenth Amendment, of a great deal of power to the states. The result is that "one of the enduring consequences of the American federal structure is that policy conflicts tend to turn as much on jurisdictional questions as on the merits of policy alternatives" (Robertson and Judd 1989: 31). In other words, many debates are as much over which level of government should do something as whether something should be done.

Because the federal government assumed regulation of interstate commerce and because economic growth was considered vital to the young nation's prospects, Congress's role was largely focused on promoting commerce. Congress, however, had many other powers, as shown in Table 3.1, which reproduces Article I, section 8, of the Constitution, listing all the things Congress has the power to do. Some of these clauses may seem dated (such as the regulation of commerce with the Indian tribes in Clause 3), or appear obscure (such as Clause 17, which declares federal authority to establish a

TABLE 3.1 Article 1, section 8, of the Constitution

Perhaps the most important passage of the Constitution, particularly for students of public policy, is Article 1, section 8. If "public policy" is "what the government does or chooses not to do," it is worthwhile to review what the founders had in mind:

Clause 1: The Congress shall have Power To lay and collect Taxes, Duties, Imposts and Excises, to pay the Debts and provide for the common Defense and general Welfare of the United States; but all Duties, Imposts and Excises shall be uniform throughout the United States;

Clause 2: To borrow Money on the credit of the United States;

Clause 3: To regulate Commerce with foreign Nations, and among the several States, and with the Indian Tribes;

Clause 4: To establish an uniform Rule of Naturalization, and uniform Laws on the subject of Bankruptcies throughout the United States;

Clause 5: To coin Money, regulate the Value thereof, and of foreign Coin, and fix the Standard of Weights and Measures;

Clause 6: To provide for the Punishment of counterfeiting the Securities and current Coin of the United States;

Clause 7: To establish Post Offices and post Roads;

Clause 8: To promote the Progress of Science and useful Arts, by securing for limited Times to Authors and Inventors the exclusive Right to their respective Writings and Discoveries;

Clause 9: To constitute Tribunals inferior to the supreme Court;

Clause 10: To define and punish Piracies and Felonies committed on the high Seas, and Offences against the Law of Nations;

Clause 11: To declare War, grant Letters of Marque and Reprisal, and make Rules concerning Captures on Land and Water;

Clause 12: To raise and support Armies, but no Appropriation of Money to that Use shall be for a longer Term than two Years;

Clause 13: To provide and maintain a Navy;

Clause 14: To make Rules for the Government and Regulation of the land and naval Forces;

Clause 15: To provide for calling forth the Militia to execute the Laws of the Union, suppress Insurrections and repel Invasions;

Clause 16: To provide for organizing, arming, and disciplining, the Militia, and for governing such Part of them as may be employed in the Service of the United States, reserving to the States respectively, the Appointment of the Officers, and the Authority of training the Militia according to the discipline prescribed by Congress;

Clause 17: To exercise exclusive Legislation in all Cases whatsoever, over such District (not exceeding ten Miles square) as may, by Cession of particular States, and the Acceptance of Congress, become the Seat of the Government of the United States, and to exercise like Authority over all Places purchased by the Consent of the Legislature of the State in which the Same shall be, for the Erection of Forts, Magazines, Arsenals, dock-Yards, and other needful Buildings;—And

Clause 18: To make all Laws which shall be necessary and proper for carrying into Execution the foregoing Powers, and all other Powers vested by this Constitution in the Government of the United States, or in any Department or Officer thereof.

capital at what was to become known as Washington in the District of Columbia), but most of these powers remain as current and important today as they were more than 200 years ago.

The powers granted to Congress fall into two broad and overlapping categories: the management of national responsibilities, such as defense and immigration policy, and commercial responsibilities, such as coining money, setting bankruptcy rules, and building roads and post offices. The latter function was particularly important, since federal efforts to encourage communication and transportation established links between states that served to forge a new nation from separate and often distant states. Even with these features in the Constitution, this forging of a new nation took some time, and for a while states squabbled over, for example, the right to regulate interstate commerce. The classic example of this fight is found in the case of *Gibbons v. Ogden*, 22 U.S. 1 (1824), in which the state of New York attempted to require the operator of a steamboat that crossed the Hudson River from New Jersey to New York to obtain a New York State permit to cross the river and land in New York. The Supreme Court held that such a regulation was unconstitutional under the **commerce clause** of the Constitution, which reserves to the federal government the power to regulate commerce between the states. With states prevented from erecting barriers to trade between states, a national economy soon flourished.

The powers of Congress are broader in practice than those listed in Article I, section 8, because clause 18, also called the "**elastic clause**," grants Congress power to do things not explicitly listed in Article 1, section 8, to advance the goals outlined in the Constitution. For instance, Congress in this period funded canal and road building for much more general purposes than simply moving mail. Congress, in establishing and funding the army, also funded the process of westward expansion by providing military protection to the new settlers of the West.

From the perspective of the average citizen the federal government was not the most important official participant in policy making in the early days of the United States. The federal government was a distant entity; most citizens' contact with the federal government was limited to the post office. The Constitution's structure and the founders' understanding of the role of the new federal government help explain this, but other factors are equally as important, including the mostly rural nature of the nation; its sparse and generally homogeneous voting population (of course, most blacks and all women were not allowed to vote, and some places only allowed property owners to vote), a political philosophy based on limited government, individual liberty, and the protection of private property rights; and, in particular, the fact that the **Industrial Revolution** had not yet taken hold

commerce clause
Article I, section 8, clause 3, of the Constitution, which gives the Congress (and, by extension, the federal government) the power "to regulate commerce with foreign nations, and among the several states, and with the Indian tribes."

elastic clause
Article I, section 38, clause 18, of the Constitution, which allows Congress "to make all laws which shall be necessary and proper for carrying into Execution the foregoing powers, and all other Powers vested by this Constitution in the Government of the United States, or in any Department or Officer thereof," which appears to give Congress expansive powers.

Industrial Revolution The period in Europe and in the United States when industry grew rapidly due to technical innovations in production; people moved to cities and worked for wages; and a series of major social and political changes occurred, such as the growth of business power and the establishment of labor unions.

in the United States. Indeed, Thomas Jefferson was the strongest proponent of a largely rural, agricultural America populated by a virtuous class of farmers, an ideal that stood in sharp contrast to Alexander Hamilton's vision of a nation based on industry and commerce. Hamilton's vision ultimately won out over Jefferson's and with growing industry and national systems of production and distribution of manufactured and agricultural goods came greater demands on government to create policy that would foster greater uniformity throughout what was to become a great industrial nation. However, until the Federal Reserve Bank was established in 1913, the full expression of Hamilton's vision was incomplete, in large part due to the important features of policy restraint in politics and in the constitutional order. The broader point is this: change can occur, but the full expression of an idea can take years to be adopted and implemented.

State Activism

The next era—state activism—spans the period from the 1870s to 1933. This was a period of great change and turmoil as the nation shifted from a predominantly rural, farming-based economy to a modern urban, industrial economy, powered by both native and immigrant labor. This urbanization led to great wealth for some people and great poverty for others, particularly those living in the urban ethnic ghettoes as well as in the "company towns" set up and run by large mining and industrial monopolies. The presence of disease and crime in these newly industrialized cities, mass popular uprisings in the cities, such as the Haymarket Riot in Chicago in 1886, severe labor strife, such as the Pullman Strike of 1893–1894, and the ongoing problem of large industrial disasters prompted the states to seek solutions to some of the most overt ills wrought by the rapid industrialization and social change of this era.

Civil War Amendments
The Thirteenth, Fourteenth, and Fifteenth Amendments to the Constitution that were enacted right after the U.S. Civil War. The Thirteenth Amendment banned slavery and the Fifteenth Amendment provided the vote to all men

Many states sought to regulate industry in general and to rein in the excessive power exercised by many of the largest industrial monopolies. But individual states could only regulate businesses operating wholly within their states, and the fact that these monopolies existed across state boundaries made regulation by individual states difficult, if not impossible. Because these firms were engaged in interstate commerce, many people felt that the federal government needed to step in and regulate business under the commerce clause of the Constitution.

As the Industrial Revolution continued, Congress reacted to the problems of railroad rate setting by establishing the Interstate Commerce Commission (which was dissolved by Congress in 1995). And in 1890, Congress passed the Sherman Antitrust Act, which, combined with later efforts by Theodore Roosevelt and others, led to the breakup of the "trusts," the term used then for monopolies or near monopolies, most notably the Standard Oil Trust, which was the parent firm of what we now know as Exxon, Mobil, Chevron, and others. Exxon and Mobil have since merged into ExxonMobil, bringing together two old members of the Standard Oil Trust, while Chevron merged with Texaco, a firm outside the original oil trust.

On the social front, the federal government began to tackle the problems of integrating former slaves into the political community—problems that vexed those who wanted to see former slaves rapidly enjoy the fruits of equal citizenship with whites, and those who wanted blacks to remain servile and uninvolved in deciding their own fate as well as that of their nation. The primary step in addressing these problems was the enforcement of the **Civil War Amendments**—the Thirteenth, Fourteenth, and Fifteenth Amendments to the Constitution. In addition, Congress passed several comprehensive civil rights laws, including the 1866 and 1875 Civil Rights Acts, intended to grant basic civil rights to African-American men, such as voting, property rights, and the right to equal public accommodations, such as schools or railroad cars. For a short period, these acts, enforced by federal agencies such as the Freedman's Bureau and by federal troops occupying much of the South during Reconstruction, created a political system open to the participation of African Americans. But the highly controversial election of Rutherford Hayes in 1876 ended Reconstruction, and with it any concerted federal effort to enforce civil rights laws. The South was thereby free to engage in a policy of segregation laws known as **Jim Crow laws**. In keeping with this change in federal priorities and national politics, the Supreme Court, in ***Plessy v. Ferguson***, 163 U.S. 537 (1896), allowed the Southern states to pursue policies of racial segregation in all aspects of social, political, and economic life. Racist and segregationist policies and practices were also evident outside the South, and some of the more difficult political conflicts against racism during the civil rights movement that started in the 1940s were seen in the North and West (see the case study in this chapter).

Similar to the failure of the federal government to ensure civil rights in this era was the federal government's weakness in its efforts to regulate industry. Corporate power was protected from government interference by a

regardless of race. The Fourteenth Amendment provided new due process of law and equal protection guarantees for citizens of each *state*, not just citizens of the United States, in their relationships with the national government.

Jim Crow laws
The laws primarily enforced in the South that discriminated against African Americans with regard to housing, jobs, the use of public accommodations, and other civil rights. Some laws were directly discriminatory, while others encouraged racial discrimination in private establishments, such as restaurants and hotels.

Plessy v. Ferguson The Supreme Court case that made it Constitutional to create "separate but equal" accommodations for blacks and whites; this decision was the underpinning for the racist Jim Crow laws, enforced primarily in the South.

laissez-faire economics
A system of economic regulation in which government leaves business totally, or almost totally, unfettered. This term has negative connotations, referring as it does to the freewheeling and sometimes abusive business practices of the late nineteenth century.

Lochner v. New York Supreme Court case that held that state work hour laws were unconstitutional restraints on the right of workers to enter into labor contracts with their employers. The court relied on a concept called substantive due process. This decision made regulation of wages and hours very difficult for the federal government and the states. The decision was overturned in 1937.

conservative judiciary that interpreted constitutional law to protect business from even minimal regulation. At the same time, starting in about 1900, public demands for federal and state action focused on industrial safety and labor relations. Federal policy in this area can be defined as purposefully noninterventionist. The federal government and, in particular, the Supreme Court, supported **laissez-faire economics** and identified the role of the government as allowing states and individuals to conduct their business without government intrusion.

For example, the Supreme Court, in **Lochner v. New York**, 198 U.S. 45 (1905), ruled that the cities and states could not regulate the wages and hours of workers (in this case, the wages and hours of bakers) because such regulation interfered with the workers' right to freely contract their labor with their employers. In this way, a regulation intended to protect the health and welfare of workers was construed as a threat to liberty—both that of the worker, and of the employer, to engage in an economic transaction. This decision sparked serious controversy, because the workers were *not* very free to negotiate the terms of their labor and were often compelled to work very long hours or risk losing their jobs. The *Lochner* doctrine ignored the obvious power disparities between workers and employers, and put a serious damper on workplace regulation for the next three decades. Thus, the federal courts, under the *Lochner* doctrine, and Congress, often influenced by business interests, failed to enact policies that would substantially limit industry's freedom of action, even when this freedom caused hardship and upheaval. Effective regulation of wages and hours did not extend fully to most workers until 1936, when the Supreme Court upheld a minimum wage law in Washington State, in *West Coast Hotel Co. v. Parrish*, 300 U.S. 379 (1937).

Still, this period was not completely without government action to address the needs of a growing national, industrial economy. Congress established the Federal Reserve System in 1913, establishing the central bank that is vital to a modern economy. In 1914, Congress further regulated monopolies by adding the Clayton Act to the Sherman Act. While both the Sherman and Clayton acts required additional legislation to clarify their meaning, they laid the groundwork for modern antitrust law. In response to muckraking journalists such as Upton Sinclair, Congress also passed the Pure Food and Drug Act. This act was intended to remedy the severe problems in food packaging revealed by Sinclair in his novel *The Jungle*, about a working-class community and its meat-packing plant, where insects, rodents, and other filth were introduced into canned meat. But even this act was passed with the active support of the major food-processing firms, which sought such laws to instill public faith in their products; its fate without their support might have been tenuous. Drugs were regulated when it became clear that many popular remedies were often useless or, sometimes, more harmful than beneficial. However, the Federal Reserve was still dominated by private banking interests and Congress significantly weakened Woodrow Wilson's proposed antitrust legislation. In sum, the federal and state governments were not completely inactive between 1905 and 1937, but many of their activities were constrained by an economically and socially conservative federal judiciary that blocked government initiatives while containing the backlash against capitalism.

Still, we must keep in mind that the states were powerful political entities in the state activism period, even more powerful than today, in most cases. Before the Civil War, the federal Constitution only restricted federal action against citizens, while state constitutions governed the relationships between individuals and states. In other words, under the notion of dual citizenship, one was a citizen of the United States *and* of the state in which one resided. Because the federal government didn't have much to do with the daily lives of Americans, most people didn't see the federal government as very important, and many promising political leaders preferred to serve in their state legislatures or courts, or as governors, rather than as members of Congress or the federal courts. State governments mattered more to people's daily lives, and state offices held higher prestige because, under our constitutional system, *most policy was made at the state level.* Indeed, most people considered themselves New Yorkers, Ohioans, or Kentuckians as well as Americans.

The concept of dual citizenship is present in ***Barron v. Baltimore***, 32 U.S. 243 (1833). John Barron owned a successful business: a wharf in Baltimore harbor. While making street and drainage improvements, the city of Baltimore caused changes to the flow of streams that caused the water to become shallower, thereby making Mr. Barron's wharf less useful for shipping. Mr. Barron sued in the Maryland courts, claiming that his property had been illegally taken, without proper compensation, by the city of Baltimore, which was created by the state of Maryland. Mr. Barron repeatedly lost in state court, and appealed to the U.S. Supreme Court, arguing that the *state* was bound to respect his Fifth Amendment right under the *federal* constitution to be compensated when his property was taken from him. But the court disagreed, stating that the *federal* Bill of Rights did not apply to the actions of the *states*.

Barron v. Baltimore
This decision held that people in the United States were both citizens of their states *and* of the nation, and that they therefore had to seek relief under their *state* constitutions, not the U.S. Constitution, if they felt their rights had been violated.

Thus, if a *state* abridged a person's rights of free speech, or assembly, or due process of law, or property ownership, that person had to appeal to the *state* courts, not the federal courts, for matters deemed to be solely state matters. One could bring a case in *federal* court if one's *federal* rights were violated *by the federal government.*

It wasn't until the ratification of the Fourteenth Amendment, which says that "no state shall make or enforce any law which shall abridge the privileges or immunities of citizens of the United States; nor shall any state deprive any person of life, liberty, or property, without due process of law; nor deny to any person within its jurisdiction the equal protection of the laws," was an avenue opened for the application of the national standard of the Bill of Rights against the states. That avenue was the "equal protection clause," of the Fourteenth Amendment, one of the most important parts of the modern Constitution. But the idea that there are fundamental rights that states and the federal government must respect didn't begin to take hold until the 1890s and gained momentum in the 1920s and 1930s. Even so, the *incorporation doctrine*—the idea of setting the *national* constitution's rights and protections as the minimum standard for the states—does not mean that every provision of the Bill of Rights is "incorporated against" the states. In particular, the courts have never fully incorporated the Second or Seventh Amendments against the states. This is a fascinating aspect of our constitutional history, but it's also an important feature of policy making, because the emergence of the incorporation doctrine plus major changes to occur in the 1930s led to historic levels of national power.

incorporation doctrine The idea that the Fourteenth Amendment's due process clause "incorporates" all the provisions of the Constitution's Bill of Rights against the states, meaning that states cannot violate the federal standard in these matters.

National Activism

The third era—national activism (1933–1961)—was marked by the demands placed on the national government by the Great Depression and then by the demands created by **New Deal** programs and the postwar boom. Soon after his inauguration, President Roosevelt called Congress into session and presented sweeping proposals to end the Depression and to maintain confidence in business, industry, and finance. These ideas, most of which became law, included greater regulation of banking and securities, the National Industrial Recovery Act (NIRA), and the Civilian Conservation Corps. The conservative Supreme Court, operating under the *Lochner* doctrine, struck down the NIR in *A.L.A. Schechter Poultry Corp. v. United States*, 295 U.S. 495 (1935).

New Deal The program of policy changes and reforms associated with President Franklin D. Roosevelt's administration that intended to alleviate the Great Depression.

The Supreme Court's restraining influence on policy was so great that, after his 1936 re-election, President Roosevelt attempted to break this constraint by proposing a new way of organizing the Supreme Court. Arguing that old age was making it difficult for some justices to do their jobs well, Roosevelt proposed to add one justice to the Court for every justice who was age 70 or older. This would have resulted in a 15-member court at the time, dominated by Roosevelt appointees, who presumably would be more favorable to the president's plans. People across the political spectrum vigorously opposed Roosevelt's "court-packing" plan, and Roosevelt's enthusiasm for the plan was further diminished after two justices seemed to change their philosophy in favor of New Deal legislation, in what became known as the "switch in time that saved nine." As it turned out, a number of justices did retire, in part due to their age, during the Roosevelt administration, so that, by 1940, the Supreme Court, consisting mostly of Roosevelt's appointees, became more amenable to the president's program; this, more than the proposed reform in staffing the Court, was likely FDR's ultimate goal (Carson and Kleinerman 2002).

The most important outcome of the New Deal history is its promotion of active federal involvement in national policy making. By 1937, the New Deal had created a vast system of governmental regulatory bodies, including but not limited to the Federal Communications Commission (FCC), the Civil Aeronautics Administration (later the Civil Aeronautics Board, or CAB), the Securities and Exchange Commission (SEC), the Federal Deposit Insurance Corporation (FDIC), and the Federal Home Administration (FHA). The government entered businesses that were traditionally private, such as power generation, with the creation of the Tennessee Valley Authority (TVA) and the Bonneville Power Authority (BPA). Indeed, the TVA had a broader goal of fostering economic development in the once-isolated Tennessee Valley, while the BPA provided cheap electricity to the factories that refined aluminum, which was a key input in the West Coast's aviation industry during and after World War II. These agencies continued to influence American policy and politics after the New Deal and World War II.

World War II era programs further enhanced the influence of the federal government: the G.I. Bill, which funded the postwar education of many servicemen and servicewomen; the FHA, which made mortgage loans easier to obtain; and the FDIC, which guaranteed the safety of bank deposits, laid the groundwork for the postwar economic boom. These and other programs, such as Social Security, became so entrenched in the national psyche that by

PHOTO 3.1
Photographs such as this one, which became known as "Migrant Mother," by photographers working for New Deal agencies, both reflected the need for New Deal programs and provided political support for a continued and strong federal government role in relief.

Source: Library of Congress.

the 1950s, most Republicans realized that they could not resist their popularity and that efforts to repeal them would be unpopular and futile. The result was a bipartisan consensus on the political sanctity of Social Security that persists to this day, even as controversies over how the system is funded recur.

After World War II, U.S. foreign and defense policy establishments grew significantly, setting the tone for U.S. postwar foreign policy. The term **national security** first came into common use after the war, and the defense establishment of the United States was substantially reorganized in 1947. The North Atlantic Treaty Organization, or NATO, was formed in 1949 as an alliance intended to contain the threat of Soviet expansionism. Fears of

national security
The collection of policies, practices, and ideas that seek to protect the United States from foreign military or terrorist threats.

communist subversion led to ethically questionable congressional actions to root out subversion, such as the creation of the House Un-American Activities Committee (HUAC) and the crusade against communism led by Senator Joseph McCarthy (R-WI). At the same time, the expansion of the federal role in defense policy slowed under the Eisenhower administration because of Americans' desire for a somewhat slower pace of change. Still, the seeds of important federal initiatives, such as the space program and the construction of the Interstate Highway System, were planted in the late 1950s.

National Standards

The final period in Robertson and Judd's formulation, the era of "national standards," runs from 1961 to the present, although, as I argue later, there was what may have been an era of "the end of big government" that started in about 1980. The 1960s were a fertile period for domestic policy making, akin to the New Deal era in the 1930s. Under President Lyndon Johnson's **Great Society** program, federal efforts to address policy problems again accelerated. Great Society programs addressed poverty, racial discrimination, educational problems, barriers to access to healthcare for the poor and elderly, mass transportation, urban renewal, environmental issues, and myriad other problems. It is not a coincidence that the 1960s also saw the birth of the scientific study of public policy and public problems, as researchers asked, what are the most pressing public problems; what causes the problems; and do we have the policies and techniques to solve these problems, or to reduce their effects? This scientific study was undertaken because the federal government was starting to set national standards for the states and other actors to follow in the pursuit of policy goals. At the same time, the states' capacity to make and enforce policy grew rapidly, particularly in leading states such as New York and California.

Great Society
The package of domestic programs advanced by President Lyndon Johnson to alleviate poverty, improve education, and foster civil rights during the 1960s.

Richard Nixon's election in 1968 was viewed by some as a return to more conservative federal policy making; indeed, many of Nixon's proposals and programs were intended to cut back federal activities in various problem areas. The Nixon administration pursued a policy of "New Federalism," in which discretion was returned to the states, and federal block grant programs were developed to replace the highly descriptive, top-down policies that characterized many Great Society programs. But the Nixon administration was not afraid to use federal power and policy making to address national programs. The Environmental Protection Agency (EPA) was established and the National Environmental Policy Act (NEPA) was passed under the Nixon administration, although the Trans-Alaska Pipeline, built to transport oil from Alaska's North Slope to the ice-free port of Valdez, was approved and explicitly exempted from NEPA requirements over the objections of environmentalists. Nixon attempted to stem inflation through wage and price freezes imposed at the federal level, but the administration's New Federalism and block grants programs were attempts to move power from the federal level to the state level.

From a policy-making perspective, the Nixon years were also important because this period witnessed major changes and reforms in Congress. President Nixon often angered Congress by not spending funds that were appropriated for particular uses, which is called "impoundment," and Congress prohibited the practice while reforming the budget process in the 1974 Budget and Impoundment Act. The president's ability to commit troops to overseas actions was somewhat constrained by the 1973 War Powers Resolution. And the power and prestige of the executive branch in general were dulled by the Watergate scandal and Congress's investigations into the activities of the Federal Bureau of Investigation (FBI) and Central Intelligence Agency (CIA). From a policy perspective, the important change here was the reassertion of congressional power in its relationship with the presidency.

The End of Big Government?

Perhaps the most important post-New Deal shift in government and attitudes toward policy was the 1980 election of President Ronald Reagan. Because he ran on a consistent program of cutting "big government," his perceived mandate was to do just that. In some ways, he aggressively did so, particularly in social welfare programs. His mandate to cut big government did not run, as it turned out, to the defense department. Nor were his policies strictly designed to reduce the federal budget deficit, a figure often used by small-government activists to highlight the problems with a large federal establishment.

But it is important to remember that efforts to shrink government and decentralize it were also undertaken by President Nixon and President Jimmy Carter, and that efforts to make the government more "efficient" and effective have been a staple of postwar policy and politics. Carter foreshadowed his desire to make the federal government smaller and more efficient in his inauguration speech, in which he declared:

We have learned that "more" is not necessarily "better," that even our great nation has its recognized limits, and that we can neither answer all questions nor solve all problems. We cannot afford to do everything, nor can we afford to lack boldness as we meet the future.

And in his 1979 State of the Union speech, after listing the challenges faced by the nation, Carter said, "At home, we are recognizing ever more clearly that government alone cannot solve these problems." Later in his speech, Carter, in language sounding very familiar to that of Reagan supporters, claimed:

We must begin to scrutinize the overall effect of regulation in our economy. Through deregulation of the airline industry we've increased profits, cut prices for all Americans, and begun—for one of the few times in the history of our nation—to actually dismantle a major federal bureaucracy. This year we must begin the effort to reform our regulatory processes for the railroad, bus, and the trucking industries. America has the greatest economic system in the world. Let's reduce government interference and give it a chance to work.

The deregulation of the airline industry is perhaps the most-remembered regulatory action taken by the Carter administration; it opened airlines to price competition and allowed people of modest means to fly, although some have argued that deregulation was not a complete success (Dempsey 1990; Pogue and Pogue 1991; Dempsey and Goetz 1992). But while Carter sought to reform and rearrange, to some extent, the government's approach to regulation, Reagan was much more opposed to the idea that the government could solve problems. In his first inaugural address, Reagan stated that "Government is not the solution to our problem; government is the problem." But by the mid 1980s, an aroused Congress was tempering the Reagan program, and Reagan suffered a major setback in his prestige during the so-called Iran-Contra scandal. Before then, however, Reagan had substantially increased American military spending, which signaled a return to American willingness to project military power overseas, in places such as Grenada, Panama, and the Middle East. This tendency continued in the G.H.W. Bush, Clinton, G.W. Bush, and Obama administrations, which used the military in Iraq, Afghanistan, Somalia, Bosnia-Herzegovina, and Kosovo, and in various counterterrorism activities throughout the world, with varying degrees of real or perceived success.

The post-Nixon legacy of distrust in government—a sentiment that presidents Carter and Reagan both appealed to, although on different ideological grounds—continues to influence policy making and government action. Indeed, a 2008 Rasmussen poll found that "59 percent agree with Ronald Reagan—government is the problem."[1]

More significantly, the rhetoric and the actual policies created by Reagan spawned an America in which Bill Clinton could remark in his 1996 State of the Union speech, driven possibly by his party's stinging defeat in the 1994 congressional elections and his failure to pass major healthcare reform, that "the era of big government is over." This sentiment may have changed during the Clinton administration when the federal budget deficit became a budget surplus, as discussed in Chapter 2. Still, we continue to live in an era in which the federal government is mistrusted. On the other hand, state governments, while for the most part not able to develop vast new programs, are often perceived as better positioned to address local needs and appear to be more responsive to citizens' needs, even as they come under significant fiscal stress (Erikson, Wright, and McIver 1993).

The drive for smaller government continued in earnest through both George W. Bush administrations. The major legislative achievement of the Bush administration before the September 11, 2001 terrorist attacks was a significant and controversial tax cut. This tax cut, coupled with the economic downturn that began before the September 11 attacks (but that was likely accelerated by the attack) and the costs of fighting the war in Afghanistan and Iraq, caused an increase in the federal budget deficit. It did not, however, lead to a major increase in the size of the deficit compared with the gross domestic product, as discussed in Chapter 2.

But the appeal of "small government," while very popular in the broadest sense, often flags when confronted with more immediate challenges. For example, after the September 11, 2001 terrorist attacks, Congress enacted the USA Patriot Act, which gives the government greater powers to investigate terrorism and other crimes, at some potential cost to individual rights and liberties. And while new government departments are often anathema to small-government proponents, the Bush administration created an entirely new department, the Department of Homeland Security (DHS). This expansion of government authority was bipartisan. Congressional Democrats—in particular, Senator Joseph of Connecticut, promoted the creation of DHS. It is hard to say whether the department constitutes growth in government, or merely a reorganization of existing government programs and agencies. But regardless of ideological commitments to "smaller government," government will grow if policy makers perceive the need for greater government activity, such as in counterterrorism.

The election and re-election of Barack Obama has thrown the small-government idea into even greater doubt. And, if nothing else, there's apparently no conflict between the ideas of "national standards" and "smaller government," at least rhetorically. For example, the controversial No Child Left Behind program enacted during the Bush administration set national standards for school performance, to which education aid dollars are attached. And, at least in recent years, government *spending*, if not government itself, has grown substantially. Even before President Obama took office, the Bush administration had committed extraordinary sums of money to support the banking and financial system after the collapse of the Lehman Brothers investment firm—a controversial but certainly understandable intervention, considering how banking and investment institutions in the United States are at the center of international finance.

These policies continued on about the same course under the Obama administration, which also promoted programs to remove old "clunker" cars from the roads, to provide relief for people with major mortgage problems, to invest in high-speed passenger trains, to promote alternative energy, and so on. After significant Republican electoral losses in the White House and Congress in 2008, the Tea Party materialized out of frustration from a failing economy and perceived reckless spending by the federal government, as exemplified by the new president's stimulus package, which was designed to spark economic growth. The movement energized a demoralized right-wing base and quickly grew into a national movement. Tea Party supporters eventually became an important electoral force, influencing the 2010 midterm elections by mobilizing a disillusioned conservative base and shaking up the Republican party establishment. Regardless of whether the Tea Party as a movement or as a faction of the Republican party endures, the Tea Party is simply the most recent example of mass expressions of discontent with the size and scope of the federal government (Karpowitz et al. 2011; Williamson, Skocpol, and Coggin 2011), which means that, if nothing else, the perception of a "too large" federal government persists and has been a consistent theme in American politics for at least 40 years.

Big government or small, ambitious or cautious, policy making in America reflects the flexibility and stability of our constitutional system. Without this flexibility, the constitutional order itself might not be able to endure; the Civil War demonstrated the ability of the Constitution to bend but not break in the face of major upheavals. Given the importance of stability in the American political system, the discussion now turns to this important aspect of American politics. One should not conclude from this review that policy stability is solely a result of the constitutional structure. Nor should one conclude that policy change does not happen. As we will see throughout this book, policy change can and does happen under the proper conditions. But in the end, anything more than incremental policy change is difficult to achieve in the United States given our constitutional structure and our political culture.

STABILITY IN AMERICAN POLITICS AND POLICY MAKING

Policy restraint in the United States is both a cause and a consequence of key cultural and historic features that have made the United States one of the most politically stable nations in the world. Consider the sweep of American history compared with that of our Asian and European allies. The United States ratified its Constitution in 1789 and the 48th state was admitted into the union in 1912. Two more were admitted in 1959. The United States' gravest national crisis—culturally and politically, involving nothing less than the survival of the United States—was the Civil War, fought between 1861 and 1865, and followed by a lengthy period of reconstruction. But at the same time, the rhythms of national political life have changed relatively slowly, even as the details were altered by policy changes such as the popular election of senators starting in 1913, the extension of voting rights to more people, and the number of states in the union.

Since the founding of the United States, Germany and Italy have both become national states. Great Britain amassed and then, following World War II, lost its worldwide empire, as did France. France itself went through profound national crises, from the French Revolution to the founding of the Fourth Republic in 1956. Japan did not become a modern state until the 1870s and the opening of Japan to Western trade. Japan's growth as an industrial power was extremely rapid, but its modern constitution is little more than 60 years old and was largely written by the American occupiers of Japan after its defeat in World War II. Japan, France, Germany, and other parts of Europe were utterly ruined after the war, and, with help from the United States, were rebuilt. In just 70 years, Germany evolved from the unstable Weimar Republic, through the Nazi period, to the occupation period at the end of World War II, and to two separate states, communist East Germany and social-democratic West Germany. These two parts of Germany were reunified in 1990.

This extremely brief history is a reminder that the United States' political institutions and national ideology are remarkably stable compared with other prosperous nations. This stability is something that Americans value very highly. The shocking terrorist attacks of September 11—or, for that matter, the two world wars, the Cold War, and the domestic turmoil of the 1960s—did not substantially change the most stable features of American political life and our political institutions. Neither did the economic crisis that gripped the world from 2008 through 2010. James Anderson (2003) argues that the United States has four kinds of stability: ideological stability, political stability, policy stability, and stability in power (Table 3.2).

TABLE 3.2 Elements of American Political Stability

	What this means	Examples in action
Ideological stability	Americans tend not to stray from a set of ideological precepts based largely on our national experience.	The United States has not had a labor party or workers' movement like European nations, because our ideological stability includes some suspicion of "class warfare."
Political stability	Politics in the United States tend to be fairly stable.	Our constitutional structure has changed little since 1789, although practices under it have changed. In 1800, Thomas Jefferson, whose views were quite different from his predecessor's, took office.
Policy stability	Policies tend to change very little over time.	Policies such as laws governing business practices, social welfare (social security, aid to the poor), environmental protection, and many others remain stable over time.
Stability in power	Changes in power tend not to cause major policy, political, or social upheavals.	The transition from one president to another, or the transition in party dominance in a house of Congress, is generally smooth, democratically accepted, and results in little sweeping, immediate change.

Source: Derived from Anderson (2000).

Ideological and Political Stability

Ideological stability refers to the fact that Americans' basic political beliefs do not change rapidly. Since the colonial era, Americans have strongly valued personal liberty and equality, although, as Deborah Stone has noted, this belief in liberty and equality is rather diffuse, with considerable disagreement as to what these terms mean in practice (Stone 2011: Chapter 2). With this broad belief in personal liberty and equality comes the belief that the highest power in government is (or should be) held by the people. The high value placed on liberty and equality is accompanied by a strong belief in the rule of law, free-market economics, free enterprise, and private property. While attitudes have changed considerably on things such as slavery and racial discrimination, the rights of women and children, voting rights, and the role of religion in society, the core beliefs on which the nation were founded are durable, adaptable to new problems and conditions, and rarely threatened by those who seek policy change. The important question in politics is not whether liberty and equality are good things, but rather to whom should we extend the blessings of liberty and equality? Full equality and liberty has still not been established, but it is remarkable how much progress was made over the last 60 years in extending civil rights and liberties to everyone.

The acceptable range of ideology along the traditional "left-right" scale—and therefore the range of policy preferences—in the United States is considerably narrower than the range of ideologies represented in political institutions in Europe, ranging from the extreme right of the French National Front to the German Greens on the left. Because our electoral system makes it very difficult for third parties to gain much influence, the two political parties in the United States have both tended to accommodate a relatively broad (in American terms) range of opinions because only two parties can reasonably contest elections in the United States. This broad accommodation of ideologies has changed in recent years, as more politically conservative people, including many former Southern Democrats, have shifted to the Republican Party, while, to a lesser extent, more moderate-to-liberal Republicans have moved to the Democratic Party (Fiorina and Abrams 2008; Levendusky 2009). Historically, when a party drifts too far from the ideological center, it becomes more likely to lose an election, as happened with the Democratic Party, whose candidate for president was soundly defeated in 1972, and with the Republican Party in 2008; of course, the location of the "center" can also change over time, as public sentiment moves toward more liberal or conservative attitudes.

Some of the beliefs Americans hold are contradictory; for example, equality and capitalism often clash, depending on one's definition of "equality" (Stone 2011: Chapter 2). Battles over workers' rights versus owners' prerogatives have been fought, mostly politically but sometimes violently, in the United States. However, even working-class people often display attitudes that generally support American notions of capitalism, business, and success, even when these values, in operation, work against their group or class interests. This agreement on basic ideology across social classes may explain the lack of a powerful labor movement as one sees in much of Europe.

Political stability is a key element of our overall national stability. The United States has operated under the same constitutional structure since 1789. While that structure has certainly been altered, as we have discussed, the general outline of the rules remains, including a structure that promotes a two-party system, the method of electing the president through the electoral college, the Senate based on state representation and a House of Representatives based on apportionment by population, and so on. Beyond the structural features, our political preferences have varied within a narrow range; when change does occur, it usually occurs over decades, not suddenly, with some exceptions, for several reasons. First, the American governmental and constitutional system is not designed to be quickly responsive to national needs or desires. The three branches of government were not designed to foster rapid, coordinated action among the branches; rather, they were intended to serve as checks on each other's power.

Two historical examples illustrate this. The first is the Supreme Court's consistent blocking of policies intended to regulate industry and working conditions, culminating with the Court's blocking of Franklin Roosevelt's New Deal programs. Policy changes to address the problems of the Great Depression were accepted by the Court only when President Roosevelt, in his second term, was able to appoint more ideologically friendly justices and when some justices began to change their positions. In the end, considerable policy change did occur, but it took many years before Roosevelt's plans were fully in effect.

A second example is President Clinton's failure to get his healthcare reform proposals passed by Congress. The reform package failed to pass partially because it was very complex and because many interests—insurers, employers, health maintenance organizations, many individual citizens—mobilized to aggressively oppose the Clinton proposals. Others have attributed the failure of this reform to the secretive process by which one very large bill was assembled in very little time, making for a very complex reform package that was advanced before a strong constituency in favor of reform could be mobilized (Starr 1994; Oberlander 2007; Wilson 2015). Regardless of the reasons, we can see healthcare reform as a stark example of how policy change is stymied when the president and Congress cannot agree. In this case, the dominant coalition in Congress did not even agree with the president that there was a problem requiring congressional action; in other words, when there is little agreement on a problem, there is likely to be little agreement as to potential solutions.

Because the founders designed the constitutional system to delay policy change, not expedite it, one can say that the failure of the healthcare reform was predictable simply because of the structure of American politics. Had the United States been established as a parliamentary system, in which the chief executive was the prime minister, health reform and other legislation would likely be easier to pass because prime ministers are the leaders of a cohesive majority party or coalition until their party loses or the coalition collapses. In such a system, it is likely that any previous Democratic administration could have enacted some sort of national healthcare policy. The Obama administration has therefore succeeded in accomplishing something that few others had achieved: reform of healthcare policies in the face of significant structural barriers to policy change, and, even then, the reforms were not as great as some would have hoped.

The separation of powers between Congress and the president can slow policy change, as can the federal system of divided power between the national government and the states. As James Madison, a leading founder, constitutional scholar, and the fourth president of the United States, explained in *Federalist No. 10*, a primary benefit of federalism is that it contains policy fads or fast-moving popular movements within one or a few states, thus preventing the growth or expansion of conflict to the national level. But there is a more affirmative and positive rationale for federalism. Federalism fosters state innovation and induces states to improve their capacity to address problems that the federal government does not address (Walker 1969, 1971; Osborne 1990). This has induced many students of policy to call states the "laboratories of democracy" because innovations can be developed state by state and then adopted and adapted by other states. For example, California is widely viewed to be the leader in developing policies to reduce the damage caused by earthquakes, for obvious reasons (Geschwind 2001), while New York was long a leader in developing and implementing social welfare policy and is still more active in this area than most other states. Indeed, the **devolution** of federal programs to the states is often justified in terms of the notion that the states are more innovative and responsive than the too-large federal government. As Tallon and Brown note in writing about welfare reform, "If nothing is very new about the stakes of devolution, why not craft a block grant, turn states loose, and record what transpires in the federal system's famous laboratories of democracy?" (Tallon and Brown 1998). Indeed, this very debate is now being held over how to provide disaster relief to states hit hard by major natural disasters: should the states receive federal money to spend as they see fit, within reasonable boundaries, or should the funds come with very tight controls from Washington? The answer to these questions of devolution versus control hinges on the assumption that states will make faithful efforts to build capacity to do the things the federal government seeks to accomplish with the **block grant**, which is a grant of money to states that carries with it far fewer restrictions than many funded programs. This is why the debates over these programs can be fierce: some believe that the states cannot or will not implement a program the way the federal government wants it; others argue that too much federal control fails to account for local differences, and that these "one-size-fits-all solutions" are ultimately less efficient and more prone to fail.

While federalism can be justified by the "laboratories for democracy" argument, this is not the justification provided by James Madison. Rather, according to Charles Beard (1956), Madison and the other founders justified the constitutional system to their countrymen saying it served to maintain the social and economic status quo, thereby maintaining *stability in power*. The status quo that Madison sought to preserve revolved around promoting the sanctity of free enterprise and private property, particularly among wealthy (male) property owners (this was 1787, after all). These interests are clearly different from those of the mass public, most of which held little property, had few political rights, such as office holding and voting, and relatively little influence on the drafting or ratification of the Constitution.

Because of this orientation, among the most enduring features, benefits, or problems—depending on your perspective—of the federal system are the structures that preserve the status quo. The interests that have the most advantages and are in power are motivated to maintain the status quo and are organized to do so. However, not all powerful interests seek to maintain the status quo all the time. Rather, they will push for change to the status quo when it suits their interests, and usually within the existing institutional

devolution
The process by which federally designed and administered programs are turned over, in whole or in part, to the states to manage as they see fit, based on their needs and conditions. This is often justified by the sense that the states are more innovative and responsive than the too-large federal government.

block grant
Government funding provided to state and local governments as a "block," with very broad rules on how the funds are to be used; this allows the states great flexibility in using the funds, but with a loss of some control and accountability.

rules created by the Constitution (Plotnick and Winters 1985; Cigler and Loomis 2012; Brulle 2014; Fu and Li 2014). The status quo orientation of the Constitution, coupled with its inherent protections of private wealth and property, gives the advantage to these groups over, for example, the poor and racial minorities, so much so, argue Gilens and Page (2014), that mass publics' desires for policy change have far less to do with actual policy change than do the preferences of socioeconomic elites.

The realities of the power structure in America severely limit the ability of some groups to exercise influence. To have power in Washington, a group must be organized, active, well financed, politically sophisticated, and well represented by elected and appointed officials. Washington is loaded with groups that meet these standards, but mostly they represent interests dedicated to the preservation of the status quo. Indeed, this orientation toward the status quo and the denial of political power to many people have led many historians and social scientists to conclude that the American "revolution" was far less "revolutionary" than the changes wrought by the Civil War, which was fought over fundamental national questions, such as states' rights and the civil and equal rights of individuals (Moore 1966; McPherson 1990). The federal Constitution, on the other hand, was in many ways a counterrevolutionary document, drafted in the wake of domestic insurrection and the obvious failures of the Articles of Confederation to protect the interests of the dominant classes of the day (Beard 1956). Indeed, there were few ideas in the Declaration of Independence or the Constitution that could be considered "radical" at the time of the founding; rather, the question was whether these ideas could be sustained in practice over more than a few decades: as Lincoln said in the Gettysburg Address, the United States was "conceived in liberty and dedicated to the proposition that all men are created equal," and the Civil War was being fought to test "whether that nation, or any nation so conceived and so dedicated, can long endure."

Still, even though the founders—and later national leaders—had their own doubts as to whether the arrangements they created could endure, the brilliance of the constitutional design deserves our respect. The constitutional design provides for deliberative government—that is, government that takes the time to consider the various aspects and affected interests in any legislation. The founders sought, by providing a two-house legislature, to provide both a voice of the popular will (the House of Representatives) and a means of restraint against policy fads or impulsive social movements (the Senate). And to some extent, the courts provide another restraint against popular passions or the tyranny of the majority (McCloskey and Levenson 2010). From this structure comes the considerable policy moderation and restraint that is an essential part of American political stability. Others, however, have concluded that structural features of American politics create so much restraint that the system prevents government from addressing some of the key problems of the day through means supported by a majority of citizens (Robertson and Judd 1989).

Basic Rules and Norms

James Anderson notes that political actors and institutions operate both under the Constitution and under a system of "basic rules and norms" that go beyond the very broad guidelines set out in the Constitution. For example, in the United States Senate, one senator can **filibuster**, holding the floor and speaking nonstop, tying up the body for hours or days until enough senators vote for cloture to stop the filibuster. In many cases, filibusters are successful in allowing one or relatively few senators to thwart the legislative preferences of a majority of the Senate. The House of Representatives operates under different rules, and the filibuster is not allowed there, but there are other procedural techniques that one can use to slow the progress of legislation, although less so than in the Senate.

The norm of seniority in Congress meant that, for years, committee chairmanships were held by conservative Southern Democrats, who tended to stymie legislation proposed by their liberal colleagues from both parties. Today, seniority is more evenly distributed nationally, and the ideological distinction between the parties is sharper, so while this norm is still important, it is not as important as it was before major congressional reforms were instituted in the early 1970s. Congress's procedural rules, intended to preserve decorum and order in the legislature, have been highly successful in maintaining at least some level of collegiality in the Congress, but at the cost of making legislating a slow and sometimes frustrating process.

filibuster
A parliamentary technique unique to the U.S. Senate, in which one or a few speakers can take the floor and dominate discussion and debate, effectively shutting down the Senate unless enough senators vote for *cloture*, which ends the debate (cloture requires 60 votes). This method is used to kill legislation when the side opposing the legislation lacks a legislative majority.

Fragmentation

The fragmentation of the American political system is a feature that is underappreciated by most Americans and, perhaps, overstated by those who argue that policy change and progress are impossible in the United States. There are two dimensions of fragmentation in American politics: the

Brown v. Board of Education
The 1954 Supreme Court case in which the court unanimously held that laws requiring separate (and inherently unequal) schools for racial minorities was an unconstitutional violation of the Equal Protection clause of the Fourteenth Amendment. This case is the legal basis for school desegregation plans and orders that followed in the 1950s through today. A 1955 case under the same name required that schools desegregate with "all deliberate speed."

separation of powers among the branches of government, and the division of power between states and the federal government, or federalism.

The separation of powers in the federal government, as well as most state and local governments, was intended to check the power of any one element of the government through the exercise of power by the others. The founders drew upon emerging European political theories that held that there are three major functions of governments: a legislative function, in which the laws are made; an executive function, in which the laws passed by the legislature are implemented, enforced, or executed; and a judicial function, in which the laws are interpreted, disputes over matters of fact or law are settled, and meaning is given to the enactments of the legislature, as implemented by the executive. While these powers are separate, they also serve to check each other and to overlap to some extent, as shown in Table 3.3.

When the states disagree with the federal government, considerable delay in the implementation of policies can result (Pressman and Wildavsky 1984; Goggin et al. 1990). The early years of the civil rights movement are a remarkable example of how states can delay policies thought to be in the national interest. After **Brown v. Board of Education**, 347 U.S. 483 (1954), made it unconstitutional for states and their local school districts to segregate the schools on the basis of race, many Southern districts continued to do so well into the 1960s. The federal courts continually sought to compel compliance, but there is strong evidence to suggest that it took financial incentives from the federal government, in the form of school aid tied to desegregation, to impel the South to desegregate its schools (Rosenberg 2008). Not all state delay or resistance is bad, however. As Malcolm Goggin et al.

TABLE 3.3 Separation (and Sharing) of Powers

	Congress	President	Courts
Legislative	**Make laws**	Recommend laws; veto laws; make regulations that have the force of law (quasi-legislative powers)	Review laws to determine legislative intent; new interpretations = law making
Executive	Override vetoes; legislative vetoes of regulations	**Enforce and implement laws**	Review executive acts; restrain executive actions (injunction)
Judicial	Impeach judges and president; call witnesses in hearings	Pardon criminals; nominate judges	**Interpret laws**

Note: The primary function of each branch is indicated in **bold italic** text.

(1990) argue in their study of intergovernmental policy implementation, sometimes states engage in "strategic delay" in implementing federal mandates, to learn more about the policy and how to implement it to address unique local situations. This ability to shape policy in this way is perhaps a primary strength of federalism.

Discussion of the fragmentation and separation of power in the United States is sometimes met with dismay by students of the process. After all, why does it have to be so slow? Can't we find ways to make the system more efficient so that it can react more quickly to address what we feel are the most pressing problems? But before calling for a more "responsive" government, remember that the founders concluded that deliberation—a time of thinking, discussing, and debating issues—was good, and that policies should not be made hastily.

A Rationale for Stability

It is important to recognize that other goals—such as deliberation and public participation—are at least as important as rapid and efficient policy-making action. Lest we think the American system is entirely hamstrung, however, it is important to remember that rapid policy making is possible during, for example, wars and other serious national crises. But during normal periods of policy making, the political and constitutional order makes it possible and quite common for a minority of citizens to thwart the apparent will of the majority in seeking policy change—this blocking is accommodated by the constitutional structure and the norms of the legislative process. Furthermore, this blocking is entirely healthy and justified if it prevents the passage and implementation of dangerous, unconstitutional, or unfair policies.

Policy does not change radically because much of the public does not support such rapid change—rather, years of electoral experience and public opinion data suggest that Americans value political and policy stability and are rather unwilling to see the government take large steps toward certain goals. Starting in the late 1970s and early 1980s, there was a diffuse public sense that the government had grown too big and that the Reagan administration was justified in dismantling a great deal of it. At the same time, public opinion also registered disapproval of President Reagan's attempts to significantly reduce federal commitments to environmental protection. In short, change is often welcomed by the public, as long as it is not radical change. When a social movement or a crisis does sweep the nation, change can be remarkably swift, as occurred during the Civil War, the New Deal, the Great Society era, and the movement to shrink government that began under President Carter and accelerated in the Reagan administration.

CASE STUDY: CIVIL RIGHTS AND THE DELIBERATE PACE OF CHANGE

Despite the enduring strength of the Constitution, the original document did not provide for equal rights for racial minorities. Indeed, the original Constitution prohibited any change to the Constitution related to slavery until no earlier than 1808, or about 19 years after ratification. For the purposes of census counts, slaves were counted as three-fifths of a person, giving the Southern states a disproportionate amount of power in the national government compared to the eligible electorate in these states. This disproportionate representation of Southern states, and the move away from agriculture to a more industrial economy, led to building national tensions over the nature and ultimate fate of slavery. These tensions resulted in the Civil War, one that was fought over slavery but that also established that states may not leave the Union at their own discretion.

After the war, Congress passed and the states ratified the Civil War Amendments, at which point one might assume the matter was settled: slavery was abolished, the *states* were required to respect due process of law and the equal protection of the laws, and the Fifteenth Amendment made clear "The right of citizens of the United States to vote shall not be denied or abridged by the United States or by any State on account of race, color, or previous condition of servitude." But the Fourteenth Amendment was less clear: it promised that no state shall not "deprive any person of life, liberty, or property, without due process of law; nor deny to any person within its jurisdiction the equal protection of the laws." Later, the Fourteenth Amendment was interpreted to mean that the drafters of this amendment intended to apply the same federal standard of civil rights and liberties to each and every state. But this interpretation took over 60 years to take root in constitutional law.

Congress attempted to enforce the spirit and meaning of these Civil War amendments through the Civil Rights Acts of 1866, 1870, 1871, and 1875. The Civil Rights Act of 1875 provided that all persons within the jurisdiction of the United States shall be entitled to the full and equal enjoyment of the accommodations, advantages, facilities, and privileges of inns, public conveyances on land or water, theaters, and other places of public amusement; subject only to the conditions and limitations established by law, and applicable alike to citizens of every race and color, regardless of any previous condition of servitude.

Congress also provided for fines and an enforcement mechanism, but the Act was held unconstitutional in what became known as *The Civil Rights Cases*, 109 U.S. 3 (1883). The Court held that Congress did not have the power to regulate *individual* discrimination, only state action, although Justice John Marshal Harlan, from whom we will hear again, dissented from the majority opinion.

There was not another civil rights act until 1957, or 82 years after the 1875 act. And it wasn't until 1964 that Congress passed a constitutionally acceptable law to require equality of access to public accommodations. Why did this take so long? Part of the reason is the major shift in American politics in the 1876 election, in which Rutherford Hayes, Republican of Ohio, became president even though he lost the popular vote to Democrat Samuel Tilden of New York. Some historians say that this "Compromise of 1877" allowed Hayes to become president in exchange for a promise to the Democrats—the more popular party in the South—to end the federally imposed, highly unpopular policy of "*Reconstruction*." With that, 1876 begins the period of "Jim Crow" laws that sought to keep blacks from enjoying the same constitutional rights and liberties as whites. The Supreme Court, in *Plessy v. Ferguson*, 163 U.S. 537 (1896), ratified the idea that it was permissible to provide "separate but equal" public accommodations—not just on the trains, from which this case derived, but also in the broadest range of public accommodations and institutions, from schools to parks, to restaurants to public buses.

By the mid 1930s, the obvious problems of the separate but equal doctrine were becoming quite clear. The courts had to confront separate but unequal voting laws in the Texas primary cases (*Nixon v. Herndon*, 273 U.S. 536 [1927]; *Nixon v. Condon*, 286 U.S. 73 [1932]), in which the whites-only Democratic primary was struck down as unconstitutional violation of voting rights and equal protection. And the beginning of the end of "separate but equal" occurs in three cases involving graduate education (*Missouri ex rel Gaines v. Canada*, 305 U.S. 337 [1938]; *McLaurin v. Okla. State Bd. of Regents*, 339 U.S. 637 [1950]; *Sweatt v. Painter*, 339 U.S. 629 [1950]), when the court held that policies that would send blacks out of state for law school, segregate blacks in a graduate program, and build a separate and clearly inferior black law school were unconstitutional violations of the equal protection clause.

A watershed occurred in 1954 when the U.S. Supreme Court ruled in *Brown v. Board of Education*, 347 U.S. 483 (1954), that separate schools were inherently unequal; a year later, the Court stated that the schools must be desegregated "with all deliberate speed." *Brown* gave a powerful legal, moral, and rhetorical weapon to those forces that sought to desegregate American society.

Efforts in the courts and in other venues in government sought to speed the pace of desegregation and racial equality. In the face of strike threats from railroad porters, led by porters' union and civil rights leader A. Philip Randolph, President Franklin Roosevelt issued Executive Order 8802 in 1941, which established the Fair Employment Practices committee to enforce equal employment opportunities in defense plants (Kersten 1999). Many blacks were able to work as a result of this order, although wages for blacks and for women still lagged behind those of white men.

The National Association for the Advancement of Colored People (NAACP), one of the first civil rights organizations, was founded by a "multiracial group of activists" in 1909. A separate entity, the NAACP Legal Defense Fund, was founded in 1940, and was led for years by Thurgood Marshall, the lead counsel on many civil rights cases and, later, the first African American to be appointed to the Supreme Court, in 1967 by President Lyndon Johnson. The Congress of Racial Equality (CORE) was founded in 1942, as the Committee of Racial Equality by students in Chicago, but drifted until the galvanizing events of *Brown* and the 1955 Montgomery Bus Boycott (Congress of Racial Equality 2014).[2]

The Montgomery (Alabama) bus boycott was triggered by Rosa Parks' refusal to relinquish her seat on a transit bus, thereby violating local custom, although not technically violating the law (she was already sitting in the "black section" of the bus).[3] This act of defiance triggered the formation of a group that later became the Southern Christian Leadership Conference (SCLC), led by a young preacher, Dr. Martin Luther King Jr. The bus boycott so financially damaged the bus system that the rules were changed, thereby ending the boycott 381 days later, in 1956. This was also a period of sit-ins, marches, and other direct protest, the majority of which were nonviolent protests, at least on the part of the protesters. The Student Nonviolent Coordinating Committee (SNCC, pronounced "Snick") was founded by North Carolina college students impatient with the SCLC's more measured approach, and adopted lunch counter sit-ins as a major element of its protest strategy. Again, these were nonviolent—at least on the part of the protesters, many of whom were yelled at, spat upon, or beaten by those opposed to their cause or their methods.

By the 1960s, civil rights had become a major issue in American politics, as you have seen in this chapter. While there was a Civil Rights Act of 1957 and 1960, both of which were generally toothless attempts to increase black voting, the most important events in the civil rights movement in the 1960s were the marches on Washington in 1963 and the Selma to Montgomery march in 1965. The 1963 March on Washington was organized by the "big six" civil rights leaders: A. Philip Randolph, Roy Wilkins (NAACP), James Farmer (CORE), John Lewis (SNCC, and a future U.S. Representative from Georgia), Whitney Young Jr. (Urban League), and Martin Luther King (SCLC). This march is best known for King's stirring "I have a dream" speech and for the image of a quarter of a million people packed into the National Mall, from the Washington Monument to the Lincoln Memorial.

In 1965, a group of protestors demanding voting rights sought to march from Selma, Alabama, to Montgomery, the state capital. On their first attempt, on "bloody Sunday," March 7, 1965, 600 marchers barely got out of Selma before being stopped by police wielding billy clubs and tear gas. Martin Luther King became involved, the federal courts stepped in, and ultimately 25,000 marchers made it to Montgomery on March 25. Later that year, President Johnson signed the federal Voting Rights Act, the law that finally, nearly 100 years after the Fifteenth Amendment was ratified, ensured that blacks could vote. The voting rights act was just one of several civil rights-oriented bills passed in rapid succession, which included the 1964 Civil Rights Act (which finally did what the 1875 act couldn't), the Voting Rights Act, and the Fair Housing Act, which was title VIII of the Civil Rights Act of 1968. These acts marked substantial progress.

Of course, the civil rights movement of the 1960s was not a series of unambiguous victories. Even as these laws were passed, there were riots and violent confrontations in cities such as Los Angeles, Newark, and Detroit. But by 1970, we can say that, from a legal and constitutional perspective, the promise of the Civil War amendments had been achieved. Indeed, in the face of continued Southern foot dragging (what the Southerners themselves called "massive resistance") on school discrimination, the Supreme Court, in *Alexander v. Holmes County Board of Education*,[4] emphatically rejected the "all deliberate speed" doctrine of *Brown* with the command that schools must immediately desegregate.

More than 50 years after the anniversary of *Brown*, many people wonder how far we have come since this historic decision. One highly visible indicator is the fact that the current president, Barack Obama, is the first person of African descent ever to be president of the United States, winning an outright majority of the votes cast on Election Day 2008. President Obama was born in 1961, seven years after the first *Brown* decision, which suggests how long we have come. Furthermore, racial segregation in schools, from preschool to graduate education, is illegal. So is discrimination on the basis of race for hotel rooms, jobs, housing, and other public accommodations.

Yet, even in the face of this remarkable accomplishment, there are still vestiges of segregation and inequality that have proven very difficult to address; it is difficult to claim that any racial minority has achieved civil and economic equality with whites. Certainly, travel and public accommodations are much more open to all Americans than they were 60 years ago. But, even today, some landlords still work hard not to rent to racial minorities, and some employers, either unwittingly or purposefully, don't hire qualified minority workers (Bertrand and Mullainathan 2003). And the extent of residential segregation— driven less by overt racism and more by more subtle social and economic forces—remains stubbornly high (DeFina and Hannon 2009). And blacks tend to go to jail at a higher rate than the general population, have less education, and make less money than the population as a whole. And protests over police tactics in Ferguson, Missouri, Staten Island, New York, and Cleveland, Ohio—to name just three examples—reveal the considerable divides in the perceptions of the degree to which progress has been made since the peak of the civil rights movement.

What features of American history, politics, and government do you think caused the nearly 100-year delay in redeeming the promises made in the Civil War amendments? What made it possible for there to be so much change in relatively few years between 1964 and 1970? What do you think remains to be done on this issue? What features of our current political environment—our history, the current partisan balance in politics, and the structure of our political system—will either help advance civil rights, or inhibit their achievement? And, finally, do you think that President Obama's election is an aberration—a one-time event? Or do you think that his election signals an opportunity for, in the future, blacks, women, and members of other ethnic groups, such as Hispanics and Asians, to aspire to the nation's highest office? What did President Obama's first term reveal about race relations in the United States?

SUMMARY

Many structural and historic factors influence the making of public policy and constitute, in part, the environment in which public policy is made. These environmental factors are not fixed in time; rather, they are long-standing features of American politics and daily life that can change—and have changed—over the course of our history. But change in the policy environment is relatively slow compared with the daily give and take of politics. Successful actors in policy making will understand and accommodate the enduring features of the policy-making environment and the ways in which the environment can change to enhance or retard the possibility of policy change.

KEY TERMS

Articles of Confederation
Barron v. Baltimore
block grants
Brown v. Board of Education
Civil War Amendments
commerce clause

devolution
elastic clause
federalism
filibuster
Great Society
incorporation doctrine

Industrial Revolution
Jim Crow laws
laissez-faire economics
Lochner v. New York
national security

New Deal
Plessy v. Ferguson
separation of powers
Shays' Rebellion

QUESTIONS FOR DISCUSSION, REFLECTION, AND RESEARCH

- What were the weaknesses of the Articles of Confederation?

- What are the strengths and weaknesses of the Constitution?

- Why did the founders include the "elastic clause" in the Constitution?

- How did the American Industrial Revolution affect public policy during the era of "state activism?"

- Why is it important for a government to set national standards in pursuit of policy goals? Should there even be national standards? Why not leave standards to the states?

- Why is openness important in a democracy? What laws have been passed that have made government more transparent?

- What does it mean when we say that environmental factors help shape public policy? What are environmental factors in this context?

- Why is the Fourteenth Amendment to the Constitution significant? Do you think the Fourteenth Amendment has been fully implemented? What would "fully implemented" look like?

- The election of Ronald Reagan is said to have ended the "era of big government." Has government gotten smaller since 1980? Collect some data that would measure the size of government. Here are some ideas on what sort of data you would gather, and where you can get it:

  - The size of the federal budget (in real dollars, and adjusted for inflation).

- The size of the federal workforce.

- The size of the federal budget as a proportion of the gross domestic product (GDP).

- The per capita size of the federal budget (per capita means the size of the budget divided by the number of people in the country).

- The size of the budget compared with the range of problems that the national government is asked to address.

- The size of all budgets: state, local, and federal.

Don't limit your questions to just these, though; think of the many ways in which one might measure the size of government and what it does. Some places to find data for these questions include:

- www.census.gov: the U.S. Census website provides data regarding the American people and economy, including information on demographics, housing, income, communities, and public program participation.

- www.bls.gov: the United States Bureau of Labor Statistics, with a wealth of economic statistics, including inflation, trade, labor, and other economic data. If you like numbers, you'll enjoy this site.

- www.usa.gov: the federal government's main page and search site.

- www.whitehouse.gov/omb: the Office of Management and Budget (OMB) in the White House, the executive branch agency charged with drafting and managing budgets. Contains current budget information.

- www.cbo.gov: the Congressional Budget Office (CBO), the legislative branch's counterpart to the OMB, which is also a good source for historical budget data. The CBO's projections of economic growth have generally been more accurate than the OMB's or private forecasters' projections.

- Once you've done your analyses, explain what you found. Can you find in the data an argument that government is too big? Or that it isn't very big or isn't big *enough* to address national problems? What data do you rely on to make your argument?

ADDITIONAL READING

I found three books particularly useful for understanding the development of American public policy. Of course, this chapter is thoroughly influenced by David B. Robertson and Dennis R. Judd, *The Development of American Public Policy: The Structure of Policy Restraint* (Glenview, IL: Scott, Foresman & Company, 1989), and I find their division of American policy history into the eras outlined in this chapter remarkably useful. Predating these eras was the Constitution, and one of the best books on the drafting of this document is Catherine Drinker Bowen's *Miracle at Philadelphia: The Story of the Constitutional Convention, May to September, 1787* (Boston, MA: Little, Brown & Company, 1986). The classic text, first published in 1966, recounts the history of the Constitutional Convention and how the Constitution took shape. It is remarkable to learn how quickly the document came together and how the compromises that shaped the document were formed. Finally, one of my favorite historians is James H. McPherson, and his small book *Abraham Lincoln and the Second American Revolution* (New York: Oxford University Press, 1990) is a fascinating explanation of how the Civil War, and President Lincoln's efforts to define the meaning and purpose of that war, were in many ways more revolutionary than the American Revolution itself, as the Civil War ended slavery and began the long process of bringing political equality to racial minorities. Read this book, and then, the next time you are in Washington, visit the Lincoln Memorial, climb the stairs, turn to the right, and read Lincoln's second inaugural address, perhaps the most moving document of this second American Revolution.

NOTES

1   Rassmusen Reports, October 3, 2008, www.rasmussenreports.com/public_content/politics/elections2/election_20082/2008_presidential_election/59_agree_with_ronald_reagan_government_is_the_problem, accessed May 11, 2015.
2   Congress of Racial Equality, "The History of CORE," www.core-online.org/History/history.htm, accessed September 22, 2009.
3   An excellent profile of Rosa Parks is Diane McWhorter, "Rosa Parks: The Story of Her Sitting Down," *Slate*, October 25, 2005. www.slate.com/id/2128752/, accessed February 11, 2015. In recent years, there has been coverage of a similar action taken by a teenager, Claudette Colvin, who refused to move to the back of a bus in Birmingham, Alabama, earlier in 1955. See Brendan I. Koerner, "Is Barbershop Right About Rosa Parks?" *Slate*, September 27, 2002, www.slate.com/id/2071622/ and Margot Adler, "Before Rosa Parks, There Was Claudette Colvin," *National Public Radio*, www.npr.org/templates/story/story.php?storyId=101719889, both accessed December 7, 2009.
4   396 U.S. 19 (1969).

REFERENCES

Anderson, James E. 2000. *Public Policymaking*, 4th ed. Boston, MA: Houghton Mifflin.

Anderson, James E. 2003. *Public Policymaking*, 5th ed. Boston, MA: Houghton Mifflin.

Beard, Charles A. 1956. *An Economic Interpretation of the Constitution of the United States*. New York: Macmillan.

Bertrand, Marianne and Sendhil Mullainathan. 2003. "Are Emily and Greg More Employable Than Lakisha and Jamal? A Field Experiment on Labor Market Discrimination." (No. W9873). National Bureau of Economic Research. Accessed July 4, 2015. www.nber.org/papers/w9873.pdf.

Brulle, Robert J. 2014. "Institutionalizing Delay: Foundation Funding and the Creation of U.S. Climate Change Counter-Movement Organizations." *Climatic Change* 122(4): 681–694. doi: 10.1007/s10584-013-1018-7.

Carson, Jamie L. and Benjamin A. Kleinerman. 2002. "A Switch in Time Saves Nine: Institutions, Strategic Actors, and FDR's Court-Packing Plan." *Public Choice* 113(3/4): 301–324. doi: 10.2307/30025848.

Cigler, Allan J. and Burdett A. Loomis. 2012. *Interest Group Politics*. 8th ed. Washington, DC: CQ Press.

Congress of Racial Equality. 2014. "The History of Core." Accessed January 10, 2014. www.core-online.org/History/history.htm.

DeFina, Robert and Lance Hannon. 2009. "Diversity, Racial Threat and Metropolitan Housing Segregation." *Social Forces* 88(1): 373–394. doi: 10.2307/40345050.

Dempsey, Paul Stephen. 1990. *Flying Blind: The Failure of Airline Deregulation*. Washington, DC: Economic Policy Institute.

Dempsey, Paul Stephen and Andrew R. Goetz. 1992. *Airline Deregulation and Laissez-Faire Mythology*. Westport, CT: Quorum Books.

Erikson, Robert S., Gerald C. Wright, and John P. McIver. 1993. *Statehouse Democracy: Public Opinion and Policy in the American States*. New York: Cambridge University Press.

Fiorina, Morris P. and Samuel J. Abrams. 2008. "Political Polarization in the American Public." *Annual Review of Political Science* 11(1): 563–588.

Fu, Qiang and Ming Li. 2014. "Reputation-Concerned Policy Makers and Institutional Status Quo Bias." *Journal of Public Economics* 110: 15–25. doi: 10.1016/j.jpubeco.2013.11.008.

Geschwind, Carl-Henry. 2001. *California Earthquakes: Science, Risk, and the Politics of Hazard Mitigation*. Baltimore, MD: Johns Hopkins University Press.

Gilens, Martin and Benjamin I. Page. 2014. "Testing Theories of American Politics: Elites, Interest Groups, and Average Citizens." *Perspectives on Politics* 12: 564–581. doi: 10.1017/S1537592714001595.

Goggin, Malcolm L., Ann O. Bowman, James P. Lester, and Laurence J. O'Toole Jr. 1990. *Implementation Theory and Practice: Toward a Third Generation*. Glenview, IL: Scott Foresman/Little Brown.

Heritage Foundation. 2014. "The Case against Obamacare: Health Care Policy Series for the 112th Congress." Accessed January 7, 2015. www.heritage.org/research/projects/the-case-against-obamacare.

Karpowitz, Christopher F., J. Quin Monson, Kelly D. Patterson, and Jeremy C. Pope. 2011. "Tea Time in America? The Impact of the Tea Party Movement on the 2010 Midterm Elections." *PS: Political Science & Politics* 44(2): 303–309. doi: doi:10.1017/S1049096511000138.

Kersten, Andrew E. 1999. "Jobs and Justice: Detroit, Fair Employment, and Federal Activism During the Second World War." *Michigan Historical Review* 25(1): 76–101. doi: 10.2307/20173794.

Levendusky, Matthew. 2009. *The Partisan Sort: How Liberals Became Democrats and Conservatives Became Republicans*. Chicago, IL: University of Chicago Press.

McCloskey, Robert G. and Sanford Levenson. 2010. *The American Supreme Court*. 5th ed. Chicago, IL: University of Chicago Press.

McPherson, James H. 1990. *Abraham Lincoln and the Second American Revolution*. New York: Oxford University Press.

Moore, Barrington. 1966. *Social Origins of Dictatorship and Democracy: Lord and Peasant in the Making of the Modern World*. Boston, MA: Beacon Press.

Oberlander, Jonathan. 2007. "Learning from Failure in Health Care Reform." *New England Journal of Medicine* 357(17): 1677–1679. doi: doi:10.1056/NEJMp078201.

Osborne, David. 1990. *Laboratories of Democracy: A New Breed of Governor Creates Models for National Growth*. Cambridge, MA: Harvard Business School Press.

Plotnick, Robert D. and Richard F. Winters. 1985. "A Politico-Economic Theory of Income Redistribution." *The American Political Science Review* 79(2): 458–473.

Pogue, Lloyd Welch and John Marshall Pogue. 1991. *Airline Deregulation, Before and After: What Next? National Air and Space Museum Occasional Paper Series, No. 2*. Washington, DC: National Air and Space Museum, Smithsonian Institution.

Pressman, Jeffrey L. and Aaron B. Wildavsky. 1984. *Implementation: How Great Expectations in Washington Are Dashed in Oakland: Or, Why It's Amazing That Federal Programs Work at All, This Being a Saga of the Economic Development Administration as Told by Two Sympathetic Observers Who Seek to Build Morals on a Foundation of Ruined Hopes*. Berkeley, CA: University of California Press.

Richards, Leonard L. 2002. *Shays's Rebellion: The American Revolution's Final Battle*. Philadelphia, PA: University of Pennsylvania Press.

Robertson, David B. and Dennis R. Judd. 1989. *The Development of American Public Policy: The Structure of Policy Restraint*. Glenview, IL: Scott, Foresman & Company.

Root, Damon. 2012. "The 4 Best Legal Arguments against Obamacare." Accessed January 7, 2015. http://reason.com/archives/2012/03/24/4-best-legal-arguments-against-obamacare.

Rosenberg, Randall. 2008. *The Hollow Hope*, 2nd ed. Chicago, IL: University of Chicago Press.

Starr, Paul. 1994. "What Happened to Health Care Reform?" *The American Prospect* 20 (Winter): 20–31.

Stone, Deborah A. 2011. *Policy Paradox: The Art of Political Decision Making*. 3rd ed. New York: Norton.

Tallon, James R. and Lawrence D. Brown. 1998. "Who Gets What? Devolution of Eligibility and Benefits in Medicaid." In *Medicaid and Devolution: A View from the States*, edited by Frank J. Thompson and John J. DiIulio Jr., 235–257. Washington, DC: Brookings Institution Press.

Walker, Jack L. 1969. "The Diffusion of Innovations among the American States." *American Political Science Review* 63: 880–899.

Williamson, Vanessa, Theda Skocpol, and John Coggin. 2011. "The Tea Party and the Remaking of Republican Conservatism." *Perspectives on Politics* 9(1): 25–43. doi:10.1017/S153759271000 407X.

Wilson, Anthony. 2015. "Why 'Hillarycare' Failed and 'Obamacare' Succeeded." Accessed January 10, 2015. www.americanhealthline.com/analysis-and-insight/features/why-hillarycare-failed-and-obamacare-succeeded.

CHAPTER 4

Official Actors and Their Roles in Public Policy

OVERVIEW

For years after the establishment of political science as a distinctive discipline, political scientists focused their research on the texts of constitutions, laws, and other written statements of policies, and studied the relationships between formal government institutions—the three branches of government and the states, for example. In the 1950s, **institutionalism** began to be dominated by **behaviorism**, in which the political motivations of individuals, acting singly or in groups, were analyzed, often through sophisticated polling, game theory, and statistical techniques.

While behaviorism dominates social science research, the study of institutions and the people that compose them is neither obsolete nor unimportant, and we continue to study the behavior of actors within institutions and the interactions between institutions. Moreover, our definition of institution has changed. The older notion was of discrete, formally created bodies, such as Congress, the Supreme Court, and the presidency. Institutions are now described as organizations as well as systems in which individuals interact and achieve political and policy goals through explicit or implicit rules that evolve over time through cooperative means (Ostrom, Cox, and Schrager 2014). The latter concept, called **neo-institutionalism**, has become prominent in political

institutionalism
The study of politics and policy based on the interaction of formal institutions in government, such as the legislative, executive, and judicial branches. Compare with behaviorism.

behaviorism
The approach, pioneered in the late 1930s and 1940s, that sought to study social phenomena based on the postulated and observed behavior of individuals. Behaviorism was a response to the more common approach of its day known as institutionalism.

neo-institutionalism
The study of politics and policy that retains the focus on institutions, but which incorporates a great deal of behaviorist thinking as well.

official actor
A participant in the policy process whose involvement is motivated or mandated by his or her official position in a government agency or office.

science, and new insights into the behavior of individuals and organizations are being derived from it. Indeed, as B. Dan Wood notes, "a series of studies [has examined] the presidency, the Congress, and the courts to make clear that institutions do make a difference when explaining public policy outcomes" (Wood 1991). In this chapter and the next, I share this neo-institutionalist approach and consider the network of actors, institutions, and rules involved in policy making.

In this book, I categorize participants in decision-making into two broad groups: *official actors* and *unofficial actors*. The term "official" or "unofficial" is not meant to suggest that particular participants are more "legitimate" actors in the policy process. Rather, official actors are involved in public policy because their responsibilities are sanctioned by laws or the Constitution and they therefore have the power to make and enforce policies. The legislative, executive, and judicial branches are clearly official institutions, because they are explicitly mentioned in the Constitution. In this sense, official actors play important institutional roles. Unofficial actors include those who play roles in the policy process without any explicit legal authority (or duty) to participate. These individuals and the groups to which they belong are not called upon or compelled to participate in the policy process. Indeed, these groups are involved because they have the right to be, because they have important interests to protect and promote, and because, in many ways, our system of government simply would not work well without them. As we will see in Chapter 5, interest groups have become more prominent because they have proven to be an effective way for many people to collectively express their desires for policy.

Another important group of unofficial actors is the news media, which enjoy first amendment press freedoms because of their "watchdog" role—that is, the news media exist as a check on government overreach and abuse. News outlets illuminate the actions of government. They have no formal, guaranteed role in policy making, but our democracy relies on serious journalism. Under certain conditions, such as matters of national security or personal privacy, the media have been denied access to policy-making information and processes. This denial of access to information sometimes raises controversy that is out of proportion to the value of the information being withheld.

LEGISLATURES

We begin with the legislative branch because it is the first listed branch in the federal and most state constitutions, and because the founders considered it the major policy-making branch. This derives from the idea that popular will would be exercised in the legislature, while the executive branch largely exists, in this view, to carry out what Congress enacted (Wilson 1887). The judiciary was meant to interpret the laws as enacted by the people's elected representatives. This ideal view of the three branches of government is incomplete, but this *idea* was considered by many to be the way the system did and should work well into the twentieth century. It is still the popular conception of American government, but the relationships between the branches are actually much more subtle and less separate.

The legislative branch has many duties, but, given its name, a primary responsibility is to make statute law—the laws that go into the United States Code, or the various state codes and statutes. This function consumes a considerable amount of the legislative branch's time and energy. If we use the number of bills introduced as a rough measure of the process, we can estimate how busy Congress is. Some figures for the 105th and 113th Congresses are shown in Table 4.1.

With over 7,000 bills to consider in the House, and over 3,500 in the Senate, it is easy to imagine that Congress is remarkably busy simply dealing with the volume of legislative work: drafting bills, assigning them to committees, keeping track of them, and so on. Compared with the late 1990s, the volume of legislative business has increased. However, lest we believe that Congress is overworked, it is important to bear in mind that the 535 members of Congress have ways to lighten this load. Members of Congress have staff people who help them draft, read, sift through, and understand the volume of legislation that they process every year. Other staff members manage the day-to-day workings of Congress, from providing security to maintaining the Capitol and the House and Senate office buildings.

In the United States, the national and state legislatures pass substantive laws that establish how various programs will run, how money will be distributed, what public works projects will be funded, and so on. The vast majority of bills fail to move past their initial introduction and assignment to a committee. In some cases, bills duplicate or nearly duplicate each other, so that the key ideas and some of the language from several bills can be merged into one. Members also introduce bills to satisfy group demands for,

unofficial actor
A participant in the process who does not have constitutionally or legally created incentives or mandates to be a part of the process, such as experts, researchers, and reporters, all of whom are important to the policy process.

TABLE 4.1 Measuring Legislative Activity: Bills, Amendments, Joint Resolutions, and Concurrent Resolutions in the 105th and 113th Congresses

	105th Congress (1997–1998)		113th Congress (2013–2014)	
	House	Senate	House	Senate
Bills	4,874	2,655	5,884	3,020
Joint resolutions	140	60	131	47
Concurrent resolutions	354	130	125	44

Definitions:

Bills: Bills are the most common form of legislation; they may be public or private. Bills have the prefix "H.R." when introduced in the House, "S." when introduced in the Senate, followed by a number assigned sequentially as bills are introduced. Most legislative proposals are in the form of bills, dealing with either domestic or foreign issues. Authorizations (establishing federal programs and agencies) and appropriations (actually providing the money for these programs and agencies) are both in the form of bills.

Public bills deal with issues of a general nature. If approved by both houses of Congress (the House and the Senate) in identical form and signed by the president (or repassed by the Congress over a presidential veto), they become *public laws*.

Private bills deal with matters of concern to individuals, such as claims against the federal government, immigration or naturalization cases, or land titles. They become "private laws" if approved by Congress and signed by the president or enacted over his veto.

Joint resolutions: There is little practical difference between bills and joint resolutions, although the latter are not as numerous as bills. Usually joint resolutions concern limited or temporary matters, such as a continuing or emergency appropriation. Like bills, joint resolutions also have the force of law, upon approval of both houses of Congress and the signature of the president.

A joint resolution is the legislative vehicle used for proposing amendments to the Constitution. This type of joint resolution is not presented to the president for his signature, but instead becomes part of the Constitution when three-fourths of the states have ratified it.

Concurrent resolutions: Concurrent resolutions are limited in nature. They are not legislative in character and are not presented to the president for action. They are used to express facts, opinions, principles, and purposes of the two houses, such as fixing the time and date for adjournment of a Congress. Annual congressional concurrent resolutions set forth Congress's revenue and spending targets for the coming fiscal year, and thus have great impact upon other legislation. Upon approval by both chambers, they are published in a special part of the *Statutes at Large*. They do not require presidential approval and do not have the force of law.

Source: Definitions and data found at Library of Congress, www.congress.gov/.

at least, some basic level of action. And introducing bills can also move ideas onto the agenda. Interest groups know that the seemingly symbolic gesture or courtesy introduction of a bill could spark its rapid movement up the legislative ladder or mark the beginning of a slow but still successful movement to spur policy change. Legislation that is primarily symbolic and noncontroversial moves through the process relatively quickly. For example, H.R. 433 of 2015 would "designate the facility of the United States Postal Service located at 523 East Railroad Street in Knox, Pennsylvania, as the 'Specialist Ross A. McGinnis Memorial Post Office.'" It is very likely that this bill will be enacted into law by the time you read this.

Legislators do more than simply introduce bills and make laws. Legislators are remarkably busy people, particularly during a congressional or legislative session, often maintaining a dawn-to-dusk schedule of meetings, hearings,

PHOTO 4.1
Tourists visit the U.S. Capitol building. Why do people visit buildings such as the Capitol, the White House, and the Supreme Court?

Source: Alamy. Used with permission.

campaign and fundraising appearances, news media interviews, communications with constituents, and a host of other activities that make service in the legislative branch a full-time job, even in states where legislators are considered and paid as part-timers. While a full treatment of the legislature's activities is beyond the scope of this book (see, for example, Arnold 1990; Ripley and Franklin 1991; Fiorina 2004; Baker 2008; Davidson et al. 2014), it is important to consider two other functions that have gained considerable importance in recent years: casework and oversight.

Casework refers to the tasks undertaken by a legislator (or, more commonly, the legislator's staff) to help constituents solve problems with government agencies or to gain a privilege or benefit from the government. Examples include writing letters of recommendation for admission to military academies, resolving immigration or passport problems, and resolving problems with federal benefits, such as social security or veterans' benefits.

casework The tasks undertaken by a legislator (or, more commonly, the legislator's staff) to help constituents with problems with government. Examples include writing letters of recommendation for admission to military academies, resolving immigration or passport problems, and resolving problems with federal benefits, such as Social Security.

Casework provides elected officials, particularly members of the House of Representatives, with opportunities to reach out to constituents and demonstrate concern for their needs in a way that is neither ideological nor partisan. Indeed, this sort of service is actively promoted by many members of Congress and, while the direct electoral influence of casework remains unclear, most members of Congress believe that when they help an individual constituent resolve a frustrating agency-related problem, the constituent will overlook party and ideological differences and vote for the incumbent (Fiorina 1981; Johannes and McAdams 1981; McAdams and Johannes 1981; Yiannakis 1981; Romero 1996). While the extent to which a member of Congress can influence agency response can be quite limited (Peterson 2010), we can see casework, and its management by members of Congress, as a form of feedback from citizens to legislators on the implementation of public policy.

oversight The process by which Congress supervises the executive branch's implementation of laws and programs.

Oversight has grown far more important since the late 1970s and early 1980s, as overall trust in government and belief in its efficacy have declined.[1] Oversight refers to the process by which Congress oversees the implementation of policies. Congress has a number of methods by which it can oversee the implementation of programs. Congress often pursues its oversight function by holding public hearings about policy issues and problems. Sometimes these hearings are triggered by sudden, newsworthy events: Congress often holds hearings very soon after highly visible events, such as plane crashes, natural disasters, terrorist attacks, or spectacular crimes, such as the Columbine High School shooting in 1999. Congress also holds hearings when scandal or actual or claimed policy failure is revealed, such as the hearings held in the wake of the Watergate, Whitewater, and Iran-Contra affairs, and after major disasters such as the September 11 attacks and Hurricane Katrina.

These hearings serve at least three functions. First, they help Congress and the public to understand issues by bringing together various interests to testify; their testimony is often reported in major national news outlets. Second, the hearings reveal shortcomings in current policies. After Hurricane Katrina in 2005, hearings revealed the gaps in federal and state policies relating to disaster preparedness, response, and recovery. These hearings paved the way for passage of an improved set of policies contained in the Post-Katrina Reform Act of 2006. To show how complex lawmaking can be, and how Congress often bundles issues together, note that this law is Title VI of the Department of Homeland Security appropriation bill for FY 2007, which is PL 109-295. Congress often includes reform legislation in appropriation bills, thereby linking money to the desired reform.

Finally, a political party or a group of members can use oversight hearings to score political points, usually against the executive branch. This strategy is particularly likely if the executive branch is of a different party than the party controlling Congress as a whole, or the House or Senate alone. A particularly useful technique for highlighting an issue is the **field hearing**, in which a committee or subcommittee holds a hearing in the community where an accident or disaster occurred or where a scandal has had the most impact. Members hear testimony and give speeches expressing their concern and endorsing the complaints of local citizens. These hearings are symbolic, providing local officials and citizens with an opportunity to vent their frustration, but the hearings can also provide useful feedback to legislators and create and enhance popular pressure for changes in policy.

Congress does not need to hold hearings to gather important oversight information. Congress can informally gain a great deal of information from constituents, from interest groups, which often provide information to Congress, and from the news media, which often report on problems relating to the implementation of public programs (Aberbach 1990). More formally, Congress's investigative arm, the Government Accountability Office (GAO) (known as the Government Accounting Office before 2004) studies public programs and makes recommendations to improve efficiency, effectiveness, and accountability to elected officials. By investigating public programs, the GAO helps Congress to monitor the implementation of the policies it enacts. But GAO's own analytic capacity is limited. GAO reports and investigations are limited by the same time, resource, and expertise constraints that affect any evaluation research. And GAO's findings may conflict with other legislative goals—for example, a finding by GAO that a program is "inefficient" may not fully account for the political benefits of a government program to the members of Congress that support it. Congress also gets information on programs and problems from other sources; in particular, the Congressional Research Service, an arm of the Library of Congress, researches issues and prepares briefings for Members of Congress.

Organization

Many people who have visited the Senate or House galleries or have watched their proceedings on **C-SPAN** find the action on the floor slow and dull. Television coverage of the House or Senate may not reveal that the member

field hearing
A legislative hearing held outside Washington, DC, often for the purpose of highlighting a local issue; capitalizing on an accident, disaster, or scandal; or providing local residents with an opportunity to make their views known to their elected officials.

C-SPAN The Cable-Satellite Public Affairs Network, which is owned in common by the cable TV industry to provide video coverage of Congress and of related public affairs broadcasting. C-SPAN offers television, and also has a radio station in Washington, DC, that runs the audio of some C-SPAN channels. It is also available online at www.c-span.org.

is speaking to a camera in an empty or near-empty chamber. While "speechifying" seems silly to some, this activity, recorded and shown on C-SPAN and other outlets, is an important way for members to communicate their positions on issues to their constituents, each other, and the nation.

The empty chambers and the highly technical and procedural activity that seem so boring when Congress is in session represent only a fraction of the activity that happens in offices and the committee rooms. The bulk of Congress's work is done in committees, which review legislation, propose and vote on amendments, and, in the end, decide whether a bill will die at the committee level or will be elevated to consideration by the full body. The legislative process, which you may have learned as "how a bill becomes a law," is presented with some elements of the regulatory process in Figure 4.1.

Congress is a large body, and needs to organize itself to handle its large workload. Political parties are one form of organization in Congress. Each party elects majority and minority leaders in the two bodies, and various other leadership positions, such as the majority and minority whips, and the chairs of the respective congressional campaign committees. One position that is slightly different is the speaker of the House, who is the speaker of the whole House, not just the leader of a party. The speaker is therefore elected by all members of the body, not just by one party, but, as a practical matter, the speaker is elected on a strict party-line ballot and serves as a leader of the majority party in the House. Indeed, the office of speaker has become more visible and partisan in recent years, starting with the respectful but often intense rivalry between Speaker Thomas "Tip" O'Neill (D-MA) and President Reagan. This continued through the tumultuous tenure of Speaker Newt Gingrich (R-GA), although the office became somewhat less visible during the term of Speaker Dennis Hastert (R-IL), who sought to tone down some of the sometimes overheated partisanship. Then the position became more visible again when Democrat Nancy Pelosi of San Francisco was elected the first female speaker of the House during the George W. Bush administration. Upon the election of President Barack Obama, a Democrat, Speaker Pelosi—and her Senate counterpart, Majority Leader Harry Reid (D-NV)—have been more supportive of the executive branch, as is typical when the Congress and the White House are held by the same party. But this is not to say that these leaders march in lockstep with the president, because institutional and party leaders—regardless of their party label—are sensitive to the powers and prerogatives of the Senate and House of Representatives as specified in

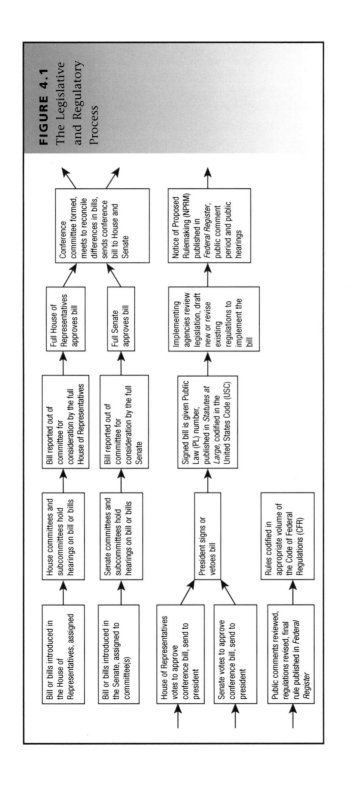

FIGURE 4.1

The Legislative and Regulatory Process

Bill or bills introduced in the House of Representatives, assigned → House committees and subcommittees hold hearings on bill or bills → Bill reported out of committee for consideration by the full House of Representatives → Full House of Representatives approves bill → Conference committee formed, meets to reconcile differences in bills, sends conference bill to House and Senate

Bill or bills introduced in the Senate, assigned to committee(s) → Senate committees and subcommittees hold hearings on bill or bills → Bill reported out of committee for consideration by the full Senate → Full Senate approves bill → Conference committee formed, meets to reconcile differences in bills, sends conference bill to House and Senate

House of Representatives votes to approve conference bill, send to president → President signs or vetoes bill

Senate votes to approve conference bill, send to president → President signs or vetoes bill

President signs or vetoes bill → Signed bill is given Public Law (PL) number, published in *Statutes at Large*, codified in the United States Code (USC) → Implementing agencies review legislation, draft new or revise existing regulations to implement the bill → Notice of Proposed Rulemaking (NPRM) published in *Federal Register*, public comment period and public hearings

Public comments reviewed, regulations revised, final rule published in *Federal Register* → Rules codified in appropriate volume of the Code of Federal Regulations (CFR)

the Constitution. And, starting in 2011, when the House of Representatives returned to Republican control, and again in 2015, when both houses of Congress had Republican leadership, political conflicts arose between the Democratic president and Republican majorities. Again, it is important to understand that while much of this tension between the president and Congress is partisan, at least some of it is also institutional, or both.

Congress and state legislatures are also divided into committees that help divide the legislative workload among the members. Most state legislatures are not as large and complex as Congress, but Texas, New York, and California have legislatures that rival Congress in size and complexity. In both Congress and large legislatures, legislators generally do not pore over every line of every bill; their staffs brief them about the bills' essential details, and the members rely on other members who become legislative specialists on issues. This doesn't mean that the members always agree with these specialists. It shocks some of the public and less-informed journalists that members of Congress do not read each and every word of every bill, even major legislation such as healthcare reform. And while such claims can yield populist annoyance and partisan bickering, expecting each member to read each bill is unrealistic, particularly since they have staffs that can read and distill the technical aspects of legislation in a way that can keep members informed while allowing those members to attend to the challenges of their very busy workdays.

The committees serve as gatekeepers for legislation, in both the organizational and political sense. Organizationally, the committees help Congress prioritize the legislation that it will hear: the routine but mandatory issues that Congress must address every year, such as the budget, are higher priority than less pressing business, and crises will often overwhelm all other priorities (Walker 1977). The breadth of issues that committees deal with is reflected in Table 4.2.

Committee chairs are senior, but not necessarily the most senior members of the majority party, and the majority party holds more seats on a committee than does the minority party. The ranking member of the committee is the senior member from the minority party who would presumably be chair if the minority were the majority party. The chairs and the ranking members usually work closely together to ensure the smooth conduct of routine business—and a lot of Congress's activities are routine from year to year. The committee chairs wield considerable political power when they decide which bills will be debated and advanced to action by the full House or Senate and make decisions about the committees and Congress's agenda to advance their

TABLE 4.2 Committees in the 114th Congress

House Committees	Senate Committees
Agriculture	Agriculture, Nutrition, and Forestry
Appropriations	Appropriations
Armed Services	Armed Services
The Budget	Banking, Housing, and Urban Affairs
Education and Workforce	Budget
Energy and Commerce	Commerce, Science, and Transportation
Ethics	Energy and Natural Resources
Financial Services	Environment and Public Works
Foreign Affairs	Finance
Homeland Security	Foreign Relations
House Administration	Health, Education, Labor, and Pensions
The Judiciary	Homeland Security and Governmental Affairs
Natural Resources	Judiciary
Oversight and Government Reform	Rules and Administration
Rules	Small Business and Entrepreneurship
Science, Space, and Technology	Veterans' Affairs
Small Business	
Transportation and Infrastructure	*Special, Select, and Other*
Veterans' Affairs	Indian Affairs
Ways and Means	Select Committee on Ethics
	Select Committee on Intelligence
Special, Select, and Other	Special Committee on Aging
House Permanent Select Committee on Intelligence	
	Joint
House Select Committee on Benghazi	Joint Committee on Printing
	Joint Committee on Taxation
Joint	Joint Committee on the Library
Joint Economic Committee	Joint Economic Committee
Joint Congressional Committee on Inaugural Ceremonies	
Joint Committee on Taxation	

Source: Websites of the House and Senate, www.house.com and www.senate.com.

individual or party's policy agenda. This power is entirely consistent with the way in which Congress is organized, and both parties realize that control over the partisan balance in Congress means control over the legislative agenda.

For the student of public policy, the legislative branch is an important center of policy making, the institution we most often study when trying to assess what issues are gaining and losing prominence and which alternative policies are being weighed. This is also true at the state level, although state legislative activities have not been as thoroughly tracked and analyzed by social scientists as federal legislation has. The process by which bills become law at the state level is roughly similar to the federal process. A few states, for example, do not have conference committees that coordinate differences between the lower and upper houses' versions of bills. Many state legislatures have posted on their websites descriptions of how bills become laws in those states; indeed, the advent of the Web has made much more legislative information, at the federal and state levels, more readily available than ever before.

Public Policy and Critiques of the Legislative Branch

Many people argue that federal and state legislatures are out of touch with the wishes of the people. Why, people ask, does the legislature act against what seems to be the clearly stated will of the majority of the people? Why is the legislature so bogged down in partisan squabbling? Why can't the legislature get anything *done*? In some states, citizen frustration with the perceived failings of legislatures has led to the widespread use of the initiative process, as is most visibly seen in California.

The motivation of members seems, on its face, to be very simple: to be re-elected—and that motivation bothers a lot of people. Morris Fiorina, in *Congress: Keystone of the Washington Establishment* (2004), assumes "that the primary goal of the typical congressman is reelection." Why? Certainly, ego, fame, and power are involved, but, as Fiorina argues, many members of Congress are motivated by the desire to create or shape what they believe to be good public policy, and "even those congressmen genuinely concerned with good public policy must achieve reelection in order to continue their work." If one assumes that re-election is the primary motivation, then many other elements of politics and policy making, such as how election campaigns are financed and run, how legislators and the media interact, and how the labor is divided among committees and congressional leadership, become clearer.

Richard Fenno provides a somewhat more subtle explanation of members' motivations in his classic book *Homestyle* (2003). Fenno argues that the primary goal of members may not be re-election. Certainly, he says, they do fight to be re-elected, but this is usually in pursuit of other goals that depend on their re-election, such as making public policy. Furthermore, different members have different styles of working, both at home and in Congress itself—this reflects the old saying in Congress that there are workhorses (those who enjoy the give and take of legislating) and show horses (those who like the more public aspects of the job).

Congress as a Decentralized Institution

The decentralized nature of Congress helps explain the decisions made by the legislative branch. One can argue that for every member there is a separate agenda, and trying to reach consensus among even half of these legislators, all with their own agendas, is difficult even in the best of circumstances. This may explain why many members, as Fenno notes, run for Congress by running against it. According to Fenno, Americans "hate Congress and love their Congressmen," because there are things individual members seem to do for their home districts and constituents that Congress as a whole seemingly does not. When a member brings federal money to our individual districts, it is hailed as a boon to folks in the home district, but when Congress as a body approves spending on local projects in general, it is claimed that this simply reflects Congress's predilection for wasteful pork-barrel spending. Thus, the so-called "bridges to nowhere" in Alaska—which would have been funded by federal appropriations—received much scorn because it seemed like wasteful spending on unnecessary infrastructure. But the detractors often failed to discuss how much federal funding they had secured for their own districts. But the practice fell into considerable disfavor and the use of congressional earmarks—funds designated for particular local projects—fell into considerable disfavor (see, for example, Kraft and Furlong 2014: 107).

Before about 1974, power in Congress was rather more centralized in the hands of legendary party leaders such as Sam Rayburn in the House of Representatives and Lyndon Johnson in the Senate. But a number of events—Watergate, Vietnam, and the eroding faith in government and its leaders—combined with and contributed to the frustrations of junior and rank-and-file members of Congress. A significant number of moderate-to-liberal Democrats were elected to Congress in the historic 1974 elections that immediately followed President Nixon's resignation in the Watergate scandal. As a group, the new members were committed to reforming government in general as well as the Congress. They sought, with some success, to reduce the influence of seniority in the selection of committee chairs, to gain power for sub-committees, and to provide a voice for junior members of the body. These new members were much less patient than their senior colleagues with the old norms that junior members should quietly serve an apprenticeship period before speaking out on substantive issues.

In the 1990s, some power returned to the top party leadership, as the margins with which the majority party held control became rather narrow.

issue network
A term that describes the relationships between the various actors and interests in a particular policy issue. Hugh Heclo promoted this term because it describes a more open policy-making system that contains more actors and relationships than the older *iron triangle* concept.

policy subsystem
Another term for *policy network* or *issue network*, although the term *subsystem* implies a somewhat less open, more mutually accommodating set of relationships between members of the subsystem.

The policy implications are indirect, but include a legislative branch that is more prone to engage ideas based on ideological commitments rather than on pragmatic grounds. This was most dramatically demonstrated during the term of Speaker Newt Gingrich, who created a remarkably high degree of party discipline in the House, particularly in 1995 and 1996. Recently, Nancy Pelosi sought to re-centralize some of that power back to the speaker and the senior party leadership. These trends continue under Speaker John Boehner, although he, like other party leaders, has had to contend with Members of Congress that are more conservative than the party mainstream, just as Nancy Pelosi had to contend with those who were more liberal than the Democratic mainstream.

We should not make too much of this movement toward re-centralization of power because Congress has always been, to a greater or lesser extent, relatively decentralized. This diffusion of power and expertise allows for the creation of small **issue networks** or **policy subsystems** that, in many ways, operate to ensure the flow of benefits from the federal government to well-organized interests. These networks encompass centers of power, influence, and interests both inside and outside the legislative branch, and outside formal government.

Congress and Implications for Policy Making

What do these aspects of the legislative branch mean for policy making? Any discussion of the legislative process will inevitably reflect difficulty in actually passing laws and policies. When a decentralized Congress and its members are more concerned with its relationships with interest groups, key bureaucracies, and citizen-clients, it is difficult to make "big" policies that require substantial legislative action, particularly since members' "clients" are often as likely to resist change as they are to support it. This feature of the system became most evident during the healthcare reform debate in 2009, and subsequent attempts to repeal the legislation, where opposition to reforms arose based simply on the distaste some have for any change. Of course, we must recognize that the founders of our constitutional system purposefully created "checks and balances" that made change slow, but they also created a system in which it would be possible when a coalition of elected officials and citizens formed to promote change. But Congress's focus on politically safe casework and on avoiding the creation of new and large government programs may lead to greater tendencies to maintain the status quo—a situation in which less powerful, still striving interests find it difficult to press their case for policy change.

CASE STUDY: PARTY CONTROL OF CONGRESS AND POLICY CHANGE, 1994–2014

Those who argue that there's no real difference between the two political parties in the United States should consider significant events in recent political history: the Republican takeover of the U.S. House of Representatives during the 1994 elections; the Democrats's victories in the 2006 congressional elections, in which the Democrats regained control of the House of Representatives, and, eventually, the Senate; and the 2008 congressional elections, where the Democrats expanded their majority in the House and built a solid majority in the Senate as President Obama was elected. These events were followed by the 2010 and 2014 congressional elections, when the Democrats lost control of the House, and then failed to regain the House of Representatives and lost party control of the Senate as well.

As of 1994, the Democratic Party had controlled the House of Representatives for over 50 years, even as the Senate was under Republican control from 1980 to 1986. Led by House Minority Leader Newt Gingrich (R-GA), the Republicans put forth a bold program dubbed the "Contract with America," which made a range of promises, including balancing the budget, lowering taxes, setting limits on the tenure of committee chairs, and other substantive and procedural changes (Fenno 2003). Gingrich characterized the 1994 Republican victory as a rollback of Great Society liberalism and big government: "There are profound things that went wrong starting with the Great Society and the counterculture and until we address them head-on, we're going to have these problems . . ." (Dowd 1994).

The Republican victory was a significant setback for the Democratic Party and President Bill Clinton, suggesting that party control of the legislative majority—and the ideological commitments of the respective parties—do matter in public policy. And these changes in public policy appeared, at the time, to have some staying power. In annual averages of party identification figures in the Gallup poll, the Republican Party was favored by a higher proportion of partisans—that is, those who identify with either the Republicans or Democrats—between 1990 and 1995, and between 2001 and 2005, the latter period corresponding with voters' higher degree of confidence in the Republicans' ability to manage homeland security. However, in no year since 1969 have Republicans constituted a majority of partisans. Indeed, when either party wins, it is usually when it attracts independent voters to its cause, a task made easier by the smaller proportion of self-identified Democrats among voters since the 1960s, and by the increasing tendency of some Democrats to switch parties, particularly among self-identified conservative Democrats.

With their 1994 victory, the Republican-led House forced President Clinton to modify his proposals and to work out compromises to get his legislation passed. His plans for healthcare reform were largely dead at this point. Clinton was re-elected in 1996, but liberals were particularly bothered by his advocacy of major welfare reform in the 1996 Welfare Reform Act (technically the 1996 Personal Responsibility and Work Opportunity Reconciliation Act). Clinton was significantly weakened by the Monica Lewinsky and Whitewater scandals, political problems that might not have led to his impeachment trial had the Democratic Party held a majority of the Congress.

Although a number of factors led to the 1994 Republican House victory, political observers widely agree that Newt Gingrich played a central role in organizing it. Unlike his predecessor, Minority Leader Robert Michel (R-IL), who was more willing to work out of the public eye and to seek compromise, Gingrich was a partisan and a tough leader who was not hesitant to attack the House Democratic leadership (Dowd 1994). Earlier in his career, Gingrich had been referred to as a "backbench bomb thrower" (Lacayo 1994). For example, Gingrich's persistent pursuit of a House investigation into an ethics charge led to the resignation of House Speaker Jim Wright (D-TX). Gingrich helped craft the Contract with America that gave Republican House candidates a platform on which to effectively base their campaign. And Republicans were remarkably adept at staying "on message," with a series of substantive policy proposals in the Contract with America that appealed to a majority of the 1994 electorate. Strahan and Palazzolo believe that Gingrich's House leadership is an excellent case study for examining how the political context influences congressional leadership. In other words, can Gingrich's actions be explained more by contextual factors or by his own individual personality? This is a central issue in trying to understand political leadership. These two scholars conclude that "a satisfactory explanation of Gingrich's leadership style must include both contextual factors and individual leader effects, specifically those resulting from Gingrich's own political goals and the orientation toward leadership that follows from those goals" (Dowd 1994). His goals were much more oriented toward electoral and policy success achieved through more aggressive partisanship and rhetoric, combined with good message control and timing.

Some argued that Gingrich embodied how partisanship is both a good thing and a problem in American politics (Strahan and Palazzolo 2004). Indeed, after the Gingrich speakership, the loss of House seats to the Democrats in 1996 (a presidential election year) and in 1998, and a short period of leadership instability, the Republicans elected Dennis Hastert of Illinois—a far less polarizing figure in Congress—to be their speaker, a position he held until 2007. With the election of President Bush in 2000, the Republicans were able to dominate policy making because they held a majority in the House and Senate, even when Senator Jim Jeffords of Vermont switched parties from Republican to Independent, but caucused with the Democrats, leading to a 50–50 split in the Senate. The Republicans retained the majority because Vice President Dick Cheney, a Republican, could vote to break ties in the Senate, as provided for in Article I, section 3, clause 4, of the Constitution. In the House, the Republicans gained eight seats in the 2002 elections, which ran against the usual pattern of the president's party losing seats in "off-year" (that is, non-presidential) elections. The partisan balance of the Senate shifted by one seat between 2001 and 2003. After the 2002 elections, a 51–49 Republican majority regained control. Such a thin majority did not, however, make majority control particularly effective, due to the Democrats' ability to filibuster.

In the 2006 congressional elections, the Democrats regained majorities of the House and Senate, in considerable part due to the unpopularity of the president; unpopular presidents often hurt their party's candidates for Congress. The 2008 elections saw the Democrats' majorities increase, in large part due to the "coattail" effect of President Obama's successful campaign. Such a coattail effect is very rare in midterm elections. Indeed, the president's approval rating is nearing the level of disapproval as of this writing (late 2009), and presidential approval often declines until about the third year of a president's term.

But did the results of the 2006 and, more to the point, the 2008 congressional elections (leaving aside, for a moment, the presidential election) really presage a period of policy change in a different direction? Political scientist Jonathan Woon believed so: using various methods, he asserted that policy will take a more liberal turn under the 111th Congress, as a direct result of partisan polarization and the results of the election itself (Clymer 1998). Examples of significant policy change in the first session of the 111th Congress included the expansion of the State Children's Health Insurance Program (SCHIP) (PL 111-2), a change that had been twice vetoed by President George W. Bush; the major economic stimulus legislation (PL 111-5); the expansion of AmeriCorps and other service programs (PL 111-13); programs designed to help homeowners faced with foreclosure stay in their houses (PL 111-22); the Car Allowance Rebate System (CARS) or "cash for clunkers program" (in which the federal government offered subsidies to people to buy more fuel-efficient cars); and part of the Supplemental Appropriation Act (PL 111-32). Many—if not most—of these programs would not have been enacted under the prior Congress, as they would have been vetoed by the president (as happened in the SCHIP program) or would never have passed Congress when it was led by the Republican Party.

Of course, all these policies were and often remain controversial—if nothing else, many of them increase federal spending, and therefore the budget deficit and the national debt, which became major issues in late 2009 and early 2010. Indeed, the growth of the federal budget deficit and the belief that much federal spending was wasteful was part of the rallying cry for the Tea Party movement, the populist movement, mostly in the Republican party, that opposed additional spending, healthcare reform, and the bipartisan efforts to support the banking system in 2009 through 2010. It is difficult to attribute the Democratic Party's major losses in 2010 and 2014 to major ideological shifts, or even the actions of the Tea Party, because we know that, in off-year elections—that is, when national elections are held in which the president is not on the ballot—the president's party often loses seats in Congress. Of course, when President Obama was first elected in 2008, his party fared very well. But as of 2015, as this is written, it seems clear that Congress, dominated by Republicans, and the executive branch, dominated by the White House, will often be at loggerheads over major national issues. This is not to say that no policy change is likely at all; rather, in a system where the president is a primary agenda setter, it means that the president's key legislative ideas are less likely to be adopted than they would be in a Democrat-controlled Congress. What this means is that the president will likely be making rhetorical appeals to what *should* be done about public problems, and, indeed, will be focusing on what he believes the most important problems are. Even if the president cannot achieve his legislative goals, he retains, as Theodore Roosevelt called it, the "bully pulpit," which enables him to make his case to the public. Congressional leaders will do likewise, despite their institutional disadvantages compared with the presidency. But such debate will lay the groundwork for the 2016 presidential election.

THE EXECUTIVE BRANCH

John Kingdon, in *Agendas, Alternatives, and Public Policies*, notes that when people think about a presidential "administration," they tend to think about the president, his immediate staff, and appointees (Kingdon 2011: 21–30). This is the sense in which I discuss the executive branch; the permanent civil service, or bureaucracy, is considered separately, because it differs from the institutional presidency in key respects.

The president has some considerable advantages in policy making when compared with the legislature. First, the president can wield the **veto** against any legislation he does not like on substantive or political grounds (and these two often overlap). It is difficult to muster enough votes—two-thirds of the House and two-thirds in the Senate—to override a veto, in part because of some level of deference to the presidency and in part because it is unlikely that any one party can muster 67 Senate or 290 House votes to override a

veto The veto is the power the president has to reject legislation passed by Congress, which in turn may attempt to override the veto. This requires that two-thirds of each of the House and Senate members vote to override, which is relatively rare.

veto. This is why the mere threat of a veto is often enough to induce members of Congress to alter legislation to gain presidential approval. The president also has at his disposal the **pocket veto**, which is the ability to not return a bill, signed or unsigned, to Congress if it is in recess, which is effectively the same as an overt veto.

The veto is, however, a fairly blunt instrument—the president may want to enact much of the law presented to him by Congress, but may wish to make clear that he will enact its provisions in a particular way. In recent years, presidents have issued "signing statements" at the time they signed a bill. These signing statements explain the president's understanding of the law he has signed, and provide some clues about its implementation. The use of such signing statements became very controversial during the George W. Bush administration, not for the number of times he made signing statements, but because of the extent to which his statements contained objections—and, sometimes, multiple objections—to the legality or constitutionality of some of the provisions of the laws he would sign. He was therefore accused of violating the separation of powers and congressional intent, but it's worth noting that other presidents since Ronald Reagan have used signing statements, although not quite as forcefully as G.W. Bush (Garvey 2012; Tumulty 2014).

The president also enjoys considerable organizational advantages. The presidency has only one person—the president—at its head and a staff that works for him in pursuit of the administration's goals. There is no such single point of leadership in Congress. Even the speaker of the House commands only limited deference, particularly from members of the majority party, so one cannot say that Congress speaks with one voice in pursuit of an agreed-upon set of goals. The crosscurrents of party loyalty, constituent interests, and personal ambition make a single-minded Congress impossible, regardless of the media's attempts in recent years to portray the speaker as some sort of constitutional counterpart to the president, particularly when the president's party is not the same as the majority party in the House.

A third advantage for the president is that he gains more media and public attention than any single elected official in the United States, if not the world. As head of government and chief of state, the president symbolizes America, both domestically and worldwide. Wherever he goes, he is an important focus of media attention. In his role as head of government and head of state, the president symbolizes the whole of the United States government, not simply one branch. This attention often causes people in other countries—and,

pocket veto
This occurs when Congress adjourns before the president is given the constitutionally mandated 10 days to sign or veto a bill. Normally, a bill that is unsigned automatically becomes law, but if Congress adjourns, and the president chooses not to sign the law, it is effectively vetoed.

indeed, many people in the United States—to forget that the president is but one actor in our constitutional system, whose power is still circumscribed by the Constitution and whose influence varies with his political popularity and the nature of the policy issue.

An important advantage the president enjoys is his informational advantage over the legislative branch. For decades, Congress was at a disadvantage because the executive branch had access to most information about government: what was being done, how much was actually being spent, the nature and cause of public problems. Reforms starting in the early 1970s, with the establishment of the Congressional Budget Office, the growth of the committee staff, and the improved capacity of the Government Accountability Office, have closed the information gap, but the president continues to enjoy better information about policy initiatives than does Congress. Indeed, in 1995, the Republican Congress abolished the Office of Technology Assessment (OTA), an organization designed to help overcome the president's inherent information advantages in technology policy. By eliminating the OTA, Congress ceded even greater advantages to the executive.

Over the last 35 years, we have seen presidential influence wax and wane depending on the state of politics, current events, or what Kingdon calls the "national mood." President George W. Bush's power and influence was considerable immediately after the September 11 attacks due, in large part, to the well-known "rally around the flag" effect that improves presidential ratings during crises. He noted this phenomenon after the 2004 presidential election, claiming that he had accumulated some "political capital" that he was determined to spend wisely. But by the end of his term, President Bush was so unpopular that members of his own party openly defied him and, in the 2006 midterm elections, the Republicans were badly beaten. The pattern was somewhat similar for President Obama: he didn't have a high-visibility crisis to manage, and, while his approval ratings started relatively high in the midst of the financial crisis, his ratings, like that of most presidents, were highest in the first term, then rebounded in time for his re-election, only to drop considerably by 2014. In that year's midterm elections, Democrats fared at least as poorly as did Republicans in the 2006 midterms. These trends show that while the president enjoys considerable organizational, constitutional, and symbolic powers, these powers are variable based on the current winds of politics, and the president can enhance or squander his power to make him at various times relatively stronger or weaker than the other branches.

In policy terms, it is probably more important to remember that the executive's powers are not limitless. Indeed, many people attribute rather more power to the president than is actually apparent to the people who hold the office. In *Presidential Power*, Richard Neustadt argues that the "power of the presidency is the power to persuade" (1990). Through a number of anecdotes and case studies, Neustadt shows how the president uses the considerable prestige of the office to *persuade* people to do things; we learn that the president does not simply bark orders and have them obeyed. And, in his relations with Congress and the courts, the president is, constitutionally, the head of just one of three branches of government, and is most assuredly subject to the checks placed on the executive by the legislature and the judiciary. While the presidency is, therefore, powerful, it is perhaps not, as Arthur Schlesinger put it, an "imperial presidency" (1973), and, indeed, President Nixon—whose administration was said to have exemplified the "imperial presidency" of nearly limitless power—was forced to resign before articles of impeachment were approved by the House of Representatives. Had Nixon not resigned, he almost certainly would have been the first president impeached and convicted of "high crimes and misdemeanors," and forced to relinquish his office. The lesson here is that even very powerful presidents are accountable to Congress and to the people.

Another complicating factor for the president is that the Executive Office of the President—that is, the president and all the officials that work for him in agencies such as the National Security Council and the Council of Economic Advisors—is very large. The president cannot supervise every initiative and all the actions of his staff. He must rely on his key staff to ensure that the people who work in the executive office support his agenda and goals and are not doing anything that would detract from or embarrass his administration. Presidential scandals, such as Watergate (Nixon) and Iran-Contra (Reagan), are examples of cases of when it is claimed that subordinates to the president acted illegally or unethically without his approval. Of course, other scandals, such as the "Whitewater" scandal during the Clinton administration, which devolved into revelations of an extramarital affair, are examples of scandals directly connected to the president's behavior, and can be equally damaging to the administration.

The presidency is particularly interesting to policy scholars because of the chief executive's role in policy making. In particular, Kingdon argues that the president is more involved with agenda setting than in developing policy alternatives to address the issues and problems that he raises on the agenda.

This tendency has been quite evident in the strategies used by the Obama administration to promote healthcare reform. This agenda-setting function comes to the fore because of the president's position in the public imagination as a leader, and because of his constitutional responsibilities. In the Constitution, the president is empowered to suggest legislation and to report periodically on the state of the union.

Nevertheless, the president's powers go beyond mere agenda setting. During real or apparent crises and during times when his popularity is high, the president's power as the head of government is considerable. But the level of power is not constant over the president's time in office. As Paul Light has noted:

> The president's main task is to narrow the stream [of people and ideas] into a manageable policy agenda. By the end of the term, the stream is reduced to a trickle and the president's major task is to pass the initial programs and get re-elected.

(1982: 44)

The challenge, then, is not simply to develop endless new ideas, but to define and manage the agenda in order to ensure some policy victories, providing a positive record that will persuade voters to re-elect the president.

For example, after the shootings at Columbine High School in Littleton, Colorado, President Clinton pressed for stricter gun control legislation, an issue that was relatively high on Clinton's agenda throughout his presidency. Relatively little of his legislation was enacted, however, which illustrates the difference between elevating an issue on the agenda and actually seeing substantive change. After the murders of 32 students at Virginia Polytechnic Institute in Blacksburg, Virginia, in 2006, President George W. Bush made no effort to reform gun laws, both because his party did not see the need for gun reform (there are many other ways that one can view this problem as other than a "gun problem") and because gun reform legislation is often very contentious. Even if the president had wanted to press for gun reform legislation, he might have been dissuaded by the controversial nature of the issue. In this case, the president's ideological predisposition was to not address the gun issue, but to focus on campus safety concerns. And, in the aftermath of the Sandy Hook elementary school shootings in 2012, the president did very little to promote gun control, and what efforts were attempted in Congress to tackle the issue failed.

Beyond recommending legislation, the president can take action through executive orders and through his constitutional role as the nation's head of government to address public problems. For example, after the Columbine High School shootings, President Clinton launched a study of how the entertainment industry markets "violent" movies, music, and video games to children. By December 2014, President Obama had issued 198 executive orders, on matters as weighty as the disposition of detainees at Guantanamo Bay, the lawful interrogation and avoidance of torture of terrorists and other suspects, the legality of research using human stem cells, and the seemingly minor reorganization of the National Economic Council and other functions in the Executive Office of the President. The rate at which President Obama has issued executive orders is consistent with G.W. Bush's, and both Bush and Obama issued fewer orders per month than did President Clinton.[2] Such figures are often cited as a rough measure of presidential activism in policy making, but this is generally not a good measure of overall executive activity.

Administrative Agencies and Bureaucrats

It was Max Weber who used the term **bureaucracy** scientifically to describe the large organizations, both public and private, that manage the government programs that accompany modern economic and social life. Weber believed that bureaucracies were an important innovation of the modern age; indeed, the achievements of the last 100 or more years—major government initiatives such as the New Deal, fighting World War II, or putting astronauts on the moon—would likely not have been possible without a bureaucratic organization.

Many people use the terms "bureaucracy" and "bureaucrat" negatively. No doubt, you have said things such as "I can't believe the bureaucracy at the DMV" or "I had to argue with some bureaucrat today." I often complain to my colleagues about the "bureaucracy" involved with getting a parking permit at my university, or with dealing with health insurance claims. But Weber did not necessarily mean to put these terms in a negative light; rather, he was using them simply to describe a particular kind of organization and to help us understand the features of a bureaucracy, which include the following:

- "Fixed and official jurisdictional areas," that is, a rule-based distribution of labor and of the power to give orders.

bureaucracy
(1) A term of derision used for any complicated, cumbersome process characterized by paperwork, unresponsiveness, and slow results; (2) a system of social organization in which tasks are divided among bureaus, each of which follows particular procedures to evenhandedly administer rules; (3) the organization that administers government through rules and procedures.

- "A firmly ordered system of super- and subordination in which there is a supervision of the lower offices by the higher ones," that is, a hierarchical organization.

- "The management of the modern office is based upon written documents ('the files')." Thus, bureaucracies retain copious documentation of their decisions, which can enhance learning about what was done and why.

- Expert training of staff. This can be seen in fields such as law, accounting, and public administration, where advanced degrees are usually required for many agency careers.

- "The full working capacity of the official," meaning that the leadership of modern bureaucracies is a full-time job, not a part-time sideline, as it was before modern forms of organization became prominent.

- "The management of the office follows general rules, which are more or less stable, more or less exhaustive, and which can be learned." In today's terms, offices are characterized by standard operating procedures and rules, often codified, which lay out what an agency can do and how it can do it (Weber 1973).

These features of bureaucracy are very familiar, because all of us have lived in, worked in, or transacted business with bureaucratic organizations. Schools, universities, large private firms, government agencies, hospitals, and all manner of other institutions are hierarchically organized, with distinct division of labor, people trained to do particular tasks, and a set of rules and procedures that governs operations. If you are a student, you are in daily contact with agents of a bureaucracy—your college or university. Indeed, all your professors are, in some way, bureaucrats (although many would rather not think of themselves this way!). People who work at college or university follow the rules and perform tasks that are assigned to each person, ranging from teaching classes to managing the books, to managing computers and Internet access, to keeping the heat, cooling, and electricity working. In essence, everyone who works in a reasonably complex organization is a bureaucrat, even though we tend to think of bureaucrats as only working in the public sector. A more expansive understanding of bureaucracy and bureaucrats alters our attitude toward bureaucrats: we may conclude that it's not bureaucrats that we should worry about—it's the very nature of bureaucracy itself.

One of the most persistent complaints about bureaucratic government is its sheer size. The government has grown considerably since the founders ratified the Constitution. While the federal administrative establishment in 1800 was very small, by fiscal year 2014 (a fiscal year starts on October 1 of the prior calendar year), the federal government had grown enormous, with total outlays of almost $4 *trillion* current and over $3 trillion in constant 2000 (Figure 4.2). From 1980 to about 2000, federal government spending (the technical term is "government outlays") was generally steady at about 18 to 22 percent of GDP. The FY 2009 budget, which came during a period of significant government spending growth and a deep recession, made federal spending as a fraction of GDP the highest it had been since the end of World War II (Figure 4.3). One might argue, however, that the federal budget has grown simply because the population has grown; after all, the nation's population was well less than half of our current population in 1940. But even per person (per capita) growth in the budget has been remarkable, as shown in Figure 4.4. To summarize: the federal government spends more than it ever has, but, except for the extraordinary FY 2009 budget, the federal

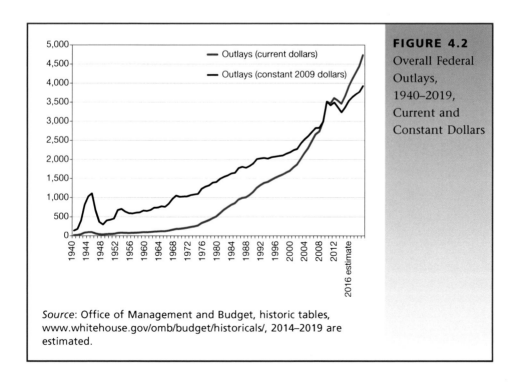

FIGURE 4.2
Overall Federal Outlays, 1940–2019, Current and Constant Dollars

Source: Office of Management and Budget, historic tables, www.whitehouse.gov/omb/budget/historicals/, 2014–2019 are estimated.

FIGURE 4.3
Federal Government Outlays as Percentage of GDP, 1940–2019

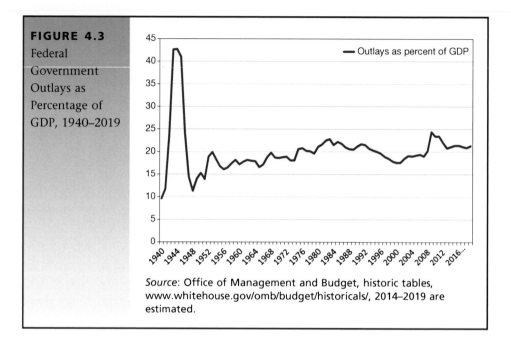

Source: Office of Management and Budget, historic tables, www.whitehouse.gov/omb/budget/historicals/, 2014–2019 are estimated.

FIGURE 4.4
Federal Government Outlays per Capita, Constant Dollars, 1940–2019

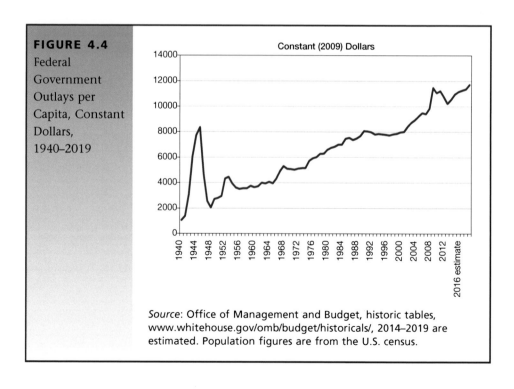

Source: Office of Management and Budget, historic tables, www.whitehouse.gov/omb/budget/historicals/, 2014–2019 are estimated. Population figures are from the U.S. census.

government's growth has been mostly proportional to the growth of the economy, as measured by GDP.

Another way to measure the size of government is to examine the number of people that work for government. In 2007, over 19 million people worked for state and local governments (Figure 4.5); taken together, about one in seven of all employed Americans worked for the federal, state, or local governments. Figure 4.6 shows that federal employment has grown, in large part due to President Obama's new federal programs. Another way to compare the growth of the federal government is to compare the amount the government spends to the number of people it employs. This comparison is found in Figure 4.7. In this figure, the amount of federal spending and the number of federal employees are indexed to a common base year, 1981. As you can see, the relative size of the federal civilian workforce has declined, while spending has increased quite a bit. This shrinkage in the workforce and increase in spending can be attributed to increases in spending on social programs that are administered by the same number of people, increases in government's propensity to contract with the private sector to provide services rather than government providing those services itself, and, in the early days of the Obama administration, to economic stimulus spending and the so-called "bailouts" of major investment banks and the automakers, yielding

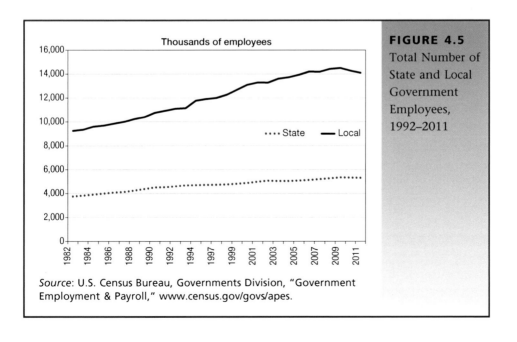

FIGURE 4.5

Total Number of State and Local Government Employees, 1992–2011

Source: U.S. Census Bureau, Governments Division, "Government Employment & Payroll," www.census.gov/govs/apes.

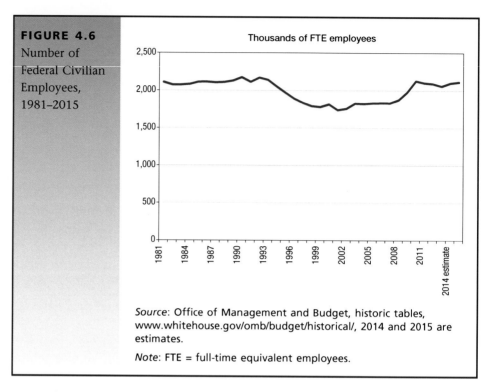

FIGURE 4.6
Number of
Federal Civilian
Employees,
1981–2015

Source: Office of Management and Budget, historic tables,
www.whitehouse.gov/omb/budget/historical/, 2014 and 2015 are
estimates.

Note: FTE = full-time equivalent employees.

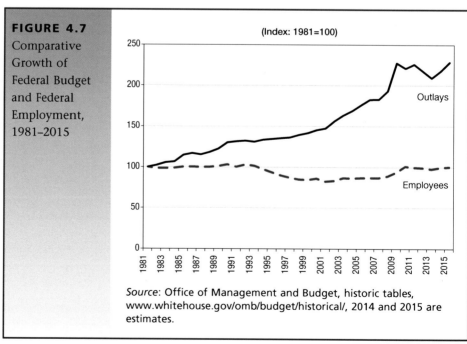

FIGURE 4.7
Comparative
Growth of
Federal Budget
and Federal
Employment,
1981–2015

Source: Office of Management and Budget, historic tables,
www.whitehouse.gov/omb/budget/historical/, 2014 and 2015 are
estimates.

greater spending without increased employment. Government's size, complexity, and growth in spending reflect, to a great degree, the size and complexity of society, government, and the economy, as well as the demands placed on government and all our social institutions by interest groups and citizens. In other words, the government is big because many of us want the various services provided by government. Adding up all these demands yields a large governmental establishment.

What Do Government Agencies Do?

In the simplest terms, government agencies provide services that are uneconomical for the private sector to provide directly, or they carry out the tasks that we demand from government but that we have chosen not to ask the private sector to provide. In general, any good that carries with it major **free rider** problems is a **public good**. Public goods are, as economists put it, indivisible and nonexclusive. Indivisible means one cannot divide a good or service among the public and let each citizen use the good or service as he or she sees fit. Rather, the goods are provided for everyone collectively. Nonexclusive means that just because a citizen uses the services of the fire department does not mean the citizen is the only one who can use the fire department. By contrast, private goods are divisible and exclusive: companies can make a fixed number of sports cars, and if you and I and some other people buy all the sports cars, there are none left for everyone else (exclusivity) and we get to enjoy them ourselves without any usefulness (utility) being provided to others (divisibility).

Free riding results when a service is provided for everyone but not everyone chooses to pay for it. Imagine a system in which roads, national defense, police and fire services, and public health and sanitation were provided by private entities—perhaps nonprofits—and we were all sent letters asking us to contribute some money for these services. Indeed, in many communities, fire and rescue squads are volunteer or semi-volunteer organizations that raise money outside regular local budgets. Where I used to live in upstate New York, we received similar appeals yearly. Many people ignore these appeals, because we might reason that many other people may contribute, that their contributions are sufficient to pay for the service, that we may be more careful about fires and thus less likely to need emergency services, and therefore we can still use—that is, free ride on—other people's contributions.

free rider A free rider is someone who consumes a good provided to everyone, but does not pay for it. This problem is called free riding, and is one rationale for the government's provision of public goods.

public goods Goods that, once provided for one user, are provided for everyone, such as national defense or police services; economists say that public goods are indivisible and nonexclusive, because they cannot be divided into parts for individuals to consume and because one person's use of the good does not deny others the use of the good.

Where voluntary action is insufficient, government provides these goods to avoid the free rider problem and ultimately to compel all beneficiaries to bear their "fair share" of costs. This is not to say, however, that the government always has to be the ultimate provider of these goods. In some communities, fire protection and prison management are contracted out to private sector firms. Still, these functions are paid for by tax dollars and are therefore not truly based on a market for these services. Thus, as Charles Cochran and Eloise Malone note, an important feature of public goods "is that they can be provided only by collective decisions" (Cochran and Malone 2010: 17), which means that institutions—in this case, government—must be created to facilitate decision-making about what goods to provide.

Communities may choose to keep certain functions in the public sector, even though the organizations that manage those functions may work like private companies. For example, in Anchorage, Alaska, where I grew up, the telephone company and the electric utility were both owned by the city because it was believed that these functions were more responsive to the public if the public owned them. Attitudes about government functions do change, however, and telephone service in Anchorage and most of Alaska is now privately managed. In many cities and states, some functions, such as public transit and intercity passenger railroad service, were once viable as private firms. Because of changing economic and social settings, they became unprofitable, so the public sector assumed their operation because they remain important to the users of these services and carry with them benefits that are not reflected in the costs of the goods.

While the complaints about bureaucracy in the United States often relate to the *size* of the administrative infrastructure, the complaints more often relate to our frustrations with what the bureaucracy *does*. These frustrations range from the extreme antigovernment position that government and its workers should have the most minimal role in our lives to the more moderate sort of complaints that what the bureaucracy does is unaccountable to the public or that the decisions it makes are erroneous or undemocratic. Most Americans probably do not know how large their government is or what its budgetary priorities are, but a broad range of the American people have direct experience with unpopular bureaucracies such as the postal service, the Internal Revenue Service, or state motor vehicles offices.

Even if these bureaucracies have improved their "customer service" functions—as the New York DMV did in the early 1990s and as the U.S. Postal Service has been doing for the last 20 years—these bureaucracies are historically unpopular. They have been perceived as slow, inefficient, and less adept at service delivery than private sector firms, particularly when the services provided by government agencies are also provided by the private sector. For example, the postal service has private sector counterparts such as FedEx and UPS that provide seemingly superior service. Such comparisons are often flawed because, again, the government is constrained to provide service to everyone. For example, the U.S. Postal Service is required to carry a letter from, say, Atlanta to Kotzebue, Alaska, or Molokai, Hawaii, for the same postage as a letter from Atlanta to Athens, Georgia—or a letter from one side of town to another (United States Postal Service 2008).

Bureaucracy and the Problem of Accountability

A more basic reason for our distrust of bureaucracy rests on the problem of accountability. The vast majority of civil servants at all levels are not political appointees; they serve in their positions based on their skills and expertise, not based on which party or leader is in power. Expertise is what the designers of modern civil service systems—reacting to the abuses of political patronage—had in mind when they developed systems based on merit, not political connections, in the late 1800s. Nevertheless, with this detachment from elected officials comes a belief that "faceless bureaucrats" make rules based as much on a thirst for power as on a desire to serve the public.

Before engaging this question of bureaucratic accountability, it is important to first consider whether the bureaucracy makes policy at all. After all, if it does not make policy—that is, if the bureaucracy does not decide who gets what—then there is no accountability problem, because we can simply assume that the bureaucracy carries out the will of the democratically accountable branches of the government, and in particular, the legislature's will.

Some of the most astute political thinkers of the 1800s and early 1900s believed that the bureaucracy is not a political or policy-making branch of government. Students of administration and politics simply assumed that agencies existed to carry out the will of the people, as expressed by the legislature. The bureaucracy's duties were to be carried out separate and apart from "politics," which is the proper domain of the legislature. This is how future U.S. president (and early president of the American Political Science Association) Woodrow Wilson viewed the relationship between the Congress and the agencies. He argued, in his classic article "The Study of Administration," that the *administration* of the laws and policies of the government stood apart from *politics*, that is, the grand and broad planning that is properly the province of Congress and the president. Consider this passage:

> Most important to be observed is the truth already so much and so fortunately insisted upon by our civil-service reformers: namely, that administration lies outside the proper sphere of politics. Administrative questions are not political questions. Although politics sets the tasks for administration, it should not be suffered to manipulate its offices . . . The broad plans of governmental action are not administrative; the detailed execution of such plans is administrative.

> (Wilson 1887: 210)

Today, we would consider this claim to be naïve. We know that agency decisions have to engage "political" dilemmas and questions. Every day, agencies make decisions without explicit instruction from Congress. These decisions require that the bureaucracy exercise administrative or **bureaucratic discretion**. This bureaucratic discretion, much like legislation, is part of the process of deciding who gets what from government. The problem, from a democratic perspective, is that unelected officials often make these decisions without popular or legislative input or oversight. Thus, those who do not get what they want from the bureaucracy—or who believe that the bureaucracy should not do what it is doing at all—often argue that the bureaucracy is unaccountable to the public and its elected officials, and its decisions are therefore suspect on democratic grounds, regardless of the substance of the decisions. (Of course, we must recognize that people and groups may make this argument when they have lost on more substantive grounds.)

Bureaucratic accountability to the broader public interest is very difficult to achieve in the American system because there is no single, easily defined "public interest" that all of us can agree upon, and because we—citizens and legislators alike—often ask the government to do many things, some of which may conflict. The bureaucracy has grown to meet these demands. Because these demands are complex—ranging from medical research to space exploration to business regulation—the citizens, through the legislature, have sought to hire many knowledgeable people that hold their jobs based on merit—that is, they serve due to their technical expertise. Many positions at the state, federal, and local levels are filled by people who have taken civil service tests to demonstrate they have the basic knowledge necessary to do

bureaucratic discretion The ability of agencies in government to make decisions without the explicit direction or consent of any other branch of government. Some agencies have a great deal of bureaucratic discretion, while others have very limited discretion.

the job. Citizens and Congress must therefore defer to the expertise of the bureaucrats on a wide range of issues.

A primary way Congress defers to administrators' expertise is by granting discretion to the bureaucracy. Discretion is the ability of the agencies to make decisions about how they will administer policies and programs with relatively little input or interference from Congress or other institutions. Congress will sometimes grant discretion to agencies to avoid having to make difficult political decisions; it is sometimes easier to leave legislation somewhat vague and let the competing interests fight over the details in the regulatory process. The more usual reason for the grant of discretion is Congress's inability to deal with the myriad issues that bureaucrats are better prepared to address.

The grant of discretion by Congress to the administrative agencies is not uniform across all agencies and problems. Kenneth Meier argues:

> The amount of discretion accorded an agency is a function of its resources (expertise, cohesion, legislative authority, policy salience, and leadership) and the tolerances of other actors in the political system. Each actor has a zone of acceptance; and if agency decisions fall within that zone, no action will be taken.
>
> (Meier 1985, cited in Theodoulou and Cahn 1995: 275)

That range of acceptance is smaller in the more active subsystems because actors in the most dynamic and contentious systems are likely to respond negatively to nearly any action taken by an agency that they feel runs contrary to their interests. Where the policy subsystem is composed of tightly connected, mutually reinforcing relationships, the agency's decisions will probably be well known to all interested parties before the decision is put into effect, but such mutually reinforcing relationships cannot be said to be open and democratic.

The next problem we must consider is to what purpose bureaucrats use this discretion. If it is exercised by bureaucrats responsive to popular pressure, voiced directly through the public's daily relationships with the agency, or indirectly through the elected branches, then we might say that the agency is broadly responsive to public demands. This situation, however, is quite rare, and in some cases it would be unworkable for the bureaucracy to respond to public pressure if the public was making demands that were contradictory, illegal, or unconstitutional. Rather, agency discretion is often exercised as a result of the agency's own perception, as signaled to it through legislation and relationships with Congress, of its relationship with the "public interest," defined more broadly than individuals or groups might prefer. Thus, the National Transportation Safety Board (NTSB) and the Federal Aviation Administration (FAA) have different conceptions of the public interest; the NTSB sees its mandate as ensuring safety of transportation, most prominently aviation, thereby protecting public safety. The FAA, on the other hand, takes its safety mandate seriously, but promotes safety by working with airlines and manufacturers to find, improve on, and codify best practices and procedures. The FAA, like many regulatory agencies, has to focus greatly on cost-benefit analysis and risk analysis, particularly when pressured by airlines and airplane makers to minimally regulate certain systems. NTSB is not constrained by its industry relationships and sees its mission differently, which is why aviation accidents are not investigated by the FAA.

Related to discretion is the question of private influence or even control over the activities of an agency. For many years, students of bureaucracy wrote about how agencies were "captured" by the interests they regulated. For example, the Federal Communications Commission was once said to be "captured" by broadcasters because its system of allocating frequencies and licenses served the interests of the industry at least as much as the broader public interest. More recently, the FAA, in working harder for airline industry interests than for safety interests, was captured and doing the bidding of the airline industry (Schiavo 1997). Private influence became even more controversial when the House Republican leadership allowed representatives from a wide range of industries (most of whom were opposed to stringent environmental regulation) remarkable access to the daily activities of committees and subcommittees after the Republicans became the majority party in 1994. This inevitably led to fears that the legislative and regulatory processes would come under the undue sway of industry representatives to the exclusion of other voices. However, these fears were not borne out in actual policy making.

We do not usually claim that an agency is wholly captured; instead, it is more useful to consider to what extent the agency demonstrates the characteristics of a captured agency. This analysis leads us to ask how much power do the regulated have over the regulators, and vice versa. The potential for regulatory capture varies with the type of policy and the coalitions that are built to deal with these issues. In summary, there are substantial problems with bureaucratic accountability. These problems relate in large part to the discussion in Chapter 5 of sub-governments or issue networks.

When we consider accountability, we must also consider the popular portrayal of government as a single-minded monolith that is completely accountable only to itself and pursues its own ends. However, bureaucratic government may be more accountable than it appears to be at first glance. B. Guy Peters describes how many government agencies and the interests related to each may serve as a check on one another:

> It is also customary to consider government as an undivided entity and to regard government organizations as monolithic. In fact, this is not the case at all. We have mentioned that American government is divided horizontally into a number of subgovernments and vertically into levels of government in a federal system. Moreover, the federal and state governments, and even single government departments, contain a number of bureaus, offices, and sections all competing for money, legislative time, and public attention. Each of these organizations has its own goals, ideas, and concepts about how to attack the public problems it is charged with administering.

(Peters 1993: 94–95)

With so much internal competition, agencies seek to advance their ideas before Congress and among their allied interest groups. In so doing, the agencies compete with and check each other and, at least theoretically, gain some accountability to the congressional subcommittees and committees charged with their oversight, particularly when the agencies seek congressional support. Again, the manner in which the FAA and the NTSB check and balance each other is an excellent example of the competitive nature of modern American government and offers some hope for greater accountability, while showing that government is not always, or even usually, a monolith.

The Courts

Alexander Hamilton argued in *Federalist 78*, "the interpretation of the laws is the proper and peculiar province of the courts," and, since the Constitution is the most fundamental of laws, the courts cannot help being responsible for ensuring that laws remain within the boundaries set by the Constitution. It is an idea that the new Supreme Court was relatively quick to claim in ***Marbury v. Madison***, 1 Cranch 137 (1803), which established the courts' power of **judicial review** over the constitutionality of the acts of the Congress

Marbury v. Madison The case in which the Supreme Court claimed the power of judicial review, which is the power to declare the acts of any state or of any federal official in the legislative or executive branch unconstitutional, and therefore void.

judicial review The power of the courts to review the acts of the legislature and the executive branch and to strike them down if the courts find them to be unconstitutional. This power was first proclaimed by the court in *Marbury v. Madison* in 1803.

and the executive branch. Judicial review gives the courts a potential veto over every act of government that is generated by the popularly elected legislature and executive. In addition, the power of judicial review allows the courts to have the "final word" in the application of laws.

While we might assume that judicial review would make the courts the center of power in the United States, the opposite has been true since the creation of the republic. Hamilton proposed that since the judiciary lacks "either the sword or the purse," it can therefore be defined as "the weakest of the three departments of power." It cannot simply spend or tax in order to encourage the citizenry to fulfill its policy goals as the legislature can do. Nor can it simply force through military strength the acceptance of its policy goals as an executive can do. Instead, the courts have only the legitimacy accorded to the law and their ability to argue their case as the sole power accorded to them. No wonder Hamilton proposed we had little to fear from the judiciary. Historically, however, the role of the courts has fallen somewhere between the impotence claimed by Hamilton and the unfettered, undemocratic omnipotence attributed to the courts by their critics, who, not coincidentally, are often associated with the losing end of the political battles that are played out in the courts.

What role have the courts played in public policy making? In a long-accepted practice, most public policy scholars have divided the courts from the other branches supporting the notion of a separation of law and politics. As noted earlier, Woodrow Wilson argued that Congress makes public policy and the bureaucracy simply carries out that policy without exercising discretion. In making this argument, Wilson implicitly embraced the notion that courts cannot be policy makers because they are engaged in the *neutral* discovery of legal principles. Where the legislature is identified with compromise and the exchange of votes in the pursuit of policy preferences, the legal system is identified with the pursuit of more abstract principles, such as justice, associated with the notion of law. Thus, the Wilsonian perspective established a distinction between law and politics in relation to policy making—politics created policy, and law ensured that such policy was implemented justly.

While the simplicity of the Wilsonian perspective has long since been rejected, subsequent public policy theories have accepted, without serious question, his implicit distinction between law and politics. For example, Easton (1965) defines the actions of political actors and institutions as structured by the constitutional order. In this context, the courts determine the boundaries of policy making by the other branches, but these boundaries are claimed to have been created neutrally; that is, without the consideration or involvement of policy making. The court is assumed not to be engaged in policy making when it sets the boundaries of acceptable policy; it is simply engaged in the practice of articulating a socially accepted and predetermined set of rules. In this way, the court is simply discovering or clarifying rules that we, as a society, have previously agreed to follow, from divinely inspired law to popularly sanctioned constitutions. For example, in *Brown v. Board of Education*, 347 U.S. 483 (1954), the Supreme Court ruled that school segregation was unconstitutional because it unfairly discriminated against and stigmatized African Americans, thereby denying them the full potential of citizenship, including political participation. Therefore, the courts stepped in to restrict the deleterious use of race in determining educational policies.

The problem with such an approach is that establishing boundaries across which "politics" may not intrude is itself a form of policy making. In the case of race, *Brown* restricted the negative use of race in state policies in a manner similar to the way in which the *Civil Rights Cases* and *Plessy v. Ferguson*[3] had first allowed race to be so used. Thus, while the courts might be setting constitutional boundaries, the changing definitions of these boundaries allow the courts to make public policy.

Even the everyday act of resolving disputes requires the courts to determine the acceptable application of many policies. As Edward Levi (2013) notes, the bargaining process inherent in legislatures and the uncertainty as to all possible future applications often requires elected officials to be purposely vague in the drafting of laws. This means that the courts are required to make choices in the application of these laws to new situations or to fine-tune laws to ensure their successful application in the real world. These choices in determining the outcome of the policies in the real world act to further draw the courts into the policy-making arena.

In 1957, Dahl claimed that:

> [t]o consider the Supreme Court of the United States strictly as a legal institution is to underestimate its significance in the American political system. For it is also a political institution, an institution, that is to say, for arriving at decisions on controversial questions of national policy.
>
> (Dahl 1957: 279)

In making this statement, Dahl was recognizing that the courts have played a significant role in policy making in a variety of areas.

CONCLUSION

Simply reading the federal Constitution, the state constitutions, and the relevant laws will reveal some sense of the institutional organization of the federal and state governments. Nevertheless, while the federal and state constitutions and laws specify the role and function of the official actors, the law is not fully clear on many aspects of their relationships, and the relationships between official actors and unofficial actors. Indeed, the substantial social, political, and economic changes that have occurred since the drafting of the Constitution are reflected in the changing balance of power among all the official actors. This change will continue as our needs change. Meanwhile, it is important to understand how these actors interact so that we can better understand the process by which some policies are enacted and others are rejected.

KEY TERMS

behaviorism	*Marbury v. Madison*
bureaucracy	neo-institutionalism
bureaucratic discretion	official actor
casework	oversight
C-SPAN	pocket veto
field hearing	policy subsystem
free rider	public good
institutionalism	unofficial actor
issue network	veto
judicial review	

QUESTIONS FOR DISCUSSION, REFLECTION, AND RESEARCH

- Why do you think that Richard Fenno says that Americans "hate Congress" but "love their Congressmen?" What implications do you think this phenomenon has for actual public policies?

- Why do you think Congress has focused so much more on oversight in recent years? Do you think Congress provides more oversight than legislation? How would you measure this? What role does oversight play in the policy process? (You may want to consider this question again as you read about theories of the policy process in Chapter 11.)

- Do you believe that partisan legislative politics is good for our form of representative democracy? Should legislative business be conducted in a partisan way? Why? If not, what should replace the partisan organization of the legislative branch? Some people argue that intense partisan competition forces each side to be a watchdog for the other, thereby achieving stability and balance. Others might argue that this highly partisan environment leads to a paralysis in policy making and detracts from tackling society's most important issues. How would you measure or test these assertions? What influence, if any, do you think this partisan shift has had on the sorts of public policies that are enacted—or are not enacted—by Congress? In light of all this, does the partisan balance of Congress matter in terms of the policies it enacts?

- What functions do congressional committees serve? Do you think there may be other or better ways to organize Congress than by committee? What would the likely policy consequences be of organizing Congress as you propose?

- We typically think of goods such as roads as public goods. But what about toll roads? Are these public goods or private goods? Is education a public or private good, considering that educational services are provided by both the public and private sectors? Are goods public or private based simply on *who* provides the good, or are there other features that characterize public and private goods?

- What essential point do you think Wilson was trying to make when he claimed that politics and administration are—or should be— separate? What do current political scientists think of this distinction? Do you think the *spirit* of his assertion is still important today?

- What are some reasons that Congress may expand or restrict bureaucratic discretion? Can you think of examples in which Congress has given the bureaucracy too much discretion? Too little?

- How different do you think policy making would be in the United States if the courts *lacked* the power of judicial review, as claimed in *Marbury v. Madison*?

- As seen during the nomination and confirmation of Judge Sonia Sotomayor, and of Solicitor General Elena Kagan to associate justices of the Supreme Court, some people argue that judges should not, in effect, *make* law, but should merely interpret the laws and the Constitution based on the intention of the framers of the Constitution or the authors of the laws. Is it possible to separate this interpretation function from lawmaking? Why or why not? How would one go about understanding the "intent" of the drafters of a law or constitution?

- Reflecting on the previous question, do you believe that those who argue that judges should merely interpret the law rather than make law have a consistent ideological approach to the role of the judiciary? Or are such arguments made by the losing side when legal trends are running against them? Does so-called judicial activism lead solely to what are popularly called "liberal" decisions? Can judicial activism support a "conservative" ideology?

- Make an appointment to speak with a member of your congressional representative's local district staff, or perhaps with your state legislator or his or her staff members. Remember, you are their constituent so they should be happy to talk with a potential voter! Ask them about how much and what type of casework they do and whether they think casework helps their members politically. Also, ask about what key issues most concern your legislator. You will likely find that a legislator specializes in a few key areas. If you talk to your federal and state representatives, consider similarities and differences between the representatives' jobs and those of their staff members.

- Did Congress become more or less partisan during the 1990s and 2000s? How would you measure this? Try by using a reference source such as the *Almanac of American Politics*; track a sample of Members of Congress (perhaps your state's congressional delegation if you live in a large state) by their voting scores issued by such groups as the Americans for Democratic Action or the National Conservative Union.

The *Almanac of American Politics* has been published since 1971, so it should be possible to track some members over several years. Newer tracking information is also available from Project Vote Smart, at www.vote-smart.org.

ADDITIONAL READING

A classic text that puts Congress at the center of policy making is Morris P. Fiorina's *Congress: Keystone of the Washington Establishment*, 2nd ed. (New Haven, CT: Yale University Press, 2004), in which Fiorina argues that there is a "Washington establishment" of interest groups, bureaucrats, the media, lobbyists, and others, but that the focal point or "keystone" of all this activity is in Congress. This book is lively and well argued, and is fascinating reading. Other works of note on Congress include R. Douglas Arnold's *The Logic of Congressional Action* (New Haven, CT: Yale University Press, 1990). A now-classic text that reveals what it is like to be a Member of Congress, particularly when interacting with the folks back home, is Richard Fenno's *Homestyle: House Members in Their Districts* (New York: Longman, 2003). The best source for summary information about Members of Congress and their states and districts is the *Almanac of American Politics*, published by the National Journal Group every two years since 1971.

The presidency has attracted a great deal of scholarly attention. The classic work in the field is Richard Neustadt's *Presidential Power*, the most recent edition of which is titled *Presidential Power and the Modern Presidents: The Politics of Leadership from Roosevelt to Reagan* (New York: Free Press, 1990). Neustadt is famous for noting that the "power of the presidency is the power to persuade," which reflects both the institutional strengths and the institutional weaknesses of the executive branch. Arthur M. Schlesinger, in *The Imperial Presidency* (Boston, MA: Houghton Mifflin, 1973), ascribes a great deal more power to the presidency, although this book is very much a reflection of the time in which it was written. Schlesinger, writing during the Vietnam and Watergate years, argued that the presidency had gained so much power that it was becoming "imperial" and therefore answerable only to itself. Experience with later administrations has tempered the belief that the presidency is unfettered by other institutions. For example, Paul Light, in *The*

President's Agenda: Domestic Policy Choice from Kennedy to Carter (with Notes on Ronald Reagan) (Baltimore, MD: Johns Hopkins University Press, 1982), found that the power of the presidency is in the power to set the agenda—that is, to cause Congress, the media, interest groups, and the public to focus on the issues he finds most important. Nevertheless, the president's power is limited; he must gather resources to advance his chosen issues on the agenda early in his term, before those resources are expended. And John Kingdon, cited throughout this book, notes, in *Agendas, Alternatives, and Public Policies*, updated 2nd ed. (Boston, MA: Longman, 2011), that the president has considerable agenda-setting power, but that Congress has greater influence in structuring alternative policies.

Those interested in studying the lives and activities of individuals might wish to look at biographies of the presidents or histories of their administrations. One such book that gained considerable attention in the 2008 election season is Doris Kearns Goodwin's *Team of Rivals: The Political Genius of Abraham Lincoln* (New York: Simon & Schuster, 2005). Perhaps the standard by which all other presidential biographies will be judged is Robert Caro's *The Years of Lyndon Johnson* series, consisting of *The Path to Power* (1982); *Means of Assent* (1990); and *Master of the Senate* (2002) (all published by Knopf). Caro continues to work on this series, with a fourth volume published in 2012 and a fifth volume to be published later this decade. Other notable books on twentieth-century American presidents include Lou Cannon, *President Reagan: The Role of a Lifetime* (New York: Public Affairs, 2000); Haynes Johnson, *Sleepwalking through History: America in the Reagan Years* (New York: W.W. Norton, 2003); David G. McCullough, *Truman* (New York: Simon & Schuster, 1992); Edmund Morris, *Theodore Rex* (New York: Random House, 2001) (on President Theodore Roosevelt); Richard M. Nixon, *RN: The Memoirs of Richard Nixon*, The Richard Nixon Library Edition (New York: Simon & Schuster, 1990); Ronald Reagan and Douglas Brinkley, *The Reagan Diaries* (New York: HarperCollins, 2007); and recent works by Bob Woodward, one of the reporters who broke the Watergate scandal: *The Commanders* (1991); *The Agenda: Inside the Clinton White House* (1994); *The Choice* (2005); and *Bush at War* (2002) (all published by Simon & Schuster).

To my mind, one of the finest books on the role of the Supreme Court is Robert G. McClosky's *The American Supreme Court*, 5th ed., edited by Sanford Levinson (Chicago, IL: University of Chicago Press, 2010). This book links the historical development of the United States to the legal doctrines that were being developed by the Court. You will find remarkable parallels between the policy-making history outlined by Robertson and Judd and summarized in Chapter 3 of this book with the historical analysis in McClosky's work. The book proceeds chronologically, from the founding until 1960. This fifth edition, edited by Sanford Levinson, updates McClosky's original work with chapters on civil rights and other topics. A major debate surrounding the courts, and the Supreme Court in particular, centers on whether it makes decisions that deviate greatly from the public's preferences, as expressed through the elected branches. Robert Dahl, in "Decision Making in a Democracy: The Supreme Court as a National Policy-Maker," *Journal of Public Law* 6 (Fall 1957): 279–295, found that the Supreme Court's decisions did not stray too far from the policy choices made by Congress, although later research has questioned his conclusions. In particular, Jonathan D. Casper, in "The Supreme Court and National Policymaking," *American Political Science Review* 70 (1976): 50–63, argued that the Supreme Court does make policy more independently of the elected branches than Dahl argued. Finally, Randall Rosenberg argues, in *The Hollow Hope*, 2nd ed. (Chicago, IL: University of Chicago Press, 2008), that the Supreme Court and the lower courts are not the powerful protectors of civil rights and venues for policy change that many social movement leaders and lay people believe them to be.

The standard popular book on the Supreme Court—and one long assigned to courses on the Court—is by Bob Woodward and Scott Armstrong, *The Brethren: Inside the Supreme Court* (New York: Simon & Schuster, 1979), which provides details on many landmark decisions and the roles played by justices and, in particular, by their law clerks. A more contemporary book on the Court is Jeffrey Toobin's *The Nine: Inside the Secret World of the Supreme Court* (New York: Doubleday, 2007).

For an illuminating discussion of Woodrow Wilson's classic article about bureaucracy and the assumptions underlying it, see Charles H. Levine, B. Guy Peters, and Frank J. Thompson, *Public Administration: Challenges, Choices, Consequences* (Glenview, IL: Scott Foresman/Little Brown, 1990), 105–107.

NOTES

1   For more information on trends of public trust over time, reference the interactive graph of trust and distrust provided by the Pew Research Center, www.people-press.org/2013/10/18/trust-in-government-interactive/.

2   These data are drawn from the American Presidency Project at the University of California at Santa Barbara, www.presidency.ucsb.edu/data/orders.php. A directory of executive orders

issued by presidents from Franklin D. Roosevelt to Barack Obama is found at www.archives.gov/federal-register/executive-orders/disposition.html.
3   *The Civil Rights Cases*, 109 U.S. 3 (1883); *Plessy v. Ferguson*, 163 U.S. 537 (1896).

REFERENCES

Aberbach, Joel D. 1990. *Keeping a Watchful Eye: The Politics of Congressional Oversight*. Washington, DC: Brookings Institution.

Arnold, R. Douglas. 1990. *The Logic of Congressional Action*. New Haven, CT: Yale University Press.

Baker, Ross K. 2008. *House and Senate*. 4th ed. New York: W.W. Norton.

Clymer, Adam. 1998. "The Gingrich Whirlwind: A Man of a Thousand Ideas and Dreams Fell Victim in the End to His Own Flaws." *New York Times*, November 8, 1998, 1.

Cochran, Charles L. and Eloise F. Malone. 2010. *Public Policy: Perspectives and Choices*. 4th ed. Boulder, CO: Lynne Rienner.

Dahl, Robert A. 1957. "Decisionmaking in a Democracy: The Supreme Court as a National Policy-Maker." *Journal of Public Law* 6 (Fall): 279–295.

Davidson, Roger H., Walter J. Oleszek, E. Lee Frances, and Eric Schickler. 2014. *Congress and Its Members*. 14th ed. Washington, DC: Congressional Quarterly Press.

Dowd, Maureen. 1994. "The 1994 Elections: Leaders: The G.O.P. Leader: G.O.P.'s Rising Star Pledges to Right Wrongs of the Left." *New York Times*, November 10, 1994. Accessed January 31, 2015. www.nytimes.com/1994/11/10/us/1994-elections-leaders-gop-leader-gop-s-rising-star-pledges-right-wrongs-left.html.

Easton, David. 1965. *A Systems Analysis of Political Life*. New York: John Wiley & Sons.

Fenno, Richard. 2003. *Homestyle: House Members in Their Districts*. New York: Longman.

Fiorina, Morris. 1981. "Some Problems in Studying the Effects of Resource Allocation in Congressional Elections." *American Journal of Political Science* 25(3): 543–567.

Fiorina, Morris P. 2004. *Congress: Keystone of the Washington Establishment*, 2nd ed. New Haven, CT: Yale Unversity Press.

Garvey, Todd. 2012. "Presidential Signing Statements: Constitutional and Institutional Implications." Accessed January 15, 2015. www.fas.org/sgp/crs/natsec/RL33667.pdf.

Johannes, John R. and John C. McAdams. 1981. "The Congressional Incumbency Effect: Is It Casework, Policy Compatibility, or Something Else? An Examination of the 1978 Election." *American Journal of Political Science* 25(3): 512–542.

Kingdon, John W. 2011. *Agendas, Alternatives, and Public Policies*. Updated 2nd ed. Longman Classics in Political Science. Boston, MA: Longman.

Kraft, Michael E. and Scott R. Furlong. 2014. *Public Policy: Politics, Analysis, and Alternatives*. 5th ed. Washington, DC: CQ Press.

Lacayo, Richard. 1994. "Bringing Down the House: G.O.P. Guerrilla Newt Gingrich Rides a Surge of Voter Anger, but Where Does He Want to Go with It?" *Time*, November 7, 1994.

Levi, Edward. 2013. *An Introduction to Legal Reasoning*. 2nd ed. Chicago, IL: University of Chicago Press.

Light, Paul C. 1982. *The President's Agenda: Domestic Policy Choice from Kennedy to Carter (with Notes on Ronald Reagan)*. Baltimore, MD: Johns Hopkins University Press.

McAdams, John C. and John R. Johannes. 1981. "Does Casework Matter? A Reply to Professor Fiorina." *American Journal of Political Science* 25(3): 581–604.

Meier, Kenneth J. 1985. *Regulation: Politics, Bureaucracy, and Economics*. New York: St. Martin's Press.

Neustadt, Richard E. 1990. *Presidential Power and the Modern Presidents: The Politics of Leadership from Roosevelt to Reagan*. New York: Free Press.

Ostrom, Elinor. 2007. "Institutional Rational Choice: An Assessment of the Institutional Analysis and Development Framework." In *Theories of the Policy Process*, edited by Paul A. Sabatier and Christopher M. Wieble, 21–64. Boulder, CO: Westview.

Peters, B. Guy. 1993. *American Public Policy: Promise and Performance*. Chatham, NJ: Chatham House.

Peterson, R. Eric. 2010. "Casework in a Congressional Office: Background, Rules, Laws, and Resources." Accessed January 10, 2015. http://digital.library.unt.edu/ark:/67531/metadc29666/m1/1/high_res_d/RL33209_2010Nov04.pdf.

Ripley, Randall B. and Grace A. Franklin. 1991. *Congress, the Bureaucracy, and Public Policy*. 5th ed. Pacific Grove, CA: Brooks/Cole Publishing Company.

Romero, David W. 1996. "The Case of the Missing Reciprocal Influence: Incumbent Reputation and the Vote." *Journal of Politics* 58(4): 1198–1207.

Schiavo, Mary. 1997. *Flying Blind, Flying Safe*. New York: Avon Books.

Schlesinger, Arthur M. 1973. *The Imperial Presidency*. Boston, MA: Houghton Mifflin.

Strahan, Randall and Daniel J. Palazzolo. 2004. "The Gingrich Effect." *Political Science Quarterly* 119(1): 89–90.

Theodoulu, Stella Z. and Matthew A. Cahn, Eds. 1995. *Public Policy: The Essential Readings*. Englewood Cliffs, NJ: Prentice Hall.

Tumulty, Karen. 2014. "Obama Circumvents Laws with 'Signing Statements,' A Tool He Promised to Use Lightly." *Washington Post*, June 2, 2014. Accessed January 1, 2015. www.washingtonpost.com/politics/obama-circumvents-laws-with-signing-statements-a-tool-he-promised-to-use-lightly/2014/06/02/9d76d46a-ea73-11e3-9f5c-9075d5508f0a_story.html.

United States Postal Service. 2008. "Universal Service and the Postal Monopoly: A Brief History." Accessed January 2, 2015. https://about.usps.com/universal-postal-service/universal-service-and-postal-monopoly-history.pdf.

Walker, Jack L. 1977. "Setting the Agenda in the U.S. Senate: A Theory of Problem Selection." *British Journal of Political Science* 7: 423–445.

Weber, Max. 1946. "Bureaucracy." In *Essays in Sociology*, edited by H.H. Gerth and C. Wright Mills, 196–244. New York: Oxford University Press.

Wilson, Woodrow. 1887. "The Study of Administration." *Political Science Quarterly* 2(2): 197–222.

Wood, B. Dan. 1991. "Federalism and Policy Responsiveness: The Clean Air Case." *Journal of Politics* 53(3): 851–859.

Yiannakis, Diana Evans. 1981. "The Grateful Electorate: Casework and Congressional Elections." *American Journal of Political Science* 25(3): 568–580.

CHAPTER 5

Unofficial Actors and Their Roles in Public Policy

OVERVIEW

Having reviewed the important official participants in the policy process in Chapter 4, we now turn to the unofficial actors. These actors are unofficial because their participation in policy making is not fully specified in the Constitution. But the First Amendment contains a set of core political rights—freedom of speech, freedom of the press, freedom of assembly (that is, to form groups), and "the right . . . to petition the Government for a redress of grievances." The way that people, groups, and the press participate in public life has evolved and grown with the nation. While some actions are controversial—those of unpopular groups and lobbyists come to mind—and some participants in the policy process arouse considerable annoyance among other actors, it is also true that our democratic system of policy formation and implementation could not function without them. As you consider these actors, consider how changes and reforms to the constitutional order—and to the nature of politics—would alter their roles and behaviors.

INDIVIDUAL CITIZENS AS POLICY ACTORS

Many studies of the policy process seem to be disconnected from the activities and preferences of individual citizens. This is because most analysis focuses on policy making undertaken at the group level, with various groups vying for attention, influence, and power. Politics in the United States is primarily a group process, and groups often make their preferences very clear, because they deal regularly with important issues of policy. By contrast, opportunities for individual participation seem to be intermittent, at best. We hold elections for national office every two years, and not every office is up for election every year. Furthermore, even when important issues are on the agenda, most Americans do not vote, although in some presidential elections turnout exceeds 50 percent.

But in state, county, city, and town elections, voter turnout is consistently low. For example, in the 2009 school board elections in Wake County, North Carolina, two slates of candidates with sharply contrasting visions of how the schools should be managed ran against one another. Despite the drastic differences in their proposed platforms and the possible significance of the results, only 11 percent of the electorate turned out to vote. The election significantly changed the composition and policy preferences of the school board. The new slate of candidates were concerned with, among other things, district policies that assigned students to faraway schools to meet ethnic and, more to the point, socioeconomic goals for the schools. Many parents and students were unhappy with these policies, and, when the new board majority took over, it forced out the school superintendent and hired a new superintendent more likely to adopt the board's new policies on school assignment, student transportation, and other policies. But the policies pursued by the new school board were sufficiently controversial—some claimed that they had the effect of re-segregating the schools—that, in the next election, 21 percent of the electorate turned out at the polls. The result of this election was a near-total sweep of the old majority's seats, leading to a reversal of much, but not all, of the prior policies.[1]

Of course, in neither case did the majority of the electorate turn out to vote. Some people might assume that the people who did not vote have no policy preferences at all, or may be satisfied with the status quo, or may believe that their vote wouldn't make a difference in the election. Whatever the reasons, it is very difficult, if not impossible, to discern the preferences of those who do not turn out. Even elections with higher turnout—over 50 percent—cannot be said to be broadly representative of public preferences, because the demographic composition of the electorate, in terms of age, race and ethnicity, and income and wealth, is not the same as the entire body of eligible voters.

Low participation rates in elections have led to widespread concern among citizens and democratic theorists that a majority of potential voters do not express their opinion on important matters of the day. This long-run trend may reflect voters' growing alienation from the political system and the decisions made in it. The 2008 election, however, saw an increase in electoral turnout over the previous presidential election (Figure 5.1).

One might argue that low voter turnout is relatively less important as long as people find other ways to meaningfully express their preferences. However, even fewer Americans find other ways to participate in politics and policy making, follow many issues very closely, or admit to being very well informed on issues. More Americans vote than write to elected officials, attend public meetings or hearings, circulate petitions, join groups and lobby officials, or even engage in peaceful protest activities. For example, a 2003 survey of college undergraduates conducted by the Kennedy School of Government at Harvard University found that only 26 percent said they had attended a political rally or demonstration and only 32 percent said that they had signed a petition or participated in a boycott. A 2006 report funded by the Pew Charitable Trusts found that 17 percent of young people between the ages of 15 and 25

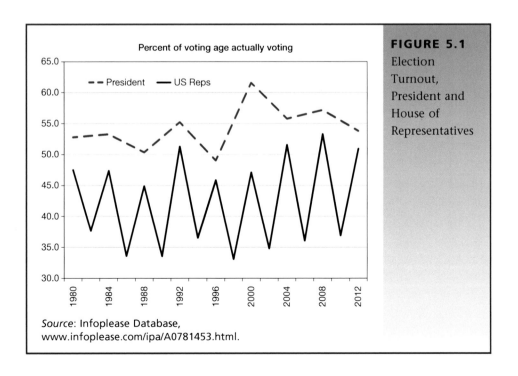

FIGURE 5.1

Election Turnout, President and House of Representatives

had participated in *none* of 19 possible political activities. At the same time, a plurality of the young people polled believed that government is generally wasteful and ineffective. Related to these results is the remarkably low level of knowledge about basic politics, particularly among the most uninvolved people. For example, only a bare majority—53 percent of respondents—knew that one had to be a citizen to vote in national elections (Center for Information and Research on Civic Learning and Engagement 2006).

The 2008 elections and the healthcare debate may have increased group mobilization slightly, but it is unclear whether there really is a long-term change in participation, or whether most Americans really followed the details of the healthcare debate, both before and after "ObamaCare's" enactment.

Expressions of concern about low voter turnout and a lack of political participation generally are based on the belief that broad-based political participation is a key feature of a healthy democracy. But one cannot simply look at political participation as voting—there's a wide range of ways that people in different communities, socioeconomic strata, age cohorts, and other categories participate (Zukin et al. 2006). And we know that policy makers are sensitive to public opinion and the probability that their actions may arouse anger among enough people to make implementation difficult or to cause them to lose elections. Thus, in the end, we can say that the general public does not often participate in policy making. Indeed, the overall level of political attention and participation—including voting and other activities—is low (Chesney and Feinstein 1993; Schachter 1997). Furthermore, to the extent that any political participation is evident in American politics, it is usually shown in voting. Notable exceptions are major social movements (described later in this chapter), such as women's suffrage and civil rights movements, which mobilized millions of people to support major policy change.

Given the low level of regular political participation, is there any way to figure out what individuals expect government to do? Political scientist Morris Fiorina suggests that the people want the most benefits at the least cost, and for other people to pay for the benefits we receive (Fiorina 1989). In essence, we *individually* define efficiency as getting the most services for ourselves while paying the least taxes for that package of services. Of course, when everyone defines efficiency that way, conflict between groups is likely because all of us cannot gain the things we want from government *and* expect that someone else will provide them; that is, we would like the benefits focused on us, but the costs spread among many people. This way of thinking about policy is discussed in greater detail in Chapter 7, where we consider policy types. Once again, the "who gets what" question in politics is starkly illustrated.

From a normative, pro-democracy perspective, it is encouraging to know that people can be **mobilized**—that is, anyone can be persuaded to care about particular issues. The sometimes-raucous town hall meetings about healthcare reform in 2009 exemplified potential group mobilization, although these meetings still drew a very small fraction of the overall public. Nonvoters and relatively uninterested people can still be sufficiently motivated to write letters, join an interest group, or take other political action. People will often act when something threatens, or appears to threaten, their livelihood or their lifestyle, such as when new commercial development may disturb their neighborhood, or when government is unresponsive to local needs for education or public safety. While some people will mobilize to try to get the government to do something about a problem, other people will often organize to get the government *not* to do something—*not* approve a new mall, *not* create a national health insurance system, or *not* raise taxes. The decision to shut down a program or do nothing is policy as much as the decision to aggressively act is, and it is often true that blocking an action is more readily achieved than moving a policy idea forward.

People may remain mobilized until the issue is somehow resolved, whether or not it is resolved to their satisfaction, and sometimes mobilization leads to the creation of interest groups. The open question in American politics is the extent to which these relatively distinct issues and mobilization episodes add up to what we might call "public opinion" or the "public mind." Because these may all involve separate issues and actors, and often involve issues of interest to only a small number of people, it is likely that the sum of all this activity is not really the same thing as "public opinion." As Theodore Lowi argues in *The End of Liberalism*, American government became less concerned with vital issues of national importance as it became more involved with the distribution of benefits to particular interests (1979). If this is true, then there is no single **public interest**, but rather sets of separate interests with separate publics and separate opinions about what should be done. This point should be stressed: it is very difficult to define and *prove* that a particular governmental action or policy would be in the broadest public interest, because there is so little agreement on what the so-called public interest really is. This does not, of course, prevent people from forming interest groups to pursue their own goals, whether or not they perceive them to be in the public interest.

mobilization
The process by which people or groups are motivated to take action, such as through lobbying, protest, or any other form of expression in response to an issue or problem.

public interest
The assumed broader desires and needs of the public, in whose name policy is made. The public interest is hard to define, but is something to which all policy advocates appeal.

INTEREST GROUPS

interest group
A collection of people or organizations that unite to advance their desired political outcomes in government and society. There are many different ways to organize these groups by types of interest (public/private, institutional, economic, etc.).

Interest groups are important—perhaps central—to the policy process because the power of individuals is greatly magnified when they form groups. Interest groups of some sort have been a part of American politics since before the founding of the republic. James Madison, one of the key proponents of the Constitution, recognized this, and one of his reasons for supporting the creation of a *federal* union was the possibility of breaking down "faction"— that is, group-based interests—into geographically contained states and their subdivisions, to prevent the spread of populist ideas from overwhelming what the founders considered to be the more reasoned deliberation of the elected officials.

Since the 1960s, the number of interest groups has rapidly expanded (McFarland 1987). Today, while many groups are local and deal with local issues, many interest groups and popular movements cannot be confined to small states or communities in the manner contemplated by Madison in *Federalist 10*. Clearly, our evolution from a group of states to a nation, aided by transportation and communication capabilities unimagined by the founders, has made it possible for groups to mobilize quickly on a regional or national scale. After all, news that took weeks to travel from New York to Pittsburgh can now move nearly instantly from New York to Pittsburgh—or to Los Angeles, Moscow, Tokyo, Beijing, or Baghdad. With this capacity to communicate, containing political conflict within one place is very difficult. Political ideas and information transcend local and national borders at a speed and volume unprecedented in world history.

The American system of democracy, with its respect for freedom of association and speech, does not place great legal burdens in the path of those who wish to mobilize and form an interest group; the major barriers are not political, but are related to organization and resource: effective interest group activity is very expensive. Grassroots organizations form almost daily to pursue myriad goals, such as halting the construction of cellular phone towers in residential areas or promoting the formation of a new charter school. However, while anyone can form a group, its mere existence does not suggest that it will have any voice in policy making. As you may have experienced directly, some groups have considerably more power than other groups. Groups that represent powerful or privileged interests are partly responsible for Americans' suspicion of interest groups or, as they are often called, "special interest groups." In fact, some groups call themselves "public interest groups" to signal that they view their mission as a counterweight to these "special" interests. Other groups simply support positions that many find controversial, such as civil rights groups in the 1950s and 1960s, women's rights groups in the 1970s and 1980s, and gay and lesbian rights groups today.

There are several reasons for the differences in power between some groups and others, particularly within a particular policy area. First, as Howlett, Ramesh, and Perl note, "One valuable resource that such interest groups deploy is knowledge, specifically, information that might be unavailable or less available to others" (Howlett, Ramesh, and Perl 2009: 69). Legislators and bureaucrats draw on this information to help them make decisions; groups that are the most effective at channeling that information to bureaucrats and legislators often have an advantage in ensuring that their definition of the problem, and the range of potential solutions, is taken into account. Communication with key decision-makers, in turn, requires substantial resources that emergent groups may not have and that established groups often have in abundance.

Money, knowledge, and information are related to the size of the group and the resources that it and its members can bring to policy conflicts. Some interest groups have very few members, and others have millions of dues-paying members. Large groups include the National Education Association, the Sierra Club, and the AARP.[2] All other things being equal, larger groups can be expected to be taken more seriously by the government. Even more powerful groupings, called **peak associations**, "may be expected to be more influential than those operating individually." The National Association of Manufacturers is a peak association in the business sector. The American Petroleum Institute, representing oil companies' interests, and the Air Transport Association (ATA), which represents the major airlines, are also peak associations. But not all peak associations are big business oriented: the Sierra Club is a peak organization in the environmental movement, and the Consumers Union is a peak association in the consumer movement. Of course, many argue that these groups' influence is nowhere near as great as business groups, because, simply, they have less money. As noted earlier, money is very important for interest groups, because it "enables them to hire permanent specialized staff and make campaign contributions to parties and candidates during elections" (Howlett, Ramesh, and Perl 2009: 70–71).

A rough calculation of the political power of an interest group (and thus of one's political influence as a group member) is derived from the size of the group's membership. A group with 500,000 members is likely to have

peak associations/peak organizations The largest and most influential groups in a policy domain. These tend to be the groups that lead other like-minded groups in advocacy coalitions. The American Medical Association and the National Rifle Association are examples of peak organizations.

more clout (or at least be "louder" in some sense) than a group with 500 members. But this isn't always the case, and we cannot assume that the larger group in this example is a thousand times more powerful than the smaller one. As social scientists have learned, it is very difficult to create a committed membership group unless there are incentives for people to join (Olson 1971). Business interest groups, such as the National Association of Realtors, can be powerful because their members are vitally interested in the issues addressed by the group. If Congress proposed to reduce or eliminate the mortgage interest tax deduction, which allows people who own houses to deduct from their taxable income the money they spend in interest on their home loans, real estate agents would take note because their livelihoods could be directly affected: fewer houses would be sold because the mortgage tax deduction works to subsidize home buying, particularly for the wealthy. There are, of course, both benefits and costs to this tax deduction (see Glaeser and Shapiro 2002).

By contrast, a person interested in animal conservation may be less *directly* affected by changes in the Endangered Species Act, even as that individual cares about such species. With no personal *economic* stake in endangered species, individuals might be less motivated to join the Sierra Club or another environmental group. Indeed, while some people join the Sierra Club because of a belief in the importance of the environment, others may join simply to feel like they support the cause and primarily because of the benefits of membership, such as a glossy magazine and various social opportunities. Indeed, there are groups, such as the American Automobile Association (AAA) or the AARP, that people join almost solely for material benefits, such as discounts on towing, travel, or prescription drugs. Many of the members of these groups are only vaguely aware of the advocacy activities undertaken by these groups on their behalf. For example, I belong to the AAA for the towing and dead-battery service, which I have used several times! But when the AAA advocates for larger share of federal transportation funding to be spent on highways, and less on mass transit, my personal preferences may not be being represented. But I am far less aware of AAA's advocacy than of the availability of emergency towing.

institutional interest group
A group of people, usually not formally constituted, whose members are part of the same institution or organization. Students at a university are an example of such a group. Contrast with a membership interest group.

Types of Interest Groups

There are many ways to categorize interest groups. One can distinguish between an **institutional interest group**, whose members belong to a particular institution, and a membership group, whose members have chosen to join. If you are a student at a university, you are a member of an institutional interest group—university students—because you share some interests with your fellow students, such as affordable tuition and quality education. If you join the National Rifle Association or your on-campus Public Interest Research Group, you are part of a membership group because you made the positive choice to join, rather than being a member simply because of your status in an organization or society at large.

One can also contrast **economic interest groups** with **public interest groups**. While the difference between the two is sometimes rhetorical—after all, almost every group believes it is acting, directly or indirectly, in the broader public interest—there is also a more technical way to distinguish between the two. Public interest groups, such as environmental groups, Common Cause, and the like, seek to create broad benefits for the entire society, not simply their members. Indeed, it is difficult to allow only public interest group members to reap the benefits of, say, a cleaner environment without providing such benefits to others. While public interest groups would like more people to join their causes, they also know that nonmembers constitute a potential force of supporters, and, as mentioned earlier, when many such people are mobilized, a social movement may result.

In economic terms, we can say that nonmembers of public interest groups are free riders who benefit from the work of the group without contributing resources such as labor or money. Economic groups, on the other hand, seek to overcome this problem by creating benefits only for the members of their groups. For example, labor unions, particularly in "closed shop" states where all workers must pay dues to the union, work to provide wage and benefit agreements that help only the members of the union. By restricting benefits in this way, the union seeks to promote cohesion and to encourage others to join the union.

Industry groups are clearly economic groups. They tend to be small groups in terms of the actual numbers of members, but they are powerful because they are collections of powerful economic interests that often enjoy considerable local, regional, or national political support. For example, the Pharmaceutical Research and Manufacturers of America enjoys considerable support in the Research Triangle area of North Carolina where many pharmaceutical companies and their jobs are located (Barrett 2009). Similarly, the American Petroleum Institute represents an industry that is very important to people in the major oil-producing states of Alaska, Texas, Louisiana, and

economic/private interest groups Groups formed to promote and defend the economic interests of their members (for example, industry associations).

public interest groups Groups formed to promote what its members believe is the broader public interest.

North Dakota, among others. Finally, we can consider professional and trade associations to be economic associations. Groups such as the American Medical Association and the American Bar Association seek to promote and protect the professional and economic interests of doctors and lawyers. They provide important benefits and services to their members, such as medical or law journals and continuing education. They also seek to protect the economic interests of their members. These associations play an active role in the education and licensing of doctors and lawyers, thereby seeking to keep the size of the profession relatively fixed. When their interests are threatened, they lobby elected and appointed officials; for example, the American Medical Association has been a traditional opponent of many plans for government-sponsored healthcare programs for those without insurance, although their position has shifted in recent years.

In both public interest and economic groups, people join because they gain some benefit. The challenge for public interest groups is to make clear what those benefits are to attract and keep members. As a rule, it is easier for economic groups to do this because their members have tangible economic interests at stake. Public interest groups, on the other hand, must appeal to motivations other than economics. Most public interest groups make an appeal to people's desire to do good, augmenting it by material benefits such as discounted nature tours, glossy magazines, calendars, and tote bags. These benefits may seem trivial, but they help to attract new members and promote group cohesion. Still, they are not as powerful as economic inducements in promoting group unity (Olson 1971).

Finally, it is important to note that many groups do not fit neatly into the public interest/economic dichotomy. In particular, the United States contains many religious and ideological groups that come together without being based on economics or a broader public interest mission. Rather, their mission is to promote their religious, moral, and ideological values among their members and, sometimes, in the broader society. These groups range from mainstream churches to fundamentalist congregations, and from the politically moderate to the politically extreme groups on both ends of the ideological spectrum. Such groups can become important players in the policy process, at least briefly, during times of social upheaval and crisis or when issues of morality and values are paramount. They often argue, of course, that their positions are in the best public interest, as do economic groups, who argue that their industries are comprised of responsible business firms that benefit all their stakeholders.

Interest groups engage in a range of activities to make group members' voices heard. Many groups engage in *lobbying* elected and appointed officials. The term "lobbying" has negative connotations, because it conjures up images of smoke-filled rooms and secret dealings between shadowy lobbyists and less-than-honest officials, often accompanied by the exchange of cash in the form of campaign contributions, or, in less savory transactions, in the form of bribes and graft. This perception is reinforced by campaign contribution practices, which have led many people to believe that they are made to ensure friendly access to elected officials and to the decision-making process. This perception was explicitly cited by U.S. Supreme Court Justice David Souter in his decision in *Nixon v. Shrink Missouri Government PAC*, 528 U.S. 377 (2000), in which he noted:

> the cynical assumption that large donors call the tune could jeopardize the willingness of voters to take part in democratic governance. Democracy works "only if the people have faith in those who govern, and that faith is bound to be shattered when high officials and their appointees engage in activities which arouse suspicions of malfeasance and corruption."
>
> (*United States v. Mississippi Valley Generating Co.*,
> 364 U.S. 520, 562 [1961])

Attempts to influence government decision-making are not, however, solely a function of campaign contributions, although campaign financing plays an important role in influencing decisions. After all, the First Amendment to the Constitution guarantees the right of people "to petition the Government for a redress of grievances," and there is no prohibition on people gathering together in groups to petition the government, nor is there anything in the Constitution to suggest that one cannot, or should not, engage the services of experts to help us petition the government. Lobbying—the organized, continuous act of communicating with the government—is one way to petition government, not only for the redress of grievances, but also to encourage government to support particular interests with various benefits.

People's objection to lobbying may not be to lobbying per se, but rather to the perception that more political power is held by well-funded interest groups in Washington and the state capitals. Furthermore, and as Justice Souter hints, many people believe that there is some sort of quid pro quo operating in Congress with respect to campaign contributions. The most basic form of this idea holds that an interest group will meet with a Member of Congress and say, "If you vote with me, I will give you this campaign contribution."

lobbying
The term applied to the organized and ongoing process of persuading the legislative or executive branches to enact policies that promote an individual's or group's interest. The term has taken on a negative connotation.

The other variant of this idea is the member of Congress saying, "I will vote to promote your interest if you give me a campaign contribution." In both cases, the implication is that there is an exchange taking place that is unfair and undemocratic.

The campaign contribution process is clearly more subtle. Attempts are made to at least make the process partially transparent; that is, certain amounts have to be reported, lobbyists need to register with state and local legislative offices, and so on. Of course, there are states, such as New York, where good government groups seek to promote transparent systems of tracking campaign contributions. But in New York, as elsewhere, even minor reforms cannot hide the fact that many stakeholders work to prevent information from being gathered and presented in a useful and timely manner (The Fog of Ethics in Albany 2009). There remains a perception that votes can be "bought" by the most powerful groups. Still, the prevailing legal theory that often strikes down campaign reform legislation is the idea that the choice to spend money to advocate for a position is a form of constitutionally protected free speech. Indeed, as noted earlier, there is nothing in the first amendment to prohibit this form of expression, and, in some cases, the *less* politically powerful can find that their collective resources can be put to use to communicate with Members of Congress.

While lobbying sometimes carries with it tawdry overtones, it is important in the policy process because lobbyists provide important information to officials in the legislative and the executive branches. Elected officials generally have large staffs, and Members of Congress have access to the work of the Congressional Research Service and the Government Accountability Office, two agencies that help Congress gather information and do its work. But interest groups can provide further information that is unknown or unavailable to elected officials. Such information has to be reasonably good— outright distortions and fabrications are likely to be exposed, and no elected official wants to use grossly inaccurate information for fear of damaging his or her credibility. Groups consequently try to feed good information to elected officials who may already be predisposed to the group's position, hoping that their supporters can use information to make a better case for the group's preferred solutions.

Of course, not all groups have equal power and equal access to elected officials. There are many instances in American history in which elected officials were actively hostile to a particular group's goals. A prime example is found in the history of the civil rights movement, particularly at the state level. Clearly, African Americans could not gain a fair hearing for redress of their grievances before the very state governments that passed and enforced segregationist laws in the first place. At the same time, a sufficiently large number of senators and representatives were unsympathetic to the civil rights cause, making policy change more difficult.

The groups involved in the civil rights movement turned then to three strategies: mass mobilization, protest, and litigation. An example of mass mobilization was the 1963 March on Washington, sponsored by several civil rights organizations and featuring Martin Luther King's "I Have a Dream" speech; the 1955–1956 Montgomery (Alabama) bus boycott, occasioned by the refusal of Rosa Parks to sit in the back of a city bus, was an example of both mass mobilization and nonviolent protest. The bus boycott actually triggered the creation, in 1957, of the Southern Christian Leadership Conference, a very prominent civil rights organization.

These actions were accompanied by litigation. The NAACP Legal Defense Fund, Inc. (known as the Inc. Fund), under the leadership of Thurgood

Source: Corbis Images. Used with permission.

PHOTO 5.1
Individuals in the United States may protest the actions of government, industries, or other people. From what you see here, does this person belong to any formally organized or informal interest groups? What is he expressing with his sign and flags?

Marshall, had, in the 1940s and early 1950s, begun to score successes in court. The Inc. Fund won cases to desegregate law schools and graduate education, but its most prominent victory was in *Brown v. Board of Education*, in which the Supreme Court ruled that "separate but equal" schools were in fact not equal.

As discussed in Chapter 4, other groups have used litigation to some advantage; those supporting abortion rights brought suit in *Roe v. Wade*, 410 U.S. 113 (1973), as a way to eliminate abortion restrictions. While litigation has long been considered a last-ditch strategy and its efficacy has been questioned, the choice of litigation as a technique is an important example of **venue shopping**, in which groups pick the branch or agency of government that is most likely to give their concerns a sympathetic hearing (see Pralle 2003, 2006; Rosenberg 2008; Baumgartner and Jones 2009).

Protest marches are also a form of political participation. Protest marches are, of course, generally legal in democratic countries, and many large events, such as the March on Washington in 1963, gain legendary status. Even smaller events, such as the several antiwar rallies in 2003 before the U.S. invasion of Iraq, a rally in Washington in 2009 to protest the Obama administration's tax and health reform policies, and the protest marches that accompanied California voters's adoption of Proposition 8, a measure designed to make gay and lesbian marriage illegal, can trigger great attention and can influence the immediate debate, even if they do not rise to historic status. Protests that turn violent or threaten violence may be labeled illegitimate by these causes' opponents, and are often condemned by other supporters, because violent protest by definition breaks the law or threatens to do so. In the United States, where the rule of law is so highly valued, extralegal forms of political expression and protest are often condemned.

Protest activities are inputs to the policy process that reflect the dissatisfaction of protestors and the people they represent. While the antiwar and civil rights protests of the 1960s may not have been the ultimate reason that the Vietnam War ended or that civil rights laws were passed, they were certainly part of the reason that policies changed. Many people attempt to delegitimize such protest activity if groups on the fringes of these events engage in the threat or reality of violence against people or property. But one cannot delegitimize an entire movement by the behavior of a few violent or rude protestors. In Seattle in 1999, where the World Trade Organization was meeting to discuss trade policy, many groups came together to peacefully protest various trade policies, but a small number of people engaged in violent

venue shopping
A term used by Frank Baumgartner and Bryan Jones to describe how groups choose which branch or agency of government to lobby or persuade; they will choose the venue where they believe their concerns will receive a sympathetic hearing.

acts, which led to heavy police response, all of which entirely overshadowed the meeting and made it unsuccessful. Similar dynamics occurred in 2014, when residents of communities such as Ferguson, Missouri, and Staten Island, New York, engaged in protest actions when the community believed that African-American men had been killed by police officers who treated these men more harshly because they were African American. In these protests, some acts of violence, including arson, vandalism, and gunfire, did occur. But the violent actions at the ideological fringes of these protests—even as they overwhelmed meetings and the peaceful protests—do not cause policy makers to uniformly ignore the very real concerns that mainstream participants in protest activity sought to highlight.

In 2009, group action took what many believe to be an ugly turn during the several "town hall" meetings members of Congress held in their home districts during the August recess, at the beginning of the nascent "Tea Party" movement. Boisterous shouting and outlandish claims about the content of proposed reforms characterized several of these meetings. Some political commentators have noted that such behavior—often inspired by interest groups that some call **astroturf groups**, or groups that appear to have emerged from the grassroots but in reality have not, crosses the line from the usual give and take of political debate and into the realm of bullying and intimidation. This is related to claims about the overall coarsening of public discourse in the United States, fueled by new media that elevate implausible stories—such as the idea that President Obama was not born in Hawaii—into subjects fit for "mainstream" journalism. While it is important to place this sort of rhetoric and protest behavior into context—the sort of rhetoric used in the early days of the republic was surprisingly personal and coarse—it is also worthwhile to consider whether group activity has worsened the nature and function of policy making. And, as in the Seattle protests, we must not lose sight of underlying motivations: legitimate concern about the direction of public policy based on uncertainty about what direction policy will take.

Social Movements and Mobilization

When groups of people mobilize and coalesce around a set of high-visibility issues, a **social movement** may result. A social movement involves far more people—although not all at a high degree of activity—than the membership of relevant interest groups. Social movements often involve a coalition of groups with similar goals, and other people support movements without a

astroturf group
An interest group that appears to have been formed by concerned citizens (that is, from the "grassroots"), but is actually sponsored by a larger interest group such as a corporation or labor union.

social movement
A broad-based effort by a large group of people to make fundamental changes in public policy and attitudes. Broad social movements are important features of history, such as the civil rights movement or the women's rights movement.

formal group affiliation. Recent social movements include the civil rights and women's rights movements, neither of which are simply historical eras, but which continue to play a role in American politics and policy making. In the 1960s and 1970s, and continuing today, women's groups promoted policies to create equal pay in the workplace, access to abortion, more stringent laws governing sexual harassment, improved laws that reduce, to some extent, the stigma attached to rape victims, and so on. These actions are the result of citizens coming together and pressing for change, both within and outside official institutions.

The civil rights movement is a classic example of a movement that lobbied or pleaded its case to government institutions—Congress, the president, and the courts—as well as appealing to the "court of public opinion." Indeed, the imagery of the civil rights movement—the police dogs in Alabama and kids being escorted to school by federal troops, for example—appealed directly to Americans' sense of justice and fairness. While not all Americans supported the enforcement of civil rights for minorities, there were certainly enough Americans to constitute an important social movement to press for policy and social change. The gay and lesbian rights movement might also be considered a social movement, against which many socially and politically conservative people have mobilized to oppose policies that offended their sense of morality and ethics. Social movements and their key issues wax and wane as the political conditions and the consequences of their work change.

The examples given here are of liberal social movements, which are historically more common given the status quo orientation of the American political system, which favors conservatism (Robertson and Judd 1989). However, in recent years, politically conservative groups have also mobilized, often to counter perceived liberal gains. Conservatives (and religious groups, often with a conservative outlook) have mobilized against abortion, in favor of restoring school prayer, and against textbooks and teaching that contradict their political or religious values. Conservatives have also formed groups to advance their views on welfare, economic regulation, and environmental protection. Clearly, there is no reason why conservatives or liberals cannot mobilize and press for change. Those that are successful will be those that respond to the current ideological, social, and political attitudes of the public; the truly successful among them will be led by people who know, intuitively or otherwise, how to gain political advantage and policy gains by helping to shape public opinion and offer policy options acceptable to a large number of people.

POLITICAL PARTIES

Political parties serve important functions in the policy process (Eldersveld 2000; Burbank, Hrebenar, and Benedict 2011; Green, Coffey, and Cohen 2014). First, party labels provide voters with cues for voting. Voters know, in general, that Republicans tend to be more socially conservative and distrustful of "big government" than Democrats, while Democrats generally favor government programs that "level the playing field" for all people. Second, political parties provide a rough way of transmitting political preferences from the electorate to the elected branches. The congressional elections of 1994, for example, in which the Republican Party took control of both Houses of Congress, may have reflected in some ways a shift in the preferences of some of the voting public; one might make a similar argument for the 2008 presidential and congressional elections, which suggested a shift in partisan affiliations and ideological self-identification. Third, political parties help elected officials and their supporters create packages of policy ideas that can be used to appeal to voters and then to shape legislation. During the 1960s and 1970s, this was not a particularly important role of the parties, but the Republican House leadership in the 1990s used its "Contract with America" as a way of packaging ideas and differentiating them from the policies proposed by the Democratic Party.

The political parties are crucial to the organization of the legislative branch. Congress and the state legislatures elect their leaders along party lines, and committee assignments and other positions are made based on party affiliation (and seniority within the party). In this way, a rough connection is made between the ideological preferences of the electorate and policy-making apparatus of Congress. Theoretically, this enhances democratic accountability, although the organization of Congress along party lines has been controversial, particularly when very senior members in very safe districts wield disproportionate power over policy.

THINK TANKS AND OTHER RESEARCH ORGANIZATIONS

The emergence of complex problems and the need for greater analytic capacity than that possessed by the federal and state governments has led to the growth of independent research organizations, often called **think tanks**.[3] Some of

think thanks
Independent research organizations, sometimes ideologically neutral but often identified with a particular political perspective.

the most famous think tanks include the Brookings Institution, the Cato Institute, the Urban Institute, the RAND Corporation, and the American Enterprise Institute. Employing scholars and policy experts, these organizations provide information that policy makers and other influential people can use to make "better" policy. Many think tanks are associated with a particular ideological position: Brookings and the Urban Institute are center-left, the American Enterprise Institute is somewhat more to the right, and Cato is libertarian. Others, such as RAND, are more closely associated with their methodological style; RAND uses very sophisticated scientific methods and statistical techniques.

The last three decades have seen the emergence of more overtly ideological think tanks, such as the Heritage Foundation, which is explicitly conservative in its orientation, and the Urban Institute, which is consciously liberal. Other think tanks seek to blur their ideological orientation while obviously advocating positions with an ideological slant. One such example, once used by a student in one of my public policy courses, is the National Center for Policy Analysis (NCPA). A review of the NCPA's reports and of its board of directors (listed on its website, www.ncpa.org) reveals a conservative orientation. This is not to say that this is the only group that blurs its ideological leanings or that one should be concerned with the formation of such groups. And, in fairness, the NCPA site provides links to other conservative and liberal think tanks and values robust policy discourse among all positions. But any consumer of analysis from think tanks should have a good sense of the ideological leanings of the organization in question, so that they can be aware of ideological commitments or blind spots in the analysis.

Other think tanks and research organizations are associated with universities and provide valuable input into the policy process. Such centers tend to be more scholarly and less ideological than some think tanks, and state and local governments often rely on them for expert advice. Indeed, one of the missions of public institutions of higher learning is to provide such politically and socially relevant research to units of government. They are often good sources of information and ideas for research on important policy issues.

COMMUNICATIONS MEDIA

Our nation's founders knew that the news media—at that time, the print media, which largely produced books, political pamphlets, fliers, and the like, as well as the emerging periodical newspaper industry—were important to politics and public policy. The founders had a keen appreciation for the value of a free press in a democracy. They believed, at least in the abstract, in press freedoms because the news media can serve as a "fourth branch" of government, thereby providing a check on the other three branches. This is known as the "watchdog" function of the media, in which it is assumed that the news media provide citizens with information about government that people can use to support or challenge policy decisions. Journalists and academics have reinforced the belief that the news media play an important role in informing citizens about issues and what their government is doing about them (Alger 1996; Cook 2005; Bennett 2012; Graber and Dunaway 2015).

The notion of a free press extends well beyond words printed on paper. The "press" today consists of traditional outlets such as magazines, newspapers, radio, and television, but also extends to websites, blogs, social networks, and the like, all of which are involved, in one manner or another, in providing the public with information about policy and politics. Of course, these new **social media** are not all about the weighty matters of our time—after all, neither are newspapers and television news. But they are alternative media that have already changed the way in which news is defined, gathered, written, distributed, and consumed, all of which matters in the policy process. For example, the social networking and microblogging service Twitter allows people to share information with each other about "breaking news" in real time, whether from the scene of the news itself, or in response to it.

There are many historic examples of the news media exposing some of the troubling activities and shortcomings of business and government. In the early 1900s, crusading journalists called **muckrakers** aligned with progressive publishers and interests to expose the problems of child labor, tainted foods, and useless medicines. Later in the twentieth century came the revelations of wrongdoing by President Nixon and his staff, as reported in a series of stories by journalists Carl Bernstein and Robert Woodward in the *Washington Post* from June 1972 until Nixon's resignation in 1974 (see Bernstein and Woodward 1999). The Pulitzer Prize for Public Service—awarded to newspapers for exemplary efforts in providing the public with vital policy and politics information—is often awarded to newspapers reporting some sort of policy failure or official wrongdoing. For example, in 1989, the *Anchorage Daily News* won the prize "for reporting about the high incidence of alcoholism and suicide among native Alaskans in a series that focused attention on their despair and *resulted in various reforms*." In 1990, a small newspaper,

social media
Internet-based systems of information gathering and publishing that rely on the actions of a broad range of people, rather than the actions of a few reporters, to find and promote information. Twitter, Facebook, YouTube, and other systems are examples.

muckrakers
The investigative journalists of the early twentieth century, whose work exposed problems such as tainted food, dangerous working conditions, and bogus medicines. The term was coined by Theodore Roosevelt.

the Washington, North Carolina, *Daily News*, won the prize for its reports "revealing that the city's water supply was contaminated with carcinogens, *a problem that the local government had neither disclosed nor corrected over a period of eight years*." The italicized portions of these quotes highlight how the media, along with other actors in the policy process, are interested in public problems.

Large newspapers often win these awards. The *Washington Post* won in 1973 for its coverage of Watergate and again in 2008 for "the work of Dana Priest, Anne Hull, and photographer Michel du Cille in exposing mistreatment of wounded veterans at Walter Reed Hospital, evoking a national outcry and *producing reforms by federal officials*." In each of these citations,[4] I have italicized the passage that indicates how the reporting led to reforms of public policy. And, reflecting the major changes in the news media in the past several years, the co-winners of the Public Service award for 2014 were the *Washington Post* and the U.S. website of the British newspaper, the *Guardian*, both for their coverage of secret surveillance conducted by the United States National Security Agency (NSA). This coverage led to pledges from the president that the NSA's ability to gather a very wide array of personal information would be curtailed (Savage 2014).

But newspapers and TV networks are, in a business sense, suffering from significant changes in the way news is gathered, written or produced, and consumed by the public. The causes of their recent financial problems include a sharp drop in advertising revenue in the recession and the huge decrease in classified advertising revenue occasioned by new media outlets such as Craigslist and in display advertising sold through companies such as Google and Yahoo.

It is tempting to blame "new media" and the Internet for the decline of newspapers, and it is true that the new media are greatly changing people's news consumption habits. But the decline of newspapers predates competition from the Internet. Overall daily newspaper circulation in the United States peaked in 1984. The total number of papers has steadily declined since 1940. In the early twentieth century, many cities had two or more newspapers; today, most cities have only one newspaper, and those few smaller to medium-sized cities with two papers have recently become one-newspaper towns. Seattle lost the *Seattle Post-Intelligencer* and Denver lost the *Rocky Mountain News*, both in 2009. As this was written, Boston was in significant danger of losing its only paper, the *Boston Globe*. The *Detroit Free Press*—in a city hard hit by the recession—is currently delivering the paper three days a week to subscribers, while publishing for newsstand sales daily. And several major papers, such as the New Orleans *Times-Picayune*, do not publish a daily edition.

While the number of newspapers and their circulation are all on the decline—and their financial viability is in even greater danger than the data in Figures 5.2 and 5.3 suggest—the major *national* newspapers remain important. The *New York Times*, the *Washington Post*, and the *Wall Street Journal* continue to be read in policy-making circles; the *Wall Street Journal* is a particularly important and respected source of business and economic news, and its editorial and opinion pages are a bastion of conservative thought. *USA Today* is a national paper launched by the Gannett Company in 1982 as a consciously colorful, entertaining national newspaper.

All of these papers have active websites that offer content undeliverable in print, such as audio reports, podcasts that can be listened to at one's leisure, extensive photos essays, videos, and interactive graphics that illustrate important trends. Many newspapers also underwrite blogs and provide opportunities for comment, although the tone of much commentary is often mean-spirited and surprisingly uninformed. And many newspapers continue

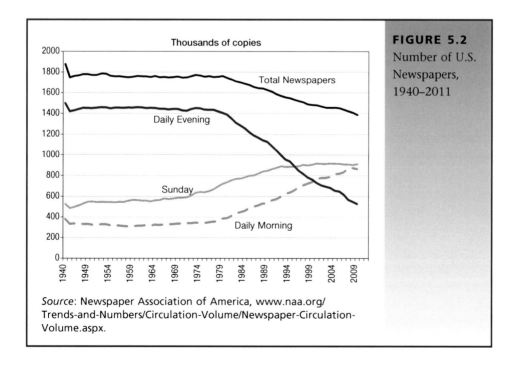

FIGURE 5.2
Number of U.S. Newspapers, 1940–2011

Source: Newspaper Association of America, www.naa.org/Trends-and-Numbers/Circulation-Volume/Newspaper-Circulation-Volume.aspx.

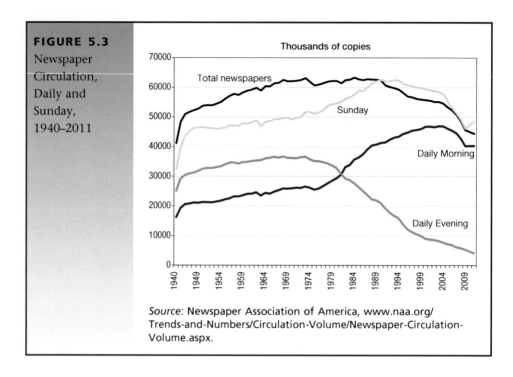

FIGURE 5.3
Newspaper Circulation, Daily and Sunday, 1940–2011

Source: Newspaper Association of America, www.naa.org/Trends-and-Numbers/Circulation-Volume/Newspaper-Circulation-Volume.aspx.

to serve important regional audiences, such as the *Los Angeles Times* or the *Chicago Tribune*, and may well be the dominant print outlets in their states, such as the *State* (Columbia, SC), the Providence *Journal*, the Atlanta *Journal Constitution*, the *Alaska Dispatch News* (formerly the *Anchorage Daily News*, which was bought out by a website!), the Portland *Oregonian*, and the Newark (New Jersey) *Star-Ledger*. But even the *Star-Ledger* is struggling, and its loss would constitute the loss of the state's major source of news about legislative activity in the New Jersey state capital. And, as noted earlier, all of these newspapers have a Web presence as well. Indeed, during a natural disaster, as was seen in New Orleans' the *Times-Picayune*'s dogged post-Katrina reporting, the website may be the only way to disseminate "print" news, at least for a short time, and, in the *Times-Picayune*'s case, its website has picked up the slack.

This drumbeat of bad news about newspapers reflects, perhaps, my personal admiration for newspaper journalism, and my preference for newspapers over other forms of news. But for decades, television has been the primary source of news for those Americans who consume news. But the influence of the Internet is so great that network television news has substantially lost viewership. The flagship broadcast of most TV networks was the evening nightly news broadcasts. You—or your parents and grandparents—may remember iconic news anchors such as Walter Cronkite and Dan Rather on CBS; Chet Huntley, David Brinkley, John Chancellor, and Tom Brokaw on NBC; and Howard K. Smith, Harry Reasoner, and Peter Jennings on ABC. Today, however, broadcast network anchors are not household names the way they once were, and ratings are far below their historic highs of the early 1980s. In 1980, over half of U.S. households watched network TV news; by 2008, that number had fallen to less than half of U.S. households, as shown in Figure 5.4, and the nightly TV news audience had grown to be much older, on average, than the overall adult population. The nightly broadcasts are now less prone to cover breaking news, and are more prone to cover health, economic, and lifestyle issues. This is because most seemingly time-sensitive stories are covered intensively by cable TV and, in recent years, on the Internet; because "hard news" is more expensive to cover; and because audiences seem to like soft news. Network news is still important because the audience remains reasonably large compared with cable news, and the

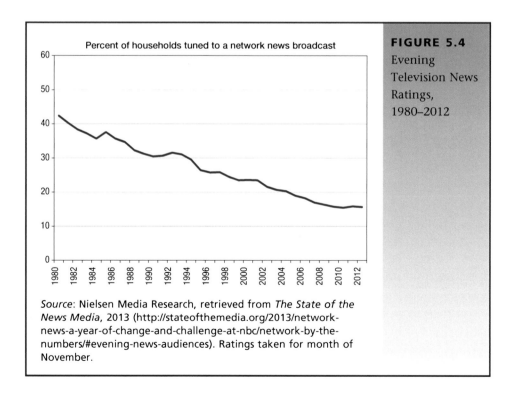

FIGURE 5.4
Evening Television News Ratings, 1980–2012

Source: Nielsen Media Research, retrieved from *The State of the News Media*, 2013 (http://stateofthemedia.org/2013/network-news-a-year-of-change-and-challenge-at-nbc/network-by-the-numbers/#evening-news-audiences). Ratings taken for month of November.

older viewership is more likely to vote than younger people. From a business perspective, however, it worries networks that their older news audience is somewhat less attractive to advertisers than the younger viewers.

Younger audiences, to the extent that they consume news programming, prefer cable TV sources such as CNN, MSNBC, and Fox News to the "big three" networks. For many years, CNN was the dominant cable TV news channel. But it has been substantially overtaken in viewership by the overtly conservative Fox News Channel, and by MSNBC, once a joint venture of Microsoft and the NBC network, which is said to lean in a liberal direction. Few congressional offices are without cable TV, and, because these channels cover breaking political and policy news, they are followed very closely.

Other cable TV outlets also play an important role, even though their audiences are quite small. C-SPAN is a set of several networks—including a radio station in Washington—established as a public service by the cable TV industry. C-SPAN devotes a considerable amount of time to unedited recordings and broadcasts of House and Senate activity, as well as news conferences and other events hosted by interest groups. Much of this activity seems tedious and incomprehensible to those with little interest in politics, but political junkies and policy entrepreneurs avidly watch these networks; in many congressional offices, at least one TV is tuned to a C-SPAN channel at all times.

Radio was once a primary source of news, but TV has supplanted its importance as a news source. Nevertheless, some larger cities have all-news radio stations, which tend to broadcast local news with traffic, weather, and sports. On these stations, the same stories repeat throughout the day, so 24-hour news stations are not airing 24 hours of new information. Most stations on the AM band have turned to talk radio (including news, sports, and other subjects), which has some news content. But some claimed that these stations have been given over to partisan and polarizing commentators. A notable exception to the radio news trend is National Public Radio (NPR), which offers several hours of news every day to its listeners, and whose audience has grown substantially since the mid 1990s; its well-educated and politically aware audience has made NPR a respected and influential news source. Policy elites tend to listen to NPR. Many public radio stations carry news programs from the British Broadcasting Corporation (BBC), a strong source of international news. Much of NPR's listener gains from 1998 to 2008 came at the expense of nightly television news (Kamenetz 2009).

Entertainment broadcasting can influence politics and policy making, such as when MTV mounts its "Rock the Vote" campaigns to encourage youth voting or when ESPN covers a sports scandal. Indeed, recent survey research suggests that people who watch late-night television shows such as *The Tonight Show*, the *Late Show with David Letterman*, and Comedy Central's *The Daily Show* are better informed on basic political events than average Americans (Annenberg Public Policy Center 2004). What is in the media and how it is presented are important inputs to the policy process and are the subjects of policy making itself.

Now that we have reviewed the many sources of news—and the breathtaking change in the news business in just the last five years—it is important to turn our attention to what effect the news has on politics and public policy. The particular importance of the media is in its *agenda-setting* function; that is, they help to elevate some issues to greater public attention. This function is very important, particularly in the major national news outlets used by key decision-makers, such as Fox News, CNN, and the *New York Times*, the *Washington Post*, and the *Wall Street Journal*. These sources can highlight the importance of certain issues and provide ideas and feedback to elected officials and bureaucrats. In political science terms, we can say that greater levels of news coverage are closely (but not identically) associated with greater levels of institutional attention to public problems. Moreover, the media's influence goes beyond its ability to pressure policy makers to pay attention to problems. The news media can expand issues from narrow groups to broader audiences, thereby creating more pressure for change, or, to use E.E. Schattschneider's term, can "expand the scope of conflict" (Schattschneider 1975). Less powerful groups and interests can gain access to media attention when their stories are sufficiently compelling to attract news coverage, thereby making access to the agenda more democratic (Schattschneider 1975) and helping to open up policy sub-governments (Baumgartner and Jones 2009).

We should keep in mind, however, that the news media are not simply passive actors in the decisions to cover certain news stories. First, interest groups often try to arouse or provoke the news media to devote greater scrutiny to an issue or a problem (Cobb and Elder 1983). Sometimes this is successful; other times it is unnecessary when dramatic and so-called mediagenic events, such as airplane crashes, crimes, and natural disasters, occur. However, the decision to cover any event or issue means that another issue will not be covered, even when the latter issues are arguably more important. In other words, what journalists call "the news hole" is limited by various constraints on traditional outlets. Time is the major constraint for TV and radio news; a half-hour nightly news broadcast must carefully pick its stories to maintain viewer interest. Even with the advent of cable TV, there are only 24 hours in the day, so decisions must be made about which topics deserve what level of coverage. Newspapers and magazines are limited in the amount of space they can devote to news; the amount of space is often a function of the amount of advertising sold in the newspaper or magazine. Thus, with the current downturn in advertising revenue—some of which is unlikely to return—less space is available for news. Further complicating this space problem in newspapers are modern shifts in consumer tastes that are reflected in newspaper design and typography, with larger print, more white space, and more pictures crowding out what used to be dense columns of text. Thus, the use of news space is determined by design aspects of a newspaper *and* by what editors believe will be most interesting to their readers and audiences. Stories of domestic crisis, particularly with a compelling human element and a sense of conflict, are often more interesting and more extensively covered than foreign policy issues, for example.

While many worry that the corporate owners of media outlets will unduly influence news content (see Timid Media Giants 1995; Mifflin 1998), the evidence of such influence is still unclear at best. After all, journalists are professionals who often believe that their first duty is to inform the public, not to ensure the profitability of their corporate owners. On the other hand, owners make decisions about how much to spend on news gathering, and recently their decisions have led to significant cuts in the capacity of traditional journalism to produce what most people think of as "news." The next decade is likely to see this conflict between journalistic norms and profitability become more intense and more public, as traditional media lose their audience.

A subtler and yet more pressing problem for our purposes relates to the biases that are introduced in news coverage based on the competitive and economic needs of news outlets, particularly in electronic media. Students of the news media have long known that the selection of stories for coverage is often influenced more by the dramatic and narrative features of the "story" than by its substantive importance (see Bennett 2012). Thus, the old expression "if it bleeds, it leads" is played out in newspapers and local TV news programs nationwide. Stories involving murder, crime, fires, grisly car accidents, and the like are presented because they are dramatic and novel and therefore easily told as a story with good guys, bad guys, winners, losers, and even a moral (e.g. crime doesn't pay, don't drink and drive).

Such stories tend to distort people's perceptions of the relative risks they confront every day. A steady diet of crime reporting on TV will lead viewers to believe that the crime rate is higher than it is, because the news is often presented out of context. Because of the time and space constraints facing news outlets, they often fail to place events in context, such as by including crime statistics in a murder story. In international reporting, news outlets tend to focus on the immediate conflict, such as between the Pakistani and Afghan governments and Taliban and al-Qaeda operatives, or between the West and Iran over nuclear issues, rather than explaining the historical roots of conflict. This historical fragmentation leads to fundamental errors in understanding, such as believing that Kurds are the same as Arabs, or that Iranians are Arabs (they are not).

In policy debates, the media focus on the conflicting positions and, in particular, the people that represent the positions is called *personalizing* the news and is used by journalists to make the news more interesting and comprehensible to readers and viewers. Personalization can reduce conflicts to sometimes-absurd depictions, such as when the media depicted the Gulf War as a confrontation between George H.W. Bush and Saddam Hussein, rather than as a war between one nation and a coalition of other nations.

Many people believe that the institutional biases of the news media might be overcome by the proliferation of so-called new media and Web 2.0, or social media products such as Facebook and Twitter. These sources have proliferated since high-speed Internet access became widespread. The Internet also provides for new forms of participation that make it possible for some people to join in political movements and political discussions. Most blogs (from the term *Web log*) are interactive, with the writer hearing back from commenters in something like a dialogue. Some of the larger blogs, such as the Huffington Post or Slate, have become more like daily newspapers that attract millions of viewers and thousands of comments every week, but it is unclear whether such websites or blogs have a substantially different effect on public policy than do traditional print sources.

The Internet allows people to select and read news and information at any time of the day, but, even more to the point, Internet news sources allow people to customize their news reading in a way that allows them to focus on the issues that they find most interesting. The growth of the Internet is important for at least three reasons: because of its influence on traditional media (or its coexistence with it); because of the potential for changes in agenda-setting processes as a result of "narrowcasting" of the news; and because of the potential for a greater diversity of news sources.

First, though, consider the speed with which home Internet access has grown. It was only in 1993 that the first widely popular Web browser was used. It wasn't until about 2000 that home Internet usage became common. Even then, 35 percent of users used slow dial-up connections, compared with about 4 percent of adults who had broadband. By 2009, over 60 percent of adults had broadband access, and dial-up had dropped to about 9 percent. Indeed, as I write this paragraph in my home office, my family are watching movies, engaging with social media, or playing games online, not watching "traditional" cable television. Indeed, with nearly ubiquitous data access via smartphones or wireless network, Facebook has become not just a social media site, but a news source for people who read and follow links to stories put up by their friends. And, in the last edition of this book, I noted that not everyone was on the Internet and using Web browsers. This remains true to some extent, but as of 2015, the explosion of smartphones and mobile cellular data has made the use of social networking and reading news even more common on a device, with the corresponding decline in consumption of print news.

With this greater penetration of broadband, as shown in Figure 5.5, users are able to consume audio, video, and text on demand, rather than on a television network or newspaper's scheduling choices. And when the Web was first becoming popular, it was believed that many people would be able to distribute (or, as is often the case, redistribute from existing sources) news and political information independently of the gatekeepers among broadcasters and editors of print outlets. This is what I call the "diversity" argument: there are thousands of outlets, so people can choose from newspapers (and their websites), TV, newsletters, blogs, or social networks to get their news, thereby breaking up the "big media" domination of news.

But there is much less diversity than one might suppose. For example, as I was writing this section, I originally wrote, "many people are able to *produce* news and political information independently." But I changed this to "*distribute* news" or even "redistribute" news because, in almost all cases, social networkers, bloggers, and the like are not gathering and writing the original news stories, but are linking to and commenting on them. This is reflected in Figure 5.6, which shows that over 60 percent of visits to Internet news sites are to traditional news sources (TV and newspaper websites) and

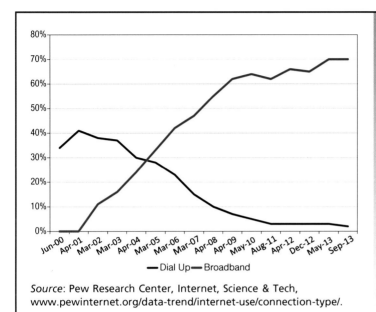

FIGURE 5.5
Trends in Home Internet Adoption, 2000–2013

Source: Pew Research Center, Internet, Science & Tech, www.pewinternet.org/data-trend/internet-use/connection-type/.

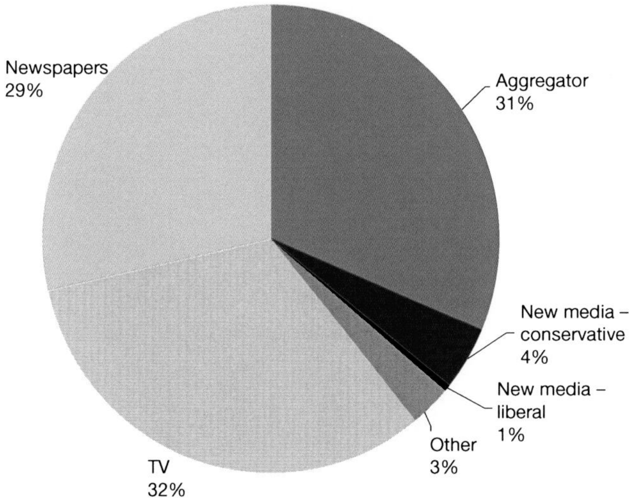

FIGURE 5.6
Most Commonly Visited Types of Internet News Sites, February 2008

Source: www.naa.org/blog/digitaledge/1/2008/03/Nielsen-Online-Names-Top-30-News-Sites.cfm, from Nielson Online.

Notes: Data are based on the top 30 most visited sites, and are percentages of unique viewers in February 2008. Newspapers include individual newspapers and news services (such as Gannett); TV includes cable TV news sites and national broadcast networks and their affiliates.

30 percent are to news aggregator sites, where the stories originate from newspapers, TV, wire services, and from other sources such as press release distributors. Wire services include the Associated Press, Reuters, and the like. Taken together, most "new media" outlets only constitute about 8 percent of the Web news audience.

Thus, the bulk of gathering, writing, and distributing news falls on traditional news organizations, whose problem is not in figuring out how to be journalists, but how to make journalism pay in a starkly changed business environment in which people are consuming news for free, or almost for free. This trend has, in particular, angered Rupert Murdoch, chairman and CEO of News Corporation, which owns the *Wall Street Journal* and Fox, among other media outlets. Murdoch argues that Google News "steals" its content when it brings up his properties (the *Wall Street Journal*, Fox News Channel, and so on) in their searches (Smillie 2009).

If journalists continue to produce news, we must remember that journalists often cover political campaigns in packs, and use the same themes in their stories. Indeed, a journalist for a mainstream publication who deviates too far from the consensus line of the story is likely to be asked why (see Crouse 1973). Pack journalism may be an exaggerated term, but years of experience show that media follow dominant themes. What's more, greater diversity—which would break down the influence of pack journalism—does not really exist. Instead, the same organizations that traditionally covered the news on radio and TV are covering the news in the new media environment. The news is still gathered by a relatively small number of journalists for mass audiences. The number of journalists is growing smaller as local newspapers cede coverage of national and international news to relatively few news services and newspapers, and all but the very largest newspapers close bureaus and lay off staff.

Even if more information—or more access to information—is a given, it is not clear that the diversity of information on the Web extends to information useful for people in a democracy. Like many social scientists, I tend to be critical of the media because of their shortcomings in providing information that citizens can use to make political and policy choices. Indeed, much of the material published online, even by sites such as CNN, is soft news such as celebrity gossip, and a great deal of bandwidth is consumed by fluff from sites such as TMZ and Perez Hilton (which is entertaining, no doubt). Other sites blur the line between news and entertainment. The website Gawker was among the first to break the news that Toronto mayor Rob Ford used cocaine while in office, and the site Mashable has begun to cover harder news.

But does this matter? The news media are not the source of information for policy makers, and are arguably a poor source. Citizens therefore may be at an informational disadvantage compared with the "insiders" if the news media do not cover important policy information and choose, instead, to give over their space to relatively unimportant topics such as personal animus among politicians, fragmented news, or feature writing or "service journalism" in favor of more traditional newsgathering. John Kingdon, in his interviews with key decision-makers in transportation and healthcare, found that relatively few of them cited the media as an important source of information and ideas (Kingdon 2011). And Howlett, Ramesh, and Perl (2009: 74) note that:

> policy makers are for the most part intelligent and resourceful individuals who understand their own interest and have their own ideas about appropriate or feasible policy options. As a rule, they are not easily swayed by media portrayals of issues and preferred policy solutions or by the mere fact of media attention. Indeed they often use the media to their own advantage.

Note that Howlett, Ramesh, and Perl are saying two things here: that *ideas* do not necessarily come from media attention or coverage pressure, but that groups still recognize the value of the media in helping them make their case. In this realization, groups and officials know what students of the media have suspected for years: that the media do not tell us what to think, but help shape the things we think *about*. And, as Baumgartner and Jones (2009) note, when the news media cover an issue intensively and "negatively" (from the perspective of the groups under scrutiny), the more likely public pressure for some sort of solution will ensue. This sort of pressure can be generated and continued in online outlets.

SUB-GOVERNMENTS, ISSUE NETWORKS, AND DOMAINS

If this chapter were to end here, you might be left with the impression that there are no patterns in the relationships between the actors in the policy process and that the process is characterized by chaos or a lack of interaction between groups. You know intuitively that this is not true: the actors in the policy process can and *must* interact with each other to advance policy proposals. Without this interaction, nothing would happen, and policy making would come to a standstill. Fortunately, we need not worry that Congress, bureaucrats, the president, the courts, the people, the media, interest groups, and all the other actors will suddenly stop making policy. Rather, our task is to make some sense of these very complex interactions. The Constitution and statute law structure many of these interactions, such as the relationships among the three branches of government. Others are informally structured but equally important to policy making.

To understand how these interactions work, we start with the idea of a **policy domain**. A policy domain is the substantive area of policy over which participants in policy making compete and compromise (Laumann and Knoke 1987), such as the environmental policy domain or the healthcare policy domain. Of course, some of these domains are so vast that they contain other domains, such as the air pollution domain, the water pollution domain, or the mental health domain. The activities that take place within these domains are influenced by other domains, and issues and ideas often spill over from one domain to the others (Kingdon 2011: 190–194). And, indeed, the boundaries between domains are often so indistinct that it is sometimes difficult to discern exactly what the "health care policy domain" or the "homeland security domain" really is (Jochim and May 2010; May, Jochim, and Sapotichne 2011).

The political culture of the nation and the existing legal environment and doctrine influence the overall environment in which policy is made in these domains. As we have seen, these environmental features are fairly stable in the short run but often change in the long run; our political culture and legal doctrines treat women and minorities considerably differently than they did 50 years ago, for example. The domain is also influenced by how people conceive of the nature of a problem, what causes the problem, and the range of potential solutions to the problem.

Contained within the policy domain is the **policy community**, which consists of actors who are involved in policy making in a particular domain. The policy community consists of those who are most expert in studying, understanding, negotiating, or explaining an issue. The nature and composition of the policy community is not, however, permanently fixed. There is variation in how easily one can join a policy community. Some are open to

policy domain
The substantive area of policy over which participants in policy making compete and compromise, such as the environmental policy domain or the health policy domain.

policy community
The group of actors—such as interest groups, government agencies, the media, and elected officials—that is actively involved in policy making in a particular domain. This group is generally thought of as being more open and dynamic than an iron triangle or sub-government.

participation by a variety of interests and actors. Others tend to be closed and operate in relative obscurity.

A considerable amount of effort has been expended by political scientists in trying to explain how policy communities organize themselves into something less than a political free-for-all in which every possible interest fights with all comers. Rather, we know intuitively that these interests and groups are likely to form connections, alliances, and coalitions. One way these participants organize is in an **iron triangle** of mutually reinforcing relationships between regulated interests, the congressional committee or subcommittee charged with lawmaking on the particular issue, and the agency charged with regulating the interests in question.

The most striking feature of the iron triangle is the mutually reinforcing nature of the relationships therein. The regulated interest, the agency, and the congressional subcommittee make policy based on their common perception of the issues and goals. The regulators tend to negotiate with the regulated, rather than imposing their ideas. Because there are benefits to all parties, this relationship has the potential for long-term stability. Baumgartner and Jones (2009) call such tightly knit relationships "policy monopolies."

For example, farm policy is largely controlled by the appropriate bureau in the United States Department of Agriculture, by its parallel subcommittee (for example, the Subcommittee on Livestock, Dairy, and Poultry), and by the interest being regulated or supported (in this case, livestock, dairy, and poultry interests). Other areas in which iron triangles are found include public works projects and big water projects, particularly in the western states, where subcommittees in the Department of the Interior committee are committed to **logrolling** (that is, trading commitments to vote on each other's bills) and promoting member interests, usually related to helping local constituents, in their districts.

The iron triangle continues to have a significant influence over the way relationships involved in policy making are depicted in texts on American politics. Given that so much policy is made outside of popular or media scrutiny, this seems sensible. But the problem with this depiction of policy making is that, as Hugh Heclo writes, the "iron triangle concept was not so much wrong as it is disastrously incomplete" (Heclo 1978: 88).

The examples of the types of policies that iron triangles address are largely distributive policies in which costs are dispersed and benefits are concentrated (I discuss these policy types in detail in Chapter 7). In such policies, few "outside" interests meddle in decision-making: bureaus, subcommittees, and

iron triangle
A particular style of sub-government in which there are mutually reinforcing relationships between a regulated interest, the agency charged with regulation, and the congressional subcommittee charged with policy making in that issue area. This way of characterizing policy-making relationships has largely given way to more sophisticated sub-government concepts, such as issue networks.

logrolling
The legislative practice of trading commitments to vote for members' preferred policies.

regulated interests dominate, and the relationships between organizations remain stable. But if we look at the other policy types, we see greater conflict, more peak organization involvement, and greater involvement on the part of committees and whole houses of Congress, rather than individual subcommittees. Due to the controversial nature of some policies, something less closed and secretive than iron triangle styles of sub-government must exist, and the iron triangle concept covers only a small part of policy making.

Even the policies that were characterized by iron triangle politics have become more prone to conflict as new actors and new voices enter and others exit the debate. Congress's assertion of its power in the early 1970s, combined with the decentralization of power in Congress itself, created more conflict between committees and more points of entry to the political and policy processes. Baumgartner and Jones (2009) argue that these multiple points of access allow interest groups to go "venue shopping" in a search for a committee or subcommittee to serve as the most likely forum for their claims. Additional access to the policy process has been afforded through greater government openness, such as through sunshine laws and the **Freedom of Information Act** (see Chapter 2), and through greater sophistication of interest groups in exploiting points of access, such as committee hearings and public comment opportunities for regulations. This is not to say that policy is generally made out in the open; rather, social scientists now believe that policy making in general is not as closed as the old iron triangle model would lead us to believe.

Heclo (1978) also notes that the federal budget and the volume of rule-making activity have substantially increased since 1950. With very large amounts of money and power at stake, politics and policy have become more contentious; the opening of government to greater citizen participation has allowed more groups to weigh in on policy, with an associated increase in conflict, number of veto points, and so forth. Heclo notes that, with greater funding being passed to state and local units of government and greater regulation accompanying these transfers of funds, more of these units of government are operating as lobbyists and serving as interest groups in their own right. All state governments, many city governments, and the key associations that represent governors, legislators, state judges, and local governments have offices in Washington and participate in federal policy making at every stage of the process. At the same time, the devolution of power to local and state governments creates new venues for interest groups to participate in policy making, because state and local governments are again very important decision-making bodies.

Freedom of Information Act
The federal law that allows citizens to gain information about government programs through a specified procedure. This act is often invoked by journalists and researchers when the government is at first unwilling to provide information; it is sometimes but not always successful in compelling the government to provide information. Of course, national security information is often unavailable.

How, then, do we describe policy-making relationships without reverting to the old iron triangle formulation? The term **sub-government** came into use in the late 1960s to describe a **policy network** or **policy subsystem** that was most involved in making policy in a particular policy domain.

Heclo proposes the "**issue network**" as a superior way of depicting sub-government politics. The issue network consists of the various government agencies, committees, groups, and interests that hope to influence an issue. This term is very similar to the idea of policy communities, which were defined earlier, and both communities and "networks are ways of describing subgovernments that are more open to information and to participation than are closed systems like iron triangles." In large and contentious issues such as healthcare reform, the policy community is vast, with hundreds of interest groups plying every member of Congress (not solely key committee members) with ideas to promote their interests.

While these depictions of issue networks and policy communities have proved useful to students of public policy, they do not help us to understand the ebb and flow of policy making over time. Baumgartner and Jones argue that policy making still involves relatively long periods of stasis punctuated by changes in the political equilibrium. Paul Sabatier provides a framework for policy making called the Advocacy Coalition Framework (ACF), which helps us to make some sense of what often look like chaotic issue networks (Sabatier 1993). We return to the ACF in Chapter 10, where we examine current models of public policy.

Finally, on the question of how we conceive of the organization of interests, we can think more broadly about the idea of a **policy regime**. The policy regime idea is particularly well suited to policies where there is no single clear, coherent policy community where people speak the same language, even as they have sufficiently similar goals that suggest that their efforts can or should work together. These "boundary spanning" problems cannot be fully described by traditional notions of policy networks and domains. Policy regime theory borrows from research on international regimes and urban regimes, and recognizes that there is more to a policy subsystem than a series of institutional arrangements. Indeed, while we understand that policy subsystems are not solely about government action—there are many other actors involved—it is understood that thinking about policy regimes moves us far away from institutions as central to policy regimes, and moves us closer to realizing that groups, interests, and ideas are central to thinking about how group politics is organized (Jochim and May 2010).

sub-government
The policy network or subsystem that is most involved in making policy in a particular domain.

policy network/policy subsystem
Another term for issue network.

issue network
A term that describes the relationships between the various actors and interests in a particular policy issue. Hugh Heclo promoted this term because it describes a more open policy-making system that contains more actors and relationships than the older iron triangle concept.

policy regime
A system of policies intended to achieve broad policy goals, such as homeland security. Policy regimes can be more or less coherent in terms of the goals and structure of the policies and of the participants in the process.

Prying Open Policy Networks

While policy scholars now think more in terms of regimes, networks, communities, and coalitions than issue networks, access to policy making is clearly not wide open. For example, in environmental policy, major business interests often dominate smaller groups with limited resources. This is particularly true when an issue is local or when the big national environmental groups, such as the Sierra Club, choose not to engage an issue. In homeland security, major defense contractors tend to dominate other participants in policy making. In healthcare policy, big insurance companies, the pharmaceutical industry, and the American Medical Association tend to dominate the debate.

But policy change is possible, as was evident in the New Deal, the civil rights movement, and the Great Society programs, all periods in which government took on more tasks and protected more groups and interests. Policy changed in the other direction during the Carter, Reagan, and Bush administrations, when more conservative preferences led to attempts to make government smaller. These changes happened because policy networks were forced to open up to other voices and participants. As a result, the nature and composition of advocacy coalitions changed, and new coalitions were created or significantly altered.

Nor are big, sweeping changes that involve great matters of state and ideology the only sorts of policy changes. There are many examples of relatively small, focused movements grabbing attention and adherents nationwide. Civil rights and environmental groups started as relatively small groups in the early twentieth century. These groups grew as concerns about equality and environmental damage became more important to more people. In the past 25 years, groups such as Mothers Against Drunk Driving (MADD) have spawned policy changes. MADD not only advanced the issue of drunk driving to the national agenda, but also succeeded in inducing states to stiffen their penalties for driving while intoxicated (DWI). In a sense, a small social movement was created calling for greater individual responsibility and stricter sanctions against those who do not exercise responsibility.

There are many ways that new and established groups can follow in the footsteps of these historic examples, all of which have one thing in common: they all created opportunities for participation in policy making where such opportunities were inaccessible. There are at least four ways to gain this access.

Exploiting the Decentralization of American Government

By definition, grassroots groups are unlikely to tackle vast federal-level problems. Indeed, James Madison, one of the founders of our Constitution, argued that the constitutional structure was designed to prevent or compartmentalize national movements. In MADD's case, drunken driving was to a large extent a state and local issue that involved establishing and enforcing DWI laws. Tackling the problem at the local level—in this case, California—made the most sense in terms of the early MADD's limited resources and because the founder of the group, whose child was killed by a drunk driver, lived in California. Modern communications media, however, make it easier for new and grassroots groups such as MADD to mobilize, expand issues, and grow in both membership and geographic reach.

Going Public

If government institutions such as congressional committees are closed off to groups promoting change, such groups are likely to appeal to others besides these institutions. Given that, at least theoretically, political power is derived from *our* consent, it is reasonable for groups to appeal to us directly in conjunction with trying to gain status within a policy network or community.

There are many ways groups can "go public." Traditionally, groups have run direct mail campaigns and phone solicitations and have placed ads in major newspapers. If you subscribe to magazines with an identifiable ideological label, you will often get mailings from groups associated with that ideology: those who subscribe to *The Nation*, for example, are more likely to get mail from the American Civil Liberties Union (ACLU) than are readers of the more conservative *National Review*. Large full-page ads run in the *New York Times* and other important journals of news and opinion, both to mobilize people to join a cause such as protesting the World Trade Organization or questioning the importance of global warming, and to influence the key policy makers who read these publications.

An emerging method of going public is the increasing use of the Internet and its possibilities for low-cost communication among group members and potential members. Kevin Hill and John Hughes argue that the Internet allows groups to communicate at considerably lower "transaction costs" than more traditional means of communication: after all, once a group sets up a website, it costs no more for one person or 1,000 or 100,000 to see it. An email message to one member of a group can just as easily be sent to several thousand simultaneously (Hill and Hughes 1998). It is fair to say that the Internet has provided campaigns and causes with important and efficient new tools for mobilizing people and advancing their policy ideas. A recent example of such a group is MoveOn.org, a liberal group that began an email campaign to press Congress to "move on" after the impeachment, but failed conviction, of President Clinton in 1998 and 1999. The group continued as an active mobilizer on the left, and its high watermark may have been its successful efforts to defeat then-Democratic Senator Joseph Lieberman of Connecticut in the 2006 primaries; its influence did not extend to the general election, however, which Lieberman won as an independent. Lieberman continues to caucus, for the most part, with Senate Democrats and MoveOn's later efforts became so controversial that their influence began to wane. But the group still exists, and has served as a model for Internet-based mobilization for liberal and conservative groups alike (Hayes 2008; Moore 2008).

CONCLUSION

Many people find it very hard to understand what the government does and how they can play a role in it. As many public opinion polls have shown, people think that the government is distant, uncaring, hard to understand, and unable to be influenced by individual action. This feeling is understandable—governments *are* large, complicated, and sometimes frustrating institutions. However, to give up on trying to understand government and to fail to participate in its decisions is to abdicate one's rights and, indeed, one's duties as a citizen. Because our government rules us, in John Locke's words, "with the consent of the governed"—that is, with *our* consent—we have a role in overseeing the government. This argument is clearly rooted in a sense of civic obligation, and induces some people to vote, keep up with the news (and not just by watching the TV), and be aware of community concerns. But doing one's civic duty is often less compelling than the desire to do a good job, be a good parent/friend/neighbor/partner, or just relax and avoid the stress that sometimes accompanies current affairs.

A more compelling reason for getting involved in making public policy is that if you and your friends fail to get involved, other people, who may very likely be working contrary to what you perceive to be your interests, may be effective in their work with the opposition. For example, you may find a book in the library that you believe contains racist, sexist, obscene, or antisocial material that is suitable for adult use only. You believe that minors' access to the book should be prohibited. If you and your friends (or political allies) do nothing, it is likely that the book will remain on the shelf. If, however, you and your political allies mobilize to restrict access to adults only, it is likely that this restriction will be imposed. Conversely, if you believe strongly in freedom of thought and information, you might mobilize to counter the actions of those who would restrict access to books.

A cynic would argue that the inequities in power and resources make it impossible to take on interests that would block policy change, and that any effort to promote change would be a waste of time. Policy making is indeed a slow and challenging process, and sometimes groups are disadvantaged and unable to do much to cause change. It is not easy to achieve social change. Indeed, the constitutional structure of the United States is in many ways explicitly designed to promote stability and hinders change (Robertson and Judd 1989). I am *not* suggesting here that policy change is easy, that you or a group that you form or join will see results immediately, or even that your policy preferences will be translated into actual governmental policy. But if a goal is worth achieving, it is worth the hard work and patience needed to achieve it.

American policy history is full of examples in which people decided not to remain on the sidelines. The women's suffrage movement, the civil rights movement, the women's equality movement, and the crackdown on drunk driving are examples of social movements that relied upon the involvement of citizens, not big interest groups with an army of expensive lobbyists.

In recent years, citizens and their attorneys have sued tobacco companies for damages caused by smoking. This success in turn emboldened states to sue the tobacco companies to recover state Medicaid costs incurred by sick smokers. In pursuit of tougher drunk-driving laws, MADD stood its ground against the restaurant, bar, tavern, and beverage interests. Labor unions have fought and won political battles with management. In addition, in perhaps the most important social change in our nation's history, people coalesced to fight institutionalized racism and to secure the rights of African Americans to vote, buy property, and seek and hold employment. Lest you think that all these movements are "liberal" in the popular sense, there are current social movements to press for abortion restrictions or prohibitions, to reduce taxes, to ensure the right to own and legally use firearms, and to introduce moral education and values in the school.

All these struggles are difficult, none have been fully resolved to everyone's satisfaction, and we may not agree on what they are trying to accomplish, but they do yield important changes in policy and in public attitudes. And regardless of whether you agree with the ideologies behind these struggles, these issues are important and worth debating and discussing, if for no other reason than to ensure the continued vitality of our political process. Unfortunately, many people do not participate in these debates, leading to atrophy in our political institutions. This trend will continue at great peril to our social, political, and economic well-being.

Why, if the odds are stacked, as they often seem to be, against the "little people," do people get involved in policy making? Perhaps a main reason is that people sense that they can influence policy, particularly at the local level, by taking a clear and public position on an issue that affects them. Often people have an intense interest in the substance of issues. Many people who care deeply about the environment, for example, feel they have a responsibility to address environmental problems to ensure a better life for future generations. Other people get involved simply because they like to participate in politics and enjoy it the same way other people enjoy sports or hobbies. Most people get involved in the policy process when something happens in their local community that mobilizes them and induces them to care deeply about a particular issue.

Those of us who are intensely interested in politics and policy should not condemn those who fail to meet our standards of passion and fascination with the process. While most people do not follow day-to-day politics, many people can be mobilized to address a particular issue when it is of interest and concern to them. Sometimes their mobilization will dismay you—if you are a liberal, you would rather not see conservatives mobilize to exclude certain books from libraries—but keep in mind that there are plenty of people who will work with your side to attempt to advance your preferred style of policy change.

KEY TERMS

astroturf group

economic/private interest groups

Freedom of Information Act

institutional interest group

interest group

iron triangle

issue network

lobbying

logrolling

mobilization

muckrakers

peak associations/
   peak organizations

policy community

policy domain

policy network/policy subsystem

policy regime

public interest

public interest groups

social media

social movement

sub-government

think tanks

venue shopping

QUESTIONS FOR DISCUSSION, REFLECTION, AND RESEARCH

- Many people have argued that there really isn't any difference between the Democratic and Republican parties—that they stand for basically the same things and that it really doesn't matter which party gains power. Do you agree or disagree? Can you think of ways one would objectively compare the differences between the policy preferences of the two parties? Would the 2008 elections change some people's position on this statement? Do you think the formation of a third party could somehow change the nature of American politics and result in noticeable policy change?

- Consider Madison's view of interest groups in *Federalist 10*. Do you think if James Madison were alive today that he would think that "special interests" have become too powerful in Washington, DC? In what ways would he be concerned? In what ways might he not be too concerned?

- Have you considered working as a lobbyist? If you could be a lobbyist, what would your dream job look like? For whom or for what interest would you lobby? Whom would you lobby? How would you influence the people you want to influence? What would be your goals and your measure of whether you successfully met your goals? Would you have to compromise your beliefs and values to be a lobbyist? Would this matter?

- Can you think of any examples of muckraking journalism today? Is such journalism—or, its modern form, "investigative journalism," very common? Why or why not? Has the advent of the Internet created more or fewer opportunities for muckraking "investigative journalism" or "enterprise journalism?" Has the rise of the Internet and new media reduced traditional journalism's capacity or commitment to investigative journalism? How might this innovation influence public policy making in a different way than was possible when most news was in print newspapers and on traditional broadcast networks?

- From which media outlets do you get your news? Radio? TV? Newspapers? Websites? Which sources among these media do you rely on most? Compare your newsgathering habits to those of your friends and family. How are they similar or different? Do people's choices vary by age or by political ideology? Which medium do you consider the most complete and most trustworthy? Why?

- In what sense are the media not passive actors? How do the media influence public policy? Many members of the news media say that they are just a "mirror" of society and that they simply reflect what happens in society. They would argue that their influence is relatively small. Do you agree or disagree with this position?

- Think of a policy area that might be characterized by an "iron triangle" style of sub-government. Why do you think this is better described as an "iron triangle" than as an "issue network?" Why does Heclo believe that an issue network is a preferable way to describe sub-government politics than the iron triangle model?

- Think of an area of public policy you care a great deal about. Using the various searching tools available at your library, find four or five years' worth of congressional hearings on a subject. Find out who testifies before Congress on these issues. Are you surprised by what you found? Do you think that some voices are over- or under-represented? Why?

- Along the same lines, search news media coverage of issues using LexisNexis or similar databases, or even Google News (provided you read quality sources, not opinion blogs). Whom do journalists quote the most in the stories you found? Are there voices that are left out?

- Search the Internet for interest groups on an issue of importance to you. One way to make sure you get interest groups is to ask Google to search only sites that end in *.org*. For example, if you were interested in endangered species, you would enter into Google this search: *endangered species site: .org*. What do you find? Are there a lot of groups or just a few? Do they seem equally large and powerful or is there some variation in their apparent power and influence? What led you to your conclusions?

- I Googled *think tanks* and found some interesting results. There is a *World Directory of Think Tanks* published by the National Institute for Research Advancement (NIRA) in Japan (www.nira.or.jp/past/). Click on Think Tank Information then NIRA's World Directory of Think Tanks. This page lists think tanks by country. Scroll down the page and click on the list of think tanks in the United States. Are some of the think tanks listed in the United States clearly ideologically based? Are others more politically neutral? How can you tell from reading their websites—if you can tell at all? (A decidedly left-leaning view of think tanks is available at SourceWatch.org, www.disinfopedia.org/wiki.phtml?title=Think_tanks.)

ADDITIONAL READING

On the question of why interest groups form, and why it is that interest groups must form to pursue their interests, the classic text is by Mancur Olson, *The Logic of Collective Action* (Cambridge, MA: Harvard University Press, 1971). The interaction of parties and groups in the policy process is taken up in two books: John C. Green, Daniel J. Coffey, and David B. Cohen, Eds. *The State of the Parties: The Changing Role of Contemporary American Parties.* 7th ed. (Lanham, MD: Rowman & Littlefield, 2014), and Matthew J. Burbank, Ronald J. Hrebenar, and Robert C. Benedict, *Parties, Interest Groups, and Political Campaigns* (Oxford: Oxford University Press, 2011). The question of whether or not one can say that the interest group universe is characterized by pluralism or elitism remains controversial in the social sciences.

There are hundreds, if not thousands, of books on the news media and politics. Many of these books are ideological attacks on the so-called liberal or conservative media. Such analyses are generally not useful for understanding the influence of the media in a scientific and rational way. More useful analyses undertaken by social scientists include Doris A. Graber and Johanna Dunaway, *Mass Media and American Politics*, 9th ed. (Los Angeles, CA, and Washington, DC: CQ Press, 2015); W. Lance Bennett, *News, the Politics of Illusion*, 9th ed. (Boston, MA: Longman); and Timothy E. Cook, *Governing with the News: The News Media as a Political Institution*, 2nd ed. (Chicago, IL: University of Chicago Press, 2005). Recent works on the Internet, politics, and journalism include Eric Boehlert, *Bloggers on the Bus: How the Internet Changed Politics and the Press in 2008* (New York: Free Press, 2009); Natalie Fenton, *New Media, Old News: Journalism and Democracy in the Digital Age* (Thousand Oaks, CA: Sage, 2009); and Philip Meyer, *The Vanishing Newspaper: Saving Journalism in the Information Age*, 2nd ed. (Columbia, MO: University of Missouri Press, 2009).

The literature on the organization of policy subsystems, networks, or sub-governments is quite rich. Among the most influential articles on this question is Hugh Heclo's "Issue Networks and the Executive Establishment," in *The New American Political System*, edited by Anthony King (Washington, DC: American Enterprise Institute, 1978). Paul Sabatier's work on the Advocacy Coalition Framework (ACF) has been particularly influential in our understanding of how policy communities are organized. See, for example, Paul Sabatier and Hank C. Jenkins-Smith, *Policy Change and Learning: An Advocacy Coalition Approach* (Boulder, CO: Westview Press, 1993).

NOTES

1   Data on this election are drawn from the Wake County (NC) Board of Elections, www.wakegov.com/elections/.

2   AARP used to stand for the American Association of Retired Persons, but the organization is simply known now as AARP because it claims to represent the interests of older Americans, whether or not they are retired. For a humorous discussion of this name change, see Fisher (2004).

3   A comprehensive listing of think tanks is available at the University of Michigan's website, www.lib.umich.edu/govdocs/psthink.html.

4   Found at www.pulitzer.org/bycat/Public-Service.

REFERENCES

Alger, Dean E. 1996. *The Media and Politics*. 2nd ed. Belmont, CA: Wadsworth.

Annenberg Public Policy Center, University of Pennsylvania. 2004. "Daily Show Viewers Knowledgeable About Presidential Campaign, National Annenberg Election Survey Shows." Accessed January 16, 2015. www.annenbergpublicpolicycenter.org/downloads/political_com munication/naes/2004_03_late-night-knowledge-2_9-21_pr.pdf.

Barrett, Barbara. 2009. "North Carolina Companies Spend Big to Influence Health Bill." Accessed January 15, 2015. www.mcclatchydc.com/2009/07/29/72683/north-carolina-companies-spend. html.

Baumgartner, Frank and Bryan D. Jones. 2009. *Agendas and Instability in American Politics*. 2nd ed. Chicago, IL: University of Chicago Press.

Bennett, W. Lance. 2012. *News: The Politics of Illusion*. 9th ed. Boston, MA: Longman.

Bernstein, Carl and Bob Woodward. 1999. *All the President's Men*. New York: Simon & Schuster.

Burbank, Matthew J., Ronald J. Hrebenar, and Robert C. Benedict. 2011. *Parties, Interest Groups, and Political Campaigns*. Oxford: Oxford University Press.

Center for Information and Research on Civic Learning and Engagement. 2006. "The 2006 Civic and Political Health of the Nation: A Detailed Look at How Youth Participate in Politics and Communities." Accessed January 15, 2015. www.civicyouth.org/PopUps/2006_CPHS_ Report_update.pdf.

Chesney, James and Otto Feinstein. 1993. "Making Political Activity a Requirement in Introductory Political Science Courses." *PS: Political Science and Politics* 26(3): 535–538.

Cobb, Roger W. and Charles D. Elder. 1983. *Participation in American Politics: The Dynamics of Agenda-Building*. 2nd ed. Baltimore, MD: Johns Hopkins University Press.

Cook, Timothy E. 2005. *Governing with the News: The News Media as a Political Institution*. 2nd ed. Chicago, IL: University of Chicago Press.

Crouse, Tim. 1973. *The Boys on the Bus*. New York: Random House.

Eldersveld, Samuel J. 2000. *Political Parties in American Society*. 2nd ed. Boston, MA: Bedford, St. Martin's.

Fiorina, Morris P. 1989. *Congress: Keystone of the Washington Establishment*, 2nd ed. New Haven, CT: Yale Unversity Press.

Fisher, Jennifer. 2004. "Becoming a 'Classic'; Everything Old Needs to Be Renamed." *Pittsburgh Post-Gazette*, August 17, B2.

Glaeser, Edward L. and Jesse M. Shapiro. 2002. *The Benefits of the Home Mortgage Interest Deduction*. Cambridge, MA: National Bureau of Economic Research. Accessed May 1, 2015. www.nber. org/papers/w9284.

Graber, Doris A. and Johanna Dunaway. 2015. *Mass Media and American Politics*. 9th ed. Los Angeles, CA, and Washington, DC: CQ Press.

Green, John C., Daniel J. Coffey, and David B. Cohen. 2014. *The State of the Parties: The Changing Role of Contemporary American Parties*. 7th ed. Lanham, MD: Rowman & Littlefield.

Hayes, Christopher. 2008. "Moveon.Org Is Not as Radical as Conservatives Think." *The Nation*, July 16. Accessed January 16, 2015. www.thenation.com/doc/20080804/hayes.

Heclo, Hugh. 1978. "Issue Networks and the Executive Establishment." In *The New American Political System*, edited by Anthony King, 87–124. Washington, DC: American Enterprise Institute.

Hill, Kevin A. and John E. Hughes. 1998. *Cyberpolitics: Citizen Participation in the Age of the Internet.* Lanham, MD: Rowman & Littlefield.

Howlett, Michael, M. Ramesh, and Anthony Perl. 2009. *Studying Public Policy: Policy Cycles & Policy Subsystems.* 3rd ed. New York: Oxford University Press.

Jochim, Ashley E. and Peter J. May. 2010. "Beyond Subsystems: Policy Regimes and Governance." *Policy Studies Journal* 38(2): 303–327. doi: 10.1111/j.1541-0072.2010.00363.x.

Kamenetz, Anya. 2009. "Will NPR Save the News?" *Fast Company*, March 18.

Kingdon, John W. 2011. *Agendas, Alternatives, and Public Policies.* Updated 2nd ed. Longman Classics in Political Science. Boston, MA: Longman.

Laumann, Edward O. and David Knoke. 1987. *The Organizational State: Social Choice in National Policy Domains.* Madison, WI: University of Wisconsin Press.

Lowi, Theodore. 1979. *The End of Liberalism: The Second Republic of the United States.* 2nd ed. New York: W.W. Norton.

McFarland, Andrew. 1987. "Interest Groups and Theories of Power in America." *British Journal of Political Science* 17(2): 129–147.

May, Peter J., Ashley E. Jochim, and Joshua Sapotichne. 2011. "Constructing Homeland Security: An Anemic Policy Regime." *Policy Studies Journal* 39(2): 285–307.

Mifflin, Lawrie. 1998. "An ABC News Reporter Tests the Boundaries of Investigating Disney and Finds Them." *New York Times*, Ocboter 19, 8C.

Moore, Art. 2008. "'Conservative Moveon.Org' Targets Hillary Case." *World Net Daily*, January 14. Accessed January 16, 2015. www.wnd.com/2008/01/45528/.

Olson, Mancur. 1971. *The Logic of Collective Action.* Cambridge, MA: Harvard University Press.

Pralle, Sarah B. 2003. "Venue Shopping, Political Strategy, and Policy Change: The Internationalization of Canadian Forest Advocacy." *Journal of Public Policy* 23(3): 233–260.

Pralle, Sarah Beth. 2006. *Branching out, Digging In: Environmental Advocacy and Agenda Setting.* American Governance and Public Policy Series. Washington, DC: Georgetown University Press.

Robertson, David B. and Dennis R. Judd. 1989. *The Development of American Public Policy: The Structure of Policy Restraint.* Glenview, IL: Scott, Foresman & Company.

Rosenberg, Randall. 2008. *The Hollow Hope*, 2nd ed. Chicago, IL: University of Chicago Press.

Sabatier, Paul A. 1993. "Policy Change over a Decade or More." In *Policy Change and Learning: An Advocacy Coalition Approach*, edited by Paul A. Sabatier and Hank C. Jenkins-Smith. Boulder, CO: Westview.

Savage, Charlie. 2014. "Obama to Call for End to N.S.A.'s Bulk Data Collection." *New York Times*, March 24. Accessed January 10, 2015. www.nytimes.com/2014/03/25/us/obama-to-seek-nsa-curb-on-call-data.html?_r=0.

Schachter, Hindy Lauer. 1997. *Reinventing Government or Reinventing Ourselves: The Role of Citizen Owners in Making a Better Government.* Albany, NY: State University of New York Press.

Schattschneider, E.E. 1975. *The Semisovereign People.* Hinsdale, IL: The Dryden Press.

Smillie, Dirk. 2009. "Murdoch Wants a Google Rebellion." *Forbes.com*, April 3.

The Fog of Ethics in Albany. 2009. *New York Times*, October 27, 2009. Accessed January 15, 2015. www.nytimes.com/2009/10/28/opinion/28wed1.html.

Timid Media Giants. 1995. *Phoenix Gazette*, December 9, B6.

Zukin, Cliff, Scott Keeter, Molly Andolina, Krista Jenkins, and Michael X. Delli Carpinin. 2006. *A New Engagement? Political Participation, Civic Life, and the Changing American Citizen.* Oxford and New York: Oxford University Press.

CHAPTER 6

Agenda Setting, Power, and Interest Groups

OVERVIEW

In *The Semisovereign People*, E.E. Schattschneider (1975: 66) asserts that "the definition of the alternatives is the supreme instrument of power." The definition of alternative issues, problems, and solutions is crucial, because it establishes which issues, problems, and solutions will gain the attention of the public and decision-makers and which, in turn, are most likely to gain broader attention. This chapter considers the processes by which groups work to elevate their issues on the **agenda** while denying other issues a place on the agenda. The discussion begins with the **agenda-setting** process and then turns to a review of current thinking about political power in the context of public policy making.

Readers who value broad-based participation in politics and policy making—that is, those who believe that American politics is characterized by **pluralism**—may find this discussion of political power dispiriting, as much of the current literature on political power and interest groups adopts the **elite theory** perspective. Elite theory suggests that relatively few people in key positions in government, industry, academe, the media, and other institutions control a disproportionate share of the nation's economic and political resources. In the discussion that follows, you will see distinct echoes of this way of thinking. At the same time, you will learn that policy elites

agenda The list of things being discussed and sometimes acted upon by an institution, the news media, or the public at large.

agenda setting
The process by which problems and alternative solutions gain or lose public and elite attention, or the activities of various actors and groups that cause issues to gain greater attention or prevent them from gaining attention.

pluralism
In group theories of politics, the theory, assumption, or belief that there are many groups that compete with each other in a reasonably open political system and that policy results from this group competition. Contrast with elite theory.

elite theory
In studies of groups and politics, the theory or belief that policy making is dominated by the best-educated, wealthiest, and most powerful elites. This position is most closely associated with sociologist C. Wright Mills. Contrast with pluralism.

do not all think alike or move in lockstep with each other to promote a unified "agenda." Also, these elites are not static. As discussed in earlier chapters and as noted here, while the American system of government and politics often favors more powerful and more focused economic interests over less powerful, more diffuse interests, often the less powerful interests—or, as I sometimes call them, disadvantaged interests—can coalesce and, when the time is right, find avenues for the promotion of their ideas.

Before we turn to this discussion, let us consider how issues reach public attention in the first place: that is, how they reach the agenda.

AGENDA SETTING

Agenda setting is the process by which problems and alternative solutions gain or lose public and elite attention. Group competition to set the agenda is fierce because no society, political system, official actor, unofficial actor, or individual person has the capacity to address all possible alternatives to all possible problems that arise at any one time (Hilgartner and Bosk 1988: 53–78). Groups must promote their issues' places among all the other issues sharing the limited space on the agenda, or to prepare for the time when a crisis makes their issue more likely to occupy a more prominent space. Even when an issue gains attention, groups must fight to ensure that *their* depiction of the issue remains in the forefront and that their preferred approaches to the problem are those that are most actively considered. They do so for the very reasons cited by Schattschneider (1975): the group that successfully describes a problem will also be the one that defines the solutions to it, thereby prevailing in the policy debate. At the same time, groups fight to keep issues off the agenda (Cobb and Ross 1997).

At this point, it is very important to understand what I mean by the term "agenda." The term has morphed, in recent political discourse, as a way to promote fear and divisiveness over another group's goals in the policy process. Merriam-Webster's online dictionary provides two definitions of the word "agenda":

1: a list or outline of things to be considered or done <*agendas* of faculty meetings>

2: an underlying often ideological plan or program <a political *agenda*>

The *Oxford English Dictionary* provides a similar second definition: "A campaign, programme, or plan of action arising from underlying principles, motivations, etc. Hence: the set of underlying motives or ideals of a particular individual or group." The term has come to take on sinister overtones about "hidden agendas," which many people associate with conspiracies or, at least, unclear motives. Of course, a group's overt agenda—that is, the implicit or explicit list of things it would like to accomplish—can be used to attack that group. A common contemporary version of this usage is in discussions of lesbian, gay, bisexual, and transgendered (LGBT) groups' efforts to achieve certain civil rights such as marriage and the ability to adopt children, or to be protected from hate crimes. Their opponents—particularly among political conservatives—use the phrase "gay agenda" to describe what they believe are these groups' efforts to promote their ideas. This terminology is equally applied to left- and right-wing groups, but it is testament to Americans' continued beliefs in political conspiracies, shadowy plots, and unclear group motivations, as famously noted by Richard Hofstadter (Hofstadter 1996). These types of arguments resonate well in a culture that, since the founding, has valued organized group action as an important part of pluralism, while also bemoaning the power of certain groups.

To help you understand groups, power, and agenda setting, I begin with a brief discussion of the idea of political power, since one of its main uses is to keep ideas and issues on or off the public agenda. I then describe how the debate over issues begins with whether something is a *problem*, about which something can be done, or a condition, about which little can be done. I then turn to a discussion of the levels of the agenda and how groups use their power to influence agenda items by advancing alternative social constructions of problems.

Central to understanding agenda setting is the meaning of the term "agenda" as it is meant in the social sciences. An agenda is a collection of problems: understandings of causes, symbols, solutions, and other elements of public problems that come to the attention of members of the public and their governmental officials. An agenda can be something as concrete as a list of bills that are before a legislature or a series of beliefs about the existence and magnitude of problems and how they should be addressed by government, by the private sector, by nonprofit organizations, or through joint action by some or all of these institutions.

Agendas exist at all levels of government. Every community and every government entity—Congress, state legislature, county commission—has a

enactment
The act of putting a decision, such as legislation or regulation, into effect. Statute laws are generally enacted in the United States when the president or a state governor signs a bill presented by the legislature or when a legislature or Congress overrides a governor or president's veto.

systemic agenda
Any issue, problem or idea that could possibly be considered by participants in the policy process, provided that the idea does not fall outside well-established social, political, ideological, and legal norms.

agenda universe
The list of all the possible ideas that could ever be advanced in any society. Compare to the systemic agenda.

collection of issues that are available for discussion and disposition. All these issues can be categorized based on the extent to which an institution is prepared to make an ultimate decision to enact and implement or to reject particular policies. Furthest from **enactment** are issues and ideas contained in the **systemic agenda**, which contains any idea that could possibly be considered by participants in the policy process. Some ideas fail to reach this agenda because they are politically far beyond the pale in a particular society; government ownership of big businesses is, for example, generally off the systemic agenda in the United States because it is contrary to existing ideological commitments. Of course, recent experience with government assistance to General Motors, big banks, and major insurance companies shows how a major crisis can change the boundaries between what is and what is not an acceptable government undertaking.

It is important to think of several levels of the agenda, as shown in Figure 6.1. The "largest" level of the agenda is the **agenda universe**, which contains all ideas that could possibly be brought up and discussed in a society or a political system. In a democracy, we can think of all the possible ideas as being quite unconstrained, although, even in democracies, the expression of some ideas is officially or unofficially constrained. In the United States, aggressively racist and sexist language is usually not tolerated in reasoned public discourse, even if it is protected, to some extent, by the Constitution. In Germany, it is illegal to write in praise of Nazism or to deny that the Holocaust happened, and Canada has laws prohibiting hate speech and expression that would probably conflict with the First Amendment of the U.S. Constitution. Ideas such as the establishment of aggressively racist, fascist, or communist policies are so far out of bounds of politically appropriate discourse that they rarely are expressed beyond a fringe group of adherents. Indeed, policy ideas are sometimes labeled as "socialist" or "fascist" to place these ideas outside the realm of acceptable discussion. For example, healthcare reforms that would involve an increase in government activity have long been dismissed as "socialized medicine," with the threat of "socialism" used to derail the idea. This often is an effective rhetorical technique because the very idea of socialism has such a negative connotation in the United States, but carries no such connotation in other countries. Many ideas in the agenda universe, however, are more or less "acceptable" in a political sense, and may come and go on the systemic agenda. President Obama's healthcare reforms have, for example, advanced on the agenda,

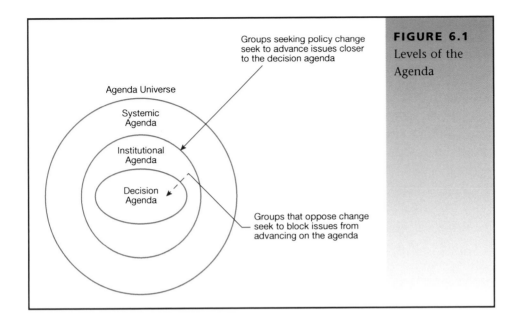

Groups seeking policy change seek to advance issues closer to the decision agenda

FIGURE 6.1
Levels of the Agenda

Agenda Universe

Systemic Agenda

Institutional Agenda

Decision Agenda

Groups that oppose change seek to block issues from advancing on the agenda

although not in the form first proposed, because some ideas were politically acceptable and others were not.

Cobb and Elder say that "the systemic agenda consists of all issues that are commonly perceived by members of the political community as meriting public attention and as involving matters within the legitimate jurisdiction of existing governmental authority." The boundary between the systemic agenda and the agenda universe represents the limit of "legitimate jurisdiction of existing governmental authority" (Cobb and Elder 1983: 85). That boundary can move in or out to accommodate more or fewer ideas over time. For example, ideas to establish programs to alleviate economic suffering have waxed and waned on the agenda when the national mood is more expansive toward the poor, as it was during the 1960s, or less compassionate, as during the 1990s. The boundary shifted in 2008 and 2009 as government intervened in the economy, as healthcare reform became more likely, and as the U.S. military's own leadership began to suggest that allowing openly homosexual people to serve in the military would not harm the armed services.

If a problem or idea is successfully elevated from the systemic agenda, it moves to the **institutional agenda**, which is "that list of items explicitly up for the active and serious consideration of authoritative decision makers" (Cobb and Elder 1983: 85–86). The limited amount of time or resources

institutional agenda The list of issues that is being currently considered by a governmental institution, such as an agency, legislature, or court.

available to any institution or society means that only a limited number of issues are likely to reach the institutional agenda (Hilgartner and Bosk 1988; O'Toole 1989). However, we have learned over the past several years that institutions can increase their "carrying capacity" and can address more issues simultaneously, either when there are many pressing issues, or when resources or technology are available to manage this increased load. Even with this increased carrying capacity, however, relatively few issues will reach the decision agenda, which contains items that are about to be acted upon by a governmental body. Bills, once they are introduced and heard in committee, are relatively low on the decision agenda until they are reported to the whole body for a vote.

decision agenda
The agenda that contains items that are about to be acted upon by a governmental body, such as bills, court cases, or regulations.

Notices of proposed rule-making in the *Federal Register* are evidence of an issue or problem's elevation to the **decision agenda** in the executive branch. Conflict may be greatest at this stage, because when a decision is reached at a particular level of government, it may trigger conflict that expands to another or higher level of government. Conflict continues and may expand; this expansion of conflict is often a key goal of many interest groups. The goal of most contending parties in the policy process is to move policies from the systemic agenda to the institutional agenda, or to prevent issues from reaching the institutional agenda.

Figure 6.1 implies that, except for the agenda universe, the agenda, and each level within it, is finite, and no society or political system can address all possible alternatives to all possible problems that arise at any time. Even though we can use resources and technologies to increase the agenda-carrying capacities of some institutions, ultimately there will still be substantial competition for what will inevitably be limited agenda space.

It is also important to understand that, even when a problem is on the agenda, there may be a considerable controversy and competition over how to define the problem, including the causes and the policies that would most likely solve it. For example, after the 1999 Columbine High School shootings, the issue of school violence quickly rose to national prominence, to a much greater extent than it had after other incidents of school violence. So school violence was on the agenda: the real competition then became among depictions of school violence as a result of, among other things, lax parenting, easy access to guns, or the influence of popular culture (TV, movies, video games) on high school students. This competition over *why* the Columbine shootings happened and what could be done to prevent future school shootings was quite fierce, more so than the competition between school violence and the other issues vying for attention at the time (see Lawrence and Birkland 2004; Birkland and Lawrence 2009).

CASE STUDY: THE SEPTEMBER 11 ATTACKS AS A FOCUSING EVENT

While it may be obvious that the September 11 attacks were major events, it is important to understand how large an influence they had on the media and congressional agendas with regard to terrorism. This case study considers the nature of agenda expansion in the mass media, using the *New York Times* as a measure of the media agenda. I use the *Times* because it is considered one of the best newspapers in the nation and because it is so large and influential. It is sometimes called the "newspaper of record" for the United States. It is read by most key decision-makers in government and business, and influences the agenda of other news outlets.

Figure 6.2 shows the relative coverage of the concept of "terrorism" in the *Times* by year from 1990 through 2002. The stories are categorized by the "desk" from which they originated—national, metro, or foreign—which helps us determine whether the *Times* treated the story as a metropolitan, national, or world news issue or problem. The index is set so that the mean number of stories per desk per year from 1990 to 2000 equals 100. This allows comparisons across desks that would be more difficult to see if we just counted up the number of stories generated every year. The data were gathered from the LexisNexis database.

There were at least three incidents between 1990 and 2001 that may have been terrorist-related: the first bombing of the World Trade Center, the 1995 Oklahoma City federal building bombing, and the unsolved Olympic Park bombing in Atlanta during the 1996 Olympics. But none of these events triggered the extent of coverage by the *Times* that the September 11 events did. Clearly, the September 11 attacks "brought home" the issue of terrorism. Terrorism became a domestic problem rather than primarily an overseas issue. Foreign news on terrorism also increased due to the extensive coverage of foreign reaction to the September 11 attacks and the escalation of violence in the Middle East.

While Figure 6.2 shows the dramatic effect of the event on the national news agenda, it also shows that news coverage of the September 11 events followed a typical trend. In general, the news media aggressively covers an issue for a short time and then coverage fades as the event recedes into the past and as political institutions decide whether or not to act in substantive or symbolic ways. However, one cannot say that news coverage of terrorism has returned to pre-September 11 levels. Through 2002, there was more coverage of terrorism across all the *Times'* various desks than in any year other than 2001.

FIGURE 6.2
News Coverage of Terrorism, by *New York Times* "Desk," 1990–2002

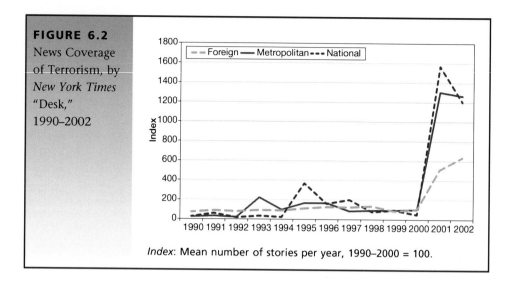

Index: Mean number of stories per year, 1990–2000 = 100.

PHOTO 6.1
The National September 11 Memorial.

Source: Corbis Images. Used with permission.

This trend continued in 2003. While I do not show the data here, preliminary analysis of more recent data shows that this trend has continued, with September 11 being the most extensively covered terrorist attack in United States, and perhaps world, history.

Like the news media, Congress has paid a great deal of attention to the attacks, but the expansion of the agenda was not as great as the media's attention to the issue. This reveals important differences between the news media and Congress. Figure 6.3 shows a significant increase in news coverage of terrorism in the two weeks after September 11, followed by a substantial drop off in coverage after that first two-week period, although not to relatively low pre-2001 figures. News coverage of terrorism as a national issue remained high, but it never returned to the levels reached in the first two weeks after September 11. Congress, on the other hand, saw its terrorism agenda expand continuously in the six weeks following September 11, and the prominence of the issue actually peaked on the agenda in March 2002, about six months after the event. Congress, as a decision-making body, cannot simply take note of an issue and then, in the manner of the news media, tackle the "next big thing." Congress is a deliberative body by design and moves slower than the media, but in many ways it is more purposive in its actions.

This case study illustrates how a large, shocking event can rapidly change the nature of the agenda, but it also shows that, in some ways, Congress is more attentive to issues over a longer period than the news media, which is more interested in the episodic nature of big events.

Are there other events in American history that you think had such a profound influence on the agenda in so little time? Are there events of similar magnitude that did not

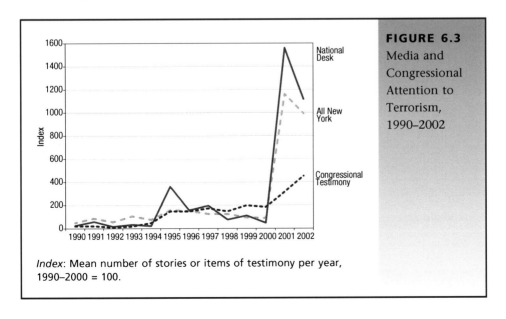

FIGURE 6.3
Media and Congressional Attention to Terrorism, 1990–2002

Index: Mean number of stories or items of testimony per year, 1990–2000 = 100.

influence the agenda? Why not? How would you gather data and track the issue in a way similar to what you see here?

THE IDEA OF POLITICAL POWER

The ability of groups—acting singly or, more often, in coalition with other groups—to influence policy is not simply a function of who makes the most technically or rhetorically persuasive argument. We know intuitively that some groups are more powerful than others, in the sense that they are better able to influence the outcomes of policy debates. This argument suggests an elite model of policy making, in which relatively few people make the important decisions affecting public policy. But power is more than this. Social scientists have developed more sophisticated ways of thinking about the sources and uses of power.

When we think of power, we may initially think about how people, governments, and powerful groups in society can compel people to do things, often against their will. In a classic article in the *American Political Science Review*, Peter Bachrach and Morton Baratz (1962) argue that this sort of power—the coercion of one person by another—is one of two faces of power. The other face is the ability to keep a person from doing what he or she wants to do; instead of a coercive power, the second face is a blocking power:

> Of course power is exercised when A participates in the making of decisions that affect B. But power is also exercised when A devotes his energies to creating or reinforcing social and political values and institutional practices that limit the scope of the political process to public consideration of only those issues which are comparatively innocuous to A. To the extent that A succeeds in doing this, B is prevented, for all practical purposes, from bringing to the fore any issues that might in their resolution be seriously detrimental to A's set of preferences.
>
> (Bachrach and Baratz 1962: 952)

In the first face of power, "A participates in the making of decisions that affect B," even if B does not like the decisions or their consequences. This is the classic sort of power that we see in authoritarian regimes, in which the government and its supporters impose policies on its citizens without their input or even approval. In the United States and other democracies, this sort of power exists because there are many groups that have very little power to influence decisions made on their behalf or even against their interests. Prisoners, for example, have little power to influence the conditions of their sentencing and incarceration because they are social "deviants" and therefore find it difficult to mobilize in defense of their very real but socially marginal interests (Schneider and Ingram 1993: 334–348). This is not to say that other people and groups do not speak for prisoners. There are several prison rights organizations in the nation, and concerns about the rate of incarceration of young black men and those who commit nonviolent drug offenses are growing. But the people who speak for people in prison are speaking for this socially deviant population that carries with it a severely negative image.

Here's another example of the first face of power that you may have experienced directly. Adults have a lot of power over children; children, as a matter of law, are generally those under age 18, at least as far as voting is concerned. Most people are not allowed to legally drink until age 21. States have varying ages at which they allow people to marry without parental consent. Why are there all these rules? Because children are not considered able to make adult decisions, because they are too young, have not yet developed key ways of logic and thinking, are potentially impulsive and impressionable, and because adults have an interest in ensuring the welfare and safety of children. Yet, remember your late teen years—did you feel that you needed this sort of "protection?" Many readers of this book may have been working and supporting themselves—and, in some cases, their families—before reaching adulthood. If we accept the paternalistic argument that children are not fully formed adults until about age 18 or 21, why are children in some states tried for serious crimes as adults and put in adult prisons? There are few good answers for this paradox, except to note that children and prisoners are, compared with other categories of people, relatively powerless.

In the second face of power, A *prevents* B's issues and interests from getting on the agenda or becoming policy, even when actor B really *wants* these issues raised. But even issues with some public support may have trouble trying to gain a place on the agenda. Environmentalism, for example, was, until the late 1960s and early 1970s, not a particularly powerful interest, and groups that promoted environmental protection at the time found that their issues rarely made the agenda because industrial interests worked to keep such matters off the agenda, and because the public did not perceive any significant problems. Not until crises such as the environmental damage done by the pesticide DDT, coupled with the writing of authors such as Rachel Carson, in her book *Silent Spring*, was the issue elevated to the point where some attention was paid to it. Even then, one can argue that actor A, representing the business and industrial sector, bent but did not break on environmental issues and is still able to prevent B, the environmental movement, from advancing comprehensive (or "radical," depending on your position) ideas that could have a profound effect on the environment.

The blocking moves of the more powerful interests are not simply a function of A having superior resources to B, although this does play a substantial role. In essence, we should not think of the competition between actor A and actor B as a sporting event on a field, with even rules, between two teams, one vastly more powerful than the other. Rather, the teams' power imbalance is as much a function of the nature and rules of the game as it is a function of the particular attributes of the groups or interests themselves.

E.E. Schattschneider (1975) explains why this is the case:

> All forms of political organization have a bias in favor of the exploitation of some kinds of conflict and the suppression of others because *organization is the mobilization of bias*. Some issues are organized into politics while others are organized out.
>
> (p. 71, emphasis in the original)

In other words, some issues reach the agenda because the bias—that is, the *tendencies* of the political system—allows them to be raised. Other issues do rise on the agenda because they are not, according to the bias of the system, fit for political consideration. There is no political right in America for people to have decent housing, or healthcare, or jobs, because the bias of the American political system is heavily influenced by cultural values of self-reliance; this has led to the United States lagging behind other nations in declaring housing, education, employment, and healthcare as matters of right. This bias is neither static nor God-given, but is continually reinforced by interests that, for whatever reason, oppose broader access to these things as a matter of right. This is not to say that groups oppose jobs, or education, or healthcare—they just seek to avoid elevating these things to the same status as other rights, such as speech or voting, because elevating these issues on the agenda could likely yield policy ideas that run counter to the interests of those who believe in maintaining the status quo, or, at least, believe in slower or different policy change.

Other scholars of political power have conceived of a third face of power, which differs substantially from the second face of power, in that large groups of people who objectively have a claim that they are disadvantaged remain *quiescent*—that is, passive—and fail to *attempt* to exert their influence, however small, on policy making and politics. This is the story John Gaventa (1980) tells in his book *Power and Powerlessness*. Gaventa explains why a community of Appalachian coal miners remained under the repressive power of a British coal-mining company and the local business and social elite. As Herbert G. Reid notes in his review of the book, Gaventa takes on the traditional idea that political participation in Appalachia is low because of the people's own shortcomings, such as low educational attainment and poverty (Reid 1981). Rather, in the third face of power, social relationships and political ideology are structured over the long term in such a way that A, the mining company, remains dominant and B, the miners, cannot conceive of a situation in which they can begin to participate in the decisions that directly affect their lives. When B does begin to "rebel" against the unfair system, the dominant interests can employ their ability to make non-decisions: in essence, they ignore the pressure for change because they can withstand such pressures. In the long run, people may stop fighting as they become and remain alienated from politics; quiescence is the result.

This necessarily brief discussion of the idea of power is merely an overview of what is a very complex and important field of study in political science in general. It is important to us here because an understanding of power helps us understand how groups compete to gain access to the agenda *and* to deny access to groups and interests that would damage their interests.

GROUPS AND POWER IN PUBLIC POLICY

Social constructionist understandings of agenda setting complement E.E. Schattschneider's theories of group mobilization and participation, which rest on his oft-cited contention that issues are more likely to be elevated to agenda status if the scope of conflict is broadened. There are two key ways in which traditionally disadvantaged (losing) groups expand the scope of conflict. First, groups go public with a problem (as noted in Chapter 5) by using **symbols** and images to induce greater media and public sympathy for their cause. For example, in early 2009, groups that opposed a major government bailout of the "Big Three" automakers (Ford ultimately didn't seek federal aid) called

symbol Something that stands for something else, usually for a broader concept. For example, "the flag" often means patriotism; a low or high unemployment rate symbolizes a strong or weak economy.

attention to company executives' use of private jets to fly to Washington—to testify before Congress—as evidence of wastefulness and company mismanagement. Tellingly, the next time the executives testified to Congress, they drove, proving how both sides can use symbols to their benefit. Of course, one might make a business case for using the jets: they are quicker, more secure, possibly safer, and allow executives to use their time more efficiently. But such arguments often fail in the face of successful depictions of things such as corporate jets as symbols of waste or privilege. In other words, the rhetoric prevails over the evidence or logic of an issue or problem.

Second, groups that lose in the first stage of a political conflict can appeal to a higher or different decision-making level, such as when losing parties appeal to state and then federal institutions for an opportunity to be heard, hoping that, in the process, they will attract others to their cause. Conversely, dominant groups work to contain conflict to ensure that it does not spread out of control. The underlying theory of these tendencies dates to Madison's defense, in *Federalist 10*, of the federal system as a mechanism to contain political conflict.

policy monopoly
A term coined by Frank Baumgartner and Bryan Jones to describe a fairly concentrated, closed system of the most important actors in a domain, who dominate or monopolize policy making; this is similar to the idea of the iron triangle.

Schattschneider's theories of issue expansion explain how in-groups retain control over problem definition and the way such problems are suppressed by dominant actors in policy making. These actors form what Baumgartner and Jones (2009) call **policy monopolies**, which attempt to keep problems and underlying policy issues low on the agenda. Policy communities use agreed-upon symbols to construct their visions of problems, causation, and solutions. As long as these images and symbols are maintained throughout society, or remain largely invisible and unquestioned, agenda access for groups that do not share these images is likely to be difficult; change is less likely until the less powerful group's construction of the problem becomes more prevalent. If alternative selection is key to the projection of political power, an important corollary is that powerful groups retain power by working to keep the public and out-groups unaware of underlying problems, alternative constructions of problems, or alternatives to their resolution (Gaventa 1980).

This thinking is a central tenet of elite theory. Many of the arguments made by elite theorists such as C. Wright Mills and E.E. Schattschneider acknowledge the shortcomings of the pluralist approach. As Schattschneider (1975: 35) famously put it, "The flaw in the pluralist heaven is that the heavenly chorus sings with a strong upper-class accent." While an accent is not the same thing as perpetual upper-class or elite domination, it does suggest that the upper classes—the social, political, and economic elites—have power disproportionate to their numbers in society.

Overcoming the Power Deficit: Ways to Induce Policy Change

Baumgartner and Jones argue that when powerful groups lose their control of the agenda, less powerful groups can enter policy debates and gain attention for their issues. This greater attention to the problem area tends to increase negative public attitudes toward the status quo, which can then produce lasting institutional and agenda changes that break up policy monopolies.

There are several ways in which groups can pursue strategies to gain attention for issues, thereby advancing them on the agenda. The first way for less advantaged interest groups to influence policy making relates to Kingdon's streams metaphor for agenda change (Kingdon 2011). "**Windows of opportunity**" for change open when two or more streams—the political, problem, or policy stream—are coupled. In the political stream, electoral change can lead to reform movements that give previously less powerful groups an opportunity to air their concerns. One example is the Great Society programs enacted under President Lyndon Johnson's administration, which sought to attack poverty, poor health, racial discrimination, and urban decline, among other problems. This package of programs was made possible by an aggressively activist president and a large Democratic majority in the Congress, the result of the Democratic landslide of 1964. Similarly, a window of opportunity to roll back government regulation of business opened when President Ronald Reagan was elected in 1980.

Second, changes in our perception of problems also influence the opening of a window of opportunity for policy change. In the 1930s, people began to perceive unemployment and economic privation not simply as a failure of individual initiative, but as a collective economic problem that required governmental solutions under the rubric of the New Deal. Similar thinking is behind the government economic stimulus actions taken in 2008 and 2009. In the 1960s and 1970s, people began to perceive environmental problems, such as dirty air and water and the destruction of wildlife, not as the function of natural processes, but as the result of negative human influences on the ecosystem. And, third, changes in the policy stream can influence the opening of a window of opportunity. In the 1960s, poverty and racism were seen as problems, but were also coupled with new and more effective policies to solve

window of opportunity
Term used in Kingdon's streams metaphor to describe the point in time at which policy change becomes more likely as the various "streams" are joined.

these problems, such as the Civil Rights Acts, the Voting Rights Act, and the War on Poverty.

Lest we think that all this change is in the liberal direction, it is worth noting that other periods of change, notably the Reagan administration, were also characterized by the joining of these streams. These include changes in the political stream (more conservative legislators, growing Republican strength in the South, the advent of the Christian right as a political force), the problem stream (government regulation as cause, not the solution, of economic problems, American weakness in foreign affairs), and the policy stream (ideas for deregulation and smaller government, increased military spending and readiness) that came together during the first two years of the Reagan administration. These factors help explain policies favoring increased military spending, an increase in attention to moral issues, and a decrease in spending on social programs.

In each of these instances, it took group action to press for change. Groups worked to shine the spotlight on issues because, as Baumgartner and Jones (2009) argue, increased attention is usually negative attention to a problem, leading to calls for policy change to address the problems being highlighted. But the simple desire to mobilize is not enough. Groups sometimes need a little help to push issues on the agenda; this help can come from changes in indicators of a problem or focusing events that create rapid attention. And groups often need to join forces to create a more powerful movement than they could create if they acted as individuals.

Indicators, Focusing Events, and Agenda Change

indicator Evidence of a problem, often based on statistics; for example, a decline in the gross domestic product or an increase in the unemployment rate are indicators of economic problems. People can, and do, argue about what indicators mean.

John Kingdon discusses changes in **indicators** and focusing events as two ways in which groups and society learn of problems in the world. Changes in indicators are usually changes in statistics about a problem; if data collected by various agencies and interests indicate that things are getting worse, the issue will gain considerable attention (Kingdon 2011). Examples include changes in unemployment rates, inflation rates, the gross domestic product, wage levels and their growth, pollution levels, crime, student achievement on standardized tests, birth and death rates, and the many other things that sophisticated societies count every year.

These numbers by themselves do not have an influence over which issues gain greater attention and which fall by the wayside. Rather, the changes in indicators need to be interpreted and publicized by interest groups, government agencies, and policy entrepreneurs, who use these numbers to advance their preferred policy ideas. This is not to say that people willfully distort statistics; rather, it means that groups will often selectively use official statistics to suggest that problems exist, while ignoring other indicators that may suggest otherwise.

The most familiar indicators, such as those reflecting the health of the economy, seem to need little interpretation by interest groups or policy entrepreneurs—when unemployment is up and wages lag behind inflation, the argument is less about whether there is an economic problem, but rather what to do about it. But even then, the choice of which indicator to use is crucial and just about any indicator is subject to multiple interpretations. For example, in late 2009, the federal Bureau of Economic Analysis announced that the U.S. GDP had grown by 2.2 percent from the second quarter to the third quarter of 2009. The second quarter showed a change of –0.7 percent over the first quarter—that is, negative growth. So is the third quarter figure good news? Some may argue yes, it is: it's growth, any growth is good, and under the circumstances—the collapse of the housing market, the fiscal crisis, the poor sales of cars—this is a good result. Others, however, may argue that 2.2 percent growth is anemic compared with the usual target of about 3.0 percent GDP growth sustained over a year, and compares poorly with good years over the last decade. In another example, the number of new unemployment payment claims in the United States at the end of December 2009 was less than had been expected. Is this good news? There are still people applying for unemployment benefits, regardless of the number. How many claims are too many? How much or how little growth and job creation can the nation reasonably expect? These are important interpretative questions, and one reason Deborah Stone argues that we can treat numbers as symbols that stand for ideas that require explanation and interpretation.

Focusing events are somewhat different from indicators. Focusing events are sudden, relatively rare events that spark intense media and public attention because of their sheer magnitude, or sometimes because of the harm they reveal. Focusing events thus attract attention to issues that may have been relatively dormant. Examples of focusing events include airplane accidents, industrial accidents such as factory fires or oil spills, large protest rallies or marches, scandals in government, and events that are inherently unusual or that may be usual but have some feature that makes them noteworthy. Peaceful protest marches, for example, are often little noted or remembered, but the outbreak of violence or the threat of violence makes

focusing event
A sudden event that can generate attention to public problems or issues, particularly issues and problems that are actually or potentially harmful.

them more compelling. Earthquakes are also fairly common, but really big earthquakes can make buildings and highways collapse and kill people, at which point the event becomes very important. Terrorist attacks worldwide are very common and are noted but do not dominate the agenda. But the September 11 attacks gained particular attention because of where they happened (New York and Washington), how they happened (flying airplanes into buildings), and the results (the World Trade Center destroyed, thousands killed).

Focusing events can lead groups, government leaders, policy entrepreneurs, the news media, or members of the public to pay attention to new problems or pay greater attention to existing but dormant (in terms of their standing on the agenda) problems, and potentially can lead to a search for solutions in the wake of perceived policy failure. The fact that focusing events occur with little or no warning makes such events important mobilization opportunities for groups that find their issues hard to advance on the agenda. Problems characterized by statistical indicators will gradually wax and wane on the agenda, and their movement on or off the agenda may be promoted or resisted by constant group competition. Sudden events, on the other hand, are associated with "spikes" of intense interest and agenda activity. Interest groups—often relatively powerful groups that seek to keep issues off the agenda—may find it difficult to keep major events off the news and institutional agendas. Groups that seek to advance an issue on the agenda can take advantage of such events to attract greater attention to the problem.

In many cases, the public and the most informed members of the policy community learn of a potential focusing event virtually simultaneously. These events can very rapidly alter mass and elite consciousness of a social problem. I say "virtually" because the most active members of a policy community may learn of an event some hours before the general public. A classic example is the grounding of the *Exxon Valdez* in Alaska in March 1989. This ship ran aground just after midnight in Alaska, or just after 4:00 a.m. on the East Coast. Most people were asleep when the spill occurred, but learned of it through the morning radio or TV news or late morning newspapers. Certain members of the policy community, however, such as key employees of the Exxon Corporation, the local Coast Guard contingent, fishers in south central Alaska, and others with a direct interest in the event, learned of the spill within minutes or hours. Still, the span of time that passed between local and national knowledge—or between elite and mass knowledge—of the spill was far too short for Exxon and its allies to contain news of the spill, which, therefore, suddenly became a very prominent issue on the agenda (see Birkland 1997). The oil spill in the Gulf of Mexico in 2010 shows similar dynamics, with the sudden explosion of the drilling rig signaling some sort of a problem with the rig, or the technology used to drill for oil offshore. However, unlike the *Exxon Valdez* spill, the magnitude of the so-called "BP oil spill" was not well known for days after the explosion, but soon the spill became a major national news story and policy problem. While the immediate news coverage of the spill started fading even before the well was successfully capped, legislative attention had only just begun to increase in mid 2010.

Group Coalescence and Strategies for Change

A major shortcoming of elite theory, and of power theories in general, is that they assume that some—or most—interests simply accept their fate, providing elites little competition for the agenda and for shaping the issues. Related to this is the assumption that the elite is somehow a monolith, single-mindedly marching toward the same goal of upper-class domination of political life. Neither of these assumptions is true. Less advantaged interests in the United States, and indeed the world, often fight against power, often against long odds and at considerable personal risk to the individuals involved. In the United States and most Western democracies, most policy disputes can be entered without the threat or reality of state suppression; this is in marked contrast with countries such as North Korea and Burma, which have created totalitarian regimes that suppress any political expression.

Powerful economic interests often conflict with each other, such as when producers of raw materials such as oil and steel want to raise prices while producers of goods that use these inputs, such as automobile makers, seek to keep raw material costs low. Within industries, vicious battles over markets and public policy can occur, as in the ongoing legal and economic battles between Microsoft and its rivals, or between different types of Internet service providers (ISPs; e.g., cable, DSL, satellite, wireless), and major airlines and discount carriers. These are not merely arguments over business matters— they often go to the heart of key public policy problems. For example, Google now allows people to make free or very inexpensive phone calls via its Google Voice service. It therefore competes with telephone companies. Does this mean that Google is now a telephone company? An ISP? Or something else? It's not an ISP, because Google does not provide Internet access directly, except for a few experimental installations. It's not really a phone company, but it provides phone services. These are real conundrums that will have real implications for phone companies, for companies such as Google and Skype, and for regulators who must figure out how, whether, and to what extent existing regulations cover these new systems and whether new regulation is required. The phone companies would like Google to be regulated as a phone company, to create what interests often call a "level playing field." Google argues that it is not a phone company. The controversy, as of this writing, is not settled (Singel 2009).

We must also keep in mind that many movements that seek policy change are led by people whose socioeconomic condition and background are not vastly different from those of their political opponents. For example, labor union leaders are often well compensated and live near powerful people, not their union members. In this section, we will review how less advantaged interests, led by bright and persistent leaders, can and sometimes do overcome some of their power deficits.

The first thing to recognize about pro-change groups is that they, like more powerful interests, will often coalesce into advocacy coalitions. An advocacy coalition, as noted in Chapter 5, is a coalition of groups that come together based on a shared set of beliefs about a particular issue or problem. These are not necessarily the core beliefs of these groups; rather, Paul Sabatier, the originator of the advocacy coalition framework, argues that groups will coalesce based on their more peripheral beliefs, provided that the coalition will advance their goals in the debate at hand.

Changes in indicators and focusing events may bring the issue to greater mass and policy-maker attention and at the same time may induce groups to form coalitions to promote their common interests. These coalitions can attract greater attention from policy makers and create greater access to the policy-making process, thereby balancing the power of elites. But where should a group begin to seek to influence policy once it has formed a coalition and mobilized its allies and members? Baumgartner and Jones (2009: 31) address this question in their discussion of "venue shopping" in the policy process.

Venue shopping, a term we first encountered in Chapter 5, describes the efforts groups undertake to gain a hearing for their ideas and grievances against existing policy (see Pralle 2003, 2006). By *venue*, we mean a level of government or institution in which the group is likely to gain the most favorable hearing. We can think of venues in institutional terms—legislative, executive, or judicial—or in vertical terms—federal, state, or local government.

The news media are also a venue, and even within a branch of government, there are multiple venues.

Groups can seek to testify before congressional committees and subcommittees where the chair is known to be sympathetic to their position or at least open-minded enough to hear their case. This strategy requires the cooperation of the leadership of the committee or subcommittee, and unsympathetic leaders will often block efforts to include some interests on witness lists. But the many and largely autonomous committees and subcommittees in Congress allow groups to venue shop within Congress itself, thereby increasing the likelihood that an issue can be heard. After a major focusing event, it is particularly hard to exclude aggrieved parties from a congressional hearing. The numerous survivors, and their supporters, who testified before Congress after the widespread failures to properly respond to Hurricane Katrina, made the problem vivid to committee members and contributed, in part, to the large amounts of money appropriated to aid in storm recovery. However, the actual pace of recovery and the speed with which aid funds are being spent are both rather slow, and reflect another aspect of event-driven agenda setting—the speed at which the issues raised by the event recede from the agenda, as public, media, and policy makers' attention wanes, as the appropriation of funds or the enactment of new laws or rules appears to "solve" the problem, and as new problems emerge and crowd the older issues off the agenda. Those older issues may not entirely disappear, but they do fade from attention. It is worth noting, however, that as issues such as the response to Hurricane Katrina recede from media and public attention, they can remain important in the congressional committees that are charged with dealing with the problem.

Groups that cannot gain a hearing in the legislative branch can appeal to executive branch officials. Environmentalists who cannot get a hearing in the House Natural Resources Committee may turn to the Environmental Protection Agency, the Fish and Wildlife Service, the various agencies that compose the Department of the Interior, and other agencies that may be more sympathetic and might be able to use existing legal and regulatory means to advance environmental goals. While an appeal to these agencies may raise some conflict with the legislative branch, this tactic can at least open doors for participation by otherwise excluded groups, particularly if the executive branch sees these groups as allies against policy proposals coming from the legislative branch.

Groups often engage in litigation as a way to get their issues on the agenda, particularly when other access points are closed to the group. A classic example of the litigation strategy involves the civil rights movement, in which black lawyers sued and desegregated law schools, graduate schools, universities, and, ultimately, all schools for blacks. While Gerald Rosenberg, in *The Hollow Hope*, argues that this litigation strategy was not entirely successful, requiring legislation to fully implement policy change, others argue that the legal strategy served as a catalyst for the civil rights movement and that landmark cases such as *Brown v. Board of Education* sparked a movement that resulted in more effective demands for change. Had the civil rights proponents not taken their fight to court, this argument holds, it is less likely that Congress and the president would have taken their claims seriously. On the idea that the courts are constrained in their ability to promote social change, see Rosenberg (2008) (for a critique of this position, see McCann 1992).

NIMBY Acronym for "not in my backyard," the usual local response to the location of unpopular public or private developments ranging from landfills to homeless shelters to wind farms. Planners have coined the term LULU (locally undesirable land use) to describe such facilities.

Groups may seek to change policies at the local or state level before taking an issue to the federal government, because the issue may be easier to advance at the local level or because a grassroots group may find it can fight on an equal footing with a more powerful group. This often happens in **NIMBY** (not in my backyard) cases, such as decisions on where to put group homes, cell phone towers, expanded shopping centers, power plants, and the like. And, of course, groups sometimes must address issues at the state and local level because these governments have the constitutional responsibility for many functions not undertaken by the federal government, such as education or, as became clear in the same-sex marriage issue, the laws governing marriage. In the latter example, it's clear that gay rights groups have adopted a state-by-state or even more local strategy because it does not make sense to seek change at the federal level as the federal government has extremely limited power over marital and family law.

On the other hand, groups may expand conflict to a broader level (i.e., from the local to the state level or from the state to the federal level) when they lose at the local level. E.E. Schattschneider calls this "expanding the scope of conflict." This strategy sometimes works because expanding the scope of conflict often engages the attention of other actors who may step in on the side of the less powerful group. The civil rights movement was in many ways contained in local actions in the South until images of violent crackdowns on civil rights protesters became more prominent on the national news, thereby expanding the issue to a broader and somewhat more sympathetic public. A more recent example of expanding the scope of conflict is found in the healthcare debate, in which the Obama administration sought to mobilize mass publics and to negotiate the cooperation of insurance companies, major industries such as the auto industry who have huge healthcare benefit expenses, and pharmaceutical companies to support a consensus on health reform. This effort was not entirely successful, but recognized the need to broaden the scope of conflict to get as many people involved as possible.

Groups and interests often seek media coverage as a way of expanding the scope of conflict. Media activities can range from holding news conferences to mobilizing thousands of people in protest rallies. These activities are more newsworthy if they address an issue of current concern, such as the gay rights Tea Party protests held in Washington, DC, in the fall of 2009. Indeed, we don't often see mass mobilization and protest over issues such as inadequate earthquake engineering or impending asteroid collisions with the earth, because the number of people directly involved in addressing these problems is small, they have other, much more fruitful avenues for political expression, and because these are broadly viewed as highly technical matters in which public input is neither offered or sought (May 1990).

Finally, gaining a place on the agenda often relies on coalescing with other groups. Many of the great social movements of our time came about when less powerful interests coalesced. The civil rights movement involved a coalition, at various times, with antiwar protestors, labor unions, women's groups, anti-poverty workers, and other groups who shared an interest in racial equality. By coalescing in this way, the voices of all these interests were multiplied. Indeed, the proliferation of interest groups since the 1950s has resulted in greater opportunities for coalition building and has created far greater resources for countervailing power.

Before concluding this discussion, we must recognize that elevating issues on the agenda in hopes of gaining policy change is not always resisted by political elites. Cobb and Elder (1983) argue that when political elites seek change, they also try to mobilize publics to generate mass support for an issue, which supports elite efforts to move issues further up the agenda. This type of effort is known as internal mobilization. Such efforts can constitute either attempts to broaden the influence of existing policy monopolies or attempts by some political elites (such as the president and his staff) to circumvent the policy monopoly established by interest groups, the bureaucracy, and subcommittees (the classic iron triangle model). The president or other key political actors may be able to enhance the focusing power of an event by visiting a disaster or accident scene, thereby giving the event even greater symbolic weight.

THE SOCIAL CONSTRUCTION OF PROBLEMS

Humans and democratic governments are problem-solvers. Many of the social and technological advances made throughout human history were solutions to claimed problems: vaccination is a solution to pandemic disease; the electrical light is a superior solution to gas lights or torches for illumination; and the wheel, the railroad, the telephone, the airplane, and the Internet are solutions to the problems posed by distance.

At the same time, many social problems remain that people believe should be "solved," or at least made better. Poverty, illiteracy, racism, immorality, disease, disaster, crime, and any number of other ills will lead people and groups to press for solutions. Often, these social problems require that governmental action be taken because services required to alleviate public problems that are not or cannot be addressed by private actors are public goods that can primarily be provided by government actors. While in the popular mind, and often in reality, economic and social conservatives stand for limited government activity, these conservatives also believe there are **public goods**, such as regulation of securities markets, road building, national defense, and *public safety*, that are most properly provided by government. It is probably best to define the problem before worrying about whether public or private actors must resolve it. Deciding whether a problem really is a problem at all is an important part of political and policy debate.

Problems can be defined and depicted in many different ways, depending on the goals of the proponent of the particular depiction of a problem and the nature of the problem and the political debate. The process of defining problems and selling a broad population on the definition is called **social construction**. It refers to the ways in which society and the various contending interests within it structure and tell stories about how problems occur. A group that can create and promote the most effective depiction of an issue has an advantage in the battle over what, if anything, will be done about a problem. In *Policy Paradox*, Deborah Stone considers how people present the background of a problem by using symbols, numbers, and stories about causes. Rather than summarize or paraphrase her argument, I will

public goods
Goods that, once provided for one user, are provided for everyone, such as national defense or police services; economists say that public goods are indivisible and nonexclusive, because they cannot be divided into parts for individuals to consume and because one person's use of the good does not deny others the use of the good.

social construction
The process by which issues and problems are defined in society.

highlight issues raised by Stone and other scholars. One of the things that problems create is uncertainty, inequity, and other burdens that some people believe are undesirable. However, many policies that reduce uncertainty for one group or one person create a burden or greater uncertainty or "annoyance" for others. Creating social welfare programs, regulating TV content, or regulating guns creates annoyance and uncertainty for, among others, civil libertarians and gun rights advocates (who are not necessarily one and the same). For some, a "problem" is really just a fact about which nothing can realistically be done; that is, the problem, as unpleasant as it is, is really a condition. People and groups will work very hard to prove that a problem *is* a problem and that a solution can be found. Merely stating a problem is not enough: one must persuade others that the problem is real or that the problem being cited is the *real* problem.

The definition of a problem is an important part of the persuasive process and affects the choice of solutions. Joseph Gusfield (1981) argues that one can look at the drunken driving problem in a number of ways. Most of us tend to look at the drunken driving problem as one of individual responsibility, which presumes that stiffer penalties to punish the responsible party are needed to address the problem. But what if we looked at the problem as one of inadequate transportation? If the United States had better systems of mass transit, it is likely that fewer people would need to drink and drive; they could drink and ride a bus or a train. Or what if the problem is deeply embedded in our culture, one that prizes recreation, relaxation, and even glamour, and links these benefits to relatively easy access to alcohol by adults?

The social construction of a problem is linked to the existing social, political, and ideological structures at the time. Americans still value individual initiative and responsibility, and therefore make drinking and driving at least as much a matter of personal responsibility as of social responsibility. The same values of self-reliance and individual initiative are behind many of our public policies, dealing with free enterprise, welfare, and other economic policies. These values differentiate our culture from other nations' cultures, where the community or the state takes a more important role. In those countries, problems are likely to be constructed differently, and different policies are the result.

Conditions and Problems

Conditions can develop over time into problems, because citizens, doctors, scientists, engineers, and so on are constantly trying to take things that we think of as conditions and turn them into problems that we can realistically try to solve. Until Dr. Jonas Salk and other scientists developed the polio vaccine, millions of children and their parents lived in fear of this crippling disease. Without the polio vaccine, this disease seemed to be a condition about which little could be done. Many communities would quarantine people with polio, and parents often voluntarily kept their kids away from swimming pools, school, camps, and playgrounds to help them avoid contracting polio. These voluntary and involuntary quarantines, and the treatments for those with polio, carried very high social costs, and were not very effective. But polio became a much more tractable problem once the polio vaccine became available. Governments—in particular, public health officials—responded by encouraging or directly providing polio vaccine to children. Today, the polio rate is vastly lower than it was just 60 years ago, and one may argue that the polio problem has been solved, except in the very poor countries where polio remains endemic. Today, the discussion of polio—and of various forms of the flu, chicken pox, measles, mumps, and other similar diseases—revolves more around the safest method of vaccine administration (oral or via injection) than around the disease itself. There is a major controversy surrounding the safety of vaccines; this controversy was rekindled in 2009 with the introduction of vaccines for the so-called H1N1 virus, or "swine" flu. Some celebrities made claims based on faulty science that the administration of these vaccines increases the risk of autism. There is no scientific evidence of such an effect (see Agency Recommends Shot Replace Oral Polio Vaccine 2000; Lifson 2000). In other words, the solution became a problem in its own right, although not as big a problem as the disease.

As technological progress continues, the original problem becomes forgotten, and when the solution to that problem is somehow disrupted, that disruption becomes the problem. Electricity was harnessed in lighting, heating and cooling, and the powering of machinery to overcome the problems posed by darkness, extreme temperatures, or the limits of human muscle power. We have now become a society so dependent on electricity that a major power outage becomes the problem. For everyone who relies on the Internet and cell phones, service interruptions are a major inconvenience. Internet outage affects email, social networking, instant messaging, and a range of other services, all of which were designed to solve some problem (social isolation, expensive communication, or business inefficiencies, to name a few). When problems such as power or Internet outages arise, people often demand government actions to solve them to ensure the lights stay on or that Internet access is not interrupted.

An interruption in electricity, the Internet, or cable TV is a problem that most believe should never happen at all! And lest we believe a power outage is a minor inconvenience with few political repercussions, consider the power outage that struck Auckland, New Zealand, in February 1998 (Lilley 1998). The outage lasted for over *10 days*, closing businesses, forcing evacuations of apartments due to water and sewer failures, and ending up costing New Zealanders millions of dollars. The cause of the outage was the failure of overtaxed power cables; but regardless of the cause, people do not expect or lightly tolerate the loss of something taken for granted for so long. Indeed, the blackouts that struck eight eastern states and two Canadian provinces in August 2003, or the one that struck Brazil and Paraguay in 2009, lasted hours, not days, for most locations, but led to significant social and economic disruption as elevators failed, subways ceased to work, computer systems shut down, and all the modern features on which urban societies rely were unavailable. Most problems are more subtle than sudden blackouts, so people have to be persuaded that something needs to be done; still more persuasion may be necessary to induce a belief that *government* needs to do something about a problem. However, there are often instances, such as in the Gulf of Mexico oil spill in 2010, where the public demands that government do even more than it is empowered to do under existing law.

Symbols

Because policy making is usually a process of political argument and persuasion, groups and individuals promoting particular policy options will work to gain whatever rhetorical advantage they can in these debates. Because a hallmark of successful policy advocacy is the ability to tell a good story, groups will use time-tested rhetorical devices, such as symbols, to advance their arguments.

A symbol is "anything that stands for something else. Its meaning depends on how people interpret it, use it, or respond to it" (Stone 2011: 157). Politics is full of symbols, some perceived as good, others as bad, and still others as controversial. Some symbols are fairly obvious; the American flag, for example, is generally respected and even revered in the United States. However, the American flag is often used outside of the United States to symbolize the alleged abuses and wrongdoings of our nation—thus, the same flag means very different things in different contexts. In most parts of the world, flying a flag bearing the Nazi swastika is considered somewhere between poor taste and an actual violation of the law, because of the extremely troubling connotations of the swastika and the Nazi regime that used it. Before the Nazis took power, the swastika was a relatively obscure religious symbol, and its use as such remains tolerated.

Deborah Stone outlines four types of *stories* that use rhetorical symbols. First, she discusses narrative stories, which are stories told about how things happen, good or bad. They are usually highly simplified and offer the hope that complex problems can be solved with relatively easy solutions. Such stories are staples of the political circuit, where candidates tell stories about wasteful bureaucrats or evil businessmen or lazy welfare cheats to rouse the electorate to elect the candidate, who will impose a straightforward solution to these problems. Stories are told about how things are getting worse, or declining, to use Stone's term, or how things were getting better until something bad happened to stop progress, or how "change-is-only-an-illusion." For example, stories may be told on the campaign trail or the floor of the legislature in which positive economic indicators are acknowledged but are said not to reflect the "real" problems that real people are having. Indeed, this sort of discourse surrounds the economic recovery the United States appears to be enjoying in 2014 and 2015. While some indicators, such as the unemployment rate and gross domestic product, are positive, wages are also stagnant, many people are underemployed considering their skills, and the degree of wealth inequality (described in Chapter 2) is at historic highs. Two different stories therefore emerge about the growth of the economy or its stagnation.

Stories of helplessness and control portray situations in which an issue or problem previously could not be resolved but a solution now exists. These stories are closely related to the condition-versus-problem tension. Helplessness-and-control stories are often cast in us-versus-them terms, such as when interest groups are called *special* interest groups because the term "special" denotes something different about these groups, and perhaps something outside the mainstream. Conspiracy theories are also a major part of these stories, as people seek to make sense of the world around them. Conspiracies include claims of hidden agendas and sinister goals. Recent conspiracy theories in the United States that gained small fringe attention include the belief that Israeli government agencies attacked the World Trade Center to incite anger toward Muslims, or theories that the collapse of buildings 1, 2, and 7 were "controlled" demolitions designed to hide secrets. Anti-vaccine proponents argue that mandatory vaccination exists primarily to enrich the makers of vaccines, or that the risks of such vaccines have been covered up. Proponents of healthcare reform are said to be conspiring to "ration" healthcare, or to grow government because the proponents just want bigger government for its own sake. There are many good reasons to question the assumptions behind healthcare reform and other policy changes, but conspiracy theories usually collapse under the weight of their own illogic and lack of evidence. But they can persuade enough people to create political problems for proponents of policies based on sound science and evidence.

Conspiracy theories are related to the stories and anecdotes people use to describe problems. Thus, the idea of the cheating "welfare queen" took hold in the 1980s, even though such people represented a small and atypical portion of the welfare population; similarly, more recent efforts to require recipients of public assistance (also known as welfare) to submit to drug testing, on the grounds that public assistance shouldn't be spent to buy illegal drugs, were based in anecdotes that poor people were highly likely to abuse drugs. There was little evidence to support this claim.

Related to such anecdotes are "horror stories" of government regulation run amok. Such stories are usually distorted: Stone cites the example of how those opposed to industry regulation claimed that the Occupational Safety and Health Administration (OSHA) "abolished the tooth fairy" by requiring that dentists discard any baby teeth they pulled; the actual regulation merely required that appropriate steps be taken to protect health workers from any diseases that may be transmitted in handling the teeth (Stone 2011: 170). The media stirred up a small controversy by reporting that OSHA was advising companies with homeworkers that they were responsible for the health and safety of telecommuters. The media, elected officials, and business interests raised the specter of OSHA invading every telecommuter's privacy to inspect their workspace; this horror story, coupled with long-standing industry dislike for OSHA and the prior propagation of horror stories, made this a very compelling and disturbing prospect. The truth of the matter was more subtle: OSHA had simply sent a letter to an employer that interpreted its existing rules on workplace safety, stating that the employer does bear some responsibility for homeworkers' safety in home offices. Regardless of this important distinction, OSHA backed away from the letter in the face of media ridicule and political pressure.[1]

You probably have heard or even told these and other horror stories about policies. Television news in particular has made an industry out of telling these horror stories, often failing to place them in their proper context. In the same way, interest groups often neglect to place stories in the proper perspective, as their main goal is to advance their policy preferences. Interest groups will therefore tell stories to gain attention from other members of the policy community and to mobilize support or opposition for a particular policy direction. In all such cases, the "truth" of such claims is contested, at best, but such arguments are part of the rhetorical and argumentative nature of policy making and politics itself.

Causal Stories

causal story
According to Deborah Stone, a narrative depiction of the causes of a public problem; such stories often contain normative statements about both the problem itself and why a particular solution will resolve the things that are said to have caused the problem.

An important part of storytelling in public policy is the telling of **causal stories** (see Stone 1989, 2011). These stories attempt to explain what caused a problem or an outcome. They are important in public policy making because the depiction of the cause of a problem strongly suggests a solution to the problem. Causal stories are similar to the causal theories of problems that are described in Chapter 8; however, in this chapter, we are more concerned with use of these stories in rhetoric and debate than in decision-making. Stone divides causal stories into four categories: mechanical causes, accidental causes, intentional causes, and inadvertent causes (see Table 6.1).

TABLE 6.1 Types of Causal Theories with Examples

Actions	Consequences	
	Intended	*Unintended*
Unguided	MECHANICAL CAUSE • machines that perform as designed, but cause harm • people who act like automatons • rigid bureaucratic routines	ACCIDENTAL CAUSE • natural disasters • fate • bad luck • machines that run amok
Purposeful	INTENTIONAL CAUSE • oppression • conspiracies • harmful side effects that are known but ignored • "bad apples" • blaming the victim ("soft versions")	INADVERTENT CAUSE • unanticipated harmful side effects of policy • avoidable ignorance • carelessness • blaming the victim ("soft versions")

Source: From *Policy Paradox: The Art of Political Decision Making* by Deborah A. Stone. Copyright © 2012 by Deborah A. Stone. Used by permission of W.W. Norton & Company, Inc.

Numbers as Indicators of Problems

Debates and controversies often involve the use of numerical information to make their points. Such numbers include the number of people living in poverty, the average amount of taxes people pay to the government, the number of people killed or hurt by various hazards, and so on. The use of numbers in policy debates is very attractive because numbers appear to have accuracy that anecdotal evidence lacks, particularly when the numbers provide a description of **aggregate data**—that is, when the data reflect a broader phenomenon. Such aggregate data include the unemployment rate, average school test scores, median family income, and the like. Indeed, I have used this sort of data to outline the policy environment in Chapter 2.

aggregate data Data based on the adding up, or aggregation, of smaller data points. For example, data on the average family income in the census is based on smaller data elements gathered then aggregated for analysis.

The use of numbers is particularly interesting, as Stone points out, because deciding to count a phenomenon is a policy decision itself. We collect data about phenomena because we want to know something more about them. We count unemployment, crime, health, education, and other statistics. Once we begin counting, there is considerable pressure to continue counting to see how problems are behaving: we want indicators of good things to go up (the GDP, wages, educational achievement) and bad things to go down (diseases and death, crime, welfare rolls). For each of these things, there is political pressure to make the problem better.

But numbers are not entirely objective measures of a phenomenon and are subject to interpretation. Numbers used in the portrayal of a problem are not always accurate. Statistics on the GDP, unemployment, inflation, and test scores, for example, have often been challenged.

The census, which the Constitution requires be taken every 10 years, is known for undercounting immigrants and minorities, placing cities at a disadvantage in the allocation of federal funds dispersed on the basis of population. On the other hand, statistical methods that might correct this undercount could introduce more error in the census than they would alleviate, or could simply stir up political opposition. Like so many other things we measure, a distinguished panel of statisticians found, ultimately, that the solution to the undercounting problem is less a technical problem than it is a social or political matter (Martin et al. 1984; Choldin 1997; Freedman and Wachter 2001). This is as true today as it was in 2000, for the same reasons: the allocation of a state's seats in the House of Representatives is directly related to census data; with the House capped at 435 members, every state that gains a seat does so at the expense of the state losing a seat.

Educational tests, such as the Scholastic Assessment Test (SAT) and other state tests, have become popular ways of assessing educational performance and are often used to assess whether students are allowed to advance in school or to graduate. Some people have challenged these tests, claiming that they are biased on the basis of race, class, and gender in favor of white males from well-to-do families and that the scores do not accurately reflect the academic potential of everyone who takes the tests (see Leonard and Jiang 1999; Young 2003).[2]

Perhaps the most questionable statistics come from the Uniform Crime Reports (UCR) collected by the U.S. Department of Justice. The UCR compiles reports of crime from police departments nationwide, but the reports include only those crimes about which the police have information. They do not include unreported crimes and some police departments may have an incentive to inflate or underreport crimes. In some cases, when police place special emphasis on particular crimes such as domestic violence, the apparent rate of crime goes up because more crime is reported and known to the police. People may report more of these crimes because they are encouraged to do so by the policy and legal authorities (see Jones 1999; Napolitano 1999; Newman 1999).

Second, even if some measures are reasonably accurate, an important question remains: is the indicator in question the best measure of a phenomenon or of progress toward a goal? For example, the GDP is a measure of all the goods and services produced in the nation. The financial press concentrates a great deal of attention on this figure and when it grows from quarter to quarter or year to year, this is said to be a good thing. Yet the GDP may not be the best measure of the nation's overall well-being. Does the GDP, for example, deduct from the value of some goods the pollution and subsequent environmental damage they cause? Indeed, if there is an environmental disaster or nuclear power plant accident, the money spent to clean the plant, evacuate people living nearby, and treat anyone injured in the accident is included in the GDP. Other things that perhaps we would not want to spend money on, such as lawyers' fees, cancer treatment, and fixing car wrecks, are all counted in the GDP. Thus, economic growth may not equate with the good life, but rather reflects all the things that we spend money on, including the things we might not really want to buy (on the environmentalist take on the GDP as a measure of well-being, see Rowe and Anielski 1999).

Many of you have taken a statistics class or two. While many of us approach such classes with trepidation, the hypothetical example of the use (or abuse) of statistics I am about to illustrate shows how useful some background in statistics can be for your own political self-defense. Being able to find and explain statistical fallacies is a very important skill in our number-driven world.

The choice of the statistic being reported has a big influence on how one is supposed to interpret the underlying idea being conveyed. Take as an example family income. In a 2003 report by the U.S. Census Bureau, the average family income in the United States was $182,381. As a measure of what statisticians call "central tendency," this figure is very misleading; because as we learned in Chapter 2, so much wealth is held by relatively few people in the United States, their income skews the average higher than the two-earner median household income of about $80,000. The median is the number at the exact middle of a range of numbers; for every family below the median, there's one above this figure. One can imagine that if you wanted to argue that American families are doing well, one would report the average; a different result would follow from reporting the median.

For example, let us take King County, Washington, the county in which Microsoft and Amazon.com are headquartered. There are at least three major billionaires in the Seattle area: Microsoft founder Bill Gates, whose wealth was about $45 billion when this example was written; Paul Allen, a cofounder of Microsoft; and Jeff Bezos, founder of Amazon.com, each were worth about $10 billion. These people have much higher family wealth than the "typical" family, so their wealth distorts the average (or, as we say in statistics, the mean) family wealth figure in King County much more than it would distort the median family wealth figure. In statistical terms, these families are called **outliers**—they fall outside the range of the bulk of the data points (see Sanchez 2000). This example shows why we sometimes talk in terms of median figures, such as median family wealth or median home prices: because if we used the mean or average of these figures, the few outliers, such as the really expensive houses or the really well-paid people, would distort the story we are trying to tell with the numbers. But if you were, say, a civic booster, you might use (or abuse) the average value as a way to make an affirmative argument about the overall prosperity of the people in King County, even if this prosperity isn't equally shared. To carry the example to its absurd extreme, let's imagine that there are 100 families in King County. Three of them are the Allen, Gates, and Bezos families, and the other 97 families have wealth

outlier
In statistics, a case (that is, a data point) that falls so far below or above the main cluster of data points that it significantly influences the mean value of all the data. A very large outlier will cause the mean to greatly exceed the median or middle value; a very small outlier will cause the mean to fall far below the median value.

of $100,000 each. The median in this hypothetical county would be $100,000, but the average would be over *$650 million*. The choice of statistic really does matter.

Finally, there are two things you should know about numbers and their depiction in policy debates. First, advocates for policy positions will choose numbers that put their arguments in the best light. This means that the use of numbers is likely to be significantly skewed or distorted for rhetorical advantage. This distortion is most often seen in charts and graphs, which citizens and policy makers must use with extreme caution. Many charts and graphs are deliberately or accidentally misleading, and it is an unfortunate byproduct of modern printing and publishing technology that allows newspapers and magazines (*USA Today* was once notorious for this), as well as anyone with a copy of Microsoft Excel, to print remarkably misleading and distorted statistical graphs that range from difficult to read to purposefully misleading. The advent of the Internet and the ease with which such distorted charts and graphs can be poorly designed means that what Edward Tufte calls "chartjunk" is widespread. Edward Tufte's work on the design of information graphics discusses these problems and will arm you with considerable defenses against chartjunk (see Tufte 1990, 1997, 2001, 2006).

As this section has shown, there is a substantial difference between a number (that is, a data point) and the interpretation of that data. There is an old saying in information management that there is a big difference between data and information: data are just the raw numbers, while information is what we get when we interpret the numbers—and as you know, that information is very much subject to the interpretation of those with a stake in the meaning of that information.

CONCLUSION

The study of agenda setting is a particularly fruitful way to begin to understand how groups, power, and the agenda interact to set the boundaries of political policy debate. To me, the relationship between ideas, the social construction of problems and solutions, the nature of agenda, the groups that are involved in agenda setting and in propagating ideas, and the very idea of power itself is not just a fascinating topic for research. I consider it the pivot point of the policy process. Groups that successfully amass resources, or that find winning rhetorical strategies, often gain power. Indeed, a winning symbol or *causal story* can, as with Mothers Against Drunk Driving, strike a chord that resonates throughout the political system and the policy process, creating pressure for policy change.

We therefore know that agenda setting, like all other stages of the policy process, does not occur in a vacuum. The likelihood that an issue will rise on the agenda is a function of the issue itself, the actors that are involved, institutional relationships, and, often, random social and political factors that can be explained but cannot be replicated or predicted. But we do know enough about groups, power, and agenda setting to know that, as Robertson and Judd describe (summarized in Chapter 3), policy restraint is still an important feature of American policy making. The struggle to shine attention on issues and on particular ways of portraying those issues is a continuing process. Those who understand the ebbs and flows of ideas and power will be better prepared to understand why policies change when they do, and how to participate in campaigns for change.

KEY TERMS

agenda	institutional agenda
agenda setting	NIMBY
agenda universe	outlier
aggregate data	pluralism
causal story	policy monopoly
decision agenda	public goods
elite theory	social construction
enactment	symbol
focusing event	systemic agenda
indicator	window of opportunity

QUESTIONS FOR DISCUSSION, REFLECTION, AND RESEARCH

- How does an elite theory of U.S. power differ from a pluralist theory? In your opinion, which theory better explains power in the United States? What evidence might you use to support your claim?

- Why are issues likely to be elevated on the agenda if the scope of conflict is widened?

- How do you think a policy monopoly would try to keep problems and underlying policy issues high or low on the agenda?

- What are the two major ways in which groups and society as a whole learn about problems? Which of these two ways will lead to the most *rapid* increase of attention to a problem?

- Why do interest groups engage in venue shopping? What are some of the different kinds of venues available to interest groups and other advocates?

- Imagine you belong to an interest group that advocates for the things you care about. In which venues would your group seek to gain attention? Why did you choose your preferred venues?

- How do a condition and a problem differ? Give some examples of each. Can you think of conditions that later became problems as the technologies or knowledge to deal with these conditions became available? Are there any conditions that will never be solvable problems? Can you think of examples of things that we thought were problems and were treated as such, but that later came to be defined as conditions?

- Think about a problem that you care deeply about. Write, in a paragraph or two, a causal story about what causes the problem that you selected. Do you think your causal story will be accepted broadly in our society? Why or why not?

- Assume that the county government plans to build a highly polluting incinerator next to your property. What actions could you take to remedy the situation?

- Choose several issues. Explain how each issue may be socially constructed depending on what political ideology a person has.

- This project may take longer than a semester, but you will find the results very interesting. Join an interest group that deals with issues you care about: for example, if you are an environmentalist, join the

Sierra Club. If you are a shooter or hunter, join the National Rifle Association. When you join, alter your name slightly for just the one group so that you can track the mail you get when these groups share their membership lists with other groups. For example, I go by Thomas A. Birkland but would sign up as Thomas B. Birkland to see how my name is shared. And now that many groups send email instead of "snail mail," you might want to set up a separate email account and/or social media presence to use these identities to join the groups you are interested in.

In several months, you may start to get mail and email from other organizations or groups, some of which you may never have heard of (if you are using email, check your spam filter—much of it will be junk, but you may be getting solicitations from other groups based on your interest in an issue). What kind of groups contacted you? Are they sympathetic to the cause you originally joined? You will likely find that your name is widely shared among other groups with similar interests. From this mail, you may be able to map the contours of the advocacy coalition to which you belong.

- An interesting way to track the importance of an issue is to follow its relative position on the agenda over time. This has been made much easier with the Policy Agendas Project at the University of Texas. At its website (www.policyagendas.org) you can find a number of data sets on congressional hearings, the *New York Times* coverage of issues, executive orders, and the like. These are all coded using a uniform subject code that allows you to compare issues across these different venues. You can download the data and use it in a spreadsheet program such as Microsoft Excel to track the agenda status of various issues. But you can also use the "Data Tools" on the project's site to do live analyses of the project's data without downloading the rather large data sets. Pick an issue you are interested in and track it over time. When does Congress, or the *New York Times*, pay more attention to an issue? For example, when I compared coverage of energy in the *New York Times* to congressional hearing activity on energy, I found that attention was relatively low until attention suddenly peaked in 1975 and again in 1979. Why do you suppose it suddenly jumped like this? Try looking at other issues and see whether they show steady activity or sudden surges or drops in attention.

ADDITIONAL READING

Nearly all discussions of agenda setting in American politics start with E.E. Schattschneider's *The Semisovereign People* (Hinsdale, IL: Dryden Press, 1975), a short, wonderfully clear book that, among other things, describes why agenda setting is so important in American politics. In the policy process, Roger Cobb and Charles Elder, in *Participation in American Politics: The Dynamics of Agenda-Building*, 2nd ed. (Baltimore, MD: Johns Hopkins University Press, 1983), provide one of the earliest and most complete treatments of how agendas are built by groups and interests. Roger Cobb and Marc Howard Ross continue this work in their *Cultural Strategies of Agenda Denial: Avoidance, Attack, and Redefinition* (Lawrence, KS: University Press of Kansas, 1997), in which they describe how groups and interests work to deny other interests access to the agenda. John Kingdon's *Agendas, Alternatives and Public Policies*, updated 2nd ed. (Boston, MA: Longman, 2011) has been particularly influential in understanding how agendas work in the policy process; so much so, in fact, that the first edition was awarded the 1994 Aaron Wildavsky Award for its continued influence on the study of public policy. Astute readers of this chapter will note that my ideas on focusing events, contained in my book *After Disaster: Agenda Setting, Public Policy, and Focusing Events* (Washington, DC: Georgetown University Press, 1997), have their genesis in Kingdon's treatment of the subject.

Such denial of agenda access is part and parcel of political power, and the oft-cited work on this topic is Peter Bachrach and Morton Baratz's "The Two Faces of Power," *American Political Science Review* 56 (1962): 947–952, in which we learn that power involves getting people to do something they don't want to do, as well as preventing them from doing what they want to do. To this formulation, John Gaventa, in *Power and Powerlessness: Quiescence and Rebellion in an Appalachian Valley* (Urbana, IL: University of Illinois Press, 1980), adds a subtle third face of power. Gaventa describes how social relations in Appalachian coal-mining communities were structured so that people at the bottom of the economic and social ladder could not conceive of ways to escape their lot.

Clearly, my thinking about how public problems are socially constructed is directly informed by Deborah Stone's text *Policy Paradox: The Art of Political Decision Making*, 3rd ed. (New York: Norton, 2011). Stone directly confronts the rationalist approach to policy analysis—she calls this the "rationality project"—by comparing rationalist notions of society (often derived from economics) as a market with a more politically and sociologically useful idea of society as the "polis." She illustrates why there are so many paradoxes in politics and policy making that cannot be "rationally" explained by "decisionist" models of policy analysis. Stone's book has the added benefit of being fascinating reading. However, it is important to ensure that you understand some of the standard policy analysis texts and techniques that contrast with Stone's approach to policy studies. These include Edith Stokey and Richard Zeckhauser, *A Primer for Policy Analysis* (New York: W.W. Norton, 1978), and David L. Weimer and Aidan R. Vining, *Policy Analysis: Concepts and Practice*, 5th ed. (Boston, MA: Longman, 2011). These concepts are also taken up in Chapter 8.

NOTES

1   See, for example, "OSHA Won't Hold Companies Responsible for Safety of Home-Offices," *Google News*, January 29, 2000, http://news.google.com/newspapers?nid=875&dat=20000129&id=qllIAAAAIBAJ&sjid=xE0DAAAAIBAJ&pg=6559,3311821; "Red-Faced OSHA Drops Rules for Home Workers," *Human Events*, January 14, 2000, 4.
2   An interest group called Fairtest has developed around this issue. See its website at www.fairtest.org.

REFERENCES

Agency Recommends Shot Replace Oral Polio Vaccine. 2000. *Indianapolis Star*, January 21, A9.
Bachrach, Peter and Morton Baratz. 1962. "The Two Faces of Power." *American Political Science Review* 56: 947–952.
Baumgartner, Frank and Bryan D. Jones. 2009. *Agendas and Instability in American Politics*. 2nd ed. Chicago, IL: University of Chicago Press.
Birkland, Thomas. 1997. *After Disaster: Agenda Setting, Public Policy, and Focusing Events*. Washington, DC: Georgetown University Press.
Birkland, Thomas A. and Regina G. Lawrence. 2009. "Media Framing and Policy Change after Columbine." *American Behavioral Scientist* 52(10): 1405–1425. doi: 10.1177/0002764209332555.
Choldin, Harvey M. 1997. "How Sampling Will Help Defeat the Undercount." *Society* 34(3): 27–30.
Cobb, Roger W. and Charles D. Elder. 1983. *Participation in American Politics: The Dynamics of Agenda-Building*. 2nd ed. Baltimore, MD: Johns Hopkins University Press.

Cobb, Roger W. and Marc Howard Ross. 1997. *Cultural Strategies of Agenda Denial: Avoidance, Attack, and Redefinition.* Lawrence, KS: University Press of Kansas.

Freedman, David A. and Kenneth W. Wachter. 2001. "Census Adjustment: Statistical Promise or Illusion." *Society* 39(1): 26–33.

Gaventa, John. 1980. *Power and Powerlessness: Quiescence and Rebellion in an Appalachian Valley.* Urbana, IL: University of Illinois Press.

Gusfield, Joseph. 1981. *The Culture of Public Problems: Drinking Driving and the Symbolic Order.* Chicago, IL: University of Chicago Press.

Hilgartner, James and Charles Bosk. 1988. "The Rise and Fall of Social Problems: A Public Arenas Model." *American Journal of Sociology* 94(1): 53–78.

Hofstadter, Richard. 1996. *The Paranoid Style in American Politics, and Other Essays.* Cambridge, MA: Harvard University Press.

Jones, Adella. 1999. "Letter to the Editor." *St. Louis Post-Dispatch*, June 14, D14.

Kingdon, John W. 2011. *Agendas, Alternatives, and Public Policies.* Updated 2nd ed. Longman Classics in Political Science. Boston, MA: Longman.

Lawrence, R.G. and T.A. Birkland. 2004. "Guns, Hollywood, and School Safety: Defining the School-Shooting Problem across Public Arenas." *Social Science Quarterly* 85(5): 1193–1207. doi: 10.1111/j.0038-4941.2004.00271.x.

Leonard, David K. and Jiming Jiang. 1999. "Gender Bias and the College Predictions of the Sats: A Cry of Despair." *Research in Higher Education* 40(4): 375–407.

Lifson, Alan. 2000. "Vaccines Have Made World a Different, Better Place." *Minneapolis Star-Tribune*, February 5, 15A.

Lilley, Ray. 1998. "Mayor Warns Blackout Could Continue for 10 Days in New Zealand." *Associated Press via LexisNexis*, February 23.

McCann, Michael W. 1992. "Reform Litigation on Trial." *Law and Social Inquiry* 17(4): 715–743.

Martin, Margaret E., Martin R. Frankel, Noreen Goldman, Daniel G. Horvitz, Joseph B. Kadane, Graham Kalton, Samuel H. Preston, Bruce D. Spencer, Michael A. Stoto, and Franklin D. Wilson. 1984. "Report of the Asa Technical Panel on the Census Undercount." *American Statistician* 38(4): 252–256.

May, Peter J. 1990. "Reconsidering Policy Design: Policies and Publics." *Journal of Public Policy* 11(2): 187–206.

Napolitano, Carol. 1999. "Why We Didn't Use FBI Numbers." *Omaha World-Herald*, November 8, 2.

Newman, Gary. 1999. "Bluffs Leads State in Violent Crime: The City's Police Chief Says the FBI Report Makes the Situation Appear Worse Than It Is." *Omaha World-Herald*, December 8.

O'Toole, Laurence J. 1989. "The Public Administrator's Role in Setting the Policy Agenda." In *Handbook of Public Administration*, edited by James L. Perry, 225–236. San Francisco, CA: Jossey-Bass.

Pralle, Sarah B. 2003. "Venue Shopping, Political Strategy, and Policy Change: The Internationalization of Canadian Forest Advocacy." *Journal of Public Policy* 23(3): 233–260.

Pralle, Sarah Beth. 2006. *Branching out, Digging In: Environmental Advocacy and Agenda Setting.* American Governance and Public Policy Series. Washington, DC: Georgetown University Press.

Reid, Herbert G. 1981. "Review of John Gaventa, Power and Powerlessness: Quiesence and Rebellion in an Appalachian Valley." *Journal of Politics* 43(4): 1270–1273.

Rosenberg, Randall. 2008. *The Hollow Hope*, 2nd ed. Chicago, IL: University of Chicago Press.

Rowe, Jonathan and Mark Anielski. 1999. *The Genuine Progress Indicator: 1998 Update-Executive Summary.* San Francisco, CA: Redefining Progress.

Sanchez, Roberto. 2000. "Medina? For Homes It Can't Be Finer." *Seattle Times*, February 20, B1.

Schattschneider, E.E. 1975. *The Semisovereign People.* Hinsdale, IL: The Dryden Press.

Schneider, Anne and Helen Ingram. 1993. "The Social Construction of Target Populations: Implications for Politics and Policy." *American Political Science Review* 87(2): 334–348.

Singel, Ryan. 2009. "Google Poised to Become Your Phone Company." *Wired.com via CNN*, November 13. Accessed January 18, 2015. www.cnn.com/2009/TECH/11/13/google.phone. service/index.html.

Stone, Deborah A. 1989. "Causal Stories and the Formation of Policy Agendas." *Political Science Quarterly* 104(2): 281–300.

Stone, Deborah A. 2011. *Policy Paradox: The Art of Political Decision Making.* 3rd ed. New York: Norton.

Tufte, Edward R. 1990. *Envisioning Information.* Cheshire, CT: Graphics Press.

Tufte, Edward R. 1997. *Visual Explanations.* Cheshire, CT: Graphics Press.

Tufte, Edward R. 2001. *The Visual Display of Quantitative Information.* 2nd ed. Cheshire, CT: Graphics Press.

Tufte, Edward R. 2006. *The Cognitive Style of Powerpoint.* 2nd ed. Cheshire, CT: Graphics Press.

Young, Jeffrey R. 2003. "Researchers Charge Racial Bias on the SAT." *Chronicle of Higher Education*, October 10, A34–A35.

CHAPTER 7

Policies and Policy Types

OVERVIEW

This chapter discusses the nature and substance of public policies—one of the key outputs of the policy process. This chapter begins with a broad definition of the term policy. It then turns to a discussion of the different ways to categorize policies into different policy types. The effort to place policies into types has consumed a considerable amount of time and effort among political scientists, for good reason. Political scientists seek to create policy typologies because we suspect, based on intuition and experience, that some policies will involve more groups in the formation and enactment of those policies, will see more conflict before and after enactment, and will be more visible than other types of policies. If we could develop sound policy typologies, we could predict what sort of politics will accompany particular kinds of policies—that is, for a given proposal about what government should do or not do, we should be able to predict who will participate and what the nature of conflict will be. There is no final word on how best to categorize policies, so when reading this chapter, it is important not to pigeonhole or force fit policies into different categories; instead, a key goal is to consider the strengths and weaknesses of each typology in telling us something meaningful about the way policy is made and what its results likely will be.

WHAT IS A "POLICY?"

policy A statement by government of what it intends to do or not to do, such as a law, regulation, ruling, decision, or order, or a combination of these. The lack of such statements may also be an implicit statement of policy.

As we discussed in Chapter 1, public policy is, in general, what the government, acting on our behalf, chooses to do or not to do. This suggests a working definition of **policy** that may seem obvious, but that is a bit more complex than the simplest definition. I define a policy as a statement by government of what it intends to do or not to do, such as a law, regulation, ruling, decision, or order, or a combination of these. For example, a law that says that those caught driving while intoxicated will go to jail for up to one year is a statement of governmental policy to punish drunk drivers. The USA Patriot Act, passed in the aftermath of the September 11 attacks, is a statement of government policy relating to national security and terrorism. Judicial decisions are also statements of policy: the Supreme Court's decision in *Brown v. Board of Education* is a statement of national policy that governments cannot constitutionally require schools be segregated on the basis of race or ethnicity. Because we also define public policy as what government chooses not to do, the lack of a definitive statement of policy may be evidence of an implicit policy. For example, the government has never declared a right to education, or healthcare, or a living wage; therefore, we can assume that the implicit policy is that one cannot get these benefits as a matter of right. Some other nations do express these services and benefits as rights, which often makes for interesting and important comparisons between the United States and other countries.

CODIFYING AND PUBLICIZING POLICIES

The simplest definition of public policy is what the government does or doesn't do. Since we more often think of individual policies as statements of the things the government does intend to know, it is useful to consider how these policies are written down and codified. After all, if policies were not made public in some way, it would be very difficult to discern what the government intends to do, and, more to the point, what it expects of the targets of the policies.

Table 7.1 summarizes how policies are codified, listed in order from the most visible and tangible types of policies to the least tangible and visible. The table starts with the most visible sort of policy change—constitutional change—and ends with the very subtle changes in individual cognition and

TABLE 7.1 Levels of Policy Codification

Level of policy	Where codified	Visibility of codification
Constitutional	In the federal or state constitutions	Highly visible at the federal level: the Constitution has been edited very few times. Some state constitutions are more easily amended for minor changes.
Statutory	United States Code, *Statutes at Large*	Highly visible through codification in statute law, publication in *Statutes at Large*.
Regulatory	Federal Register, Code of Federal Regulations	Moderately visible through the *Code of Federal Regulations* and the *Federal Register*.
Formal record of standard operating procedures	Operating Procedures Manual	Low visibility because S.O.P.s are often only internally published.
Patterned behavior by "street-level bureaucrats"	Not formally codified; evidence of a "policy" may be found in some agency records	Low visibility because these are behavioral changes with variations among actors.
Subtle changes in cognition, in emphasis on problems, etc.	Not formally codified. Often revealed by the behavior of street-level bureaucrats themselves	Very low visbility. Not codified, and changes in perceptions and emphases may be subtle.

behavior that sometimes accompany changes in the behavior of organizations that make or implement policy. Clearly, constitutional provisions are the most visible and most clearly codified statements of national policy. The Constitution is the basic law of the land, and changing the Constitution is no trivial matter. To amend the Constitution, two-thirds each of the House and Senate must vote for the amendment, and then three-quarters of the state legislatures (38 states) must ratify the proposed amendment. Or three-quarters of state conventions, called to consider the proposed change, must ratify the amendment. This was undertaken once, with the ratification of the Twenty-First Amendment, which repealed the prohibition of alcohol in the United States (the Eighteenth Amendment). All amendment provisions are laid out in Article V of the Constitution. With this many states involved, the process is very visible.

The codification of statute law and regulation is less visible than constitutional change, although the visibility of the law and regulatory processes varies with the nature of the policy being considered, as this chapter discusses in the next section. We often tend to think of policies as laws, including really famous laws such as the Civil Rights Act of 1964, the Voting Rights

Act of 1965, the No Child Left Behind Act, or the USA Patriot Act. These are, of course, among the most visible laws on the books. Other laws deal with highly technical aspects that are of greatest interest only to the most expert stakeholders. But statute laws are readily available for anyone's perusal in the United States Code, which codifies all federal laws in a way that makes laws easier to find and understand, and in the lists of Public Laws that are enacted every Congress.[1]

Federal Register
The daily journal of federal rule-making and other administrative activity. Many notices of federal administrative activity are published in the *Federal Register*, the most important of which are codified in the *Code of Federal Regulations*.

Once a law is enacted, it must be implemented, a topic taken up in Chapter 8. The regulatory process is central to the implementation of broad public policy. Congress generally delegates highly technical matters to regulatory agencies, which issue regulations that govern various activities and industries. These regulations are published in the *Federal Register* and codified in the *Code of Federal Regulations* (CFR).

It is common to hear opponents of certain regulations—or of government regulation as a whole—claim that there is "too much" regulation, and that the volume of pages published in the *Federal Register* (which runs into the tens of thousands) is evidence of this (see Friedman 2004). It is more accurate to note that the *Federal Register* is really a compendium of most of the executive branch's policy making and policy implementation activity. The *Federal Register* contains such diverse features as "Airworthiness Directives," which are regulations about the maintenance and safety of airplanes, announcements of disaster areas (published in the *Federal Register* by the Federal Emergency Management Agency, or FEMA), and, of course, actual and proposed regulations.

Code of Federal Regulations (CFR)
The compilation (in print and online) of all federal regulations. These regulations are first published in the *Federal Register* and public comment is taken into account before the regulations are codified in the CFR.

Most regulations start as a "Notice of Proposed Rulemaking," the publication of which alerts everyone to the possibility of a regulation being adopted. This allows those with an interest in the matter at hand to weigh in on policy making. Many of the pages of the *Federal Register* are devoted to summarizing the comments made during the public comment period. Thus, to the extent that the *Federal Register* is a measure of the transparency of government, one can argue that the publication of fewer pages of the *Federal Register* might reflect less transparency in government, which would have substantive meaning for public policy. In any case, while the *Federal Register* hardly qualifies as compelling reading for most people, the people whose business it is to participate in policy making read the *Federal Register*, follow the regulatory process very closely, and will comment when invited to do so to advance their policy goals or to protect their interests.

The next set of policy statements encompasses policies that are often difficult for laypeople—and, in some cases, even experts—to track and understand. First, every agency has some sort of manual of internal rules that encompass what agencies call standard operating procedures. For example, my university has a manual of rules that govern things as disparate as computer use policies, tuition and fee payment schedules, and conflicts of interest between researchers and research funders. An agency I once worked for had a manual of standard procedures that encompassed ethics rules for dealing with contractors, rules for the use of agency vehicles, and rules that prohibited sleeping on the job! (This was a state transportation department, so for many jobs, sleeping on the job could be dangerous.) All these rules govern how agencies do their work, and do have implications for policy outputs. State and local agencies that manage public services such as Temporary Assistance for Needy Families (TANF) or the Supplemental Nutrition Assistance Program (SNAP) (popularly known as food stamps) also have rules that govern how these services are delivered, and those rules can have real implications for needy people.

Finally, we have two types of policies that are often part of what we call the "tacit knowledge" of an organization's members, and that are not codified. The patterns of behavior by **street-level bureaucrats** are an important aspect of public policy. Street-level bureaucrats are the people at the front lines of public service delivery—police officers, teachers, social service caseworkers, firefighters, clerks at the post office of the motor vehicles office—whose decisions and behaviors are important to the way that programs are managed. For example, after the September 11 attacks, the security screeners at airports became much more thorough in their searches of passengers, to prevent passengers from bringing on box-cutters and other small weapons that were used in the hijackings. This was not immediately accompanied by a change in any formal policy, and, in any case, the screeners would have changed their behavior to avoid being the one responsible for such a tragedy.

Sometimes, the behavior of street-level bureaucrats can blunt the effect of a formally stated policy. In 1961, the U.S. Supreme Court held, in *Mapp v. Ohio*, 365 U.S. 643 (1961), that evidence seized illegally from suspects by the police could not be admitted in court as evidence of the guilt of the suspect. The idea was that excluding the evidence from court would deter the police from breaking this important rule on searches and seizures, as governed by the Fourth Amendment. This decision substantially changed the way that police officers testified as to how they came by important evidence—drugs—

street-level bureaucrat
A term coined by Michael Lipsky to describe the actors at the low end of the implementation chain, such as teachers, police officers, and social workers, who implement policies at the point of contact with the policy's target population.

seized by drug dealers on the streets of New York City. It is often the case that police find drugs when the alleged drug dealer drops the drugs while running from the police (attested to in so-called "dropsy testimony") or the police find the drugs frisking the alleged dealer. Researchers reported in the *Columbia Journal of Law and Social Problems* that, in the six months before Mapp:

> two-thirds of all evidence was obtained by searches of the suspect's clothing. After *Mapp*, between 80 and 90 percent of all contraband was discovered because suspects had dropped the contraband. Thus, dropsy testimony became prevalent in various courts . . . It is both unusual and unlikely that suspects would suddenly drop incriminating evidence for police to discover, in New York or any other jurisdiction.
>
> (Champion 2001: 49)[2]

This is but one example of how street-level bureaucrats can alter their behavior to conform with how they believe policy should work "on the streets," rather than as envisioned by some very distant policy maker. Teachers, social workers, air traffic controllers, and other street-level bureaucrats often make their own decisions about how to make and implement policies to achieve what they believe are important and legitimate policy goals, such as ensuring aviation safety or ridding the streets of drugs. While the example of the police testifying that drug dealers were dropping drugs at a much higher rate than before the *Mapp* decision suggests potential wrongdoing on the part of the police, it is important to understand the police officers' behavior in the face of conflicting goals: is their primary goal to arrest drug dealers and to collect evidence for their prosecution? Or is it to ensure that suspects' constitutional rights are preserved? Is there any conflict here? In the end, the police officers—like many other bureaucrats—may weigh the two goals and value one higher than the other. This sort of discretion is exercised in all manner of settings every day.

The final category of policy and of change is much more subtle than the purposive behavior of street-level bureaucrats. This level involves subtle changes in behavior of policy makers and of bureaucrats—street-level and others—triggered by a new set of beliefs or new information. For example, airport screeners may be targeting people who look "Middle Eastern" as higher risks for terrorism, even as official policy is that no such "profiling" is part of public policy. The screeners' behaviors may not be well understood even by the screeners themselves; the biases or informational shortcuts they use to identify those deserving more screening are subtle, and changes in their behavior—the sum of which yields a particular policy direction—may be discernible only after careful analysis of trend data. There is, of course, a very blurry line between purposive behavior—such as dropsy evidence—and subtle changes in behavior. But we should be, at this point, less concerned with the difference between these two types of behavior than we are concerned with the idea that the last two rows of Table 7.1 do describe public policies, but of a far more subtle and far less public and official nature than statutory or regulatory law.

CASE STUDY: AN EXAMPLE OF THE REGULATORY PROCESS

In May 1996, ValuJet flight 592, a McDonnell Douglass DC-9 airliner, crashed into the Everglades soon after takeoff on a flight from Miami to Atlanta, killing all aboard. An investigation by the National Transportation Safety Board (NTSB) determined that the plane crashed because hazardous materials were illegally included in the cargo hold of the plane with some used tires that were being sent back to Atlanta. The hazardous materials: improperly capped oxygen canisters used to provide emergency oxygen when the plane loses cabin pressure. A fire broke out among the tires, which by itself would likely have smoldered given the usual lack of oxygen in the cargo hold. But, in this case, the fire was fed by the oxygen from the illegally loaded canisters, thereby allowing a fire to breach the confines of the cargo hold, causing a series of mechanical and electrical failures that led to the plane's crash in the swamp.

Should there be a policy to make planes less likely to catch fire in flight? On the one hand, one could argue that there would not have been a crash had the illegally loaded oxygen canisters not been loaded. Indeed, the contractor that loaded the canisters on the plane, Sabretech, was later prosecuted—although not entirely successfully—and the firm ended up going out of business.

This still left the problem of a fire in the cargo hold, regardless of its cause or whether the improper loading of flammable materials could have been prevented. The National Transportation Safety Board strongly recommended that the Federal Aviation Administration (FAA) require that cargo holds be less prone to fire. Such fires can, as we have seen, cause a plane to crash. The FAA agreed, and on June 13, 1997, published proposed changes to regulations governing the construction and operation of airliners that, in essence, reclassified and strengthened the fire safety requirements for certain types of cargo holds in airplanes. This Notice of Proposed Rulemaking is lengthy—10 pages—and only about two and a half contain the actual policy itself. The remainder of this notice contains a background of the problem, the history of other fatal or dangerous fires on airliners, and a rationale for the regulation it is proposing. The NPRM also noted an important change in the attitudes of the major airlines—while they may have opposed major changes to the rules on cargo hold fire safety before the ValuJet crash, their industry group, the Air Transport Association, noted that their members had already begun voluntary measures to make the cargo holds less prone to fire, although FAA deemed these actions a good start, but still insufficient in the face of the hazard of a crash.

Perhaps most importantly, the FAA noted in this NPRM that it was seeking comment about a wide range of matters in the rule-making, ranging from what sort of chemicals are best suited to putting out fires in cargo holds, to whether and what extent the new rules would have an impact on commercial aviation in Alaska. The seeking of comments is consistent with the Administrative Procedures Act's requirements that rules are first announced as proposals, and that these comments are considered before they are finalized. The usual 90-day comment period (until September 11, 1997) was included.

The FAA did indeed receive many comments, most of which were supportive of the new rule changes. Comments were received from aviation regulators in the United Kingdom and Canada, from the Air Transport Association, and from at least one firm who wanted to make the FAA aware of its fire suppression technology. In all, over 100 comments were received. In its final rule, published February 16, 1998, the FAA adopted its proposed rule, and explained, in the *Federal Register*, its reactions to the comments and its logic for proceeding with the new rule. The new rules were codified in the *Code of Federal Regulations*, in Title 14, Parts 25 and 121; Part 25 is the section of Title 14 that regulates the construction of airplanes; Part 121 is a very extensive set of rules that regulate the operation of major airlines, like the kinds most all of us fly on.[3]

None of these actions were taken capriciously by the FAA. First, the FAA must have legal authority under federal law to regulate airlines and airplanes. This authority is provided in federal law—the Federal Aviation Act of 1958, as amended, codified in the United States Code in Title 49—in these rules, the FAA cites 49 U.S.C. 106 as its authority to regulate commercial aviation. Furthermore, other federal laws require that any regulation take into account the costs and benefits of a policy, its impacts on federalism, and on small business. In this case, there are few small businesses that run airlines, and since the regulation of aviation falls squarely within the power of the federal government, there are no federalism implications.

Why doesn't Congress just draft and apply the rules itself? First, Congress delegates the drafting of rules to others because laws are not intended to specify every element of their implementation. Lawmaking would be difficult, if not impossible, if we asked Congress to specify every aspect of the implementation of every program or policy. Even if Congress wanted to draft the detailed rules for every aspect of legislation, the public would demand opportunities for comment and input into the rule-making process, such that Congress would find itself bogged down simply in the process of making rules, particularly in highly technical areas such as aviation. The regulatory agencies have considerably greater expertise than does Congress and considerably greater resources for designing rules and managing the process. Furthermore, the bureaucracy is assumed by many as being more "neutral" than the more "political" Congress; because matters of technical expertise are assumed to fall outside of "politics," Congress can draw the broad parameters of policy and leave the bureaucracy to fill in the gaps, using neutral expertise rather than political judgment. Of course, it is extremely unlikely that the bureaucracy is truly neutral, and it is not true that Congress gives the bureaucracy free rein in all cases. For example, Congress was very clear about standards used to achieve cleaner air and water in the Clean Air and Clean Water Acts.

POLICY TYPES

An important element of the public policy process is an understanding of how various interests are organized and how various interests react to different kinds of policies. We consider these two issues in one section because the two concepts are inextricably linked—one cannot profitably discuss policy types without understanding their apparent influence on politics, including group organization, mobilization, and reaction.

In the previous section, we discussed a typology of policies based solely on the extent to which the policies themselves are highly visible and are easily found in constitutions, statutes, and regulations, or are more subtly contained in standard operating procedures and behaviors. This is a useful way to think about how policies are organized, but it does not constitute much of a theory of policy types that would allow us to describe or predict the nature of participation and conflict in policy making.

Efforts to develop policy typologies sought to do just this: explain policy outcomes by explaining and predicting key aspects of the politics underlying these policies. Like many elements of policy studies, work on creating typologies of public policies started with a great deal of enthusiasm but quickly bogged down into some major problems. We will discuss these problems, but we wish to stress that the value of at least thinking about policy typologies is still great; such typologies are useful in understanding how and why some policies are made the way they are, and why some groups do better than others in policy debates and actual enactment. Again, as I stress throughout the book, the ideas generated by these theories are often more important than the internal consistency of the theories themselves.

The earliest policy **typologies** generally separated policy into topical categories: education policy, health policy, or transportation policy, for example. This system was useful for sorting different kinds of policy domains, but it did not help us draw general conclusions about the politics that underlie these policies. The particular problem is that, by failing to tell us something more generalizable across the policy domains, these simple typologies made it difficult to learn from other types of policies and their underlying politics: by lumping together all policy types in one category, we were no closer to understanding similarities and differences among and between policies in all domains, and were therefore no closer to a useful science of public policy.

The modern era of developing policy typologies began in 1964 when Theodore Lowi laid out the classic policy types often taught in undergraduate and many graduate courses today (Lowi 1964). In the simplest terms, Lowi divides policies into three categories: distributive, redistributive, and regulatory policy. Later, Ripley and Franklin (1991) updated the typologies by dividing regulatory policy into two categories, protective regulatory and competitive regulatory (Table 7.2).

Why do we create policy typologies? Because, as Lowi argued, knowing what kind of policy we are dealing with would allow the policy designer to predict the sorts of policy conflict that would precede the policy's enactment, and what sort of conflict might arise after the policy is adopted and implemented. This would therefore be a useful predictive tool that would take policy studies beyond the realm of mere description, as it spent much of its formative years, and would provide useful problem-solving information to policy designers, in the spirit of Lasswell's call for a scientifically rigorous policy science. As we will see, this sort of theorizing had some potential, but also some significant shortcomings.

Distributive Policies

Distributive policies involve the granting of some sort of benefit to a particular interest group or other well-defined, relatively small group of bene-ficiaries. Examples of distributive policy include farm subsidies and federal spending on local infrastructure projects such as dams, flood control systems, aviation, highways, and schools. These benefits are usually distributed in the

typology
A system for categorizing things based on similar characteristics, and for differentiating things with different characteristics. A policy typology is a way of organizing a broad range of public policies into a system of policy types to aid in understanding and analysis.

distributive policy In Lowi's policy typology, this is a type of policy that takes a resource from a broad group of people and gives the resource to a narrower group; an example is so-called pork-barrel policies that send money to particular districts for local programs.

TABLE 7.2 Actors, Stability, and Visibility of Various Policy Types

Policy type	Primary actors	Relationship among actors	Stability of relationship	Visibility of decision
Distributive	Congressional subcommittees and committees; executive bureaus; small interest groups	Logrolling (everyone gains)	Stable	Low
Protective regulatory	Congressional subcommittees and committees; full House and Senate; executive agencies; trade associations	Bargaining; compromise	Unstable	Moderate
Competitive regulatory	Subcommittees; executive bureaus and commissions; small interest groups	Logrolling among favored actors	Stable	Very low; very little full congressional involvement
Redistributive	President and his appointees; committee and/or Congress; largest interest groups (peak associations); "liberals/conservatives"	Ideological and class conflict	Stable	High

Policy type	President, presidency, and centralized bureaucracy	Bureaus	Congress as whole	Congressional subcommittees	Private sector
Distributive	Low	High	Low (supports subcommittees)	High	High (subsidized groups)
Protective regulatory	Moderately high	Moderate	Moderately high	Moderate	Moderately high (regulated interests)
Competitive regulatory	Low	High (regulatory agencies)	Low	Moderate to low	High (regulated interests)
Redistributive	High		High	Moderately low	High ("peak associations" representing clusters of interest groups)

Source: Adapted from *Congress, Bureaucracy, and Public Policy*, by Randall B. Ripley and Grace A. Franklin. Copyright © 1991 by Harcourt, Inc. Reprinted by permission of the author.

process of developing authorization and appropriations bills as part of the budgeting process. While budgeting is a very important element of the policy process, it is also somewhat technical and is not taken up in this book (see Cranford 1989; Cogan 1994; Wildavsky and Caiden 2000; Anderson 2014: Chapter 5).

Distributive policy allows for a considerable amount of negotiation and distribution of benefits to members of Congress, because they cite their effectiveness in bringing home money from Washington in their re-election campaigns. Because all members benefit equally from this "pork-barrel"

interest group liberalism
According to Theodore Lowi, the dominant form of politics in the United States, in which government seeks to accommodate a wide range or relatively narrow interests, rather than attempting to weigh interests against each other and choose to support some interests more or less than others.

spending, there is a powerful incentive to engage in what political scientists call logrolling, in which members pledge to vote for each other's funding bills. For example, a member of an urban congressional district may pledge to support a rural member's farm subsidy bill in exchange for support for a mass transportation bill. This "horse trading" is probably necessary for the expeditious passage of federal spending bills, but Congress's procedures and norms also encourage this sort of negotiation, leading to more "pork-barrel" spending, which serves to allow members to "bring home the bacon" to their districts.

Distributive policy making is made even easier by the inability, in this style of policy making, to easily identify particular groups of people that are benefiting from the policy, while the costs of the policy are more broadly spread across society. Local officials and congressional representatives depict these policies as good for the local community, but as being paid for by the entire nation through general federal funds. Indeed, local spending programs are often justified as a way of gaining a community's "fair share" of federal taxes paid by the district or state's taxpayers. Because of the actual or assumed benefits to particular people without any counter groups seeking to stop spending, there is little conflict over distributive policy. It is usually made fairly quickly, easily, and with a minimum amount of scrutiny of individual spending decisions. When the news media or other members do scrutinize such spending, there may sometimes be a call for reform of this system, but the benefits of the current system of pork are so clear that the system of distributive policy endures.

This type of policy making is problematic in a democracy, as Theodore Lowi (1979) notes in *The End of Liberalism*. Because government programs often create beneficiaries and create groups to represent these beneficiaries, the United States is now characterized by what Lowi calls **interest group liberalism**, in which all claims to federal support and funding are assumed to be legitimate, and few, if any, decisions are made to separate the most compelling claims from the most minor. In such a system, the elected branches of government are more interested in servicing particular interests than in servicing the public interest—or at least something approximating it—as a whole.

Regulatory Policies

Regulatory policies are, in general terms, policies that are intended to govern the conduct of business. There are two broad types of regulatory policies.

Competitive regulatory policy involves policies designed to "limit the provision of goods and services to one or a few designated deliverers, who are chosen from a larger number of competing potential deliverers" (Ripley and Franklin 1991: 20). Ripley and Franklin cite the allocation of radio and television frequencies by the federal government, and the awarding of cable television franchises by local governments as examples. Another example is policies intended to regulate trades or professions, such as law, medicine, engineering, electrical and plumbing contractors, or hairstyling. States generally assign the power to license professions to members of that particular profession: lawyers, through the state bar associations, and physicians, through their state medical associations, are licensed and regulated by their peers. This system assures professional oversight over the activities of professionals, who must be trained and regulated to assure competent service to their clients. These policies, on the other hand, also create barriers to enter a profession, thereby limiting the number of professionals who provide a service and, possibly, maintaining fees that are higher than they might be in a fully open market.

For the most part, competitive regulatory policy is made without much public scrutiny. Much of this policy is made at the state level, further ensuring its low visibility, and the most active participants in such policies tend to be at the legislative committee and trade group levels. Much of this type of policy is relatively arcane and stimulates little public notice.

Protective regulatory policy, on the other hand, is intended to protect the public at large from the negative effects of private activity, such as tainted food, air pollution, unsafe consumer products, or fraudulent business transactions. While most businesses and their leaders are responsible citizens who do not wish to hurt or alienate their customers, businesses are also motivated by profit. Businesses often resist regulation on cost grounds, saying that it would reduce or eliminate profit margins, make products uncompetitive on the market, place firms at competitive disadvantages vis-à-vis their foreign competitors (or competitors in other states, if the policy is made at the state level), and so on.

Because businesses resist regulation while regulatory agencies insist that they are acting in the public interest, protective regulatory policy tends to be highly contentious. Congressional committees and the full body of Congress get involved, along with major trade organizations (such as the National Association of Manufacturers or the American Banking Association). Decisions are reached based on negotiation and compromise, because, in most

competitive regulatory policy These are policies designed to "limit the provision of goods and services to one or a few designated deliverers, who are chosen from a larger number of competing potential deliverers." The licensing of various professions, and of radio and TV stations, are examples of such policies.

protective regulatory policy A type of policy that seeks to protect the public and consumers from market problems, such as deceptive advertising, faulty products, or negative externalities (e.g., pollution).

cases, neither business nor the regulators can entirely dominate policy making; Congress and its committees are often put in the position of broker, mediating between the goals of the regulatory agency and business interests.

Redistributive Policies

Redistributive policy is highly controversial, involving the highest levels of government and the leaders of what are called peak associations (see Chapter 6) in policy making characterized by a high level of conflict and difficulty in changing policy.

redistributive policy In Lowi's policy typology, this is a policy that takes (or seems to take) a resource from one identifiable group and gives a benefit to another readily identifiable group. Such policies are the most controversial and contentious.

Redistributive policy is characterized by actions "intended to manipulate the allocation of wealth, property, personal or civil rights, or some other valued item among social classes or racial groups" (Ripley and Franklin 1991: 21). Based on this definition, obvious examples include welfare, civil rights for racial or social minorities, aid to poor cities or schools, and the like. While there has been considerable redistributive policy making in the United States since the Roosevelt administration, these policies are difficult to pass because passage requires that the less powerful prevail over the more powerful interests, or at least persuade more powerful groups that it is right and just to approve the redistribution of some resource to the less powerful.

It is worth noting, however, that redistributive policy can involve the transfer of resources from the less well off to the better off. During the Reagan administration, the recipients of federal redistributive benefits—the poor, urban areas, economically depressed areas—were depicted as unworthy recipients, and the policies intended to help them were severely criticized. The growing costs and apparently unrealized goals of federal social programs, coupled with the disdain felt by many people for these programs' recipients, created a political atmosphere in which it became easier—and even politically acceptable—to propose policies such as tax cuts that shifted benefits from the poor to the wealthy (see Phillips 1990). These same conditions made it possible for a Democratic president, Bill Clinton, to approve significant reform legislation in the late 1990s, which was enacted as the Personal Responsibility and Work Opportunity Act of 1996 (PL 104-193), which, among other things, reduced the length of time that individuals would receive public assistance ("welfare") benefits. And, perhaps most spectacularly, the tax code in the 2000s was substantially modified so as to allow more wealth to flow to the very wealthy, while income and wealth remained stagnant or flat for members of the "middle class" and below.

PHOTO 7.1
A homeless man holds a food voucher. This sort of aid is often considered "redistributive" policy, and, as such, is accompanied by fierce political debates over these policies' desirability. Why do you think this is so?

Source: Corbis Images. Used with permission.

Still, some people do speak for the less powerful, and any redistribution of resources—money or rights—is expected to engender controversy. Such policies include the classic welfare policies and also civil rights and liberties policies. The civil rights example is a good illustration of this notion of at least the perception of the redistribution of rights. When blacks began to demand the rights and resources guaranteed them under the Constitution—rights such as equal educational, housing, and job opportunities, the right to vote, and the right to due process in criminal proceedings—many people resisted these policies because they believed that they would somehow be losers if blacks were "winners" of these rights. Civil rights legislation was passed in the mid 1960s, but only with high-level governmental participation and after intense and rancorous debate that suffused political and social life from Washington to Main Street.

The issue of "gay marriage" also exhibits these characteristics, in which opponents of marriage rights for gay and lesbian couples argue that by providing this right to these groups, it devalues the institution of traditional heterosexual marriage. Proponents of gay marriage argue that there would be no such devaluing of marriage, and that, indeed, allowing gay marriage would elevate marriage and family even more. In the end, these arguments about redistribution can be very difficult to analyze because the nature of the redistribution involves features of the good itself—which may be tangible, such as money, or intangible, such as a right or social position—and of the perceptions of the people from whom something is "taken" and something is "given." Redistribution also assumes that, in many cases, politics is a zero-sum game, but, as Deborah Stone argues, politics and policy making are not often zero-sum propositions.

Since the example of the tax code and the shifting of wealth to the wealthy was noted above, it is important to also acknowledge the perceptions of various people in the tax policy debate to explain why many people do not consider existing tax policy to be redistributive. Many people who compared Senator John McCain's and then-Senator Barack Obama's tax plans during the 2008 presidential election were very concerned that taxes would increase on "middle income" earners, even though both candidates, in one form or another, made clear that tax code changes would affect upper income earners. But most people in the United States, across a very broad income range, self-identify as "middle class." Statistically, that family income range is between about $40,000 to $60,000, and more broadly between $20,000 and $100,000. But people who self-identify as middle class have household incomes ranging from $40,000 to $250,000—a huge span, even though the high end of that range is among the highest 3 percent of family incomes in the nation (Cashell 2008). Thus, concern about middle-class tax increases is likely to be as great among families making near the low end as among the high end of the range. And, most important for this case, many people and families at the lower end of the middle-class range aspire to move up that range, so that a threat to top earners is a threat to their aspirations, even if taxing people higher at the top end somehow benefitted people at the lower end. This shows why some redistributive policy may not be perceived as controversial, as the power of the people to whom the benefit is being distributed—and of the people who aspire to higher economic status—overwhelms the political power of lower-earning families.

Lowi's ideas continue to be quite influential, and for good reason. As Daniel McCool argues, Lowi is a leading theorist of policy types because he approaches policies not merely as outputs of government, but as something that shapes and is shaped by political conflict. Thus, in the typology described in Table 7.2, the nature and visibility of political conflict will differ considerably with the type of policy in question.

JAMES Q. WILSON: CONCENTRATED AND DIFFUSE COSTS AND BENEFITS

A persistent criticism of Lowi's typology of policies is that it is difficult to assign policies to just one category. Some policies have redistributive and regulatory attributes, such as the regulation of consumer product safety that redistributes the responsibility for risk away from consumers and to the companies that manufacture products. Is this regulatory policy, or is it redistributive policy? Depending on how one looks at this policy, it can be both. James Q. Wilson responded to criticisms of Lowi's policy types by developing a system that rejects ambiguous policy types. Instead, Wilson arranges policies in terms of the extent to which their costs and benefits are focused on one particular interest, or are spread across numerous people or interests. This typology is depicted in Table 7.3.

What might be the easiest policies to advocate and enact? In Wilson's **cost-benefit typology**, a policy that provides an obvious benefit to one group would motivate that group to press for enactment of the policy; its task would be made even easier if the costs of the policy are hard to assign to a particular group, that is, if the costs are distributed broadly throughout some larger group. Wilson cites as examples the Civil Aeronautics Board (CAB, which, before 1978, regulated air fares and airline routes) and the Federal Communications Commission (FCC, which regulates broadcasting and communications industries) as two agencies that administer this kind of client-oriented

cost-benefit typology A policy typology based on James Q. Wilson's idea that one can understand the politics related to a policy by understanding which categories of people bear the greatest or least costs for a policy, and which gain the greatest or least benefits from it.

TABLE 7.3 Wilson's Cost-Benefit Policy Typology

		Benefits	
		Concentrated among very few people	Distributed among many people
Costs	Concentrated among very few people	Interest group politics: conflict between groups that would benefit and those that would bear the costs. Treated as a "zero-sum" game.	Entrepreneurial politics: groups and their leaders seek to persuade policy makers to regulate in the public interest, in the face of opposition from the groups that would bear the cost.
	Distributed among many people	Clientele-oriented politics: close "clientele" relationships between policy makers, regulators, and the regulated interest.	Majoritarian politics: relatively loose groups of people, or those acting on their behalf, who seek a substantive or symbolic statement of policy. Often leads to weak, ambiguous policies.

Source: Derived from James Q. Wilson, *Political Organizations* (Princeton, NJ: Princeton University Press, 1995).

policy, in which the regulated organizations' interests are afforded equal or greater importance than the broader "public interest." In a more contemporary example, a tax benefit enacted in 2009 will allow large home building companies to count their losses in 2008 and 2009 against their profits from previous years, thereby reaping refunds of as much as $400 million from the federal government. In this case, the policy in question is obscure, the beneficiaries are a few companies that would generally like to keep this benefit quiet, and the ultimate cost for this policy will be borne by taxpayers (Morgenson 2009). In a similar way, the FCC's policies for licensing broadcasters ensure that the number of radio and TV stations in a market remains relatively fixed, thereby benefiting broadcasters by providing some sort of predictability, at the potential expense of the general public, which may favor a greater number of broadcast voices. In nearly all these examples, however, there are few organized interests to work against these policies, they are therefore "policies without publics," and policy making is generally conducted under relatively closed systems that benefit a few interests.

On the other hand, if the costs are easily pinned to a particular group or interest, it is likely that the cost-bearing group will take steps to oppose the policy. If the costs and the benefits are concentrated on identifiable groups, a style of policy making involving interest group conflict becomes prominent. Wilson's example is the battle between labor and business interests in the field of occupational safety. In particular, both the enactment and the implementation of the Occupational Safety and Health Act, and its administration by the Occupational Safety and Health Administration (OSHA), have led to fierce battles between labor unions and business, because the participants in this debate believe that the benefits of this policy flow to a relatively small number of interests (labor) and are paid for by a relatively small number of interests (business).

It is not difficult to find many examples of policies that seek to impose costs on one group in favor of benefits for another within the broader business sector. The regulation of pharmaceutical prices, for example, would pit health insurance companies against drug makers. Tariffs on steel can benefit the domestic steel industry, but can hurt manufacturers who use lots of steel, such as carmakers. These examples show that, in many cases, "big business" is not monolithic—that industry sectors have interests that conflict with the interests of other industries.

What results, however, if both the costs and benefits of a policy are diffuse? Wilson uses as an example the Sherman Antitrust Act. This law prohibits firms from creating anticompetitive "trusts," which was the term used in the late nineteenth and early twentieth centuries to describe monopolies or near-monopolies that stifled business competition and raised prices in the absence of competition, thereby harming customers. Since so few companies are in a position to create a "trust" or a monopoly, there are very few firms that feel the cost of this policy; at the same time, the benefits of promoting competition are often diffuse, affecting many people a little rather than having a major influence on our individual economic decision-making. This sort of policy is therefore called majoritarian policy making because majorities of the public want antitrust legislation as a means of symbolically reining in business. Anti-"big business" sentiments were translated to policy without much heated opposition, in large part because the language of the law was so ambiguous—prohibiting "combinations in restraint of trade"—that "it was not exactly clear what was aimed at" (Wilson 1989: 79) (see also Wilson 1995; Stillman 2004). This is not to say that antitrust law is a quaint vestige of an earlier age; indeed, some of the most complex and expensive antitrust cases have been brought in the last decade in the computer industry, where companies such as Intel and Microsoft have been sued by governments or rivals for allegedly illegal business practices.

The value of Wilson's typology is not, however, in the names of the policy types; instead, Wilson notes that we should think of the concentration of benefits and costs as tendencies or as ends of two continua rather than as two dichotomies adding up to a four-cell matrix. This said, we can see some relationships between Wilson's and Lowi's ways of thinking about policy types and their connections to issue networks or sub-governments. For example, clientelism is closely associated with Lowi's distributive policy type, in which interest groups gain benefits that are "paid for" (financially or otherwise) by the bulk of society. This in turn is associated with the sub-government or "iron triangle" model of interest relationships, in which interest groups, bureaucracies, and congressional subcommittees work together in a mutually reinforcing relationship (Stillman 2004). However, we should not make too much of this idea of sub-governments, as current research suggests that policy making is rather more open in most cases than the old sub-government notion would suggest. On the other hand, policies that seek to redistribute costs and benefits—redistributive policies—are highly contentious because they are often perceived as zero-sum situations, in which any gain for one interest is accompanied by an equal and opposite loss by the other. The current discussion of healthcare reform is a classic example of this conflict. Opponents to healthcare reform claim that certain groups of people—the elderly under Medicare or the already-insured under employer-paid health insurance—will lose their benefits so as to pay for benefits for those without insurance. Proponents, on the other hand, argue that reforms will benefit both those with and without health insurance.

But it is important to understand that this distribution of costs and benefits may be as much a social construction as the result of a real calculation of costs and benefits. If a group believes or is convinced that it will bear the costs of a policy, it is likely to act against the policy. Thus, a policy that seeks to reduce youth crime by providing after-school services may be resisted by a large number of citizens because they believe that they are paying a high cost for a less-than-obvious benefit to themselves. This illustration shows the difficulty of linking policies to actual benefits, but also illustrates how benefits and costs seem to be as much in the eye of the beholder as a carefully calculated accounting exercise.

If these attributes of policy (cost/benefit, distribution/redistribution) are so prone to perception, then what good is any exercise in assigning policy types? Lowi noted in 1964 that "it is not the actual outcomes but the expectations as to what the outcomes can be that shape the issues and determine their politics" (1964: 707). Peter Steinberger also addresses this issue by "conceptualizing some of the ways in which participants tend to define policies" (1980: 189). In other words, policies may not have inherent meanings in terms of any policy typology but may gain their meanings only when groups discern meanings and propagate them among friendly and hostile audiences. For example, many safety innovations in automobiles and other consumer products cost relatively little per item produced, but manufacturers and their allies believe that the additional cost will make their products unprofitable. This argument will help persuade groups to mobilize in a particular way based on a perception of policy.

OTHER POLICY TYPOLOGIES

The Lowi and Wilson typologies are not the only ways to categorize public policies. Following are four additional and not mutually exclusive ways we can categorize policies. Of course, as in any typology, policies may not fit into perfectly delineated boxes or cells, but thinking about policies in these different ways may help you gain insight into the features of policy that are most important from an analytic perspective.

Substantive and Procedural Policies

James Anderson (2003) reminds us of the very important difference between policies that set the rules for policy making and the more familiar policies that actually provide the goods and services we expect from government. He defines the difference between **substantive** and **procedural polices** as what government does versus how it does it. Nevertheless, procedural policies are very important and actually have, in the end, a substantive effect on politics.

Anderson cites the federal **Administrative Procedures Act (APA)** of 1946 as a particularly important procedural policy; the states also have similar laws. The APA establishes the procedure by which government agencies make, issue, and enforce rules and regulations as they implement the laws passed by Congress. If a regulation (or a "rule," in the language of the act) is established by an agency following the processes laid out by the APA, then it is assumed to have the force of law (like statute or case law). The APA governs how federal agencies let citizens know that they are going to make a rule and how the public can comment on the rule and offer suggestions or express their opposition to the rules, as we saw in the case study earlier in this chapter.

While the details of federal rule-making sound pretty dry, overall we can say that the APA is a very important policy. How would American government be different if there was no one way for the federal government to make rules in the open, accessible to public comment and opposition? Could certain interests be benefited and others harmed if the regulatory process were kept a secret? It would seem so, which is why, in future enactments, Congress amended the APA to make government even more open through the Freedom of Information Act of 1974, the Government in the Sunshine Act, and the Privacy Act of 1974. The overall goal, while procedural, is to ensure fairness in governmental dealing with citizens, which is substantively important as well (see Levine, Peters, and Thompson 1990: 169–170).

In most cases, procedural policy itself is not controversial. After all, procedural policy in the United States and in most democracies has been devoted to creating more transparent government, with more opportunities to participate in the process.

substantive policy A policy that explains how the government will go about its policy goals in a particular area. Contrast with symbolic policy and procedural policy.

procedural policy A policy that determines how the government's procedures—the way it goes about its work—are to be governed. The Administrative Procedures Act is an example of a procedural policy; such policies can have a substantive influence on policies.

Administrative Procedures Act (APA) A federal law (5 U.S.C. 551 *et seq.*) that requires regulatory agencies to follow particular procedures in rule-making, such as public notice of new rules, public comment periods, publication of rule-making activity in the *Federal Register*, and the like.

While procedural policies are generally noncontroversial, the procedures are important in the history and resolution of many controversies. In recent years, organizations and interests that have been the subjects of regulation have sought to mobilize their supporters to respond during the public comment period for proposed regulations. Indeed, in the late 1990s and early 2000s, General Electric sought to mobilize public support against EPA decisions to require that they dredge the Hudson River in New York to reduce water pollution caused by their manufacturing plants. The pollution, from PCBs, was considered by many to be a human health hazard, but GE opposed dredging on cost grounds, and claimed that dredging would stir up more pollutants than it cleaned. By inspiring thousands of comments, GE delayed the final regulation, and the regulatory process generated more paper than it otherwise would have. Thus, the rules that allow public access to the regulatory process can benefit both regulated interests and the people supportive of regulation. On the other hand, agencies are becoming savvy about huge amounts of comments on regulations that are generated by interest groups and that are provided as part of a mass mailing or emailing campaign, in which opposition to (or, rarely, support for) a new regulation is expressed by nonexperts in a repetitive and redundant way (Shulman 2009).

Material and Symbolic Policies

symbolic policy
A policy that satisfies public demand for statements of principles or values, without any resources to support them. The naming of post offices, highways, and airports after famous people, or the TV networks' adoption (in the face of FCC and congressional pressure) of a voluntary system of television content ratings similar to those of movies, can be seen as symbolic policies, although the line between symbolic and substantive policies is not always clear.

Another way to categorize policies is to examine whether the policy is material or symbolic. While the distinction between these two is not absolute, one can distinguish between material policies, which provide a material (that is, tangible and obvious) benefit to people, and **symbolic policies**, which simply appeal to people's values without any resources or actual effort behind them. A material policy, for example, may be a federal grant that provides money to local communities to hire police officers, as was implemented in the Clinton administration. Examples of symbolic policies include anti-drug efforts such as the "just say no" and Drug Abuse Resistance Education (DARE) campaigns and legislation and proposed constitutional amendments that would prohibit burning the flag (such laws were held unconstitutional by the Supreme Court in *Texas v. Johnson*, 491 U.S. 397 [1989]). As Anderson (2014: 16–18) notes, these policies appeal to our values and our sense of idealism, but do not really deliver any particular benefit, whether they claim to or not. Sometimes symbolic policies claim to have an impact, but this is often based on faulty causal reasoning. For example, the system of TV show ratings was developed in response to a widespread belief that various social ills, particularly among children, result from violent or sexually expressive TV shows. There is little research to substantiate this, but the TV industry implemented a voluntary ratings scheme to preempt federal legislation. In this case, TV ratings systems are the symbolic policies intended to address the perceived problem. By enacting the symbolic policy, various actors can claim to have "done something" about a problem, even when the action taken is more symbolic than anything else.

CASE STUDY: THE CHALLENGES OF POLICY TYPOLOGIES: WHEN IS A SYMBOLIC POLICY NOT MERELY SYMBOLIC?

When is a policy strictly symbolic, and when does it have important material implications? Many resolutions have been passed by Congress to recognize a particular event, person, or achievement. These resolutions typically do not require any funding or change in government activity. There merely are resolutions to state for the record that recognition is given the Congress to a particular matter. In every sense, this is purely symbolic legislation.

As you know, Congress passes a great deal of symbolic legislation every year. For example, the House passed a resolution, H.Res.342, "Supporting the National Railroad Hall of Fame, Inc., of Galesburg, Illinois, in its endeavor to erect a monument known as the National Railroad Hall of Fame." The resolution is sponsored by Rep. Lane Evans, who represents Galesburg in Congress. The bill is almost entirely symbolic, as it commits no funds or anything else of value to the National Railroad Hall of Fame. But it certainly recognizes the community and the people working to create the Railroad Hall of Fame, and many Americans who like trains may well support this gesture.

But there are two examples of policies that might appear to be merely symbolic acts, but that have important material consequences. These examples are the Martin Luther King holiday, and the attempts to ban desecration of the United States flag.

Since 1986, on the third Monday of January every year, Americans celebrate the birthday of the Rev. Dr. Martin Luther King Jr., the renowned civil rights leader who was murdered in Memphis in 1968. Legislation to create the Federal King holiday was signed by President Reagan in 1983. The holiday results in all federal offices closing, and as of 1999 all the states have also joined in the celebration by closing government facilities and public schools on the same day. The main purpose of the holiday is to observe and honor the great civil rights leader and to provide an opportunity for reflection on his legacy and on the civil rights movement in general.

Many people may view the King holiday as merely symbolic, as just a day off from work in January. But even though it may be viewed as primarily symbolic, the establishment of a King holiday created notable controversy among the states over the years. It wasn't until 1999 that New Hampshire became the last of the 50 states to fully observe the holiday. In 1991, the New Hampshire legislature had passed a law on the same day declaring it Civil Rights Day without referring to Dr. King at all (Goldberg 1999). For a time, Arizona rescinded its observance of the King holiday. And many Southern states chose to make the same day "Robert E. Lee Day," and this designation remains on the books in many of these states.

One may argue that holding a King holiday is a material policy because it grants millions of federal workers a paid holiday. This benefit costs the government millions of dollars each year. Yet, the primary reason for passing this legislation was not simply to give a federal worker another vacation day. Rather, the intent of the law was to signal that Rev. King's birthday is deserving of the honor previously afforded to presidents Washington and Lincoln.

The second example of a policy that may seem largely symbolic is legislation that seeks to prohibit the burning or desecration of the United States flag. Proper flag etiquette requires burning a worn or dirty flag in an appropriate manner, but many Americans were deeply disturbed when Gregory Johnson burned a flag in protest at the 1984 Republican national convention. For this act, Johnson was convicted of desecrating the flag in violation of Texas law. In 1989, the Supreme Court, 5–4, affirmed the Texas Court of Criminal Appeals' ruling that flag burning is a protected form of speech that cannot, under the First Amendment to the United States Constitution, be abridged by the states (*Texas v. Johnson*, 491 U.S. 397 [1989]).

The dissenting justices in this case, like many Americans, point to the long history of reverence for the flag as a justification for affording it greater protection against desecration. Chief Justice Rehnquist quoted liberally from poetry, from the "Star Spangled Banner," and explicitly noted the extremely evocative image of the Marines planting the flag on Iwo Jima during World War II; this image found an echo in the raising of the flag by three firemen over the wreckage of the World Trade Center in 2001.

After the court's 1989 decision, Congress and the states have several times sought to protect the flag from desecration, but have come up short, usually running up against the First Amendment, or against the inherent difficulty involved in amending the Constitution to include a provision prohibiting flag desecration. And, of course, one person's desecration may be another person's free speech, or even a fashion statement (Heller 2004). The question here, though, is whether this symbol—the flag—has deeper material importance and meaning. Justice Rehnquist believes it does, when he writes, in dissent:

The American flag . . . throughout more than 200 years of our history, has come to be the visible symbol embodying our Nation. It does not represent the views of any particular political party, and it does not represent any particular political philosophy. The flag is not simply another "idea" or "point of view" competing for recognition in the marketplace of ideas. Millions and millions of Americans regard it with an almost mystical reverence regardless of what sort of social, political, or philosophical beliefs they may have. I cannot agree that the First Amendment invalidates the Act of Congress, and the laws of 48 of the 50 States, which make criminal the public burning of the flag.

Like other types of typologies that try to categorize policies, the symbolic versus material policy typology should be viewed as a continuum and not as separate absolute categories. Would you say that the King holiday is more symbolic or material? If a law were passed that put people in jail or fined them—as would the Texas flag desecration law—would the law be merely symbolic? Or does it have material implications? What do these examples tell us about the advantages and disadvantages of the various policy typologies?

Public versus Private Goods

One of the main ways we distinguish between what should be provided by government and what is better provided by the private sector is by analyzing whether a good is a **public good** versus a **private good**. Again, public goods are goods that, once provided for one user, are available to all in a society and cannot be exclusively consumed by a single person or group of people. Private goods are goods that can be used by only the immediate consumer and whose enjoyment is then denied to others. One rationale for government is that it exists to provide public goods that would ordinarily not be provided by the private sector in the normal course of business.

Laws that provide for clean air and water are classic examples of public goods: a decisions to clean up the air or water for one person requires that everyone be provided with a better environment. Similarly, it would be difficult to set up a system of police protection in which only those who subscribe to police services receive protection against crime.

The public-private goods distinction, like most typologies, is not a fine distinction. There are other factors to take into account besides the consumption of a particular good. For example, the United States Postal Service (USPS) is a quasi-governmental corporation that provides document and package delivery services. FedEx, United Parcel Service, Airborne, and

public goods
Goods that, once provided for one user, are provided for everyone, such as national defense or police services; economists say that public goods are indivisible and nonexclusive, because they cannot be divided into parts for individuals to consume and because one person's use of the good does not deny others the use of the good.

private goods
Goods that can be provided in the open market without major free riding problems. Contrast with public goods.

other firms are also in the same business. Why, then, should the USPS continue in business if private firms can do the job? After all, mail and parcel delivery has all the hallmarks of a private good: the service is consumed individually, when a person decides to send a letter or package.

But the USPS exists because of a goal that the private sector firms do not pursue: universal service. A person can send a letter from Key West, Florida, to either Miami (about 150 miles away) or Kotzebue, Alaska (thousands of miles away), for the same postage. Many private firms would not serve Kotzebue, a remote village on the shores of the Arctic Ocean, because it is not profitable. Federal law therefore requires that certain kinds of mail can be carried only by the USPS, because the profits made on easily delivered mail, such as from Manhattan to Queens, cover the costs of delivering remote mail. When categorizing a good as public or private, the system of providing that good may be as important as the good itself.

For this reason, some European countries, for example, consider other goods to be public or quasi-public goods, or choose to provide goods through publicly owned corporations. The federal government subsidizes intercity rail service through Amtrak, but attacks on Amtrak have been nearly yearly battles over the nature and future of this mode of transportation. Yet, as our experience in the late 1960s showed, the railroads could or would not provide this service; if it was to be provided at all, it would be provided by government. Most European countries, on the other hand, assume that transport is a public responsibility, and they have owned and subsidized these services. They do so in order to assure that service is widely available and to support other policy goals related to industrial development, urban planning, and the like. The United States does not generally view rail transport in this way, and often looks at Amtrak through a private sector lens—"it doesn't make a profit"—without considering the extent to which other modes of transportation are public goods, such as roads and air traffic control systems, which also are generally unprofitable.

Liberal and Conservative Policies

This is perhaps the most commonly employed typology in everyday discussion of politics. In fact, to many people, the terms "conservative" or "liberal" are applied to people, parties, or policies as terms of pride or of crticism, depending on the intent of the terms' user. During the 1980s, the term "liberal" was used by President Reagan and his allies as a term of scorn for the failed social policies of the 1930s and 1960s, while self-described liberals use the term to identify themselves as believing in the power of government to better the lives of everyone, rich or poor. In today's usage, a conservative is one who believes in the primacy of individual initiative and effort over government action. Conservatives are likely to believe that government is too big, that it tends to be as much or more an instrument of mischief as of progress. Liberals, on the other hand, believe that government can and should work to equalize differences between the wealthy powerful and the poor and less powerful. These terms tend to carry with them positive or negative connotations, and those connotations shift with the tenor of the times. For example, the term "liberal" was in such disrepute during the 1980s, as part of a successful effort by the Republican Party to discredit the term "liberalism" by associating it with failed policies. But the term has lost some of its negative connotations during the early months of the Obama administration, when policies associated with "conservatives," such as light banking regulation, were said to have led to the financial crisis of 2008 and 2009.

Of course, this description is written in remarkably broad strokes. Not all conservatives think that government is evil, just as no liberals believe that government is always a force for good. Indeed, when we analyze the sorts of policies that people who self-style themselves as liberal or conservative propose, it becomes clear that these distinctions become very blurry. Conservatives prize individual liberty, yet often propose more stringent anti-crime measures than liberals. Liberals pursue governmental initiative to solve problems, yet are often the most concerned with government incursions on privacy and liberty. In the end, it is quite hard to characterize a policy as merely liberal or conservative.

CONCLUSION

There are many ways to think about how decisions are made on what to do about a policy problem. These theories of how decisions are made lead explicitly to theories of how decisions should be made. As you study and participate in public policy, it is worthwhile to ask yourself whether the decisions that are being made could be made better. When you do so, however, remember to think carefully about what you mean by "better." The theorists really do not have an opinion about what a better policy is; a rationalist would argue that the best policy is the policy that is most likely to solve a problem; you might have different goals and values that would make defining the "best" policy as much a political as it is an analytical problem.

KEY TERMS

Administrative Procedures Act
(APA)
Code of Federal Regulations (CFR)
competitive regulatory policy
cost-benefit policy typology
distributive policy
Federal Register
interest group liberalism
policy

private goods
procedural policy
protective regulatory policy
redistributive policy
street-level bureaucrats
substantive policy
symbolic policy
typology

QUESTIONS FOR DISCUSSION, REFLECTION, AND RESEARCH

- Why is there so much complexity in designing a policy within the American system of government? Why can't one just point to one document to understand a public policy?

- Why are there agencies that issue regulations, particularly since these agencies are not headed by elected officials? Why doesn't Congress just draft and apply the rules? How does Congress delegate policy-making responsibility while maintaining some sort of accountability?

- List and describe Lowi's three classic policy types. Then think of policies that would fit in each policy type. Is it easy to fit policies within one type, or are you having trouble finding one category into which a policy will fit? Does Wilson's cost-benefit typology make this task of categorizing policies any easier? Why do we use these typologies at all?

- We make a distinction between procedural policies—policies that set the rules for making other policies—and substantive policies, which are about particular policy areas (such as health policy and education policy). But does procedural policy have substantive meaning in the policy process? That is, does it matter what the rules to the game are? Why do you think we have the Administrative Procedure Act? What would policy look like if agencies didn't have to first announce rules and regulations in the *Federal Register* before they are published in the *Code of Federal Regulations*?

- Why is clean air considered a public good? Can you think of any ways to make clean air a private good that would be traded in a market? Are there other goods that were once considered public goods that are now broadly considered private goods, or vice versa?

- Is the conservative/liberal policy typology a useful way to describe and analyze policy? Why or why not? What are the benefits and shortcomings of labeling an idea, organization, or person as a liberal or a conservative?

- Give examples of material and symbolic policies. Then consider the debates over these policies. Why do you think that some debates over symbolic policies—which don't really provide any tangible product or service—are among the most contentious and emotional in politics and policy making?

- Think of an issue you care deeply about, such as welfare reform policy, or environmental policy, or healthcare, or any policy of your choice. Using the tools available in your library, such as LexisNexis, or via the Internet (www.gpoaccess.gov/fr/index.html), search the *Federal Register* to see whether there is any current regulatory activity in your area of interest. In particular, you may wish to look at "Notices of Proposed Rulemaking" or NPRMs, to see what sort of rules government regulators are thinking about implementing. What did you find? Are the rules highly technical? Or are they in language that you, your friends, your family, or other like-minded people could understand? Do you feel qualified to submit comments to the regulatory agency regarding the NPRM you found? Based on what you see, why do you think that comments come mostly from regulated interests and technical experts, rather than from the general public?

- This project would work best in a group of people in your class. Gather a group of between four to six people. Then develop a list of about 10 to 12 different policies (either specific laws, such as the No Child Left Behind Act, or general policy areas, such as "education policy") and attempt to place them within Lowi's distributive–redistributive–regulatory typology. Do you find that some policies fit into more than one category? Then repeat the process using Wilson's focused-diffused cost-benefit typology. Which typology do you find is more usable? Which is most useful in helping us to understand how the types of policies can influence politics?

ADDITIONAL READING

Clearly, in a discussion of policy types, the place to start reading is at the beginning of the efforts to create policy typologies: Theodore Lowi, "American Business, Public Policy, Case Studies, and Political Theory," *World Politics* 16 (July 1964): 667–715. Randall Ripley and Grace Franklin made good use of Lowi's typology to explain policy making in *Congress, Bureaucracy, and Public Policy*, 5th ed. (Pacific Grove, CA: Brooks-Cole, 1991), which adopts and extends Lowi's distributive–redistributive–regulatory policy typology to illustrate the relationships among Congress, the bureaucracy, and interest groups in the policy process. An alternative to the Lowi typology is provided by James Q. Wilson in *Political Organizations* (Princeton, NJ: Princeton University Press, 1995), in which Wilson more carefully discusses his concentrated-diffuse cost-benefit typology of public policies.

NOTES

1 The United States Code is available through many online sources. I prefer the site maintained by the Legal Information Institute at Cornell University: www.law.cornell.edu/uscode/. Findlaw.com's website, while rather difficult for novices to navigate, has powerful search features for federal and state law: www.findlaw.com/casecode/.

2   The study on which this is based was published in "Effect of *Mapp v. Ohio* on Police Search and Seizure Practices in Narcotics Cases," *Columbia Journal of Law and Social Problems* 4 (1968): 87.

3   Specifically, they were codified as 14 CFR 25.855 *et seq.*, and 14 CFR 121.314 *et seq.*

REFERENCES

Anderson, James E. 2003. *Public Policymaking*. 5th ed. Boston, MA: Houghton Mifflin.

Anderson, James E. 2014. *Public Policymaking*. 8th ed. Boston, MA: Wadsworth.

Cashell, Brian W. 2008. *Who Are the "Middle Class?"*. Washington, DC: Congressional Research Service. Accessed May 1, 2015. http://assets.opencrs.com/rpts/RS22627_20081022.pdf.

Champion, Dean J. 2001. *Police Misconduct in America: A Reference Handbook*. ABC-CLIO Contemporary World Issues Series. Santa Barbara, CA: ABC-CLIO.

Cogan, John F. 1994. *The Budget Puzzle: Understanding Federal Spending*. Stanford, CA: Stanford University Press.

Cranford, John. 1989. *Budgeting for America*. Washington, DC: Congressional Quarterly.

Friedman, Milton. 2004. "Freedom's Friend." *Wall Street Journal*, June 11, Opinion. Accessed January 23, 2015. www.wsj.com/articles/SB108691016978034663.

Goldberg, Carey. 1999. "Contrarian New Hampshire to Honor Dr. King, at Last." *New York Times*, May 26, A24.

Heller, Steven. 2004. "Separated at Birth: Capture the Flag." *Print*, September/October, 10.

Levine, Charles H., B. Guy Peters, and Frank J. Thompson. 1990. *Public Administration: Challenges, Choices, Consequences*. Glenview, IL: Scott Foresman.

Lowi, Theodore. 1964. "American Business, Public Policy, Case Studies, and Political Theory." *World Politics* 16: 677–693.

Lowi, Theodore. 1979. *The End of Liberalism: The Second Republic of the United States*. 2nd ed. New York: W.W. Norton.

Morgenson, Gretchen. 2009. "Home Builders (You Heard That Right) Get a Gift." *New York Times*, November 14. Accessed January 23, 2015. www.nytimes.com/2009/11/15/business/economy/15gret.html.

Phillips, Kevin P. 1990. *The Politics of Rich and Poor: Wealth and the American Electorate in the Reagan Aftermath*. New York: Random House.

Ripley, Randall B. and Grace A. Franklin. 1991. *Congress, the Bureaucracy, and Public Policy*. 5th ed. Pacific Grove, CA: Brooks/Cole Publishing Company.

Shulman, Stuart W. 2009. "The Case against Mass E-Mails: Perverse Incentives and Low Quality Public Participation in U.S. Federal Rulemaking." *Policy & Internet* 1(1): 23–53. doi: 10.2202/1944-2866.1010.

Steinberger, Peter J. 1980. "Typologies of Public Policy: Meaning Construction and the Policy Process." *Social Science Quarterly* 61 (September): 185–197.

Stillman, Richard J. 2004. *The American Bureaucracy*. Belmont, CA: Wadsworth, Cengage Learning.

Wildavsky, Aaron and Naomi Caiden. 2000. *The New Politics of the Budgetary Process*. 4th ed. New York: HarperCollins.

Wilson, James Q. 1989. *Bureaucracy*. New York: Basic Books.

Wilson, James Q. 1995. *Political Organizations*. Princeton, NJ: University Press.

CHAPTER 8

Decision-Making and Policy Analysis

OVERVIEW

This chapter presents two related aspects of public policy making: the nature and practice of policy analysis in the policy process, and how people and organizations make decisions. This discussion is not a how-to guide or a toolkit for policy analysts or decision-making. There are many fine books on these subjects, ranging from the theoretical to the applied, and many of those are cited in this chapter. Instead, this chapter describes the role that policy analysis—and policy analysts, however defined—play in the policy process and support decision-making. This relationship to the policy process is sometimes, but not always, discussed in books and courses on policy analysis as a professional activity and as a profession, as policy analysis has evolved into a field that people study, and then do, in various forms and contexts.

As described in Chapter 2, systems models of the policy process call laws, decisions, regulations, and the like **outputs** of the policy system. Policies regulating environmental health or national security are one type of output; the actual services provided by the government in monitoring pollution or in securing airplanes are also outputs. Outputs are generally easily understood, both conceptually and in concrete form. It is much harder to measure the **outcomes** of all this effort. Both outputs and outcomes are important to measure, but for different reasons. Outputs allow one to figure out how to link resources to the output of an organization. Consider the

outputs
The measurable things an agency or organization produces, such as the number of traffic signals installed, the number of students taught, or number of restaurant inspections conducted. These are not the same as measures of outcomes, which assess the effects of these outputs.

outcomes
The substantive results of the implementation of a policy. Outcomes can be intended or unintended, positive or negative. This differs from outputs, which are laws, regulations, rules, and the like; or the effort that government expends to address problems. For example, more teaching hours provided by a school district is an output; the outcome would be, one hopes, an improvement in students' educational achievement.

college or university you attend. How do we measure the performance of the university? Through factors such as number of students graduated, the graduation rate, time to completion of degrees, and so on. But these figures are outputs, not outcomes. Outcomes are the result of what happens when your college or university graduates all these students and they enter the world. Are students prepared for the job market? Will they be able to compete with others on the job market? Will they make significant contributions to society through artistic expression, scientific discovery, or excellent business management or entrepreneurial enterprise? Policy analysis engages these sorts of questions.

But many observers of what we might call "traditional" policy analysis would argue that policy analysis cannot answer these questions, because these things are very hard to quantify. For example, those of us in higher education say that education makes people better people (see, for example, Bruni 2015). But how? Are educated people smarter? More compassionate? Better able to earn a living? How can we measure this? What are the social and economic implications of a college education, or, more practically, of a particular level of public funding for higher education? These outcomes are often hard to measure because the concepts defy measurement, and, even then, these are not all equally valued outcomes. How do we measure whether someone is "well rounded?" By being well-educated citizens? Or by getting high-paying jobs? Keeping track of the career path of every alumnus is quite complicated. Teachers, in particular, object greatly to outcome measures of their performance as teachers, such as test scores, because the data may not really measure what we want to know—the so-called validity problem—and because there are so many variables influencing student outcomes outside of the teacher's control.

POLICY ANALYSIS IN THE POLICY PROCESS

With this in mind, it may be easy to understand why many agencies measure outputs; that is, they measure what they *do*, not their effect on particular problems (Affholter 1994). It is possible, with some care, to link actual outcomes to results. This requires a good *causal model* of a policy, that is, a model of how the effort expended *causes* a particular outcome. But how do we know if the causal model is correct? That is, how do we know that a given input, of time, labor, money, or other resources, yields a given output?

And how efficiently is that output—and, perhaps more importantly, the outcome—realized? Policy analysis can help address these questions. But policy *analysis* and policy analysts are not the sole actors in the policy process.

More precisely, we might think of the *practices* of **policy analysis**, because, as you recall in the public policy morphology, Table 1.2, I show four different approaches to the study of public policy. This book focuses primarily on one particular approach, the policy process approach. But when many students and professionals think about "public policy analysis," they have in mind a style of technical policy analysis that relies on tools and techniques developed by economists. The quantitative, economic style of analysis is what I discuss in this section, although these are not the only kinds of tools that policy analysts use. Furthermore, where once we thought of policy analysts as simply neutral "policy scientists," the role of the policy analyst and the nature of the profession has changed considerably in the past two decades, which makes the profession more varied, while changing the nature of policy analysis as an element of the policy process.

It is important to consider policy analysis' role in the policy process for at least two reasons. First, many students, including readers of this book, will be keenly interested in becoming some kind of policy analyst as a career path. Second, understanding the nature and uses of policy analysis can help us better understand the dynamics that characterize the policy process.

policy analysis
The practice by which policy analysts use various analytic tools, often derived from fields such as operations research, statistics, and economics, to understand the likely outcomes and benefits of particular policy ideas.

A Brief History of Policy Analysis

One can trace the history of policy analysis to the Renaissance and to Machiavelli, although this sort of policy analysis was, as deLeon and Martell (2006) note, more about "man behind the throne" political advice than it was about systematic, scientifically motivated policy analysis. Another early foreshadowing of policy analysis is found in the brief that Louis Brandeis, a future Supreme Court justice, wrote to defend the regulation of wages and hours for women in *Muller v. Oregon*, 208 U.S. 412 (1908). In this case, instead of relying heavily on the law, Brandeis expanded the brief to include a remarkable body of scientific and social scientific data that demonstrated that the State of Oregon had a strong interest in protecting the health of women by limiting the hours they could work in a day, because long work hours were, indeed, bad for one's health.[1] The brief showed that a form of empirical analysis could be used as important information for decision-makers.

Muller v. Oregon
A case in which the Supreme Court considered a legal brief defending the right of Oregon to regulate the work hours of women. The brief was an early example of policy analysis, for it contained a great deal of empirical data designed to help support Oregon's decision.

This kind of empirical analysis became possible when American universities:

> at the turn of the 20th century housed a number of disciplinary approaches, such as political science, anthropology, geography, law, psychology, sociology, and public health, that were the natural precursors to the study of public affairs in general and the activities of government in particular.
>
> (deLeon and Martell 2006: 32)

With this new knowledge, coupled with the policy demands of the New Deal, the role of advisors in government transcended the legal and institutional advice that had begun to develop in government (Heineman 2002; Radin 2013). Principles of organization and rationality were adopted to address economic and governmental problems.

During the World Wars and the Great Depression, the number of policy advisors within the government increased. That period led to the expansion of government in general. Processes generated to rationally solve problems related to war, such as operations research (Budiansky 2013) provided new analytical techniques to assess policies in other areas. Among the social scientists adopting the new approaches was Harold Lasswell, widely considered to be the first to state the idea of "the policy sciences" as an intellectual endeavor. He was, in his early work on the subject, "concerned with explaining the policy-making and policy-executing process" (Lasswell 1951: 14, cited in McCool 1995: 1) both "in and of" government (deLeon and Martell 2006). The new policy science would use the insights and techniques of a number of disciplines or "sciences," in order to improve decision-making and governance. The policy sciences approach therefore shares three key principles: an orientation toward problem-solving, the multidisciplinary nature of the policy sciences (going well beyond public administration and political science), and a value component that holds that "in order to understand a problem, one must acknowledge its value components" (deLeon and Martell 2006: 32), or, put another way, the idea that, in a democracy, decisions are made in a *political* system in which values are as important as neutrally derived "facts."

This new policy science would, among other things, deal with major policy issues, would require interdisciplinary knowledge, would be empirical and based in sophisticated theory, and would be an applied science dedicated to improving public policy through improved information and policy discourse. As McCool (1995) notes, the call for a policy science was not immediately taken up, not only because of the lack of computing and analytical power, but also because of the lack of self-identified policy analysts, the normative and applied nature of the enterprise, which ran against social scientific norms of neutral observation and interpretation, and because the policy sciences threatened the fairly well-drawn lines between disciplines in the social sciences, including political science and economics.

These barriers did break down, however, and the policy analysis field became a proto-discipline of its own; I call it a "proto-discipline" because its boundaries as a discipline were, and are, remarkably fuzzy, and because the practice of policy analysis is consciously interdisciplinary, even as its practitioners share key assumptions and values. By the 1960s, demand was high for this sort of analysis given the increasing complexity of government programs during the Great Society, and questions about whether the programs were really achieving their goals. And, as the discipline of policy analysis emerged from the call for policy sciences, its practitioners drew upon a wide range of disciplines and tools, most notably those from economics, to promote a more "rational" way of making policy, and began to lament the messiness, contingency, and sometimes irrationality of politics as a system for defining problems and framing solutions.

By the 1960s, analytic techniques and computing power had evolved to provide the nascent policy analysis profession with the tools to undertake the sort of analytic work Lasswell had foreseen. These methods included cost-benefit analysis, zero-based budgeting, operations and systems research, forecasting based in econometric tools, and Planning, Programming, Budgeting Systems (PPBS). At the same time, important policy analysis offices and systems were being implemented at various levels of the federal government, including in the Department of Health, Education and Welfare (HEW) and the Department of Defense. Such efforts were sometimes controversial, but were broadly embraced by, among others, President Johnson, who placed considerable faith on the ability of these operations to improve policy performance (Radin 2013: 17). The creation of these policy analysis operations formalized what had previously been separate efforts among a small group of professionals to apply policy analysis techniques to their agencies' key problems.

Early ideal models of policy analysis sought to emulate, if not fully implement, the rational-comprehensive approach to policy analysis. Rational-comprehensive decision-making is characterized by a series of stages: define a problem, identify the goals and objects in addressing the problem, consider the range of all alternative solutions, evaluate the alternatives and make a recommendation, or choose the alternative with the greatest likelihood of solving or at least ameliorating problems. As we and policy analysts know, the rational-comprehensive approach cannot often be applied, usually because of limitations on information, time, and human capacity to gather and analyze vast amounts of data (as I discuss later in this chapter); policy analysts know this, but sought to create better, more efficient ways of gathering information to overcome, to the extent possible, shortcomings in analysis. While Eugene Bardach's (2012) popular text on practical policy analysis outlines something that looks like a rational-comprehensive approach, Bardach and others note that one cannot gather *all* the relevant information needed to reach decisions. And, in many cases, a series of decisions—even if made in a careful, consciously rational way—will ultimately yield a process that looks more like incrementalism, as I discuss in the section on decision-making (Lindblom 1959, 1979).

By the late 1960s, this highly technical form of policy analysis was firmly established as a profession. Political scientist Yehezhel Dror, an early proponent of policy analysis, called for policy analysis operations consisting of well-trained professionals with a high degree of turnover so as to maintain fresh perspectives (Dror 1971, cited in Radin 2013). At the same time, the field became even more institutionalized with new policy programs established at, among other places, Harvard, the University of California at Berkeley, Carnegie Mellon University, the University of Chicago, and later at schools such as Washington, Minnesota, Indiana, and North Carolina at Chapel Hill. Dror's original vision was that policy analysts would be valued for more than their technical skills, but as Radin (2013: 26) notes, the analysts with technical skills tended to fall more into a technician's role, and less into a policy entrepreneurial role, which would be characterized by both high political *and* high technical skills.

Meanwhile, the typical tools of policy analysis as a profession and practice, as defined by its textbooks, are strongly oriented toward economic and formal mathematical models of the policy process. The leading textbook in the field, Weimer and Vining's *Policy Analysis: Concepts and Practice*, focuses on topics including efficiency, market failures, "distributional and other goals," and "policy problems as market and government failure," as well as a chapter on cost-benefit analysis (2011). It's important to note that they title their chapter on *efficiency* "Efficiency and the Idealized Competitive Model," reflecting that many of the assumptions made in economic analysis are ideals, subject to the constraints of actual politics. This distinction between an idealized economic logic and the logic of politics is taken up next.

Politics, Policy, and Policy Analysis

Because the term "rational" has such a positive connotation, and "irrational" a negative one, most people would want to see policy being made "rationally." But what rationality are we to adopt? While certain policies might be better from a technical perspective, they may not be politically acceptable. For example, we know that the best way to reduce the losses of life and property damage from damaging floods caused by heavy rain or coastal storms is to move people and buildings away from rivers, streams, beaches, and the like—to retreat from the riskiest areas. Or we might increase flood insurance premiums to a point where people cannot afford to live in really risky areas. Indeed, Congress sought to adopt a version of this idea, only to repeal it when the political backlash against very expensive flood insurance premiums became too great (Simpson 2014). In this case, the democratic will, as expressed through elected officials, dominated the technical excellence of the solution. Was this, therefore, irrational? From a risk-analysis perspective, it was: the original policy was intended to reduce risks, and repealing the policy is likely to return risk to its prior state. Which, as Bardach notes, is not the "do nothing" alternative as much as it is the "allow present trends to continue" alternative— which, in this case, creates even more risk. But we then must ask: what rationality was at work here? The original decision to raise premiums was based in economic logic, while the decision to repeal was based in political logic. Which was the right decision? I would argue, on risk and economic grounds, that repealing the original policy was wrong and costly, but the people who felt most directly harmed by the huge insurance premium increases, the repeal made economic sense to them. It also made political sense to members of Congress, even those who supported the original bill.

Another example is requiring drug tests for people on various forms of public assistance or welfare programs. The idea is that finding and weeding out drug users from the welfare rolls would save scarce public resources, and had a certain degree of moral satisfaction. Why, after all, should the taxpayers support someone's illegal drug use, if not habit? In essence, the claim that such "waste" of public funds was perceived as a problem, and drug testing, the solution. As it turned out, there was no significant problem to solve, as Florida soon learned:

> Ushered in amid promises that it would save taxpayers money and deter drug users, a Florida law requiring drug tests for people who seek welfare benefits resulted in no direct savings, snared few drug users and had no effect on the number of applications, according to recently released state data.
>
> (Alvarez 2012)

From a policy analytic (particularly a cost-benefit) perspective, this policy made little sense. But its proponents disagreed: "But supporters of the law said four months of numbers did little to discredit an effort they said was based on common sense. Drug users, no matter their numbers, should not be allowed to use taxpayer money, they said." Again, the political logic and the rational-analytic logic clash. In this case, the stories told about the users of drugs and welfare recipients trumped analytical efforts, in large part because many people are wary of welfare programs generally, and certainly do not support, as a Florida state representative said, allowing people to buy drugs with taxpayer dollars, regardless of how little such activity actually occurs.

These examples show that we cannot fully replace the political process with sophisticated policy analysis, and thus illustrate Radin's account of the "two cultures" of politics and analysis. She finds that politics and analysis have cultures that "are distinct and not equal. The political culture puts pressures on the norms of analysis (e.g., systematic thought and freedom from deliberate bias). In a sense the two cultures exist as master and servant" (Radin 2013: 125). And politics remains the master because elected officials are the ones who are accountable to the public, and who can bring other information, values, constituency and personal preferences, and myriad other types of information to the policy process. The orthodox view of policy analysis is that the analyst should make all assumptions transparent and should use a consistent method to compare policy alternatives; political actors are under no such obligation, and, indeed, will use information strategically, releasing favorable information and suppressing unfavorable information. In noting this, I offer no value judgment as to the "correctness" of these two logics of policy making, except to note that, in a democracy, the people and their officials do take into account a wider range of information than is provided by policy analysts.

One of the most-cited, and most critical, books on the shortcomings of the economic and mathematical logic of policy analysis *as a model of politics* is Deborah Stone's *Policy Paradox* (2011). Stone's book is a rejoinder to, and a reaction against, the application of economic logic to political phenomena.

She starts by pointing out how that early policy analysis scholarship and practice was strongly influenced by economics and "rationality":

> The new field of policy science, supposedly devoted to improving governance, was based on a profound disgust for the ambiguities and paradoxes of politics. By and large, the new science dismissed politics as an unfortunate obstacle to clear-headed, rational analysis and good policy (which were the same thing).
>
> (Stone 2011: 9–10)

Stone asks: what would policy making look like if it were removed from the realm of politics and to the realm of economic analysis? Normatively, most Americans believe that our system is or should be democratic in the sense that the popular will should be respected when policies are made on the public's behalf. Of course, whether and to what extent we have a democracy today is a question raised by scholars of democratic theory, but for now we can distinguish between politics and economics. If we understand politics, we can understand why policy appears economically or analytically "irrational" but is politically rational. With that in mind, the policy analyst also needs to understand politics:

> Policy analysts need a sophisticated understanding of the political process for a number of reasons: (1) an understanding of the political process can explain some policy outcomes ... that might not otherwise make any sense; (2) an appreciation of the political process can help us design effective democratic institutions or to refine the institutions we already have; (3) policy analysts who understand the political process can operate strategically and, therefore, effectively within the system.
>
> (Wheelan 2011: 180)

The first of these reasons is a clear reflection of how, "from inside the rationality project, politics looks messy, foolish, erratic, and inexplicable" (Stone 2011: 10). After all, Stone argues that *politics* is full of paradoxes and ambiguity that are not amenable to rationalist analysis (see also Zahariadis 2014); these paradoxes, she argues, are the very essence of politics. She therefore argues that the application of economic assumptions and logic to political decision-making is bound to fall short as long as democracy remains valued above government by experts, also known as technocracy.

To understand the difference between understanding policy making as a political phenomenon and as an economic matter, Stone asks us to consider three "models" of thinking: a model of reasoning, a model of society, and a model of policy making. She uses the terms "market" and "polis" to contrast economic and political models. She does so to offer an alternative to what she calls the "Rationality Project" in policy analysis and policy studies, which is the attempt to impose an economic logic on policy making. Such logic does not explain the many "policy paradoxes" that she describes in the book.

Stone argues that analysts who adopt the rationality project as a *normative* foundation on which policy *should* be made assume that people—from citizens to high-level decision-makers—are utility-maximizing rational actors with a great deal of good information at hand to make decisions. They weigh policy options and come up with the best solution based on the weighting of these options, and the sum of these decisions yields net social welfare. But we cannot conceive of politics this way. Markets, she argues, are competitive, and people compete to maximize their own interests. Politics, on the other hand, is about the public interest, however that is defined, and requires more in the way of cooperation, persuasion, and the careful use of information, as well as competition and the pursuit of self-interest. Markets are also based in voluntary transactions based on sound information (without which rational utility maximization is difficult), whereas politics, as a process by which a *society* collectively makes decisions, has strong coercive elements—require tax paying or obedience to a law or regulation, for example—that makes everyone a participant in the policy process, whether they are fully engaged or entirely indifferent to, or even hostile to, the ultimate decisions that our political system makes.

As Stone explains the market and the polis, it is clear that these are ideal types that stand in opposition to each other. Because these are ideal types, Stone's depiction of economic logic may be too limited, and economists know that these notions of net benefit and information are related to market failures, such as negative externalities that harm the broader public interest. Their models attempt to account for these problems, but such attempts are still based in economic logic, not political logic.

Stone's critique of the rationality project is a sound exploration of the shortcomings of economically focused policy analysis and of theories of political interaction based on the oft-disproven assumptions of classical economic theory. But her argument is, in many ways, more an indictment of the original vision of the policy sciences than it is of current policy analysis in practice. She seems to claim that policy analysts do not take politics seriously or account for its ambiguity and variability. This may have been true during the early generation of policy analysis, but, as Radin argues, today's policy analysts are not simply driven by, or trained in, a doctrinaire focus on economic rationality. Indeed, the rationality project has likely become a more accurate depiction of a form of political rhetoric about how policy *should* be made, rather than as a depiction of how policy analysts actually go about their work.

Modern and Dynamic Policy Analysis

Policy analysis, and scholars' treatment of it as an activity and profession, has evolved considerably in the last 50 years. Beryl Radin's recent book (2013), in tracing the history of policy analysis, employs three characters to illustrate the emerging field and the self-image of policy analysis. The first of these is John Nelson, who, with his Ph.D. in Economics earned in 1959, was recruited by the RAND Corporation because of his expertise in cost-benefit analysis related to defense procurement. He then went to work for the Department of Defense during the whiz kid era, and went to work on the first implementation of the Planning, Programming, and Budgeting System (PPBS). This concept gained interest in other parts of government, and Nelson took his expertise to the Department of Health, Education, and Welfare, a new cabinet-level agency in the Johnson administration. He found the work there very challenging, and, by the late 1960s, returned to California to establish, with former RAND colleagues, a consultancy focusing on military matters.

The second character, Rita Stone, is a 1989 graduate of Duke University, with a strong interest in the Head Start educational program. She began an internship at the Children's Defense Fund, a nonprofit agency, where she learned of the complexity and unintended consequences of many education policies. Her interests stimulated, she decided to enter the rigorous MPP program at the University of Chicago, after which she received a coveted Presidential Management Intern (PMI) placement in the Office of the Assistant Secretary for Management and Budget in the Department of Health and Human Services. She left government service for a time, to return as a political appointee in HHS at the beginning of the Obama administration.

The third character is Veronica Lopez, a medical doctor who also received a master's in Public Health (MPH) degree after her interest was piqued by working with children with infectious diseases, particularly HIV/AIDS. She accepted a position at the Centers for Disease Control in Atlanta, and began to understand the health system features that policy makers needed to know to make better policies. Her expertise and Spanish language skills led to her being asked to join the Pan American Health Organization, where she applied her expertise on HIV and on immunization of childhood diseases. From there, she became director of Latin American health programs for the Bill and Melinda Gates Foundation, one of the world's most prominent nongovernmental organizations (NGOs).

What these three characters represent is the way in which policy analysis is quite a bit more varied as a profession—in terms of its practitioners' backgrounds, expertise, and goals—than what was originally envisioned to be a wholly scientific and technical pursuit motivated by neutral analysis alone. Of course, all three of the characters Radin portrays have important technical skills. But Don Nelson is the only one of these characters whose analytic career was driven by an affinity for learning and using particular analytic tools; Ms. Stone and Dr. Lopez, by contrast, came to be analysts and advocates for particular policy ideas by virtue of their substantive interests in a particular policy. With this in mind, the *field* of policy analysis struggles with its identity—much as other social science disciplines or professions do—even as the activity of policy analysis is an important part of the political process. And these characters, because they represent different eras in policy analysis, also represent different attitudes toward policy analysis since the emergence of the field.

Radin makes clear that, in particular, the two younger analysts in her narrative are interested in policy analysis as a way to advance particular policy prescriptions. And, indeed, no book or course in policy analysis is entirely divorced from political reality. Both Wheelan's (2011) and Wiemer and Vining's (2011) texts recognize that policy analysis operates in a political environment, that the economic logic on which many analyses are conducted is not the same as the political logic that underlies ultimate decisions, and that policy analysts are not merely neutral actors, but are active participants in policy making. What makes a professional policy analyst different is their self-image as professionals, as Weimer and Vining discuss in Chapter 3 of their textbook. That self-image includes a commitment to ethics and to methodological rigor and fidelity to the tools of the trade. These concepts of the policy analyst are shown in Table 8.1.

To summarize, the original vision of policy analysis—as a highly technical, scientifically based endeavor that provides better information to decision-makers—has evolved from its origins as a highly technical endeavor and profession to a broader understanding of policy analysis as both a technical

TABLE 8.1 Three Views on the Appropriate Role of the Policy Analyst

	Analytical Integrity	Responsibility to Clients	Adherence to One's Concept of Good
Objective Technician	Let analysis speak for itself. Primary focus should be predicting consequences of alternative policies.	Clients are necessary evils; their political fortunes should be secondary considerations. Keep distance from clients; select institutional clients whenever possible.	Relevant values should be identified but trade-offs among them should be left to clients. Objective advice promotes good in the long run.
Client's Advocate	Analysis rarely produces definitive conclusions. Take advantage of ambiguity to advise clients' positions.	Clients provide analysts with legitimacy. Loyalty should be given in return for access to privileged information and to political processes.	Select clients with compatible value systems; use long-term relationships to change clients' conceptions of good.
Issue Advocate	Analysis rarely produces definitive conclusions. Emphasize ambiguity and excluded values when analysis does not support advocacy.	Clients provide an opportunity for advocacy. Select them opportunistically; change clients to further personal policy agenda.	Analysis should be an instrument for progress towards ones' conception of the good society.

Source: Weimer and Vining (2011), Table 3.1, page 42.

and political profession in which analysts draw on a number of tools to not only analyze policies, but to participate in debates over what policies to adopt, and what tools to use to achieve policy goals. In this way, policy analysts don't simply participate in the policy process, but they rely on their skills to be important participants in the policy process.

DECISIONS

Ultimately, in our political system, highly placed elected officials, appointed officials accountable to elected officials, and senior civil servants make public policy decisions. Once a set of goals or desired outcomes have been made, someone or some institution in the policy process has to make a decision. Decisions can be about matters as complex as President Kennedy's decision, in 1961, that the United States should send an astronaut to the moon and back by 1970. Or they can be as simple as the decision by a police officer to give a motorist a warning rather than a speeding ticket. The decision not to do something is as important as the decision to do something, and a non-decision is also a policy output. In the moon flight example, a considerable amount of momentum had built behind the space program for various reasons, so the decision to not go to the moon, or to mount a more modest space program, would have had a profound influence on future developments in aerospace (McDougall 1997). At about the same time, the decision to not pursue the supersonic transport (SST) airplane program in the late 1960s had profound influence on the aviation and aerospace industries. Our historical decisions not to create a system of university national health insurance (and "ObamaCare" is not such a system) have a profound effect on our national health system, much as even a partial solution, such as ObamaCare, has had.

Our constitutional system is structured in a way that often prevents decisions from being made very quickly. To be sure, the constitutional order does allow for very quick decisions during crises, such as in the bombing of Pearl Harbor, the September 11 attacks, or even the near-failure of the nation's largest banks. But these examples are atypical. The numerous points that bills must pass before they become laws, that proposed regulations must pass before they become actual regulations, and that laws must pass before they are effectively implemented make any sort of final and authoritative decision difficult to reach; even then, policy change is often characterized more by incremental changes than by grand, sweeping changes. Thus, when analyzing policies, it is as important to specify what has not been done as it is to specify what has been done.

In this section, I briefly explain some key concepts in the study of how decisions are made about what to do, once the decision has been reached that something is to be done. While public policy is as much about what government chooses not to do as it is about what government actually does, for illustrative purposes I will focus primarily on how decisions to do *something* are reached. And, as is true throughout this book, when I discuss Congress or the presidency, we can apply the same ideas to the state legislatures and governors, although it remains to be studied whether and to what extent our models of the policy process, which rely heavily on studies of the federal government, translate well to state and local government (Robinson and Eller 2010).

For now, we continue our focus on the federal level, and, for simplicity's sake, we can say that the decision-making process begins after an issue or problem is placed on the agenda and makes its way through the legislative process until it comes close to the decision agenda. The decision agenda is that relatively small collection of things about which an organization must make decisions. In Congress's case, the process usually begins by winnowing down a set of alternatives that are, for the most part, debated and formulated in the committees. The goal is to link potential problems to potential solutions.

Many of the models of decision-making presented here are both *positive* models (that is, neutral explanations of how a system works) and *normative* models (explanations of how decisions *should* be made). I will not delve deeply into the normative dimensions of these issues; that is, I will not spend much time on whether the rational comprehensive decision-making model is superior or should be used in making governmental decisions. This is a task for you, the reader, to decide as you weigh the relative merits of these perspectives both as normative models and as reasonable models of how the policy process works. What's more, like so much in public policy studies, it is difficult to argue that any model or perspective holds true across all time and circumstances.

Rational-Comprehensive Decision-Making

Most discussions of decision-making begin with a discussion of the "**rational comprehensive**" or "rational actor" as an ideal type of decision-making that is rarely, if ever, achieved (Levine, Peters, and Thompson 1990). Yet for years the rational actor model was widely assumed to be a primary method of decision-making in public and private organizations, and the quest for this sort of rationality persists today. After all, wouldn't it be best if all our decisions were made rationally, based on the best information we have available?

There are several assumptions that underlie the rational model. Decision-makers are presented with a problem and a goal (involving solving or ameliorating the problem) and are set to the task of solving or addressing, to the extent possible, the problem. In so doing, decision-makers gather all the possible information they can on the problem—its societal and economic costs, for example—and on possible solutions to the problem. Multiple options are analyzed, including the option to "let present trends continue," which some incorrectly call the "do nothing" approach (Bardach 2012).

This model is often set up as a straw man against which other models of decision-making are compared; an example of this straw man is Model I (the rational actor model) in Graham Allison's *Essence of Decision* (1971). The reason why the ideal rational model is a straw man is simple: several features of the rational model render it an unrealistic model of decision-making. First

rational comprehensive
A model of decision making in which it is assumed that decision makers have nearly all information about a problem, its causes, and its solutions at their disposal, whereupon a large number of alternatives can be weighted and the best one selected. Contrast with incrementalism and bounded rationality.

is the problem of goal consensus. Often, when a problem is identified, it is hard to understand what goals the various proponents of policies have in mind. Often, goals are left purposefully ambiguous so that legislation can gain passage; it is then left to the implementers to try to figure out what the most important goals are. Because solutions are so often tied to goals, some solutions to a problem will foster political conflict, even if the solution seems the most "rational." For example, liberals might see welfare as a form of societal compassion to help less fortunate people overcome the conditions that lead to poverty. Conservatives, on the other hand, may view welfare as a temporary boost to help people while they look for employment; the conservatives' support is based more on economics than compassion. Thus, the same problem can be seen as having two rather different goals. One can imagine both the decision-making *and* the policy analytic challenges under conditions of unclear goals.

Another problem with the rational model is that the information-processing demands are too great for human minds in human institutions. It is impossible to gather all the information about a particular problem; one could spend a lifetime and not find a final answer. Even with today's vastly improved information storage and retrieval systems, it is very difficult for decision-makers, confronted as they are with significant resource constraints and time pressure, to gather all the information needed, weigh the information, and make a decision.

An additional problem with attempts at highly rational decision-making comes with the nature of information itself. Because decision-makers deal with social phenomena, and social phenomena are notoriously difficult to track and analyze, it is difficult to find the proper information about goals, values, costs, and benefits needed to make a rational decision. This is one of the key criticisms of **cost-benefit analysis** (CBA). In CBA, the analyst tries to count up, often in monetary terms, the cost of pursuing a certain policy and the benefits to be derived from it. The problem is that the costs of an action are sometimes easier to count up than are the benefits. For example, we might know that the cost of cleaning up a toxic waste site is $50 million, and the result is that we might reduce the rate of cancers and other illnesses by somewhere between 2 and 10 percent. What is the benefit, in dollar terms, of this reduction? How can we make this reduction more certain? This depends on our calculation of how much each life is worth, which is very difficult to calculate. Again, this does not mean we should not try to use CBA. But we do need to realize that we cannot reduce all social problems to

cost-benefit analysis
Sometimes called cost-benefit-risk analysis, a technique of policy analysis that seeks to understand the costs of a course of action and its benefits. When risk is introduced, the risk of something bad happening is also taken into account.

economic costs and benefits, since other values may be important, such as equality or liberty.

Many of the critiques of the rational actor model suggest that rationality is so difficult, or nearly impossible, that other models of decision-making are more accurate. But it is important to keep rationality in mind as, at least, a goal, if not the realistic end. After all, if complete rationality were possible—that is, if we had complete (or very nearly complete) access to all relevant information and that information was adequate—we would be able to make better decisions. This is why people continue to develop information systems and analytic techniques: to move us toward improved, more rational decision-making.

Bounded Rationality and Incrementalism

James March and Herbert Simon provide us with a way of thinking about rationality that recognizes the limits on resources and human abilities to process information. This concept is called **bounded rationality** (March and Simon 1958). To be boundedly rational means that one behaves as rationally as one can within certain bounds or limits, including limited time, limited information, and our limited human ability to recognize every feature and pattern of every problem; we can try to enhance these skills, but they are still inherently limited.

Charles Lindblom applied these ideas in a now-classic article, "The Science of 'Muddling Through'" (1959), in which he argued that people make decisions in relatively small increments, rather than in big leaps. They do so because key sources of information include what we know about the current nature of an existing problem, our accumulated knowledge about what steps have been taken before, if any, to address the problem, and whether those steps appeared to be successes or failures. This description of the policy process, known as **incrementalism**, is both a model of how decisions are made and a description of how contending interests behave in making policy, and is offered in contrast to the idealized rational-comprehensive model (Table 8.2).

Lindblom calls the rational-comprehensive method of decision-making the "root" method, because decisions start from the "root" of the issue or problem; incrementalism is the "branch," he argues, because it uses and builds on what is already known, without relying on reanalyzing everything about what is currently being done. In this way, the incremental method allows the

bounded rationality
A term, used most prominently by James March and Herbert Simon, that describes how decision-makers seek to act as rationally as possible within certain bounds or limits; these limits include limited time, limited information, and our limited human ability to recognize every feature and pattern of every problem.

incrementalism
A model of decision-making in which policy change is accomplished through small, incremental steps that allow decision-makers to adjust policies as they learn from their successes and failures.

TABLE 8.2 Rational-Comprehensive Decision-Making and Bounded Rationality (incremental decision-making)

Rational comprehensive	Bounded rationality
1a. Clarification of values or objectives distinct from and usually prerequisite to empirical analysis of alternative policies.	1b. Selection of value goals and empirical analysis of the needed action are not distinct from one another but are closely intertwined.
2a. Policy-formulation is therefore approached through means-end analysis: First the ends are isolated, then the means to achieve them are sought.	2b. Since means and ends are not distinct, means-end analysis is often inappropriate or limited.
3a. The gist of a "good" policy is that it can be shown to be the most appropriate means to desired ends.	3b. The test of a "good" policy is typically that various analysts find themselves directly agreeing on a policy (without their agreeing that it is the most appropriate means to an agreed objective).
4a. Analysis is comprehensive; every important relevant factor is taken into account.	4b. Analysis is drastically limited: (i) Important possible outcomes are neglected; (ii) Important alternative potential policies are neglected; (iii) Important affected values are neglected.
5a. Theory is often heavily relied upon.	5b. A succession of comparisons greatly reduces or eliminates reliance on theory.

Source: Reprinted with permission from *Public Administration Review*. Copyright © by the American Society for Public Administration (ASPA), 1120 G Street NW, Suite 700, Washington DC 20005. All rights reserved.

decision-maker to take a fair number of shortcuts: it eliminates the need to explicitly separate means from ends, to pick the analytically "best" policy, and to rely heavily on theories that the decision-maker may have neither the time nor the inclination to use.

Two major problems with the theory (and to some extent the practice) of incrementalism are, first, that some problems demand bold decisions and, second, that some goals simply cannot be met with incremental steps. For example, President Franklin Roosevelt was elected on a pledge to tackle the grave social and economic problems associated with the Great Depression. His flurry of activity—the banking holiday, new banking and finance laws, the promotion of various measures such as the National Industrial Recovery Act—was a rather sharp departure from prior governmental practice. These innovations were occasioned, in large part, by the public's demand that the government do *something*; the gravity of the Depression was such that aggressive measures needed to be adopted.

A second example starts with President Kennedy's address to Congress in 1961, in which he urged that the United States put an astronaut on the moon and safely return him to earth before 1970. Paul Schulman calls this a "major national commitment," and the federal government, after some years of organizational and political confusion, responded to Kennedy's challenge by appropriating money and causing the rapid growth of the National Aeronautics and Space Administration (NASA) and other agencies to meet the goal (Schulman 1975). Because this task—putting someone on the moon— was undertaken even before the first American astronaut had simply orbited the earth, the space program serves as an example of a non-incremental, all-or-nothing decision. While the landing on the moon might have resulted from a more incrementalist space policy, it is likely that it would have taken longer and would have been achieved rather differently than it was.

Another example of sudden, non-incremental policy is the decision to mobilize for all-out war. Before the United States was drawn into World War II, it pursued an incremental policy of pressure on Japan to halt its expansionism and on Germany to protect shipments of war material to Great Britain. When Japan attacked Pearl Harbor in December 1941, and Germany and Italy declared war, the United States had to move from incrementalist economic and diplomatic policies to a very sudden commitment to build a large military to win a two-front war. Of course, some military commitments are incremental, such as the slowly building American involvement in Vietnam in the 1960s, followed by the slow disengagement from Vietnam in the early 1970s. But these two cases suggest that incrementalism is not the only way to characterize decision-making. Nor are they mutually exclusive: many decisions were made to increase military readiness and war preparation before 1941, but these were incremental choices compared with the very rapid buildup and deployment of the nation's forces after war was declared.

Other Models of Decision-Making

The rational-comprehensive and incrementalist models of decision-making are perhaps the two most commonly reviewed models in public policy, but other models, borrowing from these and other theories, help explain how decisions are made.

Michael Cohen, James March, and Johan Olsen developed the "**garbage can model**" to explain decision-making in what they call "organized anarchies" (Cohen, March, and Olsen 1972). They use universities as an example of organized anarchies because, as you may have noticed while at a college or university, institutions of higher learning are not rigidly organized

garbage can model A model of decision-making developed by Cohen, March, and Olsen, who argued that organizations are "organized anarchies," and make decisions based on the flow of problems, solutions, and participants into choice opportunities they call "garbage cans." This is the foundation of Kingdon's Multiple Stream Approach (Chapter 11).

and managed institutions. Indeed, members of the faculty demand and usually receive considerable autonomy in the management of their own work and of their departments. Students enjoy a degree of autonomy in their choices of which courses and majors to take, how to structure living arrangements, and what to do during free time. And administrators must manage the various interests—faculty, alumni, students, and members of the broader community—without violating the traditional prerogatives of any of these groups.

There are three elements or streams in the garbage can model: problems, solutions, and participants. In each of these streams, various elements of decision-making float about; what is perhaps most important about this model is the idea that there are solutions looking for problems as much as vice versa, and participants floating about looking for a way to participate in putting together these problems and solutions. Cohen, March, and Olsen call the decision opportunities "garbage cans" in which the three streams are mixed together. For example, the selection of a new dean is an opportunity for participants to come together in a garbage can and use the hiring to link perceived problems in the college with perceived solutions.

And not all organizations are as anarchic and unmanaged as universities; universities may very well be the extreme example. But John Kingdon's very successful application of the idea to policy making in the federal system suggests the considerable value of this way of thinking; this streams-and-garbage-cans model will, I hope, be clearer after we review Kingdon's model of the agenda-setting process in Chapter 11.

Two other models of decision-making are considered in Allison's *Essence of Decision*. He labels them organizational process and governmental politics, or Models II and III (Model I is the rational actor model). We might also call Model II the bureaucratic politics model. Model II is a model of organizational process grounded in a notion of bounded rationality. Allison argues that decisions are the result of bureaucrats applying standard operating procedures (SOPs) to problems. The model assumes that such procedures are relatively simple and that outcomes from these models are predictable. In addition, as Jonathan Bendor and Thomas Hammond (1992) note, the model suggests that SOPs will largely condition behavior in such a way that if we know the SOP, we can make relatively good guesses about decision-makers' future behavior. Finally, the model assumes that individuals seek information, that information carries with it relatively high costs, and that reducing the cost of information is therefore an important goal. From this, we can conclude that incrementalism is a key feature of this style of decision-making, remembering that information deficits make bold steps difficult, if not impossible.

Model III, the governmental politics model, is a model of political conflict. Model III echoes Neustadt's argument in *Presidential Power* that the power of any chief executive rests in his or her persuasive abilities (Neustadt 1990). Decisions in this model are the product of competition and negotiation among the president, top government executives, bureaucrats, legislators, and other interested parties. American politics is thus characterized by a high degree of fragmentation and competition, and decision-making is slow, competitive, and likely to reflect the power of the relative actors more than the ultimate desirability of the decision at hand. One can easily imagine that if the *president*'s power is mainly limited to persuasion, the power of other actors (who do not have the powers and prestige of the president) will be even more limited.

CONCLUSION

A common feature of all textbooks on the public policy process is the idea that public policy is *complex*: making policy, making decisions, explaining how decisions are made, how to weigh different policy decisions, are all elements of the policy process and are all remarkably complex. These activities require the combined efforts of thousands of people with their own skills, values, goals, and interests. All these participants seek to simplify complex processes through better analysis and decision-making. But our political system sometimes works against simplicity. Our political culture, constitutional order, political institutions, and the considerable variation in policy preferences across the nation make policy analysis and decision-making difficult and challenging. But this complexity is not a reason to abandon the effort to make better policies and better decisions about policies. We know that public policy is made even with imperfect systems of analysis and decision-making, because we know that no such system is perfect. But as we learn about how we understand public policies—how they work, their actual influence on outcomes, their influence on politics and decision-making—we can learn how to make both better policies (based on our own values and goals) and better arguments about what certain policy ideas should be adopted, modified, or rejected. This chapter provides some insight into this process so that, if you become an analyst, you can be sensitive to the give and take of politics and policy complexity as you learn and practice your profession.

KEY TERMS

bounded rationality
cost-benefit analysis
garbage can model
incrementalism
Muller v. Oregon

outcomes
outputs
policy analysis
rational comprehensive

QUESTIONS FOR DISCUSSION, REFLECTION, AND RESEARCH

- Compare policy *analysis* to the study of the policy *process*. How are they similar, and how are they different?

- What motivated Lasswell and other scholars to call for the creation of a policy science? What new developments in the social sciences, and in political problems, made such a call desirable and possible?

- Beryl Radin describes three different types of policy analysts, as summarized in this chapter, through the creation of fictional characters based on real people who work as policy analysts. What character do you most identify with? Why? What does your answer say about your possible career goals and career path?

- What skills do you think policy analysts need to be effective in providing useful, accurate information to decision-makers in the policy process? Where and how does one learn these skills?

- Does policy analysis have any influence on policy decisions? Or are political considerations more important?

- What sort of things can decision-makers do to make decisions that are more like "rational-comprehensive" decisions than like small, incremental decisions?

- Can you think of policies that have been enacted in the past several years or decades that are not incremental decisions? As you ponder this, you may want to ask: what do I need to know about a policy to know whether or not a policy is an incremental change, or a major change not explained by incrementalism?

ADDITIONAL READING

Because this chapter describes policy analysis as an important part of the policy sciences, readers may wish to look at some of the classic works in the field, such as Edith Stokey and Richard Zeckhauser, *A Primer for Policy Analysis* (New York: W.W. Norton, 1978) and David L. Weimer and Aidan R. Vining, *Policy Analysis: Concepts and Practice*, 5th ed. (Boston, MA: Longman, 2011). It is important to understand both the welfare economics traditions from which Stokey, Zeckhauser, Weimer, and Vining draw their ideas as well as the problems with using these approaches as the sole lens through which to view public policy making. Examples of research that use the welfare economics approach can be found in any issue of the *Journal of Policy Analysis and Management* (JPAM). Those who seek a more descriptive or narrative approach to policy analysis would do well to review Eugene Bardach's short volume, *A Practical Guide for Policy Analysis: The Eightfold Path to More Effective Problem Solving*, 3rd ed. (Thousand Oaks, CA, and Washington, DC: Sage/CQ Press, 2012).

Clearly, Deborah Stone's *Policy Paradox* (2011) has been very influential throughout my career as a policy researcher. Her book is very important reading not only for addressing the intellectual foundation for the policy sciences, but also for understanding the very nature of politics and why an economic logic is poorly applied to politics and policy making.

But one can come away from Stone with the belief that policy analysis is highly technical and seeks to set itself apart from politics. Contemporary policy analysis books, however, do note that policy analysis is but a part of a broader political and decision-making process. And as seen throughout this chapter, Beryl Radin makes clear that policy analysis is no longer—if it ever was—solely about neutral, value-free quantitative analysis.

The materials I've relied on for the discussion of policy analysis are classics in the field, and are staples of the public policy and public administration curriculum. Graham Allison's *Essence of Decision* (1971) remains a classic study of different modes of decision-making. Lindblom's classic 1959 and 1979 articles on decision-making remain relevant today as we understand why many—but not all—decisions are made incrementally. And, again, I turn to Bardach for clear and practical advice on policy analysis and how one can make decisions in a systematic and orderly way, thereby supporting better decision-making than if one just cast about randomly for ideas and analysis.

NOTE

1   Of course, this decision also meant that women were, indeed, considered the "frailer" gender, and one can view this decision both as an example of policy analysis and as a form of paternalistic gender discrimination. The latter is not the essential historic meaning of the *Muller* decision, but it cannot be ignored.

REFERENCES

Affholter, Dennis P. 1994. "Outcome Monitoring." In *Handbook of Practical Program Evaluation*, edited by Joseph S. Wholey, Harry P. Hatry, and Kathryn E. Newcomer, 96–118. San Francisco, CA: Jossey-Bass.

Allison, Graham. 1971. *Essence of Decision: Explaining the Cuban Missile Crisis.* Boston, MA: Little, Brown.

Alvarez, Lizette. 2012. "No Savings Found in Florida Welfare Drug Tests." *New York Times*, April 17. Accessed December 27, 2014. www.nytimes.com/2012/04/18/us/no-savings-found-in-florida-welfare-drug-tests.html/files/12458/no-savings-found-in-florida-welfare-drug-tests.html.

Bardach, Eugene. 2012. *A Practical Guide for Policy Analysis: The Eightfold Path to More Effective Problem Solving.* 4th ed. Thousand Oaks, CA: Sage/CQ Press.

Bendor, Jonathan and Thomas H. Hammond. 1992. "Rethinking Allison's Model." *American Political Science Review* 86(2): 301–322.

Bruni, Frank. 2015. "College's Priceless Value." *New York Times*, February 11. Accessed February 11, 2015. www.nytimes.com/2015/02/11/opinion/frank-bruni-higher-education-liberal-arts-and-shakespeare.html?ref=opinion.

Budiansky, Stephen. 2013. *Blackett's War: The Men Who Defeated the Nazi U-Boats and Brought Science to the Art of Warfare.* New York: Vintage Books.

Cohen, Michael D., James G. March, and Johan P. Olsen. 1972. "A Garbage Can Model of Organizational Choice." *Administrative Science Quarterly* 17: 1–25.

deLeon, Peter and R. Christine Martell. 2006. "The Policy Sciences: Past, Present, and Future." In *Handbook of Public Policy*, edited by B. Guy Peters and Jon Pierre, 31–49. London and Thousand Oaks, CA: Sage.

Dror, Yehezhel. 1971. *Ventures in Policy Sciences*. New York: Elsevier.

Heineman, Robert A. 2002. *The World of the Policy Analyst: Rationality, Values, and Politics*. 3rd ed. New York: Chatham House.

Lasswell, Harold. 1951. "The Policy Orientation." In *The Policy Sciences*, edited by Daniel Lerner and Harold Lasswell, 3–15. Stanford, CA: Stanford University Press.

Levine, Charles H., B. Guy Peters, and Frank J. Thompson. 1990. *Public Administration: Challenges, Choices, Consequences*. Glenview, IL: Scott Foresman.

Lindblom, Charles E. 1959. "The Science of 'Muddling Through'." *Public Administration Review* 19: 79–88.

Lindblom, Charles E. 1979. "Still Muddling, Not yet Through." *Public Administration Review* 39: 517–526.

McCool, Daniel C. 1995. *Public Policy Theories, Models, and Concepts: An Anthology*. Englewood Cliffs, NJ: Prentice Hall.

McDougall, Walter A. 1997. *The Heavens and the Earth: A Political History of the Space Age*. Johns Hopkins Paperbacks ed. Baltimore, MD: Johns Hopkins University Press.

March, James G. and Herbert A. Simon. 1958. *Organizations*. New York: Wiley.

Neustadt, Richard E. 1990. *Presidential Power and the Modern Presidents: The Politics of Leadership from Roosevelt to Reagan*. New York: Free Press.

Radin, Beryl A. 2013. *Beyond Machiavelli: Policy Analysis Reaches Midlife*. 2nd ed. Washington, DC: Georgetown University Press.

Robinson, Scott E. and Warren S. Eller. 2010. "Participation in Policy Streams: Testing the Separation of Problems and Solutions in Subnational Policy Systems." *Policy Studies Journal* 38(2): 199–216.

Schulman, Paul R. 1975. "Nonincremental Policy Making: Notes toward an Alternative Paradigm." *American Political Science Review* 69(4): 1354–1370.

Simpson, Andrew. 2014. "Senate Approves Bill to Curb Flood Insurance Hikes." *Insurance Journal*, March 13. Accessed February 14, 2015. www.insurancejournal.com/news/national/2014/03/13/323273.htm.

Stone, Deborah A. 2011. *Policy Paradox: The Art of Political Decision Making*. 3rd ed. New York: Norton.

Weimer, David Leo and Aidan R. Vining. 2011. *Policy Analysis: Concepts and Practice*. 5th ed. Boston, MA: Longman.

Wheelan, Charles J. 2011. *Introduction to Public Policy*. 1st ed. New York: W.W. Norton & Co.

Zahariadis, Nikolaos. 2014. "Ambiguity and Multiple Streams." In *Theories of the Policy Process*, edited by Paul A. Sabatier and Christopher M. Weible, Chapter 2, 65–92. Boulder, CO: Westview.

CHAPTER 9

Policy Design and Policy Tools

OVERVIEW

Once a problem has been identified and decision-makers place the issue on the agenda for active consideration, there is still more to do to move an idea from a successful contestant on the agenda to a fleshed-out policy. This chapter reviews two more aspects of the policy process. The first is what policy scholars call **policy design**, which is the process by which policies are designed, both through technical analysis and through the political process, to achieve a particular goal. After the policy is designed, it is enacted using policy tools and then implemented, at which point the administrative agencies translate the will of the executive and legislative branches into actual policy outcomes.

This chapter focuses on policy design and policy tools. In Chapter 10, we will apply what we learned here to better understand policy implementation. In reading about implementation, it is important to note that it is impossible to separate the process of designing policies from their implementation—much as all the stages of the policy process are hard to separate. Design and implementation are very closely related because the choices made in the design of a policy will profoundly influence the way a policy is implemented, which then influences the outcomes of these policies. In fact, policy designers often base their policy designs on experience with similar policies that have already been implemented.

policy design
The process by which policies are designed, both through technical

analysis and the political process, to achieve a particular goal.

Another reason that design and implementation are hard to separate from the rest of the policy process is that the policy design process continues during design and implementation. Congress's enactment of law does not result in a simple translation from Congress's will to actual action on the part of government agencies, or actual compliance on the part of the people whose behavior the policy seeks to change. Agencies must take what Congress has passed and figure out what it requires or allows them to do. The process of translating vague legislative commands into rules and regulations can be among the most contentious and difficult activities in the entire policy process.

Once policies are implemented, experience with it and with similar policies will often change the policy design, even when the policy and goals are supposedly in place and operating. For example, targeted federal spending on particular urban problems was once granted based on focused federal goals and specific programmatic interests. This policy changed because, to a considerable extent, implementation was not as successful as had been hoped. The targeted policy was replaced by block grants, in which state and local governments are freer to make choices about how the money is spent, provided that relatively broad federal goals are met.

PREPARING TO DESIGN POLICIES

At some point (preferably early) in the policy design process, decision-makers must explicitly consider five elements of policy design, as listed in Table 9.1.

Problems

As noted in Chapter 6, there is a substantial difference between a condition, about which little or nothing can be done, and a problem, about which some sort of private or public action can be taken. The initial debate over policy is, therefore, about whether something really is a problem, to what extent it is a problem, who it affects, and so on. The definition of the problem, as E.E. Schattschneider noted, often shapes the way the problem is treated throughout the policy process. For example, was Hurricane Katrina an "act of God," about which little or nothing could have been done before the event, or was the hurricane less a meteorological phenomenon and more a focusing event that worsened and called attention to social and technological

TABLE 9.1 Elements of Policy Design

Element	Questions to ask
The goals of the policy	What are the goals of the policy? To eliminate a problem? To alleviate a problem but not entirely eliminate it? To keep a problem from getting worse?
The causal model	What is the causal model? Do we know that if we do X, Y will result? How do we know this? If we don't know, how can we find out?
The tools of the policy	What tools or instruments will be used to put the policy into effect? Will they be more or less coercive? Will they rely more on incentives, persuasion, or information? Capacity building?
The targets of the policy	Whose behavior is supposed to change? Are there direct and indirect targets? Are design choices predicated on our social construction of the target population?
The implementation of the policy	How will the program be implemented? Who will lay out the implementation system? Will a top-down or bottom-up design be selected? Why?

problems that can be mitigated or avoided through appropriate public policy? The post-Katrina debate seems to have adopted the latter interpretation, yet, in the past—and even in many places today—the "act of God" interpretation is powerful.

We generally know about public problems through two mechanisms. In one, we learn about problems through changes in the indicators of a problem over time, rather than all of a sudden. For example, in 2009, swine flu (technically, the H1N1 pandemic) gained attention as a public policy problem when it first came to light in cases in Mexico, whereupon it spread to the United States and then worldwide. The flu did not strike all at once; rather, the sort of data that are routinely gathered by hospitals and healthcare workers began to accumulate as public health professionals and, later, elected and other appointed officials and the general public became aware of the problem.

Other problems become evident through focusing events, which are sudden events such as earthquakes, terrorist attacks, or industrial accidents. Another class of focusing event is the kind of event that affects a particularly influential member of a policy community. It is well known that when famous people contract diseases, or when a member of Congress or his or her family members have or contract a disease, more attention is paid to the problem than would ordinarily be paid.

This discussion sounds like the agenda-setting discussion in Chapter 6. But it is essential to understand that problems don't merely "exist" in the world in a self-evident way. For example, one can argue that childhood obesity is caused by the proliferation of junk food, fast food restaurants, and television and video games, all of which lead to poor diets and sedentary lifestyles. Others argue that the problem is caused by a lack of open space and by poor urban design, which makes people less likely to walk or play outside and more likely to go about in cars. Some people believe that childhood obesity may simply be a matter of poor parenting, poor self-control, and laziness. Nearly all the other aspects of policy design will flow from this definition of the problem—one can imagine policies that are intended to regulate junk food and video entertainment to cause kids to be more active, or policies that encourage activity through better urban form, or through public education activities to persuade or shame people into ensuring that kids need to be more active. Each of these policies assumes different causal theories and therefore will suggest different policy tools.

Goals

Policies are made because someone has persuaded enough of us (i.e., citizens, elected officials, or both) that something needs to be done about a problem. Policies are created to meet or at least to make progress toward these goals: policies to fund research on vaccines and to mandate their use by children; policies meant to desegregate schools, public facilities, and workplaces; policies to provide a "social safety net" for the poor and others hit by economic downturns; and policies to create jobs. All of these policies are linked to perceived problems and goals.

There are many ways to think about and categorize goals. A particularly useful way of thinking about goals is found in Deborah Stone's *Policy Paradox*. Stone lists four major categories of goals: equity, efficiency, security, and liberty. In many cases, Stone argues, these goals clash: most prominently, security often conflicts with liberty, and some political systems have tended to favor various forms of security while curtailing liberty. Efficiency can conflict with all these goals.

Indeed, these conflicts are intensified by the many different definitions of goals. Stone helps us to understand this by listing eight different ways of defining "equality." She uses the example of dividing a large chocolate cake among the members of a class. One might argue that the most equitable division is to simply count the number of people in the room and divide the cake into that number of pieces. But Stone argues that one can divide the cake a number of different ways—by the rank of the people in the room (professor, graduate students, undergraduates, for example); or by athletic or physical prowess; or by gender—and still justify the decision for dividing resources as "equal" (Stone 2011).

If this seems fanciful to you, consider traditional American notions of equality, in which we claim that we believe that everyone should have equal opportunity for success but no guarantee of equal outcomes—particularly when the opportunities themselves are not equal. Other nations, such as the Scandinavian countries, are more serious about coming closer to equality of outcome. Others will argue that, by right, some people simply shouldn't be equal to others in particular ways. Before women were given the vote and other civil rights, men (and some women) argued that women were the "fairer sex" who were unsuited to physical labor or even rigorous intellectual pursuits; they were deemed best at homemaking. Blacks were considered nonpersons—and therefore unsuited for anything such as equality—in the infamous Dredd Scott decision; and today, gays and lesbians are considered sufficiently different from others that they are unable to marry or, in some jurisdictions, to establish families and to share health insurance and other workplace benefits. Stone notes, indeed, that arguments that seek to exclude people from the recognized boundaries of a community are often invoked to deny some form of equality to these people. The current red-hot debate in the United States over the treatment of illegal immigrants is a case in point.

Defining Efficiency

Deborah Stone argues that **efficiency** is more a means to a goal rather than a goal itself, but she treats efficiency as a goal category because many policy advocates tout their ideas on purported improvements in efficiency. Efficiency is a particularly important aspect of policy making in the United States, given our emphasis on limited government and individual initiative and in the context of calls for the government to run "more like a business." An economist might define efficiency as gaining the most output for a given level of input, which means, in layman's terms, more bang for the buck. It also means the same bang for fewer bucks. If the efficiency of a program improves by 10 percent, spending on the program could be reduced by 10 percent without a loss of benefits.

This sort of thinking is commonplace, particularly among those who support smaller government or who wish to shift resources to other programs.

efficiency Gaining the most output for a given level of input, or getting "more bang for the buck." Efficiency is often thought of as getting the same output for less of a particular input, or getting more of something for a constant input.

Spending cuts or budget reallocations are often justified by the belief that one can gain considerable resources by simply cutting the "waste, fraud, and abuse" from programs. This thinking in government tends to overlook important issues. First, the public sector may not be any more or less efficient in some ways than large private sector firms, such as IBM or General Motors. The private sector tends to have fewer formal controls over such waste than the public sector, although accounting practices in the private sector will certainly reveal decreasing profitability or diminishing assets.

It is, of course, highly desirable to reduce or eliminate waste, fraud, or abuse in both the public and private sectors. However, there may not be as much waste, fraud, and abuse in government as there are decisions to provide benefits to narrower interests at the expense of the majority, as we learned in Chapter 6. People who oppose certain programs will often do so because they disagree with the substance of the policy, but find the waste, fraud, and abuse argument more successful than arguing the program on its merits, particularly because no one, including most proponents of policy, favors waste.

There are many different ways of understanding efficiency, depending on how we describe inputs and outputs. Stone argues that governmental activities provide inputs and outputs. She cites an example of how we might define efficiency in a public library system. While librarians' salaries can be seen as inputs, their earnings have a small but discernible impact on the community and therefore also serve as outputs.

polis In Deborah Stone's book *Policy Paradox*, the polis is the political community, and is contrasted with the market as a way of describing human organization and interaction.

Beyond this simple example, Stone uses a theme that extends our thinking about policy beyond economics. She posits that society can be viewed as a market or as the **polis**. The latter term refers to the "essential political society," or what I take to mean the community as a whole. The decisions we make to address our common problems are usually political (cooperation, negotiation, common or public interests) rather than market-based (voluntary exchanges between just two parties intended to increase both parties' welfare). Clearly, if more people and interests are taken into account in the polis than in the market, we could reasonably argue that the "polis model" is more complex than a simple market model. If this is true, then efficiency in political terms is quite complex, as hard to define in just one way as equity is.

For example, it is traditional to think about governmental administrative costs as wasted or "overhead" expenses that take resources away from more useful activity. As Stone (2011: 83) argues, however, "merely calling something 'administrative' as opposed to 'productive' is a way of prejudicing the argument." But how do we distinguish core instructional activities from administrative activities? Stone cites the example of a New Jersey plan to cut administrative costs by imposing penalties on schools with excessive "administrative" costs; the plan would categorize "school librarians, nurses, and guidance counselors as 'administrative.'" By categorizing these positions as administrative, New Jersey was sending a signal that the responsibilities of these positions do not contribute to the goals of a school.

What might the librarians, school nurses, and counselors think of this argument? What if the custodian were considered an "administrative" position, even if we assume that the custodian keeps the school in good working order so that teachers and students have a proper place to work? Perhaps these "administrators" would mobilize to show how their activities contribute to the goals of the school or simply make schools better places in which to spend the better part of the day. In any case, classifying these activities as "administrative" in order to achieve some level of "efficiency" is more a political decision than an objective economic or accounting decision. Because it is a political decision (in the "who gets what" sense), one then can use political rhetoric (argument and persuasion) to counter the proposal. This is not to say that one cannot or should not use economic or accounting data to make a case for or against moves to create efficiency. Rather, such arguments are likely only a part of a broader political argument regarding the desirability of programs. Such evidence is thus part of the advocacy process, not the be-all and end-all of the argument.

CONFLICTING GOALS: SECURITY AND LIBERTY

Two other goals that seem to conflict are security and liberty. Clearly, there are significant conflicts between these two goals: the more security one desires from the government, the more liberty one must be willing to surrender. This dilemma and the solutions to it go back at least as far as Thomas Hobbes' famous work of political theory, *Leviathan*, first published in 1651. Hobbes argues that people are naturally aggressive and that they want to acquire things for themselves: they will, therefore, in the "state of nature" (that is, the state of humankind without civil government), seek to deny those things to or take them from other people. Thus, people in the "state of nature" will fight with each other for wealth and power, and this constant striving will yield constant "war of man against man," resulting in a society in which life is "solitary, nasty, brutish, and short." To prevent this conflict, Hobbes argues, all of us in civil society have surrendered a considerable number of our liberties to the state, which holds the most coercive power in our name to prevent us from engaging in this war against all.

If we take Hobbes at his word, we might create an authoritarian or totalitarian system to protect ourselves from each other. Instead, the United States followed a path laid out by John Locke and extended by the founders of our Constitution, who believed that political power comes from our consent; thus, we surrender to the government or "leviathan" only those things that we believe government should manage to create and maintain a civil society. Under such a system, citizens retain considerable rights and privileges of citizenship until they have breached the laws of civil society, in which case individual liberties can be taken from the individual in order to make all of us more secure. The obvious example is criminals, who are largely free to act until they commit a crime, an affront to civil society, whereupon we restrict the liberties of criminals by imprisoning them, or, in extreme cases, by denying them life itself.

The problem with this trade-off is that greater security for some or all of us comes at the expense of a loss of liberty to some or all of us. Let's consider some contemporary examples. First, consider this: would you be willing to surrender some of your rights—your Fifth Amendment right not to be forced to incriminate yourself or your Fourth Amendment right to "be secure in [your] persons, houses, papers, and effects, against unreasonable searches and seizures"—in exchange for more aggressive law enforcement against vandals, murderers, and drug dealers? Your decision may presume that the constitutional protections against unfair criminal procedure apply only to actual criminals, not suspects and certainly not private citizens. However, the founders believed that the protections contained in the first eight amendments protect all of us against a heavy-handed central government. Nearly every protection provided under the Bill of Rights has its historical roots in the colonial experience, when the British government routinely violated what we now call "due process of law." Yet, at the same time, many people argue that criminals have too many "rights" and that the victims of crimes are afforded no constitutional rights. While one can reply that the Bill of Rights is at least as valuable as a set of restraints against government as it is a set of protections of "criminals" (actually, suspects), the niceties of political theory and constitutional law are not always observed in policy debates. And one can argue that crime is prosecuted by the state because crime is an offense against the entire community—the polis—and not against individuals. But the pain of crime is clearly most heavily borne by the victims.

Now, let us imagine that the police search your house without a search warrant. Such a search is a violation of the Fourth Amendment that guarantees against warrantless searches. But what if the search yields evidence that you or someone in your house (a relative or a roommate, maybe) committed a crime? (Remember the case study from Chapter 7 on "dropsy" evidence.) Then the evidence is what lawyers call "probative" in that it shows that the individual may have committed a crime for which he or she should be punished. In such a case, should the evidence be admitted at trial because it is proof of guilt? Or should it be excluded because it was seized in violation of your constitutional rights? What if excluding the evidence allows you to go free, even if the evidence very strongly suggests your guilt?

These questions are not easily and definitely answered, because they are important political questions that both influence and reflect the nature of the political community involved and the nature of the information available to people when they make these decisions about liberty. For example, early in the year 2000, the economy was sound, unemployment was at historic lows, inflation was low compared with the high rates in the 1970s and early 1980s, and people were freely spending money on houses, cars, computers, and other accoutrements of the good life, twenty-first-century style. At the same time, crime was also at a historic low, and drug-related crime in particular had been substantially reduced.

In such an environment, people may be more willing to take risks and to seek greater liberty because they feel more secure. But when the economy is performing poorly, terrorism seems to continue unabated, and the future prosperity and quality of life are in doubt, people may find that their interests shift to greater security, as reflected in the case study that follows. Thus, there is no one answer to what the appropriate balance of these goals should be; rather, what is important to examine is the extent to which conflicts exist and how they are resolved.

AMBIGUITY AND GOAL CONFLICT

Beyond the different ways of thinking about goals, policy design can also reveal conflict over **policy goals**. Because policies and their goals are often vague when they are originally established, it is sometimes difficult for the

policy goal
A desired outcome of a policy; these goals can be explicitly stated or implicit in the policy and other factors found in its legislative history.

agencies charged with implementation to satisfy the demands of everyone involved in formulating and approving the broad policy. For example, Congress could mandate that the secretary of the Department of Health and Human Services create a program to reduce the teen pregnancy rate. The goal and how attainment is measured are clear: reduce the pregnancy rate. There may be other goals, such as reducing welfare dependency, increasing educational attainment, promoting morality, and other benefits that derive from this, but the main goal is to reduce the teen pregnancy rate.

There are multiple ways to reduce teen pregnancies. Two commonly cited methods are to provide family planning services, particularly birth control, to teens, particularly teen girls, or to stress abstinence to teens through schools, public education campaigns, and the like. Clearly, the choice of one or the other of these methods to reach the goal will raise controversy. Some will argue that providing family planning services will encourage rather than discourage promiscuity and will result in more pregnancy and moral decay. Others may argue that abstinence relies too heavily on a mistaken **causal theory**; in particular, they would argue that appeals for abstinence would be ignored or even mocked by teens rather than thoughtfully and respectfully heeded. Others might argue that the abstinence-only policy, while well intentioned, simply does not yield the outcomes the policy's proponents believe it will (see Trenholm et al. 2007).

causal theory
A theory about what causes a problem and how particular responses would alleviate that problem. Different from a causal story (see Chapter 6).

We might call this conflict an agreement on ends, but not on means. The reason for the agreement on the ends in the first place is due to contending groups' interests in attaining their own goals. Socially conservative groups may see the reduction of teen pregnancies as meeting a moral goal, while liberal groups may view the same result as a step toward particular social goals. The goal of reducing teen pregnancy is used because both groups can agree to it while feeling that their own interests—either social or moral goals—are thereby promoted. The disagreement comes later, when the decision is implemented; that is, when an agency takes specific steps to lower teen pregnancy rates, such as distributing contraception or promoting abstinence.

When the goals themselves are in dispute, or when Congress or other legislatures have specified the method for implementing a program, these post-enactment goal conflicts are less likely, because they would have been explicitly stated in the legislation or at least strongly embedded in the policy design. Nevertheless, because legislation is usually the product of compromise, sometimes the means are unspecified and the ends are fuzzy until the policy takes shape during the design phase.

Some goals can conflict with other goals in other policy areas, as well. Helen Ingram and Dean Mann argue that one can claim that, because the United States has so many illegal aliens living within its borders, its immigration policies have failed. This is true if the goal is to control the number of immigrants entering the United States. What about other, perhaps more important, goals? One example, Ingram and Mann argue, is the desire to maintain friendly relations with Mexico, the source of most of our illegal aliens. A crackdown on illegal immigration may create social, economic, and political problems in a nation whose cooperation we hope to cultivate. Another goal is to keep food prices down; many argue that illegal immigrants, because they accept lower wages for farm work that legal citizens choose not to do, help keep food prices low (Ingram and Mann 1980).

Whether one agrees that these are important goals is less important than a realization that a policy can conflict externally with other policies. For example, sociologists Edward Laumann and David Knoke tell the story of an oil exploration executive who read in the *Federal Register* that the Federal Aviation Administration (FAA) was proposing to require pilots of small airplanes to file flight plans for nearly all flights, regardless of the flight's length or whether the pilot planned to fly visually or on instruments. While the goal here was to promote and improve aviation safety, the oil executive opposed the new rule because it could reveal where aircraft owned by oil companies fly when they do aerial surveys of potentially oil- and gas-rich areas. Thus, the goal of encouraging the development of our energy resources was hindered by an entirely unrelated program and goal (Laumann and Knoke 1987).

The point of this review of goals is not to lead you to believe that all policy is hopelessly complex or that goals are never set and attempted. Rather, my aim is to simply highlight how difficult it is to set and reach goals in a complex policy environment. Often, once conflicts are resolved and the means for achieving goals are developed, one is able, through a review of the record surrounding the enactment of a policy, to isolate the important goal or goals and assess the extent to which they are met or believed to have been met. This is sometimes difficult when many other activities are taking place simultaneously.

Adding to the complexity of goals is the fact that there are different types of goals. One must ask a series of questions about goals to fully understand what the policy is intended to achieve. One must ask whether the goal is to eliminate a problem, hold steady in the face of a growing problem, or reduce a problem to some better level. For example, the Clean Water Act's goal that the nation's waters be "drinkable, swimmable and fishable by 1985" seeks not to eliminate all pollution, but rather the level of pollution that renders our waters unusable for these purposes.

Similarly, national economic policy makers tend not to believe they can get rid of unemployment entirely, but they do work to bring down the level of unemployment to 4 percent, the goal specified in the Full Employment and Balanced Growth Act of 1978, also known as the Humphrey-Hawkins Act after its sponsors (Lipford 1999; Reissman 1999). On the other hand, in 1995, the FAA and the NTSB announced their goal of zero fatal accidents in American commercial aviation; this is an absolute goal to eliminate deaths from air disasters. The type of goal may reveal a great deal about what the policy designers believe is possible to do given current techniques for solving or alleviating problems.

CASE STUDY: THE USA PATRIOT ACT AND AIRPORT SCREENING: LIBERTY VERSUS SECURITY

In the heat of the moment after the September 11, 2001 terrorist attacks, and in the midst of the frightening anthrax attacks on Congress and on major media figures, Congress quickly passed a law awkwardly titled the "Uniting and Strengthening America by Providing Appropriate Tools Required to Intercept and Obstruct Terrorism Act," better known as the USA Patriot Act. President George W. Bush signed it into law on October 26, 2001. The goal of this act was to greatly increase government powers to fight terrorism and related crimes. The act consisted of ten Titles:

TITLE I: Enhancing Domestic Security against Terrorism

TITLE II: Enhanced Surveillance Procedures

TITLE III: International Money Laundering Abatement and Anti-Terrorist Financing Act of 2001

TITLE IV: Protecting the Border

TITLE V: Removing Obstacles to Investigating Terrorism

TITLE VI: Providing for Victims of Terrorism, Public Safety Officers and Their Families

TITLE VII: Increased Information Sharing for Critical Infrastructure Protection

TITLE VIII: Strengthening the Criminal Laws against Terrorism

TITLE IX: Improved Intelligence

TITLE X: Miscellaneous

It would be a mistake to argue that this law sprung from thin air after the September 11 attacks. Many of the provisions of the act were long known to be among conservative policy makers' preferred policies. Many of the provisions of the Patriot Act were relatively noncontroversial, such as the money laundering aspects in Title III, or the support for victims in Title VI. The most controversial provisions were contained in Title II and Title IX.

In particular, Title II of the Patriot Act allows any federal district court to issue warrants for electronic surveillance outside of that court's district, under section 219. It allows the federal government to demand records of electronic communications from Internet service providers (ISPs; but not necessarily the contents of the messages themselves) under section 215, and makes it illegal for any ISP or organization so ordered to disclose the fact of that request. A particularly important provision is found in section 209, which allows for the seizure of voice mail with only a search warrant, rather than under the old rules, which required a wiretap order, which is more difficult to get. Another extremely important section of the act is section 206, which allows the government to tap communications of suspects regardless of their location or of the device or instrument used in communication; this makes it easier for the government to collect information on those using email and cell phones, particularly the prepaid cell phones popular with terrorists and criminals.

The ultimate goal of the law is to provide government broader powers to fight terrorism. Operationally, the FBI focuses on gathering domestic intelligence. The CIA is empowered to direct FBI domestic surveillance operations for the first time, while the U.S. Treasury Department is required to establish a financial monitoring system that the CIA may access (much of which is contained in Title III). The CIA also now has the power to acquire evidence obtained by criminal wiretaps and federal grand juries (section 218) (McGee 2001). While many of these provisions were due to expire under various *sunset provisions* in the original Patriot Act, most of these sections—or the substantive policies contained in the policies— remain in force, having been extended by legislative action in 2005 (PL 109-177, USA Patriot Improvement and Reauthorization Act). Interestingly, this bill was overwhelmingly passed in the wake of the 2005 London bus and subway bombings (Barrett 2005). The main provisions that were not permanently extended were set to sunset on December 31, 2009; while Congress has enacted short-term extensions of the law, the long-term extension of these provisions has not been taken up by Congress, due in part to increasing political opposition to many Patriot Act provisions. This opposition is made possible by, one might argue, the amount of time that has passed since the attacks.

Critics of the Patriot Act argue that it erodes the liberties guaranteed under the Constitution, and that the law was made hastily in a climate of great fear. This view holds that the Patriot Act places security higher than liberty—the very freedoms that define

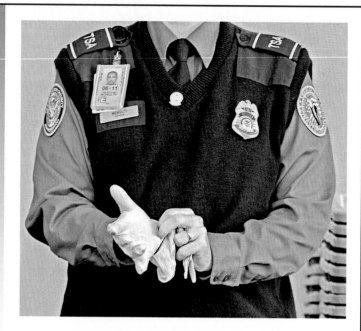

PHOTO 9.1

A Transportation Security Administration Agent. Do you think our system of aviation security was designed through careful policy analysis? Or as a result of persuasive appeals to "do something" after the September 11 attacks? Or both, or other reasons?

Source: Corbis Images. Used with permission.

America. While they believe that liberty and security involve a balancing act between these two goals, opponents of the Patriot Act maintain that it has gone too far toward promoting security at the expense of liberty. According to this position, the act is open to abuse by overly aggressive law enforcement and intelligence agencies. Despite these concerns, and because of the tenor of the times during which the law passed with an overwhelming vote by Congress (357–66 in the House, and 98–1 in the Senate), and with the strong backing of President Bush, the law has not been significantly altered since its enactment.

An important architect of the Patriot Act, former U.S. Assistant Attorney General Viet Dinh, defended the Patriot Act on the grounds that it enhances liberty and security. Dinh states that "[s]ecurity is the means by which we achieve our fundamental freedoms" (Lacayo 2003). Supporters of the Patriot Act believe that the September 11 attacks so fundamentally changed our notions of national security that the government must take strong action at home to prevent an even more deadly attack, possibly one involving weapons of mass destruction such as nuclear, biological, or chemical weapons. And these supporters would concede that it may be more important to curtail some constitutional liberties so that the republic may survive. They often cite a famous 1810 letter from Thomas Jefferson to John B. Colvin of Maryland, in which Jefferson argued that:

> A strict observance of the written laws is doubtless one of the high duties of a good citizen, but it is not the highest. The laws of necessity, of self-preservation, of saving our country when in danger, are of higher obligation. To lose our country by a scrupulous adherence to written law, would be to lose the law itself, with life, liberty, property and all those who are enjoying them with us; thus absurdly sacrificing the end to the means.

Jefferson appears to argue in this passage that some restrictions on liberty are justified if they make the nation more secure.

The controversy that the Patriot Act generates is not whether the United States should defend itself against terrorism. The controversy is whether the act goes so far in the name of security—whether it really promotes it or not—that the very liberties on which the nation was founded are undermined. The Patriot Act includes a wide variety of provisions to empower intelligence and law enforcement agencies to pursue suspected terrorists, which have sparked fierce controversy. Under the act, the FBI and the U.S. Justice Department sent out letters to college and university officials requesting information on foreign students to compare it with information on suspected or known terrorists. Academics strongly objected, stating that it violated privacy laws (Eggen 2002). It requires various financial institutions, including money-services businesses, securities firms, broker dealers, mutual funds, credit card companies, and other types of financial institutions, to both monitor suspicious transactions and to establish anti-money laundering programs (Title III) (O'Harrow 2002). And librarians and booksellers have complained strongly about Patriot Act provisions (in section 215) that appeared to allow intelligence agencies to monitor a person's library borrowing and book buying (see Hudson 2004), although it is unclear how many times this power has been used in an investigation.[1] However, the expanded Patriot Act provisions were used to prosecute the biggest Las Vegas strip club owner and several local government officials in a sting operation for money laundering and bribery, none of which had anything to do with terrorism (Isikoff 2003). Indeed, it may well be that the September 11 attacks were an opportunity to advance long sought-after changes to the criminal law that enhanced governmental powers. Roger Pilon, vice president for legal affairs at the Cato Institute, the libertarian research group, claimed that "[The administration is] taking language off the shelf that's been ready to go into any vehicle" (Greenhouse 2002). This "coupling" of ideas with events is a staple of agenda setting and alternative selection in the public policy process (Kingdon 2011).

After some time had passed, and the implications of the hastily assembled and passed Patriot Act were considered, political opposition to the act from both the left and the right emerged. The House of Representatives very nearly repealed the library and book-buying provisions of the Patriot Act in 2004 (Lichtblau 2004). And many cities and counties have passed resolutions indicating their opposition to portions of the law (Egan 2004), such as the library provisions (Foderaro 2004).

Amid all the controversy over whether the Patriot Act erodes constitutional liberties, one must consider the most basic question: does the Patriot Act make us more secure? In other words, has the act been successful in the war on terror? In a 2004 report, the U.S. Department of Justice argued that it "has charged 310 defendants with criminal offenses as a result of terrorism investigations since the attacks of September 11, 2001, and 179 of those defendants have already been convicted." The department's report argues that the Patriot Act has been central to these efforts, and that it is providing the necessary tools to prosecute terrorism without undue limitations on individual liberty. Indeed, the department argued that:

> Security and liberty are interrelated and mutually reinforcing, not conflicting, goals. Under the leadership of the President and the Attorney General, the Department of Justice has been, and remains, dedicated to using the USA Patriot Act in service of both aims.

> (United States Justice Department 2004)

Do you agree with Dinh and the Justice Department that the Patriot Act protects liberty by promoting security? In other words, do you agree that one need not sacrifice a great deal of liberty to gain a great deal of security? Or do you believe that the Patriot Act was a rapid reaction to a sudden shocking event that may, in the long run, erode liberty to achieve security? Do you agree with Jefferson's claim that some restrictions on liberty may be necessary to preserve the republic and the remaining liberties that exist? Or do you agree more with Benjamin Franklin, who said: "Any society that would give up a little liberty to gain a little security will deserve neither and lose both"?

PROPER CAUSAL THEORY

If the participants in policy making can at least approximate goal consensus, then the next thing they must do is understand the causal theory that underlies the policy to be implemented. A causal theory is a theory about what causes the problem and what intervention (i.e., what policy response to the problem) would alleviate that problem. Without good causal theory, it is unlikely that a policy design will be able to deliver the desired outcomes.

Rather, performance measurement will remain focused on effort, because implementers and researchers will find the connection between effort and outcome so difficult to make.

If the laws made by the legislature are vague or if the legislature defers to the expertise of agency officials, then developing the best causal theory and then settling on the policy design are the responsibility of the agency staff. But if Congress specifies a particular solution or set of solutions to a problem, then the causal theory is implicit in the legislation. For example, after the Exxon Valdez oil spill in 1990, Congress passed the Oil Pollution Act of 1990, which contained two key provisions: a requirement that oil tankers have double hulls by a certain date and an increase in the monetary liability limit for shipowners whose tankers spill oil. The explicit theories here are, first, that single-hull tankers leak more oil than double-hull tankers and, second, that an increase in liability will deter companies from recklessly moving oil in U.S. waters.

Because social problems are very complex, it is not surprising that developing causal theories about how the social world works is very difficult. If one develops the wrong causal theory, no policy, no matter how well crafted, is likely to have a positive impact on the problem under consideration.

Deborah Stone has found the issue of causes so important that she devotes an entire chapter of *Policy Paradox* and an article in *Political Science Quarterly* to this element of policy making (Stone 1989). You may have correctly guessed that Stone finds that isolating the causes of problems is much more complex than opposing camps might believe at first glance. After all, as Stone argues, we can distinguish between cause and effect in the natural world and in the social world: "The natural world is the realm of fate and accident, and we believe we have an adequate understanding of causation when we can describe the sequence of events by which one thing leads to another" (Stone 2011: 189). On the other hand:

> in the social world we understand events to be the result of will, usually human but perhaps animal. The social world is the realm of control and intent. We usually think we have an adequate understanding of causation when we can identify the purposes or motives of a person or group and link those purposes to their actions.
>
> (Stone 2011: 189)

Because of these different ways of understanding causation, Stone argues, we can do things to change the outcomes of human, purposive action, while few interventions will change natural phenomena such as the weather, tides, or earthquakes.

Thus, an important way of understanding how people argue about causes is to look at whether they attribute a problem to an act of God or to acts of human causation, either purposive or negligent. For example, one can argue that when a hurricane damages a city, it is an act of God that we cannot avoid and we should simply feel compassion for victims, give aid to recover from the disaster, and move on. Another view is that hurricanes (or earthquakes, or floods, or other disasters, for that matter) do not cause anything but high winds, heavy rains, too much water, or shaking ground. It is the presence of human activity and the consequence of human activities that cause the damages, such as building houses too close to rivers or beaches or in such a way that they do not stand up to shaking ground or high winds. The choice to build in such places and in such ways is a human decision that can be altered by changing policy to induce "better" decisions that help reduce the damage from such events.

Stone (2011) argues that we can take this analysis further and, considering actions and consequences, identify four types of causal theories, as discussed in Chapter 6. These stories include depictions of intended and unintended consequences. For example, environmental groups often portray environmental disasters—chemical leaks, oil spills, or leaking toxic waste dumps—as the result of carelessness (corner cutting, perhaps) or omission (failure to perform a task that would prevent an accident). The owner of the industrial facility in question will attempt to move the discussion from the realm of inadvertence, which implies liability and carelessness, to a causal theory implying that the accident was caused by weather or a completely unforeseeable event that Stone calls "machines that run amok."

This move between explanations is important because the causal theory strongly implies the appropriate actions that government and society might take and that may be codified in public policy. A causal theory that a problem is caused by carelessness and omission means that policies are likely to be adopted that more strictly regulate the activities in question, to prevent or at least penalize these actions. But a causal theory that undesirable effects are caused by accidents implies a much different set of policies, which may emphasize self-regulation over governmental action, particularly if one can make the claim that accidents are random, without any pattern that is somehow caused or worsened by the industry's action or inaction. In these ways and others, debates over policy are debates over causes and effects, with each side trying to tell a story that leads to its own most desired result. These causal theories also imply what sorts of policy tools will be used to address the problems.

POLICY TOOLS

Closely related to the causal theory is the choice of **policy tools**, or policy instruments, which can be used to create a desired outcome. Anne Schneider and Helen Ingram (1997: 93) define policy tools as "elements in policy design that cause agents or targets to do something they would not do otherwise or with the intention of modifying behavior to solve public problems or attain policy goals." Lester Salamon and Michael Lund (1989: 29) provide a simpler definition of a policy tool as "a method through which government seeks a policy objective."

policy tools
According to Lester Salamon and Michael Lund, "a method through which government seeks a policy objective."

Types of Policy Tools

We create categories of tools because while there are many different government policies, there should be relatively few types of tools used to achieve the goals set out in policy (Salamon and Lund 1989: 28). We can then learn more about how government works to achieve its goals by carefully thinking about the broad types of tools and how government uses them to achieve certain ends.

Thinking about the tools of government is important because, according to Salamon, the nature of the world and the nature of government have changed. Salamon notes that, in recent years, there has developed "a set of theories that portrays government agencies as tightly structured hierarchies insulated from market forces and from effective citizen pressure and therefore free to serve the personal and institutional interests of bureaucrats instead" (Salamon 2002: 1). Salamon continues that governments have already begun to restructure to take into account the reform theories intended to make government more nimble and responsive to modern needs. As a result of this restructuring:

> a massive proliferation has occurred in the tools of public action, in the instruments or means used to address public problems. Whereas earlier government activity was largely restricted to the direct delivery of goods or services by government bureaucrats, it now embraces a dizzying array

of loans, loan guarantees, grants, contracts, social regulation, economic
regulation, insurance, tax expenditures, vouchers, and more.

(Salamon 2002: 1–2)

The balance of Salamon's edited volume is a rich and nearly exhaustive
discussion of all these tools. The challenge for the student of public policy
is to understand what these tools are, the assumptions underlying how they
work, and, in particular, how we might categorize these tools. Thinking about
tools is particularly useful because, as Salamon and Lund argue, there are
"central characteristics" of tools that distinguish some tools from others. The
key would then be to find the central characteristic of the various tools. One
can do so by looking at four dimensions of tools. The first is "the nature of
the activity in which government is engaged." Examining this dimension
gives us a general sense of what it is that the government is doing to achieve
a goal. There are, say Salamon and Lund, four broad categories of such activities: "outright money payments . . . provision of goods and services, including
information . . . legal protections, such as monopolies or guarantees . . . [and]
restrictions/penalties," such as regulation or criminal laws.

The next dimension is the "structure of the delivery system." The delivery
system reflects the extent to which implementation is likely to be more or
less complex. Salamon and Lund broadly categorize delivery systems as
"direct" and "indirect." Direct service delivery involves systems in which the
federal government is the sole actor in the delivery of a service. Salamon and
Lund cite Social Security as one such example; others would be air traffic
control, provided by the FAA, and regulation of broadcasting through the
Federal Communications Commission. Indirect service provision involves
the delivery of service through an intermediary, such as another level of
government, or a private actor, such as a business or nonprofit agency.
Examples of these types of programs include Community Development Block
Grant programs, which go to local governments, loan guarantees, which are
given to banks to encourage lending at lower rates or to riskier borrowers,
and research grants, which are given to nonprofit universities or research
institutes.

Related to but not exactly the same as the structure of the delivery system
is what Salamon and Lund call the "degree of centralization." In general, we
can be fairly certain that the more directly service is provided, the more the
administration of the program is centralized. The management of Social
Security is centralized in Washington because the federal government,
without the assistance or participation of intermediaries, directly administers

it. However, some federally provided services are also relatively decentralized. For example, the activities of the U.S. National Park Service (a unit of the Department of the Interior) and the Forest Service (a unit of the Department of Agriculture) are managed both by central offices in Washington and by expert staff in the field, who have some managerial and programmatic latitude because they need to respond effectively to local conditions.

Finally, Salamon and Lund describe the "degree of automaticity" of a policy tool, or, in other words, "the degree to which [programs] require detailed administrative action." Tax incentives, they argue, are largely self-executing because individuals will seek them out, thereby promoting the goals of the policy. The mortgage tax deduction is a virtually effortless way for the government to promote home ownership, because homeowners know that they can take the deduction and actively wish to do so. On the other hand, welfare programs that rely on a determination of eligibility "require almost case-by-case administrative decision making" that requires a substantial degree of management effort.

Other Categories of Policy Tools

Salamon and Lund provide a particularly well-developed system of thinking about policy tools, but many other scholars have also sought useful tool typologies. Howlett, Ramesh and Perl (2009) provide two broad categories of policy tools: "economic models" and "political models." Economic models of policy tools focus on individual freedom, initiative, and choice, therefore tending to value non-coercive tools over those that are more coercive. Howlett and Ramesh do note, however, that welfare economists, whose focus is on overall societal well-being rather than the aggregation of individual well-being (the focus of neoclassical economists), do acknowledge the need for more coercive tools (such as an income tax) to correct some of the flaws of laissez-faire economics. In both cases, however, economists look at the selection of a policy tool as a positive, technical question in which the problem to be solved, the agent to solve it (government, private sector, or some combination), and the nature of the tools themselves are matched with each other to find the best possible solution to a problem.

By contrast, those who look at policy tool choice from a more political perspective tend to follow this to avoid using the most coercive policy instruments (Howlett, Ramesh, and Perl 2009: 158). Clearly, this is not merely a technical matter: if the selection of how to deal with a problem is at least partially a function of societal pressures to favor one policy tool or another, then "politics" is involved not only in the understanding of the problem, but also in the ways we choose to solve it. For example, the decision to treat as adults young people who commit violent crimes, thereby leading to much more stringent sentences, is not a technical decision based on an economic and criminological analysis of these crimes and their perpetrators. Rather, it is a response to a society that seeks to "get tough on crime."

Still, there are important shortcomings to thinking about instruments from a solely political perspective. First, the matter of substitutability of one tool for another is not so simple, because political systems are constrained in their choice of tools, both ideologically and legally. On the legal side, for example, federal policy making on any number of issues, most notably civil rights, is predicated on the notion that government could regulate a wide range of activities under the commerce clause of the Constitution. These efforts have historically been successful; so successful, in fact, that Congress, in passing federal legislation making it a federal offense to have a gun within 1,000 yards of a school, justified its action in terms of the commerce clause, saying that school violence hinders interstate commerce. In *United States v. Lopez*, 514 U.S. 549 (1995), the Supreme Court, however, disagreed, noting that the connection between the goal and the commerce clause was so tenuous that the law was unconstitutional on federalism grounds. It is unclear whether this case went beyond the Court's sense of the appropriate application of the commerce clause, or if this signals a new era of legal doctrine surrounding the clause. In any case, this is an obvious constraint on various policy tools.

A potential problem with the economic way of thinking is that economics often makes too many assumptions about what is possible in policy making, on two levels. First, it assumes we really know what the problem is. In the give and take of policy making, an agreement to do something about a problem is often easier to achieve than an agreement on what precisely has to be done. This challenge is faced by those who write regulations and seek to implement government policies without creating controversy and disagreement over the means to the ends specified by the policy makers. Second, the economic perspective assumes that we have reasonably reliable information on how policy tools work. As with much of politics and policy making, it is very hard to know the causal connections in any policy system. While we may start with a causal theory, these theories are often flawed.

Given these two ways of thinking about tools, let us turn to a discussion of some of the current ways policy scholars categorize tools, as summarized in Table 9.2. I have sought to show where the names and concepts overlap, but, as you can see in Table 9.2, there are many different terms, from the more general to the more specific, that we can use to arrange policy tools.

Perhaps the most useful way to think about tools is the extent to which they are coercive or non-coercive. The more coercive a policy, the more likely compliance with the policy can be achieved, but the more likely it is that considerable resources will have to be devoted to providing the coercion needed to create compliance. Non-coercive policies such as incentives and hortatory policies are much easier to administer by virtue of their design and of the assumptions we make about how people will behave, but the likelihood of success is highly variable.

In the end, while the categories of tools are useful descriptors of the types of tools that one can use to achieve a set of goals, they do not tell us much about the relative strengths and weaknesses of these techniques. Levine, Peters, and Thompson (1990) provide a scheme for assessing the strengths and weaknesses of each tool. They acknowledge the tentative nature of these criteria, given what we know and do not know about how government works, but they are helpful in thinking about what tools might be best for particular goals. The scheme of Levine and colleagues is adapted and shown in Table 9.3.

Tools and Choices in Policy Design

Policy designers must consider a number of elements when selecting a policy tool. One of these elements is political feasibility. Because policy making is at least as much a political process as it is a technical process, even technically superior policy tools may not be adopted because they are politically unpopular. For example, the United States has an all-volunteer military and relies heavily on the military reserves for personnel, such as during the wars in Iraq and Afghanistan. An all-volunteer military is a more politically feasible way of meeting personnel needs than the draft, which was very controversial during the Vietnam War and would be very controversial today, given Americans' historic opposition to conscription. Other countries with different needs and political cultures, such as Israel, require compulsory military service; clearly, the political and security dynamics in Israel are different from those in the United States.

A second factor in the policy tool choice is the resources available to implement policy. For example, there may be two ways to battle the problem

TABLE 9.2 Types of Policy Tools or Instruments

Peters	Levine, Peters, and Thompson	Schneider and Ingram	Anderson	Description	Examples
Law	Law and regulation	Authority tools	Directive power	Pronouncements of policy that carry the force of law; that is, they compel particular behaviors and compliance.	Criminal law, environmental regulations, antitrust law.
Services	Direct provision of services or goods		Services	Services provided directly by the government to users.	Postal services, air traffic control, weather forecasting.
Money	Transfer payments		Benefits	"Transfer" of money from government to various interests.	Social Security, food stamps, veterans' benefits.
	Intergovernmental grants				
	Contracting out		Contracts	Contracts with private firms to provide goods or services.	Contracts to run prisons, hospitals; contracts to supply complex goods to government, such as military equipment, computers, space vehicles.
			General expenditures	General spending done by the government every day on the people, goods, and services it needs to function.	Personnel costs, supplies, utilities, etc. (government spending on these items has a substantial national and local economic effect).
			Market and proprietary operations	Government activities that have private counterparts, and that have economic and policy consequences.	Public corporations such as Tennessee Valley Authority (electrical power generation), market activities of the Federal Reserve Bank (interest rate setting, buying, and selling securities to influence the market).
Taxes	The tax system (tax expenditures)		Taxes	Policies intended to alter behavior by making some activities more or less economically desirable.	Tax credits (such as for student loan interest), tax deductions (mortgage tax deduction, medical expenses), taxes on tobacco and alcohol, called "sin taxes," to raise revenue and discourage consumption. Tax policies to encourage economic development in particular areas, such as Urban Enterprise Zones.
Other economic instruments	Loans and loan guarantees		Loans	Loans to induce economic activity or other desirable activity.	Small Business Administration (SBA) loans, student loans.

Type	Tool	Description	Examples
	Subsidies	Payments to ensure the economic viability of an activity, particularly when that activity addresses some broader goals.	Farm subsidies; subsidies to sports franchises; subsidies to business to locate in particular communities.
	Insurance	Provision of insurance where it is not generally available in the private insurance market.	Flood insurance, federal deposit insurance.
Suasion	Hortatory tools	Attempts to persuade people to engage in desirable behaviors or to avoid engaging in undesirable behaviors.	Public campaigns to discourage smoking or drinking, anti-drug campaigns, pro-exercise campaigns.
Inducements and sanctions	Sanctions	Tools that induce "'quasi-voluntary or quasi-coerced' actions based on tangible payoffs" (Schneider and Ingram).	Fines for violating regulations; bonus payments for timely completion of contracts.
Capacity-building tools		"Training, technical assistance, education, and information needed to take policy relevant actions" (Peters) and empower other agencies.	Technology transfer, training, the provision of information products to local government; cash transfers to hire more staff.
Learning tools		Tools to help understand the relevant aspects of policy problems.	Focus groups, opinion polls, censuses, basic and applied research (for example, National Institutes of Health [NIH], National Science Foundation [NSF]).
	Inspection		
	Licensing	Government authority to engage in an activity that is prohibited without such a license.	Driver's licenses, professional licensing (physicians, lawyers, engineers, and the like). Licensing of hospitals, permits, corporate charters (Anderson).
	Informal procedures	Procedures not specified in law or regulation to resolve problems.	Exchange of correspondence between taxpayers and IRS to resolve disputes; plea-bargaining in criminal process.

Sources: B. Guy Peters, American Public Policy: Promise and Performance (Chappaqua, NY: Chatham House/Seven Rivers, 1999), pp. 6–13; Charles H. Levine, B. Guy Peters, and Frank J. Thompson, Public Administration: Challenges, Choices, Consequences (Glenview, IL: Scott, Foresman/Little Brown, 1990), pp. 64–73; Anne Larason Schneider and Helen Ingram, Policy Design for Democracy (Lawrence, KS: University Press of Kansas, 1997), pp. 93–97; James E. Anderson, Public Policymaking, 4th ed. (Boston, MA: Houghton Mifflin, 2000), pp. 233–244.

TABLE 9.3 Characteristics of Policy Instruments

	Certainty	Timeliness	Less Cost	Efficiency	Effectiveness	Flexibility	Visibility	Accountability	Choice
Explanation	Certainty of the administrative process and the compliance of targets	Extent to which the tool works quickly	Expense of the tool	Extent to which the tool creates maximum outputs for a given input	Extent to which the tool is likely to achieve its goals	Ease with which the tool can be altered to changing needs and circumstances	Extent to which the program is well known or less well known (sometimes invisibility is an important goal)	Extent to which implementers are accountable for their actions	Degree of which imple-citizen menters are choice accountable afforded by for their the policy actions
Direct service provision	+					–	+	+	–
Transfers	+					–	+	–	+
Grants	–					–		+	+
Tax expenditures	–			+				–	+
Regulations	+						+	+	–
Loans	–	–	+				–	–	+
Insurance	+	–	+				–	–	+
Contracts	–	–		–		+	–	–	+
Licensing	–					–			
Informal procedures	–		+			+			
Capacity building	–	–					–	–	
Inducements	–	–	+					–	
Sanctions	+	+	–					–	
Hortatory tools	–	–					+		+

Note: Plus signs indicate the presence of an attribute; minus signs indicate the absence of that attribute.

Source: From Public Administration: Challenges, Choices, Consequences by Charles H. Levine, B. Guy Peters, and Frank J. Thompson, Exhibit 3.1. Reprinted by permission of Addison-Wesley Educational Publishers, Inc.

of forest fires: post thousands of lookouts and firefighters in the forests or employ a public education program to tell people that only they can prevent forest fires. Smokey the Bear is the well known symbol of fire prevention efforts. The U.S. Forest Service slogan is now "only you can prevent wildfires" to address the broader fire hazard.

The U.S. Forest Service emphasizes the hortatory tool—educating the public about fires—because it is much less expensive than more aggressive efforts to detect and prevent fires caused by carelessness. Of course, the public education campaign may not be fully effective in addressing the forest fire risk, and many fires are still started by carelessness, but this campaign and others, such as encouraging people to stop smoking and to wear seat belts, was successful in inducing behavioral change among a large enough proportion of the population to justify its costs. Such campaigns can also become problematic in the face of newer science. We now know that occasional fires are necessary for the forest ecosystem, that routine fire actually burns accumulated fuel—dead wood—without damaging live trees, and aggressive fire suppression techniques can often make more fuel accumulate, thereby making big fires worse. This is the persistent danger of public education tools—the difficulties involved in altering public behavior or attitudes when new information becomes available.

The resource question actually falls within a broader category Salamon and Lund (1989: 41) call "administrative feasibility," or "the degree of ease or difficulty involved in establishing and operating a program." Clearly, operating any public program is likely to be much more difficult if adequate resources are lacking.

A third element of policy tool choice is based on the behavioral assumptions about the target populations. Policy targets are the entities—people or organizations—whose behavior the policy seeks to alter. The choice of the policy tool is a function of the assumed behavior of the policy target. The choice of a coercive tool reveals something about the assumed behavior of the targets that the choice of a set of incentives would not. This link between the policy target and the policy tool falls under a broader category that Salamon and Lund call "effectiveness," which can be assessed on two levels: the "supply effectiveness" of the program in providing a necessary level of output to induce changes in the target population, and the "targeting effectiveness" of the program in altering policy targets' behaviors.

This discussion tends to suggest that policy tools are sometimes used in isolation. Yet there is nothing to suggest that multiple policy tools are not used, and, indeed, it is often true that multiple policy tools are used to address a problem. For example, in drug policy, we have stiffened punishment for drug dealing, have attempted to seize drugs before they enter the country, and experimented with public education programs, such as the Just Say No campaign, the DARE program, and current efforts by the Partnership for a Drug-Free America to promote better parental knowledge of what their kids are doing and with whom they are socializing. The tendency to "bundle" policy tools into packages of tools that are all intended to achieve similar goals is noted in recent research, which shows that certain types of local economic development tools are likely to be bundled into an overall strategy (Kassekert and Feiock 2009).

CONCLUSION

This chapter focused on the things policy makers must consider when designing policies. As has become a recurring theme in this book, this process is much more complex than it might initially appear. Goals conflict with each other or are ambiguous, and policies are often designed without a sound causal theory to help policy makers know whether a particular kind of policy will work. All these aspects of design are important because policy design will have a considerable influence on the choice of tools employed to achieve the stated goals of a policy.

The next chapter discusses the implementation of public policies, and how we can learn from policy failure. Policy design, including the choice of policy tools, and policy implementation are inextricably linked to each other. The choice of policy tools both influences implementation and is influenced by implementation, as we will see in the next chapter. Furthermore, the choices of tools and implementation design reinforce each other throughout the implementation process. As you read Chapter 10, consider whether and to what extent we can explain implementation success or failure by understanding the strengths or weaknesses in the design of the policies being implemented, including the choice of policy tools being adopted.

KEY TERMS

causal theory	policy goal
efficiency	policy tools
policy design	polis

QUESTIONS FOR DISCUSSION, REFLECTION, AND RESEARCH

- Why is it difficult to separate policy design and implementation?

- What role does ambiguity play when there are conflicting policy goals? How does ambiguity help promote policy making? How does goal ambiguity make policy design more difficult?

- Why is it essential for policy makers to have a causal theory when creating a policy design? Can you think of examples of a poor policy design in which it appears that the causal theory is incorrect? How would you redesign such a policy to fit the better causal theory?

- Why does Deborah Stone argue that efficiency should not be the sole goal of implementing public policy? Are there public policies that exist that are inefficient but that serve other, more important social goals? Does this imply that there are more important goals than efficiency? What are these goals?

- You may find this to be an interesting exercise in policy ambiguity and perceptions of problems. Gather up a group of four to six people; your classmates, perhaps, or friends, roommates, or family. Then think of a public problem that you all agree should be addressed. Once you agree that something is a problem, jot down your responses to these questions:

  - *What* causes the problem you have agreed is a bad thing?

  - What *tools* or interventions would you use to alleviate the problem you all identified?

> Discuss what you conclude among yourselves. Are your causal theories different? If so, are your proposed interventions or policy tools different or similar? Why?

ADDITIONAL READING

My thinking about policy goals is greatly influenced by Deborah Stone's *Policy Paradox*. She also has a thoughtful section on policy tools, although the terminology she uses is not the same as much of the current scholarship on policy tools. Readers interested in the many ways of thinking of policy tools might browse Lester M. Salamon and Odus V. Elliott's *The Tools of Government: A Guide to the New Governance* (New York: Oxford University Press, 2002). This book is an encyclopedic treatment of the various methods of government intervention, written by top scholars in the policy sciences.

An important book on policy design is Anne Larason Schneider and Helen Ingram, *Policy Design for Democracy* (Lawrence, KS: University Press of Kansas, 1997). Additional advanced (and often highly technical) works on policy design include Robert Agranoff and Michael McGuire, *Collaborative Public Management: New Strategies for Local Governments* (Washington, DC: Georgetown University Press, 2003); Huib Pellikaan and Robert J. van der Veen, *Environmental Dilemmas and Policy Design* (New York: Cambridge University Press, 2002); and David Edward Michael Sappington, *Principles of Regulatory Policy Design* (World Bank, Office of the Vice President, 1994). Sound sources on policy tools themselves include Christopher Howard, "Testing the Tools Approach: Tax Expenditures versus Direct Expenditures," *Public Administration Review* 55, no. 5 (1995): 439–447; Lester M. Salamon, ed., *Beyond Privatization: The Tools of Government Action* (Washington, DC: Urban Institute, 1989); and Anne Schneider and Helen Ingram, "Behavioral Assumptions of Policy Tools," *Journal of Politics* 52 (May 1990): 510–529.

NOTE

1   The provision in question is contained in section 215(a)(10) (amending 50 U.S.C. 1861 *et seq.*).(a)(1) "The Director of the Federal Bureau of Investigation or a designee of the Director (whose rank shall be no lower than Assistant Special Agent in Charge) may make an

application for an order requiring the production of any tangible things (including books, records, papers, documents, and other items) for an investigation to protect against international terrorism or clandestine intelligence activities, provided that such investigation of a United States person is not conducted solely upon the basis of activities protected by the first amendment to the Constitution."

REFERENCES

Anderson, James E. 2014. *Public Policymaking*. 8th ed. Boston, MA: Wadsworth.

Barrett, Ted. 2005. "House Approves Renewal of Patriot Act." *CNN.com*, July 22. Accessed January 29, 2015. www.cnn.com/2005/POLITICS/07/21/patriot.act/.

Egan, Timothy. 2004. "Sensing the Eyes of Big Brother, and Pushing Back." *New York Times*, August 8, 20, 1.

Eggen, Dan. 2002. "FBI Seeks Data on Foreign Students; Colleges Call Request Illegal." *Washington Post*, December 25, A1.

Foderaro, Lisa W. 2004. "Board Rejects Parts of Patriot Act." *New York Times*, September 19, 7, 14 (Westchester Section).

Greenhouse, Linda M. 2002. "A Penchant for Secrecy." *New York Times*, May 5. Accessed January 29, 2015. www.nytimes.com/2002/05/05/weekinreview/05GREE.html.

Howlett, Michael, M. Ramesh, and Anthony Perl. 2009. *Studying Public Policy: Policy Cycles & Policy Subsystems*. 3rd ed. New York: Oxford University Press.

Hudson, David L. 2004. "Patriot Act." Last modified September 2012. Accessed January 29, 2015. www.newseuminstitute.org/patriot-act/.

Ingram, Helen and Dean Mann. 1980. "Policy Failure: An Issue Deserving Attention." In *Why Policies Succeed or Fail*, edited by Helen Ingram and Dean Mann, 11–32. Beverly Hills, CA: Sage.

Isikoff, Michael. 2003. "Show Me the Money." *Newsweek*, December 1.

Kassekert, Anthony and Richard Feiock. 2009. "Policy Tool Selection: Predicting the Bundling of Economic Development Policy Instruments Using a Multivariate Probit Analysis." American Political Science Association Annual Meeting, Toronto, ON, September 6.

Kingdon, John W. 2011. *Agendas, Alternatives, and Public Policies*. Updated 2nd ed. Longman Classics in Political Science. Boston, MA: Longman.

Lacayo, Richard. 2003. "The War Comes Back Home: Can Attorney General John Ashcroft Fight Terrorism on Our Shores without Injuring Our Freedoms?" *Time*, May 12.

Laumann, Edward O. and David Knoke. 1987. *The Organizational State: Social Choice in National Policy Domains*. Madison, WI: University of Wisconsin Press.

Levine, Charles H., B. Guy Peters, and Frank J. Thompson. 1990. *Public Administration: Challenges, Choices, Consequences*. Glenview, IL: Scott Foresman.

Lichtblau, Eric. 2004. "Effort to Curb Scope of Antiterrorism Law Falls Short." *New York Times*, July 9, A3.

Lipford, Jody. 1999. "Twenty Years after Humphrey-Hawkins." *Independent Review* 4(1): 41–63.

McGee, Jim. 2001. "An Intelligence Giant in the Making: Anti-Terrorism Law Likely to Bring Domestic Apparatus of Unprecedented Scope." *Washington Post*, November 4, A04.

O'Harrow Jr., Robert. 2002. "In Terror War, Privacy vs. Security: Search for Illicit Activities Taps Confidential Financial Data." *Washington Post*, June 3, A1.

Reissman, Frank. 1999. "Full Employment Now?" *Social Policy & Administration* 4 (Summer): 4.

Salamon, Lester M. 2002. "The New Governance and the Tools of Public Action: An Introduction." In *The Tools of Government: A Guide to the New Governance*, edited by Lester M. Salamon, Chapter 1, 1–48. Oxford and New York: Oxford University Press.

Salamon, Lester M. and Michael S. Lund. 1989. "The Tools Approach: Basic Analytics." In *Beyond Privatization: The Tools of Government Action*, edited by Lester M. Salamon, 23–49. Washington, DC: Urban Institute Press.

Schneider, Anne Larason and Helen Ingram. 1997. *Policy Design for Democracy*. Lawrence, KS: University Press of Kansas.

Stone, Deborah A. 1989. "Causal Stories and the Formation of Policy Agendas." *Political Science Quarterly* 104(2): 281–300.

Stone, Deborah A. 2011. *Policy Paradox: The Art of Political Decision Making*. 3rd ed. New York: Norton.

Trenholm, Christopher, Barbara Devaney, Ken Fortson, Lisa Quay, Justin Wheeler, and Melissa Clark. 2007. *Impacts of Four Title V Section 510 Abstinence Education Programs*. Princeton, NJ: Inc. Mathematica Policy Research. Accessed January 28, 2015. www.mathematica-mpr.com/publications/PDFs/impactabstinence.pdf.

United States Justice Department. 2004. *Report from the Field: The USA Patriot Act at Work*. Washington, DC: United States Justice Department. Accessed May 12, 2015. www.justice.gov/archive/olp/pdf/patriot_report_from_the_field0704.pdf.

CHAPTER 10

Policy Implementation, Failure, and Learning

OVERVIEW

This chapter focuses on policy implementation, failure, and learning. In reading about implementation, it is important to note that it is impossible to separate the process of designing policies from their implementation—much as all the stages of the policy process are hard to separate. Design and implementation are very closely related because the choices made in the design of a policy will profoundly influence the way a policy is implemented, which then influences the outcomes of these policies. In fact, policy designers often base their policy designs on experience with similar policies that have already been implemented.

Another reason that design and implementation are hard to separate from the rest of the policy process is that the policy design process continues during design and implementation. Congress's enactment of law does not result in a simple translation from Congress's will to actual action on the part of government agencies, or actual compliance on the part of the people whose behavior the policy seeks to change. Agencies must take what Congress has passed and figure out what it requires or allows them to do. The process of translating vague legislative commands into rules and regulations can be among the most contentious and difficult activities in the entire policy process.

Once policies are implemented, experience with it and with similar policies will often change the policy design, even when the policy and goals are supposedly in place and operating. For example, targeted federal spending on particular urban problems was once granted based on focused federal goals and specific programmatic interests. This policy changed because, to a considerable extent, implementation was not as successful as had been hoped. The targeted policy was replaced by block grants, in which state and local governments are freer to make choices about how the money is spent, provided that relatively broad federal goals are met.

THE IMPLEMENTATION OF PUBLIC POLICIES

implementation
The process by which policies enacted by government are put into effect by the relevant agencies.

Once the designers of policies have designed their policy tools, the various actors in the policy process turn their attention to the **implementation** of public policy. The study of "program implementation is concerned with what happens to a policy or program after it has been formulated" (Ryan 1995). Until the late 1960s, there were few studies of policy implementation. Few scholars had sought to systematically study what happens after legislation or some other statement of policy is enacted and then put into effect. Some studies described the implementation process, but had not set out to create a theory of policy implementation.

Of course, this description of implementation in the policy process is linear and simplistic. It assumes that policy design and tool selection occur separately from policy implementation. In fact, we know that both aspects are important to the success of public policies. But we can distinguish between the design and tools phase and the implementation phase to the extent that policy implementation relies on the behavior of the implementers and the policy targets. While these behaviors may be anticipated in the design process, one is never sure how policy will actually be implemented once the policy interacts with the various aspects of the policy environment, with the actual implementers, and the policy targets.

It is important to understand policy implementation because it is a key feature of the policy process, and learning from the problems encountered in implementation can foster learning about better ways to structure policies to ensure that they have the effects that designers of these policies seek. In addition, perhaps to a greater extent than other elements of the policy process, implementation studies have emphasized advice to policy makers as to how to structure programs to increase the likelihood of implementation success. Thus, when students of policy implementation talk about "top-down" or "bottom-up" implementation designs, they are talking about ways of studying policy design and ways of structuring policy implementation to enhance the likelihood of implementation success. In any case, we do know, and have known for some time, that policies are not self-executing, regardless of the hopes and beliefs of policy designers.

If the bureaucracy was a strictly neutral institution that, as Woodrow Wilson once argued, simply did what elected officials ordered it to do, then all the problems people have cited about bureaucracy—in particular, the problems of discretion and accountability—would never enter into the discussion of implementation. Because bureaucracies do have discretion in how they implement policies, this section reviews some ways of looking at policy implementation that see bureaucratic discretion as a problem to be overcome by sound choices in policy design. But, to complicate the picture again, even the simplest policy with the most willing bureaucracies involved in implementation confronts implementing agencies with two big questions: what does the legislative branch want done, and how do we do it? Discerning intent, and then figuring out how to meet the implied goals, is extremely challenging. Thus, as Smith and Larimer note, the implementation process replicates, in many ways, all the challenges of the policy process, starting with problems—in this case, discerning intent—through designing tools in a way that those further down the implementation change will willingly engage in the desired behavior (Smith and Larimer 2013).

Approaches to the Study of Implementation

As Smith and Larimer (2013) note, there are three main eras of policy implementation research. The first era, which emerged in the late 1960s through the early 1970s, is characterized by works such as *Implementation* (Pressman and Wildavsky 1984) and *New Towns in Town* (Derthick 1972). The authors undertook these studies to understand why particular policies, such as the Economic Development Administration's efforts to relieve poverty in Oakland or the Johnson administration's "New Towns in Town" efforts, seemed to fall short of their goals. These studies focused on individual case studies and did not create more generalizable theory that could be applied to and tested with other cases. Indeed, many studies of administration and organization discussed matters of policy implementation, even if that term was not well developed or if that aspect was not the centerpiece of the research project.

A second era of implementation studies, which began in the mid 1970s, sought to create systematic theories of the policy process that were generalizable to many cases, rather than focused on one or a few cases. As this research progressed, one could discern two separate research approaches. The first of these approaches emphasizes a "top-down" perspective on policy implementation. Its proponents claim that one can understand policy implementation by looking at the goals and strategies adopted in the statute or other policy, as structured by the implementers of policy. These studies focus on the gaps between the goals set by a policy's drafters and the actual implementation and outcomes of the policy. The second approach emphasizes a "bottom-up" perspective, which suggests that implementation is best studied by starting at the lowest levels of the implementation system or "chain" and moving upward to see where implementation is more or less successful.

Top-Down Approaches to Implementation

top-down approach A way of studying policy design and implementation that considers the goals of the highest-level policy designers, and traces the design and implementation of the policy through the lowest-level implementers.

Some representative studies in the top-down research tradition include research by Carl Van Horn (1979) and Carl Van Horn and Donald Van Meter (1976), as well as Daniel Mazmanian and Paul Sabatier's (1989) studies of the factors that condition successful implementation. The **top-down approach** is based on a set of important assumptions:

- Policies contain clearly defined goals against which performance can be measured. As Neal Ryan (1995) puts it, "Top-down implementation strategies greatly depend on the capacity of policy objectives to be clearly and consistently defined."

- Policies contain clearly defined policy tools for the accomplishment of goals.

- The policy is characterized by the existence of a single statute or other authoritative statement of policy.

- There is an "implementation chain" that "starts with a policy message at the top and sees implementation as occurring in a chain" (Dyer 1999).

- Policy designers have good knowledge of the capacity and commitment of the implementers. Capacity encompasses the availability of resources for an implementing organization to carry out its tasks, including monetary and human resources, legal authority and autonomy, and the knowledge needed to effectively implement policy. Commitment includes the desire of the implementers to carry out the goals of the top-level policy designers; a high level of commitment means that the lower-level implementers, particularly those at the "street level," such as teachers, police officers, or social workers, share the values and goals of the policy designers.

In a top-down model of policy design, the implementer assumes that these features are present or that any problems suggested by these assumptions can be overcome. The focus then is on creating the proper structures and controls to encourage or compel compliance with the goals set at the top. But there are some substantial weaknesses with this approach that you may recognize from earlier chapters in this book.

Perhaps the most problematic feature of top-down models is the emphasis on clear objectives or goals. Without a consensus on what program goals are, it is hard to set a benchmark for program success and failure. For example, in 1973, Congress established the 55-mile-per-hour (mph) speed limit on the nation's freeways as a method for promoting energy conservation, because, in most cases, driving one's car at 55 mph is more fuel-efficient than driving it at 70 mph. Yet most gains in fuel economy between 1973 and the early 1990s were a result of federal policies requiring that a manufacturer's vehicles achieve an average fuel economy of 27.5 miles per gallon for cars and 20.7 miles per gallon for light trucks. Most manufacturers comply with this standard. However, the 55 mph speed limit had a side benefit—it substantially reduced highway fatalities in the early years of its enforcement.

On what accomplishment, then, should the 55 mph limit be assessed? In terms of motorists' compliance and state enforcement, the 55 mph speed limit was generally unsuccessful, and its widespread unpopularity led to its repeal. In terms of fuel economy, the results were inconclusive, but the safety benefits were substantial. Highway safety advocates fought hard to keep the 55 mph limit in place and were successful in this fight until the late 1980s. This is an example of how advocates for a policy will redefine policy goals to justify the continuance of a program and how new groups can enter the debate to highlight new goals and benefits of programs—or to argue that a program has outlived its value. In the case of the 55 mph speed limit, by the mid 1980s the safety and fuel efficiency benefits, some argued, were less than they had been because of the aforementioned increase in automobile fuel economy (gains that had been lost to some extent in the late 1990s with the advent of SUVs, but regained in the 2000s with new federal fuel economy standards) and the increased safety of most newer cars.

Another example of multiple objectives is found in the management of the nation's forests by the U.S. Forest Service (USFS), which must administer the forests to serve "multiple uses," ranging from recreation to logging. By what goals should the Forest Service's efforts be measured? This is a constant source of conflict for the agency, as environmentalists and recreational users battle logging interests and their local allies over which aspect of forest policy— timber supply or resource conservation and recreation—should be emphasized by the USFS. When policy makers fail to provide one goal or a coherent, mutually compatible set of goals, implementation is likely to be difficult as agencies and people charged with putting policies into effect pursue different goals.

Another problem with top-down models is the assumption that there is a single national government that can successfully structure policy implementation and provide for direct delivery of services. But most policies made by the federal government require considerable state and, in many cases, local governmental cooperation. The 50 state governments have constitutionally protected rights and responsibilities, so they are often reluctant to surrender their power and prerogatives to distant agencies headquartered in Washington. One cannot say, then, that the federal government can mandate any policy it sees fit; if it attempts to do so, it may endanger state and local cooperation, and can generate indifference or outright conflict with the states. Even within the federal government itself, this assumption of a strong central government assumes a unitary method of decision making that ignores competing or overlapping agencies and their staffs, and the interest groups that have an interest in these agencies' work. While the focus of implementation may be in one agency, several other actors will have an influence on implementation success or failure. Given this dismal account, one might assume that the federal government—the "top"—cannot structure implementation at all. However, the top can set guidelines for implementation, if not hard and fast rules (O'Toole 1986; Sabatier 1986), provided government actors act carefully and work collaboratively across agencies and with the states and local actors.

How do states resist mandates from the federal government? Malcolm Goggin and his colleagues have cited instances of "strategic delay" at the state level, where states seek to slow implementation in order to develop ways to adapt the program to local needs, or to induce the federal government to provide more funding or other incentives (Goggin et al. 1990). However, not all delay is strategic—some delay or outright refusal to implement policy is a reaction to local and state desires to not implement a policy at all. This is sometimes due to local political pressures, such as when some states failed to aggressively enforce the 55 mph speed limit. At other times, street-level bureaucrats may refuse to implement a policy that comes from the top: the police, for example, may resist changes in policing procedure based on their professional experience, as the "dropsy" evidence case in Chapter 7 suggests. Top-down approaches often ignore the relative ease with which many implementers and interest groups can work to subvert the originally established goals. On the other hand, Paul Sabatier rejects the inevitability of "adaptive" implementation in which target groups and street-level bureaucrats subvert the original program's goals. Sabatier argues that top policy designers do have choices about who implements a policy and what incentives and sanctions to impose for noncompliance and can influence the expectations and needs of target groups so that adaptive compliance should be unnecessary or would be counterproductive (Sabatier 1986: 25).

Finally, top-down approaches assume that policy is contained in a single statute or other authoritative statement. The fragmented and in some ways incrementalist nature of policy making in the United States means that when one talks about "environmental policy" or "educational policy" or "health policy," one is discussing a wide collection of separate and sometimes contradictory policies. This is related to the tendency of top-down approaches to assume a relatively clear division between policy enactment, on the one hand, and policy implementation, on the other. Indeed, many of the studies of implementation from a public administration perspective tend to adopt this distinction, which may be analytically useful but runs the risk of assuming that the same pressures that work to shape policy adoption do not exist in policy implementation.

Bottom-Up Approaches to Implementation

In a reaction to the overly structured top-down research approach—in particular, to dissatisfaction with its ability to explain many unsuccessful outcomes, and in reaction to the flaws of top-down policy design—researchers began to view implementation from the perspective of "street-level bureaucrats" (Lipsky 1971). Richard Elmore, the key proponent of the **bottom-up approach**, calls this "backward mapping," in which the implementation

bottom-up approach A way of studying policy design and implementation that considers the abilities and motivations of the lowest-level implementers, and tracks policy design from that level to the highest levels of government.

process and the relevant relationships are mapped backward, from the ultimate implementer to the topmost policy designers (Elmore 1979). This approach is built on a set of assumptions that stand in marked contrast to the implicit assumptions of "forward mapping" or top-down approaches.

First, the bottom-up approach recognizes that goals are ambiguous rather than explicit and may conflict not only with other goals in the same policy area, but also with the norms and motivations of the street-level bureaucrats. As Rene Torenvlied (1996) notes, "The compliance problem arises when there is a conflict of interest between implementation agencies and politicians." Top-down models are most concerned with compliance, while bottom-up approaches value understanding how conflict can be alleviated by bargaining and sometimes compromise to maximize the likelihood of achieving the policy goals.

Second, the bottom-up approach does not require that there be a single defined "policy" in the form of a statute or other form. Rather, policy can be thought of as a set of laws, rules, practices, and norms, such as "energy policy" or "criminal procedure," that shape the ways in which government and interest groups address these problems. Thus, implementation can be viewed as a continuation of the conflicts and compromises that occur throughout the policy process, not just before it begins and at the point of enactment. This makes for a more realistic depiction of the implementation process, and clearly accommodates the type of policy tool bundling described in Chapter 8.

This bottom-up approach has a number of features to commend it. In particular, the lack of a focus on a particular program and on a fixed, top-to-bottom implementation chain means that the bottom-up approach can view implementation as working through a network of actors—much like an issue network or policy community—rather than through some rigidly specified process that fails to account for the richness of the policy-making environment. But there are also important shortcomings to consider in the bottom-up approach.

Paul Sabatier argues that the bottom-up approach overemphasizes the ability of the street-level bureaucrats to frustrate the goals of the top policy makers. Street-level bureaucrats are not entirely free agents. They are constrained to act in a particular way based on their professional norms and obligations, by the resources available to them, and by legal sanctions that can be applied for noncompliance. Police officers, for example, who use "too much" discretion and thereby ignore procedural rules for handling suspects or evidence can lose their jobs or face criminal charges; teachers who violate professional norms can be demoted or lose their jobs. States that fail to implement key features of federal policy put themselves at risk of losing substantial amounts of federal money, so states and local governments are under pressure to bring their agencies into compliance; the No Child Left Behind Act is a good example. Nor do street-level bureaucrats necessarily have the resources to thwart policy designers; they may be able to delay, but not entirely subvert, implementation. Finally, the tension between bottom-up and top-down approaches may overstate the extent to which local implementers will resist policies handed down from above. In some cases, the street-level bureaucrat may also *want* to follow the lead of the top-level designers, supporting the goals handed down from higher up, and working as best they can to implement national goals.

Bottom-up models of implementation also assume that groups are active participants in the implementation process. This is not always true, however. Peter May argues that some policies can be categorized as "policies without publics," which are developed and implemented with relatively little public input, particularly when those policy areas are highly technical (May 1990). Along these lines, Sabatier also argues that the bottom-up approach fails to take into account the power differences of the target groups. As Anne Schneider and Helen Ingram note, some target populations are more positively constructed than others, with the result that those with greater power can have a greater influence on the impact of policies that affect them than can other groups (Schneider and Ingram 1993). Clearly, business interests are going to be treated differently in implementation design than are the poor or prisoners, and these treatments are reflected in the choice of policy tools. The choice of tools is made at the top, based on the desired behavioral change and the nature of the target population itself.

While these approaches to implementation have shortcomings, it is worthwhile to consider how these two approaches to implementation contribute to our knowledge of this essential element of public policy. The top-down approach is much more useful when there is a single, dominant program that is being studied. Several times in this book, I have mentioned specific legislative enactments that made important policy changes. It would be appropriate to study the implementation of legislation such as No Child Left Behind or the Homeland Security Act from the top down. Much of the policy related to these acts was designed in Congress and the federal executive branch and, regardless of the complexity and span of issues raised in each law, they were structured from the outset to be promoted, managed, and evaluated by top government officials. Sabatier also argues that top-down approaches are appropriate when one has limited resources to "backward map" the implementation of a particular issue. It is considerably easier to look up statutes and other pronouncements issued by top-level policy designers than it is to map all the various interests, agencies, and street-level officials that will carry out a policy. If you are reading this book for a course, you may find that if you choose to write analysis of implementation, it is much more efficient to start from the most visible policy changes rather than from the bottom, where the less visible policies are made.

On the other hand, bottom-up modeling makes sense when there is no single dominant program (such as in a state's penal code, which consists of many policy statements regarding the nature and severity of crimes) and when one is more interested in the local dynamics of implementation than in the broad sweep of design. It is useful to consider the local factors, from both practical and academic perspectives, since local experience with implementation success or failure can yield important lessons for policy implementers.

Synthesis: A Third Generation of Implementation Research

Because of the relative strengths and weaknesses of the top-down and bottom-up approaches, researchers have sought to combine the benefits of these approaches into one model or synthesis that can address the structuring of policy from the top as well as the likelihood of its subversion or at least its alteration at the point of implementation.

Richard Elmore has sought to combine his idea of "backward mapping" with a "forward mapping element" (Elmore 1985). By looking both forward and backward, we can understand that top policy makers can make choices of policy instruments or tools to structure implementation, while realizing that the motivations and needs of lower-level implementers must be taken into account. Paul Sabatier (1986) also argues that a conceptual framework should be developed that combines the best of the top-down and bottom-up approaches. Indeed, at the same time that Sabatier was writing, Laurence O'Toole (1986) argued that better thinking on implementation was needed precisely to provide policy makers and designers with useful advice. The top-down approach is best where there is a dominant program (i.e., law) that is well structured and where the researcher's resources for studying implementation are limited, as when a student is researching the implementation of a program for a term paper or an implementer needs a quick analysis to investigate how to structure a program. By contrast, the bottom-up approach is best where one is interested in the dynamics of local implementation and where there is no single dominant program. One begins by analyzing diffuse street-level behavior rather than focused, top-down activity. Because of this diffuse behavior, gathering the needed data to tell the implementation story can be challenging, as multiple sources must be consulted and analyzed.

Sabatier's synthesis relies on a framework for studying public policy known as the Advocacy Coalition Framework, or ACF, which is discussed at greater length in Chapter 10. In this application of the ACF to implementation, Sabatier's synthesis starts by adopting the bottom-up perspective, which involves looking at "a whole variety of public and private actors involved with a policy problem—as well as their concerns with understanding the perspectives and strategies of all major categories of actors (not simply program proponents)" (Sabatier 1986: 39). This contrasts with the top-down focus on the topmost designers of policies. But Sabatier also adopts the top-down perspective by providing a simplified, abstract model of a complex system and by recognizing the importance of the structural features of policy emphasized by the top-down theorists. The primary reason Sabatier uses the ACF to think about implementation is that it reflects the growing sense that implementation does not take place in a one-to-one relationship between the designers, implementers, and targets, but is rather contained within a policy subsystem; the ACF is one way to think about the organization of subsystems.

Refining and reconciling the top-down and bottom-up approaches, Goggin and his colleagues have devised a theory of policy implementation that relies on the sending of *messages* between policy makers and implementers (Goggin et al. 1990). This study takes into account an important feature of most policy design: that implementation is as much a matter of negotiation and communication as it is a matter of command. Even commands are sometimes resisted because they are unclear or inconsistent with the receiver's expectations. Goggin and his colleagues sum up their argument in two key propositions:

- Clear messages sent by credible officials and received by receptive implementers who have or are given sufficient resources and who implement policies supported by affected groups lead to implementation success.

- Strategic delay on the part of states, while delaying the implementation of policies, can actually lead to improved implementation of policies through innovation, policy learning, bargaining, and the like.

The first of these propositions is a short summary of what has been learned thus far in the study of implementation analysis, but packaged as a matter of communication between various actors. In actual experience, messages are often unclear, officials often lack credibility, and implementers are often not receptive or, if they are, do not receive sufficient resources or are opposed by the affected groups. The second proposition counters some of the gloom that had settled around many policy implementation studies. Goggin and his colleagues found, in certain policy areas, that states that "strategically delayed" implementation—in order to seek clarification of a policy, raise more funds, ensure support of affected groups, and so on—often had better success in implementing a policy than did states that immediately implemented a policy. It seems that it would behoove the analyst to take a longer-term approach to policy studies, since what may at first blush look like delay on the part of a state or local government may in fact be a period of strategic positioning and adaptation of a policy that actually improves the quality of the service being delivered under the policy, as well as enhancing the likelihood of any implementation.

The debate continues in policy studies over the best approach to the study of implementation and even whether we should continue studying implementation or focus our attention on other, supposedly more fruitful avenues of research. As long as policies fail or appear to fail, implementation studies will remain important to policy makers and to students of the policy process.

POLICY FAILURE AND LEARNING FROM IT

For some reason, both journalists and policy scientists focus on bad news: journalists will report when the government has lost a lot of money, but will ignore evidence of those instances when the government has saved money through some sort of innovation. At the same time, most books on policy implementation describe policy failures. There are probably simple reasons for our concentration on policy failure. The old saying, "If it ain't broke, don't fix it," may dominate our thinking about government: after all, if a government program is reasonably successful, what need is there to describe how it works when we can learn more from failure? I am not sure that we should take this approach, and I believe we should study and learn from government successes—of which there are many—as well as government failures. Indeed, after the 2001 terrorist attacks, a prominent political scientist, Paul Light, wrote a very useful book on governmental achievements and successes—successes we should celebrate as our own because, as Americans, it is *our* government and the efforts of thousands and millions of our fellow citizens that help make things work (Light 2002). But because there are so many purported policy failures, and so much written about them, it is worth considering the reasons for these claims of failure.

No doubt you have asserted, and heard others claim, that a policy has failed. "Our policy against illegal immigrants has failed," you may argue, "because there are still thousands of people coming across the border illegally every day." Or you may conclude that aviation security has failed, in part because, in late 2009, a would-be bomber was able to hide a potential bomb in his underwear, even as security was supposed to be much improved after the September 11 attacks. Let us simply assume that these claims are at least partially true. You can then say that the policy has failed to meet its goals: to keep out illegal immigrants and to allow only legal immigrants to come to the country, or to keep bad people off of airplanes. *Why* might the policy be a failure? You might argue that the border patrol or the airport screeners are incompetent, that the officers are competent but their managers are not, or that the policy was doomed to fail because of resource shortfalls or because the goals of the policy—near-zero illegal immigrants or zero terrorist attacks— are just too difficult to achieve. Sometimes we say that a policy is unsuccessful, if not an outright failure, because the policy does not serve enough people or because resources and services are spread too thin among those it does serve. In other words, we tell causal stories of failure much as we tell causal stories of why problems exist in the first place. The actual idea of "failure" itself is defined implicitly, but not explicitly. In other words, the meaning of "failure" and the context in which it is discussed are never really specified.

Helen Ingram and Dean Mann provide us with a number of useful ways to think about policy failure. They argue that "success and failure are slippery concepts, often highly subjective and reflective of an individual's goals, perception of need, and perhaps even psychological disposition toward life" (Ingram and Mann 1980, 12). In other words, failure is perhaps in the eye of the beholder. And the beholder's vision is affected by his or her immediate perception of the policy in question: as Ingram and Mann argue, labor and management are likely to have very different perspectives on the necessity of the minimum wage. One person may argue that a policy has failed, while another person might look at it as a tentative first step toward a larger goal, such as some health programs for the poor and elderly: Medicare and Medicaid can be viewed as the first step toward more universal health services.

Other reasons for policy failure are listed in Table 10.1, which summarizes Ingram and Mann's argument. If you are active in politics and policy making or even reasonably attentive to politics, you will recognize these reasons for

TABLE 10.1 Explanations for Policy Failure

Alternatives to policies tried	Failure needs to be assessed in terms of the option to let present trends continue,[1] and in terms of the likelihood that other options would have been more or less successful.
The impact of changing circumstance	Changing circumstances can render policies less successful, such as energy policies that provided price relief before they created dependency on oil and natural gas.
Relationships of one policy to another	Policies are interrelated, and these relationships must be taken into account. For example, a stricter policy against illegal immigrants may endanger broader policy goals surrounding our relations with Mexico, such as oil supplies or drug interdiction.
The boundary question	Political boundaries (between states, for example) will influence policy success.
Excessive policy demand	We may expect too much from policies.
Realizable policy expectations	Policies sometimes fail when they go beyond what we know we can achieve now. But ambitious policy making can be the result of "speculative argumentation"[2] that seeks to induce innovation. The stated purpose of a policy may not be the actual purpose; there may be more symbolic goals than substance.
Accurate theory of causation	Policy will fail if it is not based on sound causal theory.
Choice of effective policy tools	The choice of ineffective tools will likely yield failure. But the choice of tools is often a function of compromise or ideological predisposition.
The vagaries of implementation	The problems inherent in policy implementation can contribute to policy failure.
Failure of political institutions	"Policy failure is simply a symptom of more profound ailments within our political institutions," such as the breakdown of political party power, devolution of power from congressional leaders to the committees and subcommittees.

1. Sometimes incorrectly called the "do nothing" option. See Eugene Bardachy, *A Practical Guide for Policy Analysis: The Eightfold Path to More Effective Problem Solving.* 3rd ed. (Washington, DC: Sage/CQ Press, 2012).

2. This idea is from Charles O. Jones, *The Policies and Politics of Pollution Control* (Pittsburgh: University of Pittsburgh Press, 1975).

Source: Derived from Helen Ingram and Dean Mann, "Policy Failure: An Issue Deserving Attention," in *Why Policies Succeed or Fail*, ed. Helen Ingram and Dean Mann (Beverly Hills, CA: Sage, 1980).

policy failure. There are many possible reasons for policy failure and many possible problems that can cause or contribute to it. Thus, simple storytelling about policy failure may reflect popular dissatisfaction with a policy in particular, or government in general, but fails to take into account the multiple reasons that policies can at least be perceived as failures.

But let's continue to assume that policies do indeed fail—they either fail to deliver what they promise, or they fail because of unintended or unforeseen consequences of policies, which is a strong probability given that policies are complex and all the variables are not always well known. We might assume that policy failure provides an opportunity to learn from the erroneous or incomplete assumptions of the past. Thus, it is useful to think about how policy failure induces policy change through a *learning* process. Indeed, many experts and commentators on important public issues claim that certain phenomena can induce organizations to learn from their mistakes.

For some time, social scientists, including those who study complex organizations, have been interested in understanding the extent to which *organizational* learning can take place. This is a major concern of organizations, because those that fail to understand their environment and adapt to it by acting on new information are likely to fall short.

Who learns, what is learned, and how learning is employed have been defined differently by various students of the policy process (Bennett and Howlett 1992). The main controversy in the debate over who learns is whether nonhuman entities such as institutions or organizations can "learn" or whether only individual people learn. One can argue that an organization learns through experience: when it develops and implements policies, the evaluation and feedback processes provide "learning opportunities" for the organization to change its behavior. While people learn by retaining information and experience in their minds, organizations rely on information storage and retrieval and, perhaps more important, on "institutional memory," which, to a large extent, is a function of the experiences and knowledge of key personnel who have been on the job a long time.

This is a somewhat passive definition of organizational learning. Colin Bennett and Michael Howlett note that learning can be a more active and "deliberate attempt to adjust the goals and techniques of policy in the light of the consequences of past policy and new information so as to better attain" the policy goals (Hall 1988: 8, cited in Bennett and Howlett 1992) Indeed, organizations make concerted efforts to improve their learning capacity by creating systems to store and disseminate information (Argyris 1999; Senge

single-loop learning Learning about how a policy or process works, and making adjustments to that policy or process without studying or questioning the fundamental assumptions of that policy or process.

2006). Organizations engage in two types of learning: in **single-loop learning** organizations learn about techniques (tools) that fail and make adjustments to improve them or replace them with techniques that work better. An example of single-loop learning would be the development of new and better tools to prevent would-be bombers from getting on airplanes. The agency in question may switch from using hand searches of passengers and baggage to explosives detectors, metal detectors, bomb-sniffing dogs, or even the controversial "full-body scanners" that can reveal just about anything carried under clothing. The latter tool is being adopted because airlines, airports, and government agencies learned that existing measures did not keep the would-be bomber off the December 2009 flight to Detroit that triggered these critical questions.

double-loop learning A type of learning that involves not only thinking about how a policy or process works, but also about the fundamental assumptions of that policy.

Double-loop learning is when organizations rethink the fundamental logic and values that support the entire range of actions around a goal. We can say that double-loop learning is learning about single-loop learning, because everything about all the aspects of policies intended to achieve a goal is revisited (Argyris and Schön 1978). Thus, in the 2009 bombing scare, some people focused on how to find bombs on would-be terrorists, but others have seized the apparent policy failure as a reason to question and probe *all* the actions the nation takes to protect against all terrorist threats to aviation, including passengers with bombs, cargo with bombs, and, in particular, the entire information-gathering and storage system that was supposedly reformed after September 11, 2001, to share information that would keep suspicious people off of airplanes.

policy learning As defined by Sabatier, policy learning, or "policy-oriented learning," is "relatively enduring alterations of thought or behavioral intentions which result from experience and which are concerned with the attainment (or revision) of policy objectives."

There are some conceptual and methodological problems in thinking of organizations as learning agents; in particular, organizations do not possess the cognitive abilities of people. Thus, in the policy process literature, Paul Sabatier (1988), Peter May (1992), George Busenberg (2001), and others deal with this problem by isolating individuals—agency heads, interest group leaders, academics, journalists, and so on—not institutions, as the unit of analysis in studies of policy making and learning.

Sabatier (1988: 133) provides a more specific definition of "**policy-oriented learning**" as "relatively enduring alterations of thought or behavioral intentions which result from experience and which are concerned with the attainment (or revision) of policy objectives." Sabatier's definition, by concentrating on individual actors as members of advocacy coalitions, avoids attributing cognitive processes to organizations, while broadening policy making to include influential actors, such as academics and journalists, that institutionally focused analyses tend to overlook. This focus on the individual as policy actor also overcomes the tendency to think of agencies or institutions as the agents of learning.

To summarize, we can think of learning at the organizational and individual levels, but for our purposes it is most useful to consider people as the agents of learning; these people apply what they have learned to in-group policy-making processes.

TYPES OF LEARNING

To refine our understanding of learning in the public policy process, Peter May divides learning into three categories: instrumental policy learning, social policy learning, and political learning. In all three types of learning, policy failure—politically and socially defined—provide a stimulus for learning about how to make better policy.

In the ideal case, learning reflects the accumulation and application of knowledge to lead to factually and logically correct conclusions. However, policy makers and their supporters may support policy change that is not objectively related to change in the political environment or the nature of the problem. May calls mimicking or copying policy without assessment or analysis "superstitious instrumental learning." Lotteries and tax policy to attract additional industrial development are examples of this sort of mimicking, because states believe that if they do not adopt these policies, other states will gain some economic advantage.

May's article lists what he calls prima facie evidence of these various forms of learning. **Instrumental policy learning** concerns learning about "viability of policy interventions or implementation designs." This type of learning centers on implementation tools and techniques. When feedback from implementation is analyzed and changes to the design are made that improve its performance, then this suggests that learning has happened and was successful. **Social policy learning** involves learning about the "social construction of a policy or program." This type of learning goes beyond simple adjustments of program management to the heart of the problem itself, including attitudes toward program goals and the nature and appropriateness of government action. If successfully applied, social policy learning can result in better understanding of the underlying causal theory of a public problem, leading to better policy responses.

instrumental policy learning
Learning about the effectiveness of policy tools and interventions.

social policy learning
Learning about the social causes of problems and the possible interventions to solve those problems.

Evidence of social policy learning involves learning the causes of problems and the effectiveness of policy interventions based on those problems. May (1992: 336) argues that prima facie indicators of social learning involve "policy redefinition entailing changes in policy goals or scope—e.g., policy direction, target groups, rights bestowed by the policy." There are many examples of such learning. One example concerns the way communities address prostitution. Traditionally, the police tried to control prostitution by arresting prostitutes, and doing so often enough to dissuade women from working in a particular area or community. When this policy was found to be ineffective—and, in many ways, unfair to the prostitutes themselves—communities focused instead on the men who seek out prostitutes, arresting the men and, in some cases, publicizing their arrests and convictions to shame them. In this case, the target of the policy shifted from the prostitute to the "John" because of a new understanding of the problem as being caused at least as much by demand as by supply. A similar logic is sometimes employed against illegal drugs, when attention shifts toward eradication and interdiction of drugs from abroad, rather than making smaller, seemingly less effective arrests of users at home. One can roughly equate instrumental learning with single-loop learning, and social learning with double-loop learning.

political learning
Learning about making more effective political arguments in policy debate.

Political learning is considerably different from instrumental and social learning. Peter May defines political learning as focusing on "strategy for advocating a given policy idea or problem," leading potentially to "more sophisticated advocacy of a policy idea or problem" and effective political advocacy. Political learning occurs when advocates for or against policy change alter their strategy and tactics to conform to new information that has entered the political system. For example, the breakdown of the nuclear power industry in the United States was due, in part, to the efforts of groups that mobilized against nuclear power; their efforts began before the 1979 Three Mile Island (TMI) nuclear power plant accident, but the event accelerated them. Group leaders learned that events such as TMI and the specter of the "China syndrome" were highly effective in promoting public and elite concerns about the safety and cost-effectiveness of nuclear power. Indeed, the exploitation of the more frightening or upsetting aspects of any event, from an industrial accident to the nomination of a potential Supreme Court justice, include the sophisticated use of imagery and storytelling to advance a position; these techniques have been learned and honed over time as competing groups seek to improve their competitive positions.

CASE STUDY: POLICY FAILURE AND LEARNING IN AVIATION SECURITY, 2000–2010

On Christmas Day 2009, the world was once again reminded of the vulnerability of civil aviation to terrorist attacks. Sensitivity to this issue was clearly stoked by the September 11 terrorist attacks, which starkly highlighted the challenge of keeping commercial aviation safe from terrorist and criminal attacks. But just as the 2009 attack was not entirely novel, neither were the September 11 attacks. Hijackings often occurred in the United States and overseas in the 1960s and 1970s, and terrorist bombings of airplanes were rare, but not unheard of, in the 1980s. In the last 25 years, the two most disturbing breaches of aviation security in the United States, or involving a U.S. airline, were the bombing of Pan Am flight 103 over Lockerbie, Scotland, in 1988, and the September 11 hijackings and attacks. As in most disasters, these incidents served as focusing events that drew a great deal of attention to the shortcomings existing in aviation security policy design and implementation. The two big questions that arose from these attacks were whether these events were evidence of policy failure and whether there was anything learned from these potential failures that could reduce the probability of their recurrence.

Congress and the media immediately labeled both the Pan Am and September 11 attacks as evidence of major policy failures. In the Pan Am case, attention was focused on how it was possible to smuggle enough explosives (a few pounds) into checked baggage to yield a bomb large enough to cause a plane to break up in mid-flight; after all, of all the bombs set off on airplanes between 1975 and 1999, 57 percent of those planes (35 bombings) survived. Still, this means that 43 percent of planes did not survive, and bombing is a substantial problem with huge costs for airlines and for societies in general (National Research Council (U.S.) Panel on Assessment of Technologies Deployed to Improve Aviation Security 1999). After the Pan Am 103 attack, and after the in-flight explosion of TWA flight 800 off Long Island, New York, in 1996 (an explosion that many people thought was a terrorist attack, but which was due to a rare technical fault), presidential commissions were formed that made a number of recommendations about the organization of aviation security and about the technologies available to prevent bombs from bringing down planes. Indeed, the Pan Am bombing, as well as other terrorist bombings of planes, led most aviation authorities to believe that bombing would replace hijacking as the number one threat to civil aviation. As a result, significant progress was made in bomb detection technology and in hardening cargo containers and cargo holds on airplanes so that, even if a bomb were to detonate, the damage could be contained and the plane could safely land. In this case, we can say that some instrumental policy learning occurred.

After the 1996 TWA crash, a commission headed by Vice President Al Gore made a sweeping set of recommendations on both aviation security and safety. Many, but not all, of these recommendations were studied and implemented, but the key recommendations on aviation security—that the Federal Aviation Administration (FAA) exercise greater oversight and control over passenger and baggage screening—were not implemented before the September 11 attacks. The FAA was in the process of implementing these recommendations, but opposition from the airlines delayed the process. The airlines were worried about the cost of new security requirements and about any inconvenience to passengers—inconveniences and costs that pale in comparison to the costs of the September 11 attacks.

After the September 11 attacks, it became clear to nearly all commentators, experts and lay people alike, that the aviation security system did not work, and that its failure greatly undermined public confidence in the safety of U.S. commercial aviation. As a result, in November of 2001, the Aviation and Transportation Security Act (ATSA) was enacted as both a means to improve security and as a way to attempt to restore public confidence in the nation's civil aviation system. As Cobb and Primo (2003: 120) note:

> There was [after September 11] a marked effect on the aviation industry. Security procedures in the airports and on planes came into question. All aspects of the security process were re-examined, severely affecting airline travel . . . Many policy changes in aviation safety were unprecedented in their scope and in the speed at which they were enacted, *but none of the issues was new to the political agenda.*
>
> (italics added for emphasis)

The media and expert condemnation of lax aviation security after September 11 was particularly intense, focusing on the fact that the passenger screeners—the people who staff the metal detectors and X-ray machines—were poorly trained, underpaid, possibly overworked, and experienced remarkably high turnover. But these screeners, employed by contractors that were hired by the airlines to do the screening, were cheap, and security costs were kept low. It is also important to note that the attackers used small box-cutters as weapons, which were not banned from airliners at the time. And yet, as Cobb and Primo note, and as I note in a later article (Birkland 2004), almost none of the ideas about better policy and policy failure that rose on the agenda after these attacks were new ideas. Instead, they were revived on the agenda by a focusing event.

If the Pan Am 103 bombing, reinforced by greater concern about aviation safety overall after the TWA crash, led to a reasonably broad range of ideas and legislative change to address aviation security lapses, how could September 11 have happened? There are two potential places to look for failure. Most notably, the FAA failed to fully implement recommendations from the post-Pan Am and TWA presidential commissions or to fully implement congressional intent as contained in the laws enacted after these events. The recommendations were routine but important; they included more careful screening of passengers' carry-on luggage, explosives detecting, better training for screeners to recognize suspicious passengers, and so forth. This is evidence of attempts at single-loop or instrumental policy learning in this domain, learning that was apparently unsuccessful. The second place to look is at the failure to imagine the possibility of hijacking airplanes and using them as, in essence, guided missiles. Many officials said that such a thing was "unimaginable," but there was accumulating evidence of just such a type of an attack from intelligence sources and thwarted plots (Easterbrook 2001), such that the commission set up to investigate the September 11 attacks—known popularly as the 9/11 Commission—noted that the attacks happened because of a "failure of imagination" on the part of intelligence, antiterrorism and security experts (National Commission on Terrorist Attacks upon the United States 2004). In other words, the commission was advocating that serious consideration be given to fundamentally rethinking how terrorists go about their business, which would involve something like social policy learning or double-loop learning.

We do know that, after September 11, substantial changes were made to aviation security. Regulations and laws were enacted that required locked cockpit doors on commercial airliners. The Transportation Security Administration (TSA) was created to replace the private contractors that were hired by airlines as passenger screeners; these companies had poor records well before September 11. The TSA screeners are, by and large, better educated, better trained, and more professional than the screeners they replaced. But the system was soon jolted by the so-called "shoe bomber" attempt to destroy American Airlines flight 63, flying from Paris to Miami in December 2001. Richard Reid, the alleged shoe bomber, hid explosives in his shoes that he attempted to detonate in mid-flight. His attempt failed, and, in a reflection of the changes in public behavior after September 11, passengers aboard the flight helped the flight crew subdue Reid. It is worthwhile to note that one of the explosives used in the shoe bombs was PETN, the same kind of explosive carried by Umar Farouk Abdulmutallab in his attempt to bring down Northwest flight 253 in 2009 with a bomb hidden in his underwear.

Students of the policy process have found that policy implementation is often where attention to detail flags as the belief sets in that a problem has largely been addressed (Nice and Grosse 2001). The passage of legislation removes an issue from the immediate congressional agenda, and journalists pay less attention to the issue as it moves from lurid front-page headlines to the more mundane aspects of daily administration. There are many examples of legislators and executives with unattainable expectations (both in terms of management techniques and the application of technology), such as funding and other resources failing to match the perceived needs addressed by the legislation. The expectations for perfection in the aviation security system are one such example. And given that oversight of the FAA by Congress is generally "fire alarm" oversight—that is, oversight triggered by events rather than through an ongoing process—it is unsurprising that, to the extent that there was social policy learning in the years after PAA 103 and TWA 800, these lessons became less important as Congress shifted its attention away from aviation security to other aspects of aviation, and to other matters of domestic or international importance. Meanwhile, one can argue that instrumental learning continued at TSA, to the point where its rules generated complaints. The most prominent change in aviation security since the shoe bomber incident (which has led to Americans putting their shoes in the X-ray machines at airports) is the new "3-1-1" requirement that containers of liquids and gels carried aboard the plane cannot exceed 3 ounces, that all containers must fit into a one-quart zip-top bag, and that each passenger can only have one such bag in carry-on. These restrictions were put in place in response to a thwarted plot hatched in 2006 to simultaneously bomb several flights from London to North America, a plot that, if fully successful, could have exceeded the death toll from September 11. In this case, British intelligence in particular was able to stop the plot before it escalated into something much more dangerous (Gardham 2009). While one might question the 3-1-1 rule—and many do—it is likely that the failure of this plot, and its having been thwarted by sound intelligence work, both hindered a plot and led to the discovery of a dangerous new mode of terrorism.

But the system is hardly perfect, as the December 2009 "underwear bomber" attempt demonstrated. Why did the system appear to fail in this case? First, implementation of improved policy becomes more difficult as the "low-hanging fruit" is picked. There is already evidence of this effect in the post-September 11 aviation security environment, as the more easily implemented features were addressed. The ATSA required, among other things, much more stringent passenger screening, inspection of luggage, more restrictions on the sorts of things that could be carried aboard aircraft, and, in particular, the "federalization" of the passenger screening workforce to ensure that weapons would be detected. While many of the screening processes and training for screeners had been improved shortly after the enactment of ATSA, Kenneth Mead, the inspector general of the U.S. Department of Transportation, noted in January 2002 that "while progress has been made, clearly the heavy lifting [installing explosives detection systems to screen all checked baggage and hiring a workforce] lies ahead" (Mead 2002). And explosives detection machinery, in particular, was not installed rapidly after passage of ATSA, owing to technological and practical considerations—the machines were quite large, and airports were not designed to accommodate them.

A similar set of events has accompanied the underwear bomber crisis, which involves making difficult and unpopular choices to deal with hard-to-detect threats to airliners. A great deal of interest was generated in using full-body scanners known as "millimeter-wave" or "backscatter" scanners. The advantage of this technology is that it creates an image that looks very much like a nude human body, which makes it difficult to conceal weapons or explosives on one's person. On the other hand, many people are uncomfortable with the very idea of being seen virtually nude on a computer screen, even if the screener is some distance from the security checkpoint, as current protocols require. The debate about this technology is unsettled, but it appears that this attempt tipped the balance in favor of using these machines, in yet another example of a terrorist action and a security reaction.

One reason why the 2001 screening changes were accomplished quickly, including the deployment of TSA employed screeners, is that they were symbolically important measures designed to add some measure of security (although not, of course, total security), while reassuring the traveling public that something was being done. The question is whether what was done legislatively is a good match with what really needed to be done. Again, one wonders whether the full-body scanners are a viable antiterrorism tool, or if they serve a symbolic value, suggesting, once again, that TSA and other nations' security systems are "doing something." (It's worth noting that the underwear bomber passed through Dutch security on his Amsterdam-to-Detroit flight, rending criticism of the TSA rather odd.) The TSA's reactive stance, coupled by what many people believe to be silly or ineffective ideas for security—such as the short-lived idea to ban passengers from leaving their seats or having anything in their laps during the final hour of flight—have led many critics to deride TSA efforts as "security theater" that is almost entirely symbolic.

A good case can be made that the ATSA and the TSA have addressed important issues, considering that they had been debated but hardly implemented since at least the late 1980s. The challenge was to make sure that the TSA implemented the program contemplated in the law. This is perhaps a stiffer challenge than many of us can imagine, because terrorists have shown that they have changed their tactics since the September 11 attacks, and have found other targets or methods to accomplish their goals.

Finally, the underwear bomber crisis raised, once again, a key theme of the post-September 11 investigations—the extent to which information and intelligence are or are not shared among the various domestic and international agencies. We know that the would-be bomber had been reported as a security concern by his own father to the U.S. Embassy in Lagos, Nigeria. We know that the CIA separately opened a file on him. The U.S. government had other information that would suggest that he might pose a threat. He purchased his ticket with cash and checked no baggage, two of the classic signs of terrorist or criminal activity. Also, the British had put Abdulmutallab on their terrorist watch list in May 2009 (Thompson 2009). As President Obama said in January 2010, the relevant agencies failed to "connect the dots" in a way that would have prevented Abdulmutallab from boarding the plane in the first place (Spangler 2010). This exact terminology was used to describe the intelligence failures that followed the 2001 attacks, and suggest that, in the broader sense, the nation's antiterrorism efforts are still falling short of the mark, even if aviation safety is better than it was 10 years ago.

CONCLUSION

For policy makers and public managers, policy implementation is one of the most difficult aspects of the policy process, and policy failure is one of the most frustrating parts of their jobs, because most managers and decision-makers want their ideas to work. For students of public policy, implementation is fascinating because implementation brings together many actors and forces that cooperate and clash with each other in order to achieve—or to thwart—policy goals. In that sense, it is truly a microcosm of the entire policy cycle. It is frustrating to research because the process has proven particularly hard to model; contributing to this frustration is the tension between building and testing good policy theory and implementation theory while providing useful information to policy makers and implementers on how to structure programs for greater success.

Given the complexity of our political system, it seems that policy failure—or, at best, very limited success—would be the inevitable outcome of any public program. This may not be true, however, because failure is, like so much else in public policy, a subjective condition that is more often grounded in the perceptions of a particular interest than in empirical "fact." Indeed, in areas such as crime control, terrorism, or environmental protection, one can argue that a policy has failed if it hasn't achieved 100 percent of its goal—but what would have happened if the policy had not been adopted at all? Is 75 percent worse than perfection, or better than nothing? Clearly, this depends on the nature of the policy domain—in some systems, such as aviation safety policy or policies regulating drugs, we expect near perfection. However, we can stipulate that some policies are much less successful than others and that policy makers and others concerned with the management of public programs will learn from the purported failure of the policy. In this way, policy development is an ongoing process with no discernible beginning and no obvious end, but with plenty of opportunities for refinement and fine-tuning. As more is learned about the success or failure of various tools and their implementation, policy makers and the various advocacy groups involved in a policy domain will continue to debate not only the underlying rationale for a policy, but the methods by which the policy is put into effect.

KEY TERMS

bottom-up approach

double-loop learning

implementation

instrumental policy learning

policy learning

political learning

single-loop learning

social policy learning

top-down approach

QUESTIONS FOR DISCUSSION, REFLECTION, AND RESEARCH

- What is the most important problem with top-down models of policy implementation? Cite several problems with this model. Do bottom-up approaches address these problems? Do bottom-up models have their own shortcomings? What are they? On balance, which model do you think would best aid someone who is attempting to design a policy?

- What is a street-level bureaucrat? Give several examples. With what sort of street-level bureaucrats have you had interactions? Would you argue that these individuals have a great deal of implementation discretion; that is, latitude to make decisions about how to apply policies? What are some examples of this discretion? Is it a good idea to allow street-level bureaucrats to have discretion in policy implementation? Think of your answer from both a program management and a democratic politics perspective.

- Do you believe that people in the policy process can actually learn from experience? Can you think of examples of policies that have benefited from learning from experience? Are there policies in which learning has not occurred, or in which the "wrong" lessons were learned? Is there a difference between policies where there is successful learning and policies where learning is more difficult to achieve?

- Why do Goggin and his colleagues believe that implementation is as much a matter of negotiation and communication as it is a matter of command? When considering this question, remember the organization of American government and how power is shared within that organization.

- As you know, Ingram and Mann argue that policy failure is highly subjective, and that what appears to be policy failure can be a result of, among other things, excessive policy demand, or the fact that failure in one policy area is a function of spillovers from other policy areas that prevent a policy from being fully implemented. Many stories in newspapers and on television, particularly those that claim to be "investigative reporting," contain coverage of supposed policy failures. Such stories are usually serious and are not the same as stories about personal corruption and scandal. For this activity, find a story or series of stories about what you believe is a policy failure (it is probably easier to use print media than TV and radio). What kinds of arguments in favor of failure are being made? Are any arguments presented in these news stories that contradict claims of policy failure? Are the claims of policy failure reasonable, given what you know about the subjectivity of such claims? Can you think of alternative explanations of "failure" that aren't explored in the story? Why do you think that the stories of failure that are in the media are so prominent, while others are less so?

ADDITIONAL READING

While it is indeed true that implementation concerns go back many years before the 1970s, the book that really started policy scientists thinking carefully about implementation is Jeffery Pressman and Aaron Wildavsky, *Implementation* (Berkeley, CA: University of California Press, 1984). Still required reading in many courses on public policy and policy implementation, this book describes the problems that accompanied the implementation of economic development projects at the Port of Oakland and the Oakland International Airport. The authors find that implementation is made difficult by the "complexity of joint action." Research from the "second generation" of implementation studies, which sought to create more advanced theories of implementation, include Richard Elmore, "Backward Mapping:

Implementation Research and Policy Decisions," *Political Science Quarterly* 94, no. 4 (Winter 1979): 601–616; Daniel Mazmanian and Paul Sabatier, *Implementation and Public Policy* (Lanham, MD: University Press of America, 1989); and Carl Van Horn, *Policy Implementation in the Federal System: National Goals and Local Implementers* (Lexington, MA: Lexington Books, 1979).

One of my favorite texts in the so-called third generation of implementation research is Malcolm L. Goggin, Ann O. Bowman, James P. Lester, and Laurence J. O'Toole Jr., *Implementation Theory and Practice: Toward a Third Generation* (Glenview, IL: Scott Foresman/Little Brown, 1990). This volume is a synthesis of top-down and bottom-up approaches to implementation in what the authors call a "communications" model of implementation. In their model, the top policy designers send implementation messages that are received and interpreted by targets and intermediaries.

In the late 1990s, a lively debate took place in *Policy Currents*, the then-newsletter of the public policy section of the American Political Science Association. That debate started with James P. Lester and Malcom L. Goggin, "Back to the Future: The Rediscovery of Implementation Studies," *Policy Currents* 8, no. 3 (1998): 1–9. The series of articles continues in volume 8, no. 4.

On the question of policy failure, Helen Ingram and Dean Mann's "Policy Failure: An Issue Deserving Attention," in *Why Policies Succeed or Fail*, edited by Helen Ingram and Dean Mann (Beverly Hills, CA: Sage, 1980), explores some reasons that policies fail—or are claimed to have failed. The authors argue that the question of policy failure deserves further study to determine whether policies are really failing, why they fail, and to what extent their failure is influenced by other, overlapping policies and goals. In "Policy Learning and Failure," *Journal of Public Policy* 12, no. 4 (1992): 331–354, Peter May links policy failure or the perception of failure to learning, and outlines the three different styles of learning described in this chapter.

This argument was very influential in my book *Lessons of Disaster* (Washington, DC: Georgetown University Press, 2006), as were Colin J. Bennett and Michael Howlett, "The Lessons of Learning: Reconciling Theories of Policy Learning and Policy Change," *Policy Sciences* 25, no. 4 (1992): 275–294; Peter A. Hall, "Policy Paradigms, Social Learning, and the State: The Case of Economic Policy Making in Britain," *Comparative Politics* 25 (1993): 275–296; and Paul Sabatier and Hank C. Jenkins-Smith, *Policy Change and Learning: An Advocacy Coalition Approach* (Boulder, CO: Westview, 1993).

REFERENCES

Argyris, Chris. 1999. *On Organizational Learning*. 2nd ed. Malden, MA: Blackwell Business.

Argyris, Chris and Donald A. Schön. 1978. *Organizational Learning: A Theory of Action Perspective*. Reading, MA: Addison-Wesley.

Bennett, Colin J. and Michael Howlett. 1992. "The Lessons of Learning: Reconciling Theories of Policy Learning and Policy Change." *Policy Sciences* 25(3): 275–294.

Birkland, Thomas A. 2004. "Learning and Policy Improvement after Disaster: The Case of Aviation Security." *American Behavioral Scientist* 48(3): 341–364. doi: 10.1177/0002764204268990.

Busenberg, George J. 2001. "Learning in Organizations and Public Policy." *Journal of Public Policy* 21(2): 173–189.

Cobb, Roger W. and David M. Primo. 2003. *The Plane Truth: Airline Crashes, the Media, and Transportation Policy*. Washington, DC: Brookings Institution.

Derthick, Martha. 1972. *New Towns in Town*. Washington, DC: Urban Institute.

Dyer, Caroline. 1999. "Researching the Implementation of Educational Policy: A Backward Mapping Approach." *Comparative Education* 35(1): 45–62.

Easterbrook, Gregg. 2001. "The All-Too-Friendly Skies: Security as an Afterthought." In *How Did This Happen? Terrorism and the New War*, edited by James F. Hodge Jr. and Gideon Rose, 163–181. New York: Public Affairs.

Elmore, Richard. 1979. "Backward Mapping: Implementation Research and Policy Decisions." *Political Science Quarterly* 94(4) (Winter): 601–616.

Elmore, Richard. 1985. "Forward and Backward Mapping." In *Policy Implementation in Federal and Unitary Systems*, edited by K. Hanf and T. Toonen, 33–70. Dordrecht: Martinus Nijhoff.

Gardham, Duncan. 2009. "Airline Terror Trial: The Bomb Plot to Kill 10,000 People." *Telegraph*, September 7. Accessed January 29, 2015. www.telegraph.co.uk/news/uknews/terrorism-in-the-uk/6153243/Airline-terror-trial-The-bomb-plot-to-kill-10000-people.html.

Goggin, Malcolm L., Ann O. Bowman, James P. Lester, and Laurence J. O'Toole Jr. 1990. *Implementation Theory and Practice: Toward a Third Generation*. Glenview, IL: Scott Foresman/Little Brown.

Hall, Peter A. 1988. "Policy Paradigms, Social Learning and the State." International Political Association, Washington, DC.

Ingram, Helen and Dean Mann. 1980. "Policy Failure: An Issue Deserving Attention." In *Why Policies Succeed or Fail*, edited by Helen Ingram and Dean Mann, 11–32. Beverly Hills, CA: Sage.

Light, Paul C. 2002. *Government's Greatest Achievements: From Civil Rights to Homeland Security*. Washington, DC: Brookings Institution.

Lipsky, Michael. 1971. "Street Level Bureaucracy and the Analysis of Urban Reform." *Urban Affairs Quarterly* 6: 391–409.

May, Peter J. 1990. "Reconsidering Policy Design: Policies and Publics." *Journal of Public Policy* 11(2): 187–206.

May, Peter J. 1992. "Policy Learning and Failure." *Journal of Public Policy* 12(4): 331–354.

Mazmanian, Daniel and Paul Sabatier. 1989. *Implementation and Public Policy*. Lanham, MD: University Press of America.

Mead, Kenneth M. 2002. *Challenges Facing TSA in Implementing the Aviation and Transportation Security Act*. Washington, DC: United States Department of Transportation, Office of the Inspector General. Accessed May 4, 2015. www.oig.dot.gov/sites/default/files/cc2002088.pdf.

National Commission on Terrorist Attacks upon the United States. 2004. *The 9/11 Commission Report: Final Report of the National Commission on Terrorist Attacks Upon the United States*. Official government ed. Washington, DC: National Commission on Terrorist Attacks upon the United States: For sale by the Supt. of Docs., U.S. G.P.O.

National Research Council (U.S.) Panel on Assessment of Technologies Deployed to Improve Aviation Security. 1999. *Assessment of Technologies Deployed to Improve Aviation Security: First Report*. Washington, DC: National Academy Press.

Nice, David C. and Ashley Grosse. 2001. "The Evolution of Emergency Management in America: From a Painful Past to Promising but Uncertain Future." In *Handbook of Crisis and Emergency Management*, edited by Ali Farazmand, 55–67. New York: Marcel Dekker.

O'Toole, Laurence. 1986. "Policy Recommendations for Multi-Actor Implementation: An Assessment of the Field." *Journal of Public Policy* 6(2): 181–210.

Pressman, Jeffrey L. and Aaron B. Wildavsky. 1984. *Implementation: How Great Expectations in Washington Are Dashed in Oakland: Or, Why It's Amazing That Federal Programs Work at All, This Being a Saga of the Economic Development Administration as Told by Two Sympathetic Observers Who Seek to Build Morals on a Foundation of Ruined Hopes.* Berkeley, CA: University of California Press.

Ryan, Neal. 1995. "Unravelling Conceptual Developments in Implementation Analysis." *Australian Journal of Public Administration* 54(1): 65–81.

Sabatier, Paul A. 1986. "Top-Down and Bottom-Up Approaches in Implementation Research: A Critical Analysis and Suggested Synthesis." *Journal of Public Policy* 6(1): 21–48.

Sabatier, Paul A. 1988. "An Advocacy Coalition Framework of Policy Change and the Role of Policy-Oriented Learning Therein." *Policy Sciences* 21: 129–168.

Schneider, Anne and Helen Ingram. 1993. "The Social Construction of Target Populations: Implications for Politics and Policy." *American Political Science Review* 87(2): 334–348.

Senge, Peter M. 2006. *The Fifth Discipline: The Art and Practice of the Learning Organization.* Rev. and updated ed. New York: Doubleday/Currency.

Smith, Kevin B. and Christopher W. Larimer. 2013. *The Public Policy Theory Primer.* 2nd ed. Boulder, CO: Westview Press.

Spangler, Todd. 2010. "Obama: Officials 'Failed to Connect the Dots' in Botched Attack." *Detroit Free Press*, January 5. Accessed January 29, 2015. www.freep.com/article/20100105/NEWS07/100105022/1322/Obama-Officials-failed-to-connect-the-dots-in-botched-attack.

Thompson, Mark. 2009. "Why Was the Accused Bomber Banned in Britain, Not the U.S.?" *Time*, December 28.

Torenvlied, Rene. 1996. "Political Control of Implementation Agencies." *Policy Sciences* 8(1): 25–57.

Van Horn, Carl. 1979. *Policy Implementation in the Federal System: National Goals and Local Implementors.* Lexington, MA: Lexington Books.

Van Horn, Carl E. and Donald S. Van Meter. 1976. "The Implementation of Intergovernmental Policy." In *Public Policy Making in a Federal System*, edited by Charles O. Jones and Robert D. Thomas. Beverly Hills, CA: Sage.

CHAPTER 11

Science and Theory in the Study of Public Policy

THE STUDY OF POLICY AS A SCIENTIFIC ENDEAVOR

The preceding chapters laid the foundation that will help you understand the current theories of the policy process that I describe in this chapter. These theories have dominated public policy theory for the past 25 years, and remain influential because scholars have found them to be useful for explaining important aspects of the public policy process. However, like most social science theories, they do not explain all the phenomena that comprise the policy process. This is not, of course, an indictment of this theory. Rather, it suggests that the search for a "unified theory of the policy process," or, logically, a unified theory of politics may be an impossible goal. These challenges to theory building are described in this chapter. But, as you will learn from this chapter, the scientific study of the policy process—and of building models and theories of how public policy is made—is one of the most challenging endeavors in social science, and while no "final" theory of the process has ever been developed, we can say that remarkable progress in theory building has been made since the early 1980s.

In this chapter, I begin with a discussion of the idea of policy science and about why we can think about the advanced study of public policy as a scientific endeavor. The discussion then turns to descriptions of the dominant theories of the policy process. These descriptions are, of course, no substitute for careful study of these theories, but my goal is to provide you with some basic sense of what these theories are and how they relate to each other. Many readers of this book will not ultimately engage in the advanced academic study of policy making, but these theories, as I will show, are worth consideration in helping to understand the broader sweep of the policy process, and how all the parts of the process fit together.

POLICY STUDIES AS POLICY SCIENCE

Harold Lasswell's call for a science of public policy was driven by a desire to generate sound social science, but also by the desire to solve problems, much the same way that science was used to unlock the atom or cure diseases. Lasswell, like many social scientists and reformers of the 1940s through the 1960s, felt that the increasingly sophisticated research techniques available to social scientists would allow them to study public problems and to propose solutions to them. While one use of science is to inform social decision-making on a range of issues, from nuclear war to medicine to mass transit, a great deal of scientific endeavor is not solely or simply driven by the desire to learn about individual problems and their solutions, but is also a function of a desire to gain knowledge of the social world. Many of the scholars whose work is described in this book are interested in public policy because they can apply the tools of their disciplines to social problems, thereby gaining greater understanding of society and politics as a whole and, perhaps, in the process, contributing to the change for the better.

Harold Lasswell argued that quantitative analysis and the *scientific method* were important elements of any policy science. However, you should not confuse "the scientific method" with "statistics," as many students do, particularly if their first exposure to research methods, theory building, and hypothesis testing comes in a statistical methods course. Often, these courses are more about running computer software than on what it means to develop a theory, establish hypotheses, and devise the appropriate tests. If anything, these courses focus on the latter, while assuming (often wrongly) that students have had some exposure to theory building and research design.

While Lasswell was motivated by a desire to harness science to explain the policy process and to help solve social problems, we do know that a science of public policy and policy analysis have generally fallen short of Lasswell's vision of a broadly useful policy science. But policy theory making has, at least in political science, shifted to the development and testing of *how* the system works, with less emphasis on how it *should* work—that is, we have shifted from a **normative** to a **positive** direction. This is where theory building is important in policy process studies.

But the proliferation of theory building without testing or systematic refinement led George Greenberg and his colleagues to assert that the explosion of modeling needed to yield to actual empirical testing of theories. These tests would allow policy scholars to gain a better sense of which theories work better than others (Greenberg et al. 1977). Paul Sabatier, echoing this sentiment, promotes a research agenda to improve the making *and testing* of policy theories (Sabatier 1991a, 1991b).

Why is theory important when there are real-world problems to solve? It would be simple enough to simply dismiss this question by saying that theory is what academic researchers do, across all disciplines. Unlike folk wisdom or craft knowledge, scientific researchers create theories to try to understand why it is that a particular collection of observations—for example, case studies—yield broadly similar outcomes. For example, the implementation literature has, for the most part, noted that most public policies fail to achieve all the goals their most ardent proponents claimed that they would meet. Of course, there are key differences between implementation of, say, social security programs, environmental policies, and urban development policies, all of which have been important case studied by academics and pursued by practitioners. These cases differ in important ways, but one can discern the important phenomenon shared by all these Theories are important because, by helping to make sense of this ambiguity, they allow us to develop general concepts that apply to more than one case or problem. In creating these general concepts or "rules," we can structure our thinking about the policy process and its application to real-world situations.

normative and positive arguments Normative arguments are arguments based on values and beliefs; positive arguments are those based on empirical evidence.

THE IDEA OF POLICY THEORY

Before we consider these theories of the process in greater detail, it is important to take a moment to consider just what we mean by *theory*. Theory is important because, without it, it is hard to really understand how we can generalize the process to more than some disconnected case studies. What is a theory, after all? The *Oxford English Dictionary* provides, as one of the many definitions of the term, this one:

A scheme or system of ideas or statements held as an explanation or account of a group of facts or phenomena; a hypothesis that has been confirmed or established by observation or experiment, and is propounded or accepted as accounting for the known facts; a statement of what are held to be the general laws, principles, or causes of something known or observed.

A theory is therefore not just a set of ideas—it is a *system* of ideas that helps to *explain* things that happen in the world. The definition goes on to note that theory is a hypothesis that is tested. It also says that a theory is "a statement of . . . the general laws, principles and causes" of something. In this book, we discuss theories about the policy process and how it works.

The Merriam-Webster online dictionary defines the term somewhat differently, and this definition is one that is well suited to the discussion here:

a plausible or scientifically acceptable general principle or body of principles offered to explain phenomena.

The point of this definition is that a theory is "general"—that is, it can be generalized to a broad range of phenomena within a field of study. Thus, we have a theory of the policy process, not individual theories about energy policy, environmental policy, social welfare policy, morality policy, and the like; even though these are different policy areas, and will differ in many ways, a sound theory can explain general phenomena that occur across policy domains. The different policy typologies described in Chapter 7 are examples of this sort of theory.

The difference, then, between talking about public policy and *studying* it is simple: we study it in a systematic or scientific way, which means that we develop and test theories of the process. Theories can be developed in two broad ways. We use deductive logic to develop a theory of how we believe the world works, starting from a theory, to the development of hypotheses, to the gathering of data—either by direct observation or through the assembling of data from another source—and then testing those hypotheses using various statistical and logical techniques. Or we can think inductively, and develop models based on observation first, from which we can discern apparent patterns in the world, which then lead to tentative hypotheses that are tested and refined until we develop a theory. One should not make too much of the difference between these two methods of theory construction; indeed, a very clear explanation of this process notes that "it doesn't take a rocket scientist to see that we could assemble the two graphs above into a single circular one that continually cycles from theories down to observations and back up again to theories" (Trochim 2006).

A sound theory is also one that is "scientifically" acceptable. What does this mean? Philosophers of science and scientists themselves argue that a good theory should generate a set of hypotheses about the world and subject them to tests. If such hypotheses are not falsifiable, then they are not, by definition, hypotheses. In science, we generally state a hypothesis in the form of a "null hypothesis." For example, if our theory is that "the greater number of interest groups that form around an issue, the greater the attention paid to the issue by Congress," we would lay out the null hypothesis as this: "The extent of interest group participation in an issue has no influence on the Congressional agenda." We do this because it is, as Karl Popper has argued, easier to prove something false than it is to prove something true.

A SCIENCE *OF* THE POLICY PROCESS

So far, we have discussed various models of the policy process without seriously considering what a model of the policy process *is* or how to assess whether, in Thomas Dye's words, a model "is helping or not." Dye considers this question in some detail. He says that "a model is merely an abstraction or representation of political life" (Dye 1992: 44). We can clarify this idea by thinking about the difference between, say, a model airplane and a real airplane. A model airplane is merely an approximation of the real thing: while the model airplane has wings, a propeller, a tail, landing gear, and the like, it is a much simplified version of the "real thing": it may not have a working engine or may not even actually fly. But it tells us enough to help us learn about an airplane. So models vary in their complexity and faithfulness to the actual thing they represent based on the use to which we want to put the model. And, of course, if the model becomes as complex as the thing it is modeling, it may not help much at all (McCool 1995: xx).

Similarly, we develop *models* of the policy process that do not reproduce every aspect of the policy process, for such a model would be nearly impossible to create. After all, what are "all" the elements of the process? As you've discerned from reading this book, such models are nearly impossible to create because the policy process is so complex. We therefore do not create models that account for every aspect of public policy making. Instead, social scientists strive to create "middle-range theories" that are readily testable using existing data and knowledge, a more realistic endeavor than an attempt to create a "theory of everything." We create theory in this way to explain general principles without becoming so bogged down in detail that the essence of what we seek to explain is lost. This is because good models, according to Dye, seek to order and simplify reality, identify what is significant about a system, are congruent with reality, communicate meaningful information about the policy process, direct inquiry and research, and suggest explanations of public policy. In the end, Dye (1992: 45) argues that models "should suggest hypotheses about the causes and consequences of public policy."

There's no negative connotation to the notion of "middle-range" theory. Indeed, much of science consists of middle-range theory, and we can say with confidence that policy theorists' work is scientific because it is not merely descriptive. Those of us who study social systems—how economic transactions take place, how communities coalesce, how families get along, how policy decisions are made, why there are wars, how people developed language—do not practice our science the same way as do natural scientists. We do not generally work in labs; instead, we observe societies and people, which are inherently dynamic and changing. While some disciplines have explored experimental designs, such as behavioral economics and game theory, many of us in the social sciences can only rely on "quasi-experimental" research in which we try to hold certain variables constant, with greater or lesser success (Campbell, Stanley, and Gage 1966).

But we share with scientists the desire to broaden human knowledge, which is ultimately what the word "science" means. After all, according to *Merriam-Webster's Collegiate Dictionary*, the word *science* is derived from the Latin word *scientia*, meaning "having knowledge." The dictionary thus defines *science* as "the state of knowing: knowledge as distinguished from ignorance or misunderstanding." An example will illustrate what this means. When I was in junior high school, one of our science teachers explained the differences between the ancient Greek and modern methods of pursuing scientific knowledge. He said that there was once a debate in Greece over whether men had more teeth than women. All sorts of reasons were given for men having the most teeth: larger jaw and overall body size, bigger appetites, the supposed physical superiority of men over women. The Greeks, our teacher told us, failed to do what to us is the most obvious thing: look in the mouths of men and women and count up how many teeth they have. This seems obvious to us because all of us are steeped in the logic of the Enlightenment. One of the outgrowths of the Enlightenment was the development of *empirical science;* that is, science based on the observation of a phenomenon or the collection of data about a phenomenon. Since we are so steeped in this tradition, it seems absurd to argue about the number of teeth in men's and women's mouths. Of course, this story itself may be an *anecdote* told simply to make a point about the difference between the **scientific method** and other, less successful ways of knowing things. But the story makes a useful point: that observation is an important tool in the empirical scientist's toolkit.

From a scientific perspective, evidence that is gathered and described using what we call the scientific method is superior, we believe, to evidence offered through anecdotes and stories. It is superior by virtue of its method. We seek to apply the best methods to our work—to ensure that our data and conclusions are reliable, valid, and, ultimately, useful in advancing knowledge. To achieve this goal, we try to create the strongest research designs, and we report our results in the form of aggregate data, rather than as separate, disconnected stories without some sort of method to assess whether the stories reveal any sort of trend. Scientific research sometimes runs counter to the "common wisdom" dispensed in anecdotes.

As steeped as we are in Enlightenment notions of method, evidence, and proof, we often see daily political debate reduced to the level of anecdotes or stories, rather than careful analysis. We should neither be surprised nor confused by this—day-to-day politics is not the province of theory development, testing, careful logic, and the accumulation of evidence. Rather, it is about telling stories—about health insurance horror stories that turn out not to be true (Woodward 2009); about people who buy expensive steaks with food stamps (Super 2004; DeParle and Gebeloff 2009; Rehl 2009), about how kids who commit acts of violence at school do so because of the malign influence of popular music, video games, or television (Lawrence and Birkland 2004; Birkland and Lawrence 2009); or about how New Orleans was intentionally left to wither after Hurricane Katrina because of ideological bias or institutional racism (Gilman 2006).

I use these examples to illustrate the difference between the scientific (or, at least, the careful) analysis of public policies and the political analysis of policies do not rely primarily or solely on what we usually think of as science. The stories people (and, quite often, their elected officials and journalists) tell are known as anecdotes, and the collection of anecdotes constitutes what we call **anecdotal evidence**. Anecdotes are quite powerful in the debate over

scientific method
The system most commonly used in Western science for gaining knowledge. It involves identifying a problem, gathering data, and testing hypotheses.

anecdotal evidence
Evidence offered in policy debates that is based on stories and personal experience rather than empirical evidence.

policies. President Ronald Reagan was particularly fond of using anecdotes to illustrate policy problems, and presidents and other elected officials before and since Reagan have told stories to great rhetorical effect. The problem with anecdotes is that they are little tidbits of information that are unsystematically gathered and that reflect the biases of the person relating the story. A political conservative is likely to tell stories extolling the virtues of individual initiative and limited government, while his or her liberal counterpart will often spin tales of the proper role and function of government in ensuring our quality of life. And, even if the anecdotes are based on correct information with respect to the one individual story itself, the accumulation of similar anecdotes may—or may not—serve as data to confirm or deny a trend or phenomenon. The differences between evidence and anecdote are outlined in Table 11.1.

An example that illustrates this point is the contrast between the discussion of a mining method sometimes called "mountaintop removal" mining in Appalachia on the *Diane Rehm Show*,[1] a highly regarded public affairs talk show on National Public Radio, and an article published on the subject in the highly regarded journal *Science*. On the radio show, a representative of the coal mining industry claimed that his firm, at least, does not engage in the sort of environmentally damaging practices that result in water pollution, coal dust, the destruction of streams, profound human health consequences, and other outcomes of this technique. On the other hand, the *Science* article—

TABLE 11.1 Anecdotes and Evidence

	Description	How it is used	Strengths/rationale
Anecdotes	Stories told to illustrate a problem or the failure of a policy, such as "My child took the DARE program and it worked to keep her away from drugs."	To justify starting or terminating programs by providing an easily understood story with obvious conclusions and underlying normative or moral principles.	Anecdotes are good for staking out a position on an issue, or for motivating people to believe a certain way. They are less useful as part of serious analysis, because they do not delve deeply into how programs work.
Evidence from scientific study	Conclusions reached through scientific study of a problem or of the outcomes of a policy.	To justify starting or stopping programs by providing the most scientifically sound information that policy makers can use to make decisions.	Scientific evidence is much stronger than anecdotes in understanding how and why things work the way they do. However, the results of scientific study are often controversial and unpopular, and sometimes run counter to popular expectations.

which was extensively **peer-reviewed**—reviewed a large body of existing peer-reviewed research and new water quality data to show that mountaintop removal mining had profound consequences for policy. This is a good case of science attempting to influence policy by the careful application of the scientific method, rather than stories and anecdotes. This is not to say that good natural or policy science can or will carry the day. The authors of the study strongly urge proper regulatory action: "Regulators should no longer ignore rigorous science. The United States should take leadership on these issues, particularly since surface mining in many developing countries is expected to grow extensively" (Palmer et al. 2010: 149).

Despite the weight of scientific evidence, and contradicting its own campaign promises, the Obama administration issued permits to allow a mountaintop mining operation to proceed, much to the dismay of the environmentalists and scientists who are concerned with the environmental and human impacts of this practice (Goldenberg 2010). This one small example illustrates that while we can apply scientific methods to *studying* policy, it is unreasonable to expect participants in policy making to act like a set of rational theory builders and hypothesis testers. Decision-makers often do not have the luxury of relying solely on scientific methods or findings, because the practice of politics is as much art as it is science. Indeed, so many issues in public policy, such as policies relating to pornography, abortion, teenage pregnancy, and other controversial matters of public and private morality, are so difficult to address through scientific or rational policy analysis that these are known as "trans-scientific" problems that transcend the ability of "science," however defined, to address these issues (Majone 1989: 5).

In this mining case, the president and the regulatory agencies must weigh many competing interests: miners, mining companies, the power companies that make electricity by burning coal, local residents (some of whom work at the mines, and some of whom suffer the mines' environmental damage), natural scientists, and environmentalists. How a policy maker decides what decision to make is often guided by a sense of what is possible or sensible politically, not what is the "best" policy from a scientific perspective. To a considerable extent, then, this decision is trans-scientific.

This is not to say that science has no role *in* the policy process. We do know that all sorts of natural, physical, and social science play a big role in policy. After all, it was health professionals and epidemiologists who led the efforts to contain the so-called "swine flu" (H1N1) virus in 2009–2010.

peer review
A process in which articles published in academic journals have been submitted to other experts in the same field to determine the suitability of the article for publication, based on the existing norms and body of knowledge of the profession.

Scientists and engineers led efforts to build the atomic bomb, build the great power dams, develop the Internet and other communications technologies, improve food safety, control polio . . . the list of such achievements is long, and is a symbol of the scientific and creative energy that characterized twentieth-century science in the United States, But there are often times where science's role can be controversial or even peripheral in policy debate. And, in particularly contentious policy domains, science can be actively disdained by participants in the process. The debate over global climate change is a case in point: the scientific community has been subject to withering attacks on the science, including the methods used and the substantive meaning of their research findings. Scientists' work has not been aided by those who make claims about how disasters such as Hurricane Katrina are a direct consequence of global climate change. On the other hand, it is clear that the science is either used or pilloried to make political points. As an old saying goes: politicians use science the way drunks use lampposts—for support, not for illumination.

In the end, we can say that the application of scientific and policy analytic tools to decision-making in public policy is more difficult than it has ever been before, in large part because the optimism that the proponents of scientific policy analysis brought to the enterprise in the 1960s was, by the 1970s, unredeemed. At the same time, the form of policy analysis—but not its analytical substance—had been taken up by so many participants in policy making that the language and logic of "policy analysis," based on scientific and social scientific methods, had evolved to become a part of the ebb and flow of politics generally, with no special claim to expertise or methodological excellence that would set policy science apart from decisions made in the seemingly irrational world of everyday politics (Radin 2013).

HEEDING THE CALL FOR IMPROVED POLICY THEORY

Policy studies, like many social sciences, are sometimes said to lag behind the natural sciences because we still have not developed what McCool (1995) calls a "dominant theoretical tradition," or what Thomas Kuhn (1996) would call a "paradigm." For example, McCool notes that Thomas Dye's text *Understanding Public Policy* (1992) lists and discusses eight theoretical traditions in policy study. All eight are treated as equally useful, even though some of them may actually conflict with each other, such as the theories that support pluralism versus those that suggest a more elitist model of government. And even at a less fundamental level understanding and developing policy theory can be very difficult because of the wide variation in terminology in the various texts and policy studies. Daniel McCool lists three different definitions of policy science taken from the policy literature, two definitions of policy studies, three definitions of policy evaluation, and four definitions of policy analysis. "The conceptual distinction between these terms," he argues, "is indistinct." McCool also lists five definitions of the term "theory" and four each of "model" and "concept," the definitions of which overlap considerably.

With all these overlapping and sometimes confusing definitions, it is understandable that theory seems so complex and unhelpful to theorists and practitioners alike. But theories of public policy making—and the very act of developing and testing theory—are very important because they are the very tools that help us to understand the broader questions of public policy. The proliferation of theory building without testing and refinement of something that looks like a paradigm or at least a set of principles for the study of public policy led George Greenberg and his colleagues to assert that the explosion of modeling needed to yield to actual empirical testing of theories. These tests would allow policy scholars to gain a better sense of which theories work better than others (Greenberg et al. 1977). Paul Sabatier, echoing this sentiment, promotes a research agenda to improve the making and *testing* of policy theories (Sabatier 1991b).

MAJOR MODELS OF THE POLICY PROCESS

To a considerable extent, calls for developing and testing theories have been heeded. Sabatier and Jenkins-Smith, in their 1993 text *Policy Change and Learning: An Advocacy Coalition Approach*, further refine Paul Sabatier's *Advocacy Coalition Framework* and invite other policy scholars to help test this framework. This point is important—all the major theories described here have been applied and tested by a wide range of policy scholars (Sabatier and Jenkins-Smith 1993).

Frank Baumgartner and Bryan Jones, in *Agendas and Instability in American Politics*, extensively study how issues gain or lose prominence in American politics by analyzing congressional hearings and news coverage of key policy areas. They gathered an immense database of legislative, regulatory, and media information that is available to all researchers at the Policy Agendas Project website.[2] Their research yields two important insights. First, using this evidence derived from congressional hearings and media coverage of issues, Baumgartner and Jones find that American politics is characterized by long periods of policy stability followed by sudden change in the agenda and in policy. Second, Baumgartner and Jones show how congressional hearing data can be used to track how much attention is being paid to particular issues. This methodological contribution—and their publicly available data set—may be as important as the main conclusions of the study, because it shows how one can use congressional data to study the public policy process and how one can build a fairly sophisticated model or at least a story of why policy making seems so slow or even static at one moment and highly dynamic the next (Baumgartner and Jones 2009).

Because there are so many models, and because they are analytically quite rich, space permits only a summary of three prominent models here: John Kingdon's "streams" metaphor of public policy, Paul Sabatier's "Advocacy Coalition Framework," and Frank Baumgartner and Bryan Jones's "punctuated equilibrium" model of agenda and policy processes. In this edition, I also briefly summarize Elinor Ostrom's "Institutional Analysis and Development" (IAD) approach. The creation of these theories was driven by many motivations, but one thing they have in common is an implicit or explicit rejection of the stages model as a theory of the policy process outlined in Chapter 1. This is not to deny the substantial analytic and instructional value of the stages heuristic, stages model, or whatever one calls it (Nakamura 1987; deLeon 1999). Indeed, the organization of this textbook owes a great deal to this formulation. Rather, I summarize these theories because they seek to overcome the stages model's obvious shortcomings—in particular, its failure to provide a predictive theory of policy making.

Kingdon's Multiple Streams Approach

In *Agendas, Alternatives and Public Policies*, John Kingdon (2011) argues that issues gain agenda status, and alternative solutions are selected, when elements of three "streams" come together. The notion of streams is borrowed from March, Cohen, and Olsen's idea of how ideas combine in "garbage cans" in nearly anarchic decision-making environments, such as universities, in which decision-making powers are broadly distributed in the system. March and his colleagues argued that ideas flow into and out of "garbage cans" of ideas, and get mixed and matched with other ideas, whereupon the ideas are taken up by other actors and promoted to decision-makers.

Kingdon's innovation was to organize and label these streams of ideas and facts into the problem, policies, and politics streams in the policy process. Each of these three streams contains various individuals, groups, agencies, and institutions that are involved in the policy-making process. The problem stream encompasses the attributes of a problem and whether it is getting better or worse, whether it has suddenly sprung into public and elite consciousness through a focusing event, and whether it is solvable with the alternatives available in the policy stream. The policy stream contains the potential ideas that could be advocated as solutions to a problem. The politics stream encompasses the state of politics and public opinion—the sort of public opinion variables reviewed in Chapter 2. All three streams suggest different types of variables that can be examined for their influence on the agenda and on decision-making. This way of looking at the policy process has come to be known as the **Multiple Streams Approach (MSA)**.

Within any particular problem area, these streams run parallel and somewhat independently of each other in a policy area or domain until something happens to cause two or more of the streams to meet in a "window of opportunity." This window is the possibility of policy change, but the opening of the window does not guarantee that policy change will occur. That trigger can be a change in our understanding of the problem, a change in the political stream that is favorable to policy change, a change in our understanding of the tractability of the problem given current solutions, or a focusing event that draws attention to a problem and helps open a window of opportunity. The streams metaphor is graphically represented in Figure 11.1.

It is important to note that this is not a model in which a problem is identified, followed by people going out to develop or invent solutions and bring them back. Rather, many solutions already exist, and the role of participants is to advance their solution to a problem, even when it seems that they are simply carrying a solution in search of a problem. For example, Secretary of Housing and Urban Development Jack Kemp, in the George H.W. Bush administration, strongly suggested that urban enterprise zones (UEZs)—zones in which tax laws and other regulations are relaxed to encourage development—be created in cities to provide jobs while slowing urban decay. Kemp promoted other ideas for public housing and job creation as well. In 1992, when Los Angeles exploded in rioting in the wake of the acquittal of

Multiple Streams Approach (MSA) The term used to describe Kingdon's approach to the policy process, in which we can think of the politics, problem, and policy streams coming together in a "window of opportunity" for policy change.

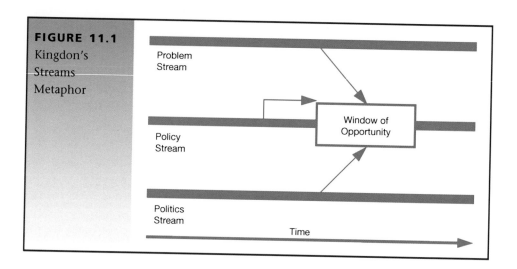

FIGURE 11.1
Kingdon's Streams Metaphor

Problem Stream

Policy Stream

Window of Opportunity

Politics Stream

Time

police accused of beating a black motorist, Kemp tied the UEZ solution to the problem of urban unrest and alienation. The riots gave Kemp an opportunity to link his potential solutions to the problem of rioting.[3]

Paul Sabatier argues that the MSA may be an incomplete description of policy making because it does not describe the policy process beyond the opening of the window of opportunity (Sabatier 1991a). However, while Kingdon is best known for the MSA as an approach to understanding agenda setting, he also devotes considerable attention in his book to the process of alternative selection, noting that different political institutions are better suited either to agenda setting, such as the president or Congress, and others have a greater role in formulating policy alternatives, such as specialist members of congress, policy analysts, and key group leaders. Furthermore, Nikolaos Zahariadis argues that the streams approach can be applied to decision opportunities, not simply agenda-setting opportunities; a *decision* to make new or change existing policy may be more likely when the streams come together (Zahariadis 1993).

For example, the decisions by agencies to adopt more stringent aviation safety and security standards were often driven by windows of opportunity that opened after crashes or terrorist attacks—often, these decisions involved the stricter application of rules or the assumption of greater regulatory power than the agency had used before. But, in many such aviation safety cases, existing ideas already were available and, once the problem rose on the agenda, the range of solutions was scanned and particular policy options were selected (Birkland 2004). Thus, Kingdon provides a rich and multilayered metaphor of policy making from the early acceptance of new ideas about public problems to the active considerations of solutions as new public policy.

The Advocacy Coalition Framework

Sabatier's **Advocacy Coalition Framework (ACF)** is an important model of the policy process, based on the idea that interest groups are organized in policy communities within a policy domain. The most recent version of this framework is depicted in Figure 11.2.

Like the streams metaphor, Sabatier's ACF encompasses a variety of individual and institutional actors, and it views policy making as an iterative process that runs over years or decades. The ACF also considers the

Advocacy Coalition Framework (ACF) A model or framework for understanding the interactions of groups and coalitions of groups called advocacy coalitions. In the framework, typically two to four coalitions form based on shared beliefs on policy issues. Paul Sabatier is the primary developer of the ACF, which has been applied to studies of implementation, policy change, and learning, and is a framework for studying the policy process as well.

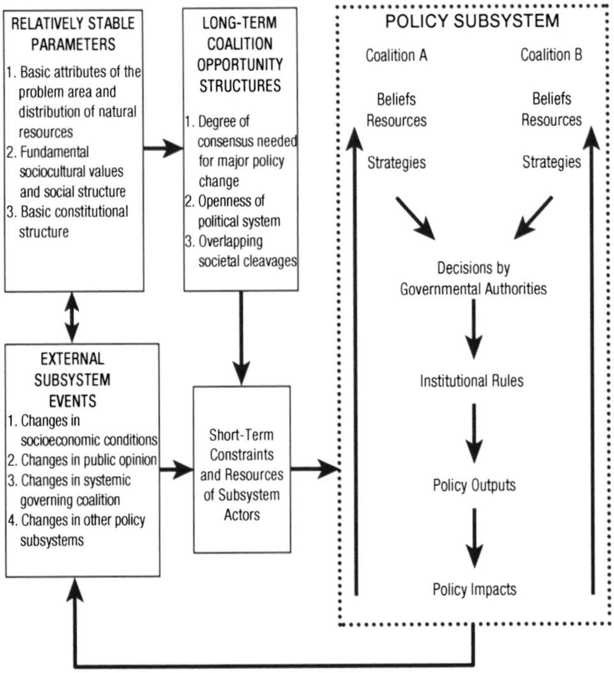

FIGURE 11.2

The Advocacy Coalition Framework

Source: From *Theories of the Policy Process*, by Paul A. Sabatier and Chris Weible. Figure 6.1. Copyright © 2014 by Westview Press, a member of the Perseus Books Group. Reprinted by permission of Westview Press, a member of Perseus Books, L.L.C.

mechanisms for policy change (not simply the possibility for change, as in the streams metaphor) and more consciously encompasses the influence of implementation and feedback on the system.

In the ACF, policy making is influenced both by "relatively stable" system parameters and by "dynamic (system) events," with the interaction between the two promoting or inhibiting policy making. The stable parameters include the basic attributes of the problem area, the basic distribution of natural resources in the society, the fundamental cultural values and social structure, and the basic legal structure, which in the United States is the constitutional framework and judicial norms.

The dynamic features of the system include changes in socioeconomic conditions and technology, changes in public opinion, changes in systemic governing coalitions (partisan balance in the legislature or the executive branch, for example), and policy decisions and impacts from other subsystems. Change in the governing coalition corresponds to one example of change in the politics stream in Kingdon's model, while changes in socioeconomic and technological conditions influence the problem and policy streams. The activities of other subsystems can influence the policy, politics, and problem streams as their activities spill over into other policy domains.

In the ACF, two to four advocacy coalitions typically form in a particular policy domain when groups coalesce around a shared set of core values and beliefs. These groups engage in policy debate, competing and compromising on solutions based on their core values and beliefs. Competition between coalitions is mediated by policy brokers who have a stake in resolving the problem, either on substantive grounds or because of their interest in maintaining political harmony in the system. These brokers are more likely to succeed when they can develop compromises that do not threaten either advocacy coalition's core beliefs and values. Policy change is much less likely if polarization of advocacy coalitions that the groups' peripheral beliefs provide little or no opportunity for shared interests.

Here's an example of how two very different types of interests can find common ground on an issue of common concern, pornography, and form alliances and a potential advocacy coalition. I will leave aside the problem of defining pornography for this discussion; the courts have found this definition extremely challenging, but, whatever it means, the example here is still apt. Perhaps we should satisfy ourselves with Justice Potter Stewart's claim that it is difficult to define, but "I know it when I see it." See his concurrence in *Jacobellis v. Ohio*, 378 U.S. 184 (1964). Political conservatives, many of whom identify as religious conservatives or evangelicals, are strongly opposed to the production and distribution of pornography on moral grounds. At the same time, many people who identify as "feminists"—that is, people who believe that women should be entitled to the same legal and social rights as men—strongly oppose the production of pornography as a matter of equality for women. They argue that women are degraded when pornography is made, distributed, and consumed. In this example, you can see how religious conservatives and feminists—who generally are considered liberal in our political spectrum—are troubled by pornography. These groups allied because of their shared opposition to pornography, a matter that's important, but part of the peripheral belief system of these groups. But this coalition, like many such coalitions, cannot last because these two groups are fundamentally opposed to each other their in core issues: gender equity in particular. While the efforts of political conservatives and feminists to restrict the distribution of what they consider to be pornography haven't been entirely successful, this example is illustrative of how groups can coalesce. Of course, this alliance is itself extremely controversial among members of these groups (see Weaver 1989; Segal and McIntosh 1993). Some writers note the fundamental differences in the *rationale* on which feminists and religious conservatives base their antipathy toward pornography (see Jelen 1986). Again, the ACF explains how these alliances are impermanent, but do form around short-term policy goals, rather than around shared fundamental beliefs. Other examples include recent examples of evangelical Christians allying with environmental groups to promote better stewardship of the earth's resources (Kintisch 2006), and liberals and conservatives coming together to oppose claimed intrusions on privacy that followed the September 11 terrorist attacks (Walker 2003; Conservatives, Liberals Align against Patriot Act 2005; Hsu 2009).

Punctuated Equilibrium

Baumgartner and Jones (2009) borrow the concept of "**punctuated equilibrium**" from evolutionary biology to describe the process by which policy is made in the United States. They argue that the balance of political power between groups of interests remains relatively stable over long periods of time, punctuated by relatively sudden shifts in public understanding of problems and in the balance of power between the groups seeking to fight entrenched interests.

punctuated equilibrium
An idea borrowed from evolutionary biology by Baumgartner and Jones (2009), in which policy change is characterized by long-run stability *punctuated* with short-term shocks that make policy change more likely.

Key to their theory of equilibrium is the idea of the policy monopoly, which corresponds with the idea of policy subsystems. A policy monopoly is a fairly concentrated, closed system of the most important actors in policy making. Such a monopoly has an interest in keeping policy making closed, because a closed system benefits the interests of those in the monopoly and keeps policy making under some measure of control. Under the iron triangle notion of policy making, this system will remain closed and stable for a long time. But Baumgartner and Jones argue that there are instances when the "equilibrium" maintained by policy monopolies will break down, greater and more critical attention to issues will follow, and rapid policy change will be the immediate result. The policy monopolies themselves can break down or at least become more open issue networks.

How do policy monopolies and their dominant construction of problems break down? First, greater media attention to an issue can begin to break open policy monopolies. Media attention to issues can grow when a small but compelling or influential group of people tell of problems with a policy to which members of the policy community do not effectively respond. Baumgartner and Jones and Jeffrey Berry use the breakdown of the nuclear power monopoly to illustrate the effect of greater attention on a problem (Berry 1989). The nuclear policy monopoly consisted of the Atomic Energy Commission (AEC), the nuclear utilities, the builders of nuclear power plants, the civil and military nuclear establishment, and the Joint Committee on Atomic Energy (JCAE), a very powerful joint committee of the U.S. House and Senate. This monopoly began to break down as interest groups and, in time, the public voiced greater concern about the safety and cost of nuclear power, and by the mid 1970s the JCAE had been disbanded, the AEC broken up, and the Nuclear Regulatory Commission created, all due to reformist tendencies in government in the early 1970s and the greater media and public attention paid to nuclear power.

This example also illustrates an important finding: that increased attention to a problem usually means greater negative attention to it. In this way, the "policy image" of various issues and policies can change. In the nuclear power case, the increased scrutiny of the industry began to break down the image of nuclear power as "the peaceful atom" creating power "too cheap to meter" to an image of danger and expense. This negative image was reinforced by the accident at the Three Mile Island nuclear plant in Pennsylvania in 1979 and the multibillion-dollar default on bonds sold to build nuclear power plants in Washington State in 1982.

Policy monopolies also break down when groups go "venue shopping" to find the best venue—that is, a level of government or a political institution—in which to press their claims. The media are one venue, and groups can seek access to the courts or other units of government to gain access to policy debate. The reform of the congressional committee system and, most important, the increasing autonomy of subcommittees starting in the early 1970s have led to a greater number of venues in Congress for groups to find a sympathetic ear to influence policy making.

An important aspect of this way of thinking about policy is the long periods of stability followed by rapid change, followed again by long periods of stability. In this way, Baumgartner and Jones argue, policy change is not merely incremental and not in a state of constant flux: rather, policy remains stable, followed by a period of rapid change, then stability again.

Institutional Analysis and Development

For those who study what we call common pool resources—that is, resources that are shared and used in common, such as a publicly owned forest, or a fishing area, Elinor Ostroms's **Institutional Analysis and Development** (IAD) framework (and she calls it a framework) encompasses a wide range of ideas about actors, institutions, and rules in the policy process, and how they work together to result in particular kinds of public policies.

The IAD framework is also called an *institutional rational choice* approach, because it is built on ideas derived from rational choice theory. Rational choice theory is based on the idea that individuals—acting alone, or within organizations—are utility-maximizing, rational individuals who are goal-oriented and use near-perfect information to weigh a range of options before adopting the optimal choice based on their calculation of costs and benefits. As we know, people are at best boundedly rational, and people often strategically shape and disseminate information to achieve particular goals. So we can say that people are boundedly rational in their decision making, that people do the best they can in making decisions, and ultimately, says Herbert Simon, people engage in **satisficing**—doing the best we can under resource and other constraints, not doing the best we can to solve problems assuming no constraints, which would be inaccurate.

Assuming that people are boundedly rational, Ostrom and those writing in her tradition come together to make public policies within "institutions" through the use of "rules." I place these terms in quotation marks because

Institutional Analysis and Development A way of understanding the policy process pioneered by Elinor Ostrom. It is rooted in ideas of rationality, of group cooperation to achieve shared goals, and in a broad definition of the meaning of "institution" within politics and society.

satisficing Making the best possible decision under constraints related to time, information, and other resources.

thus far in this book we have assumed that we have a shared understanding of these terms, particularly in political science. An "institution" to a political scientist is often an agency or branch of government, such as the Justice Department, or the Congress. Sociologists also describe social institutions like family and marriage. The behavior of members of institutions is shaped by the nature of the institution, which encompasses a set of norms and expectations of the various actors, such as the various norms for behavior in Congress. "Rules" are the decisions that institutions make to enforce their decisions. Rules can be really broad, at the constitutional level, such as rules prohibiting government interference in religion, or government promotion of it, in the First Amendment to the Constitution. Or rules can be very specific and focused, such as the laws and regulations regarding running pet stores, or having fishing licenses.

Ostrom (2007) argues that the study of institutions and rules is not so straightforward. She identifies several significant challenges to the study of institutions:

1 "The term institution refers to many different types of entities, including both organizations and the rules used to structure patterns of interaction within and across organizations."
2 "Although the buildings in which organized entities are quite visible, institutions themselves are invisible."

Let's consider these two challenges together. Ostrom argues that an institution is not just its organization and its building, but is also the rules that institutions make and that constrain the behaviors of people within those organizations. Indeed, Ostrom makes clear that institutions are best understood by how they actually use rules than by the rules that they claim are the most important; she claims that this is a distinction between "rules-in-use" rather than "rules-in-form." She then raises some important challenges for the study of institutions:

3 "To develop a coherent approach to studying diverse types of institutional arrangements, including markets, hierarchies, firms, families, voluntary organizations, national governments, and international regimes, one need multiple inputs from diverse disciplines."
4 "Given the multiple languages used across disciplines, a coherent institutional framework is needed to allow for expression and comparison of diverse theories and models of theories applied to particular puzzles and problem settings."

Here, Ostrom notes that those who study public policy really need to draw on insights from many disciplines, as you have seen throughout this book. But in the fourth point, Ostrom points to the need for some sort of shared framework for understanding how all the aspects of policy work together, across disciplinary contributions:

5 "Decisions made about rules at any one level are usually made within a structure of rules existing at a different level. Thus, institutional studies need to encompass multiple units of analysis."
6 "At any one level of analysis, combinations of rules, attributes of the world, and communities of individuals involved are combined in a configural rather than an additive manner."

In simplest terms, Ostrom is saying that rules made at a "higher" level in a government or organization will influence other levels, so if we are to understand the policy process we need to understand multiple levels of government; it is not clear, however, whether a "level" is necessarily below, above, or parallel to any particular level. Thus, in the sixth point, Ostrom argues that rules do not simply accumulate, one on top of each other. Instead, rules combine with other features of institutions to create new configurations of actors and rules.

With these challenges in mind, Ostrom has developed a framework for understanding the policy process that is shown in Figure 11.3. In this model, the existing physical world, the attributes of a community (that is, the various things that bind and define a community), and the rules-in-use that structure individual and group behavior influence the "action arena." The "action arena" includes the action situation—that is, the problem at hand—and the actors, the people and groups who will do something about this. The action situation contains the people who participate in making decisions, their positions on what they would like to see happen, the outcomes they believe should occur, or worry will occur, the connection between what is done and what will happen as a result, the nature and extent that the participants can shape or control outcomes, the adequacy of the information available to some or all actors, and the rational weighting of costs and benefits resulting from outcomes.

Actors can be individuals or groups, and include assumptions about four clusters of variables:

1 The resources that an actor brings to a situation;
2 The valuation actors assign to states of the world and to actions;

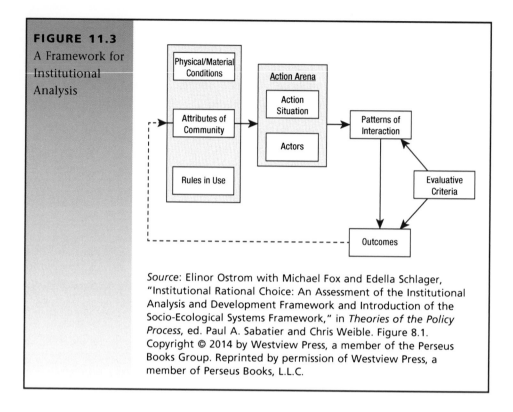

FIGURE 11.3
A Framework for Institutional Analysis

Source: Elinor Ostrom with Michael Fox and Edella Schlager, "Institutional Rational Choice: An Assessment of the Institutional Analysis and Development Framework and Introduction of the Socio-Ecological Systems Framework," in *Theories of the Policy Process*, ed. Paul A. Sabatier and Chris Weible. Figure 8.1. Copyright © 2014 by Westview Press, a member of the Perseus Books Group. Reprinted by permission of Westview Press, a member of Perseus Books, L.L.C.

3 The way actors acquire, process, retain, and use knowledge contingencies and information; and

4 The processes actors use for the selection of particular courses of action.

Both the actors and the action situation are required in an action arena for there to be any outcome. These outcomes are shaped by "patterns of interactions"—that is, the processes by which participants work in the policy process. And the activities of the participants—and the outcomes themselves—are influenced by at least six factors encompassing efficiency, equity, accountability, "conformance to general morality" (that is, following the rules), and adaptability.

This is an extremely broad-brush review of IAD, which is presented here for two main reasons. First, while it is extremely complex, if you delve into the IAD you will find that Ostrom—unique among most policy theorists—very carefully specifies the variables that should be considered throughout the policy process, in terms of the actors, the outcomes, and the process itself. Second, it is important to know a little about the IAD framework because, as

Ostrom and others have applied it, the IAD framework has become a particularly valuable contribution to the study of rules surrounding "**common pool resources**." In a well-known book, *The Tragedy of the Commons*, Garrett Hardin argues that a common area—such as a pasture, or fishing grounds—can be overused and the resource will be depleted unless it is somehow managed for the benefit of its users. Ostrom argues, using the IAD as a starting point, that many cases of shared resources show successful local management because institutions and the rules and enforcement of rules that go with these structures—in the sense described here—are formed and developed at the local or near-local level to manage the resource so that many people benefit without its overexploitation. Her and others' research has found that people can, under proper conditions, form these institutions, thereby avoiding the heavy hand of central government regulation, which often is suboptimal because it fails to equitably distribute a resource or because it creates no incentives for following the rules. And it can avoid the much-feared tragedy of the commons. Why is the IAD so well suited to this? Because the configuration of actors, action situations, and the definition of rules and institutions is more closely attuned to human behavior in communities than are most depictions of the policy process.

common pool resources
Resources that are used in common by a community, such as water supplies, fisheries, grazing land, that require some sort of regulatory system to prevent unsustainable use of the resource by one or a few people at the expense of the whole community.

CONCLUSION

While this discussion of some of the dominant theories of the policy process forms the conclusion to this book, you should not see this discussion as the final word in policy studies. This is just a taste of the ideas contained in these rich and complex theories of the process, and no summary of this sort could do justice to these models. Furthermore, the development of theory in the policy process continues apace. While these are the major theoretical traditions under which policy process scholars have worked over the past 20 to 25 years, many scholars have isolated particular aspects of these theories and have refined and modified them. It is indeed possible that these refinements and modifications could yield yet another round of highly sophisticated theory building in the field.

Finally, this is not the final word because it is my hope that you can find, in these theories, ways of thinking about what is most important to you in your studies and work in the policy process. What this means will be unique to your individual approach to policy studies, and to your motivations for studying policy. For those with a theoretical bent, I hope this book sparks your interest in the field and induces you to read and think broadly about the policy process. For those who plan to become participants in the policy process—and this may include anyone with an interest in public affairs, whether one is an academic, a professional analyst, or a civic-minded citizen— I hope you can adapt all the models we have described here to help you think about what is most important in the policy process, particularly if they help you make sound political arguments based on sound logic, good evidence, *and* strong rhetoric. If these models and if this book help you, your allies, and even those you consider your "opponents" think about how policy is made—and we can get involved to make better policy—then this enterprise is most assuredly worth the effort.

KEY TERMS

Advocacy Coalition Framework (ACF)
anecdotal evidence
common pool resources
Institutional Analysis and Development

Multiple Streams Approach
normative and positive arguments
peer review
punctuated equilibrium
satisficing
scientific method

QUESTIONS FOR DISCUSSION, REFLECTION, AND RESEARCH

- Consider the classic "stages" model of policy making. Paul Sabatier, among many other scholars, has argued that the stages metaphor has some substantial shortcomings. List these shortcomings, but then ask: What are the remaining strengths of the stages model for the student of the policy process? Does this conception still have some value to the student and researcher?

- How would you go about measuring the national mood? Is the national mood something you can measure? Or is it just something you feel intuitively? Could two people disagree about the national mood? Why would they disagree?

- As you may know, Elinor Ostrom was the co-winner of the 2009 Nobel Prize in Economics (technically known as the Swedish Central Bank [*Sveriges Riksbank*] Prize in Economic Sciences in Memory of Alfred Nobel) for her work on common pool resource management, even though her disciplinary background is as a political scientist. Spend some time reviewing the news stories and journalistic descriptions of her work. Why do you think that Ostrom was awarded a prize in economics if she is a political scientist? What does this say about the nature of her work and of the IAD framework? Or about the nature of policy science, or about the boundaries that separate social science disciplines?

- Many scholars (myself included) mix and match elements of the theories presented in this chapter to explain how specific policies are made, or to develop theory about a particular kind of policy making. Is it sensible to borrow from more than one theory of the policy process when testing theory? What does it say about theory that it is possible to borrow from different models?

- How might you use the theories outlined in this book to explain the policy outcomes in fields that interest you? This might be a particularly good question to ask yourself if you are writing a term paper for a policy class project, in which it is useful to demonstrate some knowledge of theory.

- Consider the difference between empirical scientific evidence and anecdotal evidence. Which is considered more useful to the study of public policy and why? Think of some anecdotes you use to explain why you hold particular political beliefs. Are these anecdotes backed by social science? If not, why are anecdotes still important?

- Why is methodology important to science, whether it's natural science, physical science, or social science? What would happen if we did science without a method?

- Why is creating theory about public policy important, rather than just describing specific problem areas, such as health policy or defense policy?

- Find an article on an issue of public policy in a newspaper. Consider carefully whether the people making arguments for or against a particular policy are making *normative* or *positive* arguments. Are they using anecdotes or evidence? How can you tell the difference? Whose arguments do you consider most persuasive? Why?

ADDITIONAL READING

The study of the public policy process is dominated today by three books, and by books inspired by these original studies. The first of these is John Kingdon's *Agendas, Alternatives and Public Policies*, updated 2nd ed. (Boston, MA: Longman, 2011), which was originally published in 1984. The advocacy coalition framework was published by Paul Sabatier in several forms, and was then published in a book, Paul Sabatier and Hank C. Jenkins-Smith's *Policy Change and Learning: An Advocacy Coalition Approach* (Boulder, CO: Westview Press, 1993). Paul Sabatier since supplemented this book with a broader consideration of the policy process, *Theories of the Policy Process* (Boulder, CO: Westview Press, 1999), and an updated and refined second edition (2006), and a third and expanded edition with Chris Weible in 2013. Elinor Ostrom updates her 1999 essay in the first edition of *Theories of the Policy Process* with an essay in the 2006 edition. Indeed, both volumes, which overlap to some extent, contain a wealth of theorietical information, including coverage of important theoretical questions in the field, and serious students should obtain and read both editions.

The punctuated equilibrium metaphor of agenda and policy change was broadly introduced in Frank R. Baumgartner and Bryan D. Jones, *Agendas and Instability in American Politics*, now in its 2nd edition (Chicago, IL: University of Chicago Press, 2009). Their project inspired a massive data collection effort called the Policy Agendas Project (www.policyagendas.org), which started with the data collected for 1993, but which has been extended far beyond 1993 to contain a great deal of data about Congress, the executive branch, and media coverage of key issues. Much of these data were gathered and used by the scholars who published in an edited volume, Frank R. Baumgartner and Bryan D. Jones, *Policy Dynamics* (Chicago, IL: University of Chicago Press, 2002).

There are many public policy textbooks on the market that seek to synthesize the vast amount of information on policy process theories. One of my favorite basic texts is James E. Anderson, *Public Policymaking*, 8th ed. (Boston, MA: Houghton Mifflin, 2014). For advanced students of the policy process, I recommend Michael Howlett and M. Ramesh, *Studying Public Policy: Policy Cycles and Policy Subsystems*, 3rd ed. (Toronto and New York: Oxford University Press, 2009). An excellent collection of classic readings in the policy process literature is Daniel C. McCool, *Public Policy Theories, Models, and Concepts: An Anthology* (Englewood Cliffs, NJ: Prentice Hall, 1995). Finally, a pointed and readable overview of public policy is Kevin B. Smith and Christopher W. Larimer, *The Public Policy Theory Primer*, 2nd ed. (Boulder, CO: Westview Press, 2013).

NOTES

1   The podcast for this show is at http://wamu.org/programs/dr/10/01/07.php#31354.
2   www.policyagendas.org/.
3   See, for example, William Claiborne, "Kemp Calls on Mayors for 'Audacious' Effort; Enterprise Zones, New War on Poverty Urged," *Washington Post*, June 23, 1992, A19; David Lauter, "Administration Again Divided on Urban Aid," *Los Angeles Times*, May 25, 1992, A24.

REFERENCES

Baumgartner, Frank and Bryan D. Jones. 2009. *Agendas and Instability in American Politics*. 2nd ed. Chicago, IL: University of Chicago Press.
Berry, Jeffrey M. 1989. "Subgovernments, Issue Networks, and Political Conflict." In *Remaking American Politics*, edited by Richard Harris and Sidney Milkis, 239–259. Boulder, CO: Westview.
Birkland, Thomas A. 2004. "Learning and Policy Improvement after Disaster: The Case of Aviation Security." *American Behavioral Scientist* 48(3): 341–364.
Birkland, Thomas A. and Regina G. Lawrence. 2009. "Media Framing and Policy Change after Columbine." *American Behavioral Scientist* 52(10): 1405–1425. doi: 10.1177/0002764209332555.
Campbell, Donald Thomas, Julian C. Stanley, and N.L. Gage. 1966. *Experimental and Quasi-Experimental Designs for Research*. Boston, MA: Houghton Mifflin.
Conservatives, Liberals Align against Patriot Act. 2005. *Washington Times*, June 14. Accessed January 24, 2015. www.washingtontimes.com/news/2005/jun/14/20050614-121304-2787r/.
deLeon, Peter. 1999. "The Stages Approach to the Policy Process: What Has It Done? Where Is It Going?" In *Theories of the Policy Process*, edited by Paul A. Sabatier, 19–32. Boulder, CO: Westview.
DeParle, Jason and Robert Gebeloff. 2009. "Food Stamp Use Soars across U.S., and Stigma Fades." *New York Times*, November 29, A1.
Dye, Thomas R. 1992. *Understanding Public Policy*. 7th ed. Englewood Cliffs, NJ: Prentice-Hall.
Gilman, Nils. 2006. "What Katrina Teaches Us About the Meaning of Racism." Accessed January 24, 2015. http://understandingkatrina.ssrc.org/Gilman/.

Goldenberg, Suzanne. 2010. "US Scientists Demand Government Ban on Mountaintop Mining." *Guardian*, January 7. Accessed January 24, 2015. www.guardian.co.uk/environment/2010/jan/07/us-scientists-mountaintop-mining.

Greenberg, George D., Jeffrey A. Miller, Lawrence B. Mohr, and Bruce C. Vladeck. 1977. "Developing Public Policy Theory: Perspectives from Emperical Research." *American Political Science Review* 71(4): 1532–1543.

Hsu, Spencer S. 2009. "Probe of Homeland Security Privacy Office Sought; Group Says Chief Is Enabling, Not Curbing, Surveillance." *Washington Post*, October 27, A3.

Jelen, Ted G. 1986. "Fundamentalism, Feminism, and Attitudes toward Pornography." *Review of Religious Research* 28(2): 97–103.

Kingdon, John W. 2011. *Agendas, Alternatives, and Public Policies.* Updated 2nd ed. Longman Classics in Political Science. Boston, MA: Longman.

Kintisch, Eli. 2006. "Evangelicals, Scientists Reach Common Ground on Climate Change." *Science* 311(5764): 1082–1083.

Kuhn, Thomas S. 1996. *The Structure of Scientific Revolutions.* Chicago, IL: University of Chicago Press.

Lawrence, R.G. and T.A. Birkland. 2004. "Guns, Hollywood, and School Safety: Defining the School-Shooting Problem across Public Arenas." *Social Science Quarterly* 85(5): 1193–1207. doi: 10.1111/j.0038-4941.2004.00271.x.

McCool, Daniel C. 1995. *Public Policy Theories, Models, and Concepts: An Anthology.* Englewood Cliffs, NJ: Prentice Hall.

Majone, Giandomenico. 1989. *Evidence, Argument and Persuasion in the Policy Process.* New Haven, CT: Yale University Press.

Nakamura, Robert T. 1987. "The Textbook Policy Process and Implementation Research." *Policy Studies Journal* 7(1): 142–154.

Ostrom, Elinor. 2007. "Institutional Rational Choice: An Assessment of the Institutional Analysis and Development Framework." In *Theories of the Policy Process*, edited by Paul A. Sabatier, 21–64. Boulder, CO: Westview.

Palmer, M.A., E.S. Bernhardt, W.H. Schlesinger, K.N. Eshleman, E. Foufoula-Georgiou, M.S. Hendryx, A.D. Lemly, G.E. Likens, O.L. Loucks, M.E. Power, P.S. White, and P.R. Wilcock. 2010. "Mountaintop Mining Consequences." *Science* 327: 148–149.

Radin, Beryl A. 2013. *Beyond Machiavelli: Policy Analysis Reaches Midlife.* 2nd ed. Washington, DC: Georgetown University Press.

Rehl, Christine. 2009. "Find a Way to Stop Abuse of Food Stamps." *Columbus Dispatch*, December 8, 14A, Letters to the Editor.

Sabatier, Paul A. 1991a. "Political Science and Public Policy." *PS: Political Science and Politics* 24(2): 144–156.

Sabatier, Paul A. 1991b. "Toward Better Theories of the Policy Process." *PS: Political Science and Politics* 24(2): 144–156.

Sabatier, Paul and Hank C. Jenkins-Smith. 1993. *Policy Change and Learning: An Advocacy Coalition Approach, Theoretical Lenses on Public Policy.* Boulder, CO: Westview.

Segal, Lynne and Mary McIntosh. 1993. *Sex Exposed: Sexuality and the Pornography Debate.* New Brunswick, NJ: Rutgers University Press.

Super, David A. 2004. "The Quiet 'Welfare' Revolution: Resurrecting the Food Stamp Program in the Wake of the 1996 Welfare Law." *New York University Law Review* 79(4): 1271–1392.

Trochim, William M.K. 2006. "Deductions and Inductions." Accessed January 25, 2015. www.socialresearchmethods.net/kb/dedind.php.

Walker, Jesse. 2003. "Bob Barr, Civil Libertarian." *Reason*, December. Accessed January 24, 2015. http://reason.com/archives/2003/12/01/bob-barr-civil-libertarian.

Weaver, Mary Jo. 1989. "Pornography and the Religious Imagination." In *For Adult Users Only: The Dilemma of Violent Pornography*, edited by Susan Gubar and Joan Hoff, 68–86. Blommington, IN: Indiana University Press.

Woodward, Calvin. 2009. "Fact Check: Some Obama Health Care Stories Flawed." *Associated Press Online*, September 29, 2009.

Zahariadis, Nikolaos. 1993. "To Sell or Not to Sell? Telecommunications Policy in Britain and France." *Journal of Public Policy* 12(4): 355–376.

About the Author

Thomas A. (Tom) Birkland is the William T. Kretzer Professor of Public Policy at North Carolina State University, where he is also the Associate Dean for Research and Engagement in the College of Humanities and Social Sciences. He holds degrees from the University of Oregon (B.A.), Rutgers University (M.A.), and the University of Washington, Seattle (Ph.D.). At North Carolina State, he teaches courses on disaster policy and on the policy process. Dr. Birkland's research is in theories of the policy process, focusing on agenda change, policy change, and learning. He is also an internationally known expert on policies related to natural disasters and industrial accidents. He is the author of two books, *After Disaster* and *Lessons of Disaster*, and many journal articles. His recent interests have focused on whether and to what extent people and institutions learn from disasters.

Before joining the NC State faculty, Dr. Birkland was an assistant and associate professor in the Rockefeller College of Public Affairs and Policy at the State University of New York. He also served as a program officer at the National Science Foundation in 2006. In his current role, Dr. Birkland also coordinates research and outreach programs for the College of Humanities and Social Sciences at NC State.

Index